D0124363

SURPRISE!

You may be reading the wrong way!

It's true: In keeping with the original Japanese comic format, this book reads from right to left—so action, sound effects, and word balloons are completely reversed. This preserves the orientation of the original artwork—plus, it's fun! Check out the diagram shown here to get the hang of things, and then turn to the other side of the book to get started!

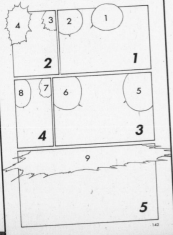

VIZMANGA

Read manga anytime, anywhere!

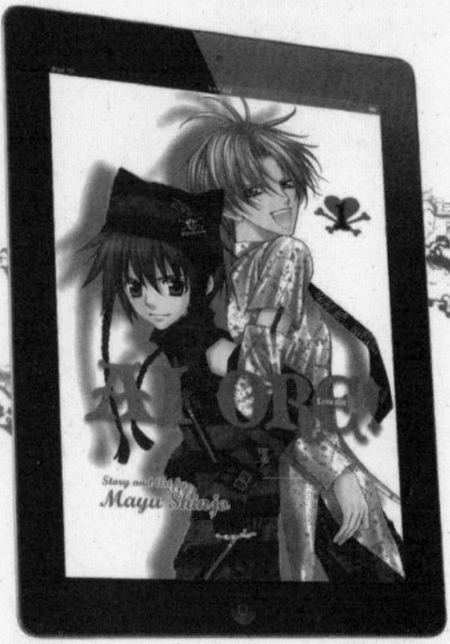
Mayu Shinjo

From our newest hit series to the classics you know and love, the best manga in the world is now available digitally. Buy a volume* of digital manga for your:

- iOS device (**iPad®**, **iPhone®**, **iPod® touch**) through the **VIZ Manga app**
- Android-powered device (**phone or tablet**) with a browser by visiting **VIZManga.com**
- **Mac or PC computer** by visiting **VIZManga.com**

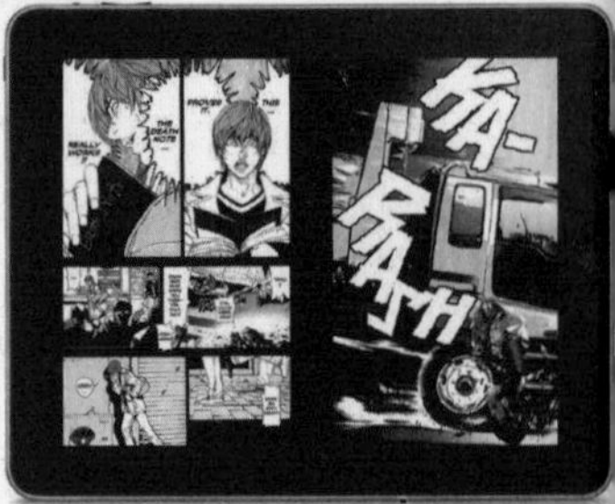

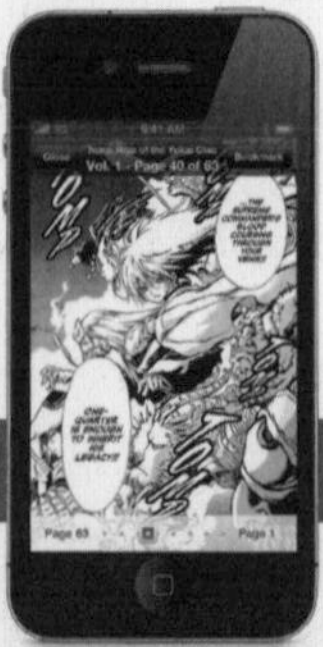

VIZ Digital has loads to offer:

- 500+ ready-to-read volumes
- New volumes each week
- FREE previews
- Access on multiple devices! Create a log-in through the app so you buy a book once, and read it on your device of choice!*

To learn more, visit www.viz.com/apps

*** Some series may not be available for multiple devices. Check the app on your device to find out what's available.**

RATED T+ FOR OLDER TEEN ratings.viz.com

viz.com/apps

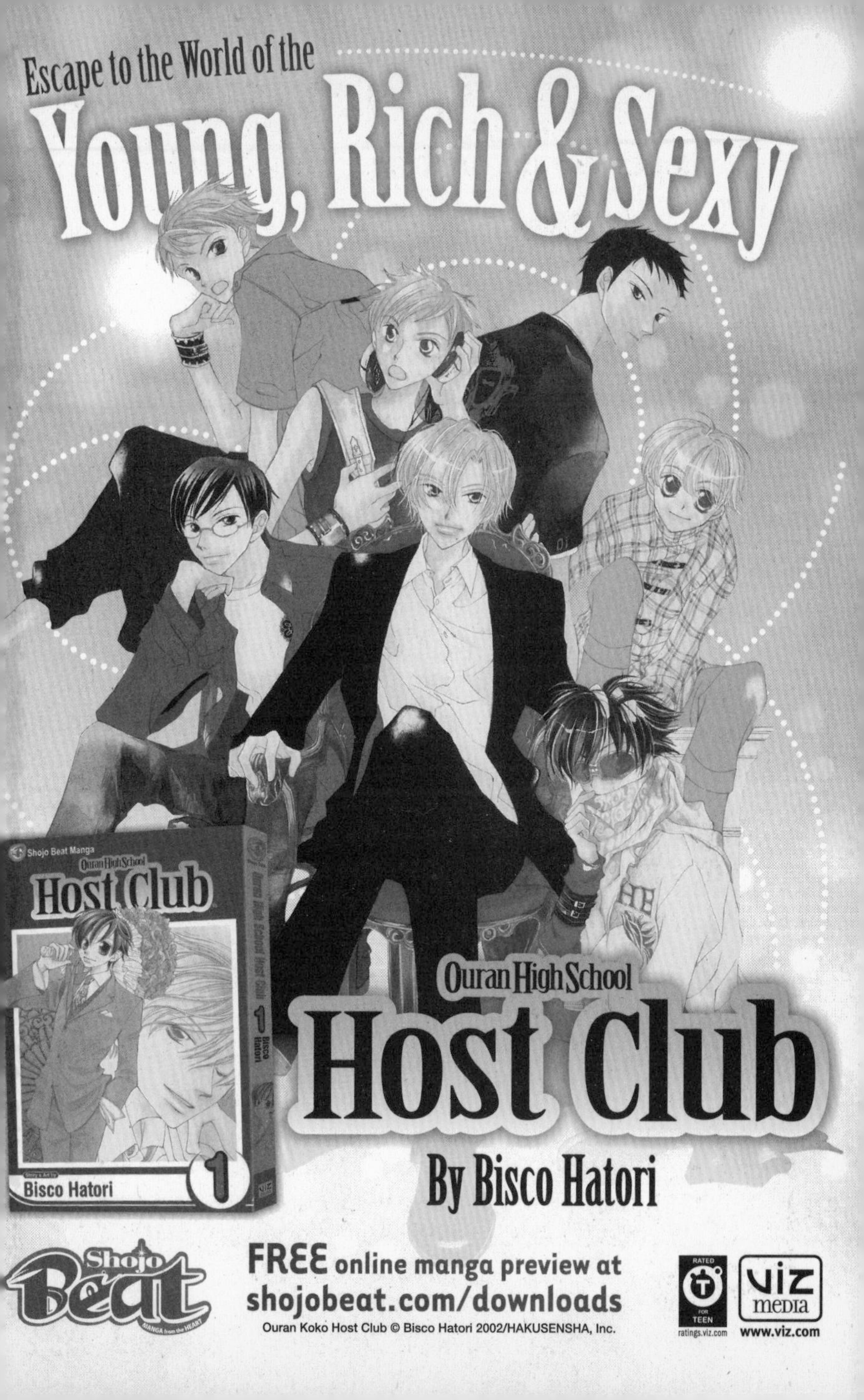
Escape to the World of the
Young, Rich & Sexy
Shojo Beat Manga
Ouran High School
Host Club
1
Story & Art by
Bisco Hatori
Ouran High School
Host Club
By Bisco Hatori
Shojo Beat
MANGA from the HEART
FREE online manga preview at
shojobeat.com/downloads
Ouran Koko Host Club © Bisco Hatori 2002/HAKUSENSHA, Inc.
RATED
T
FOR
TEEN
ratings.viz.com
VIZ media
www.viz.com

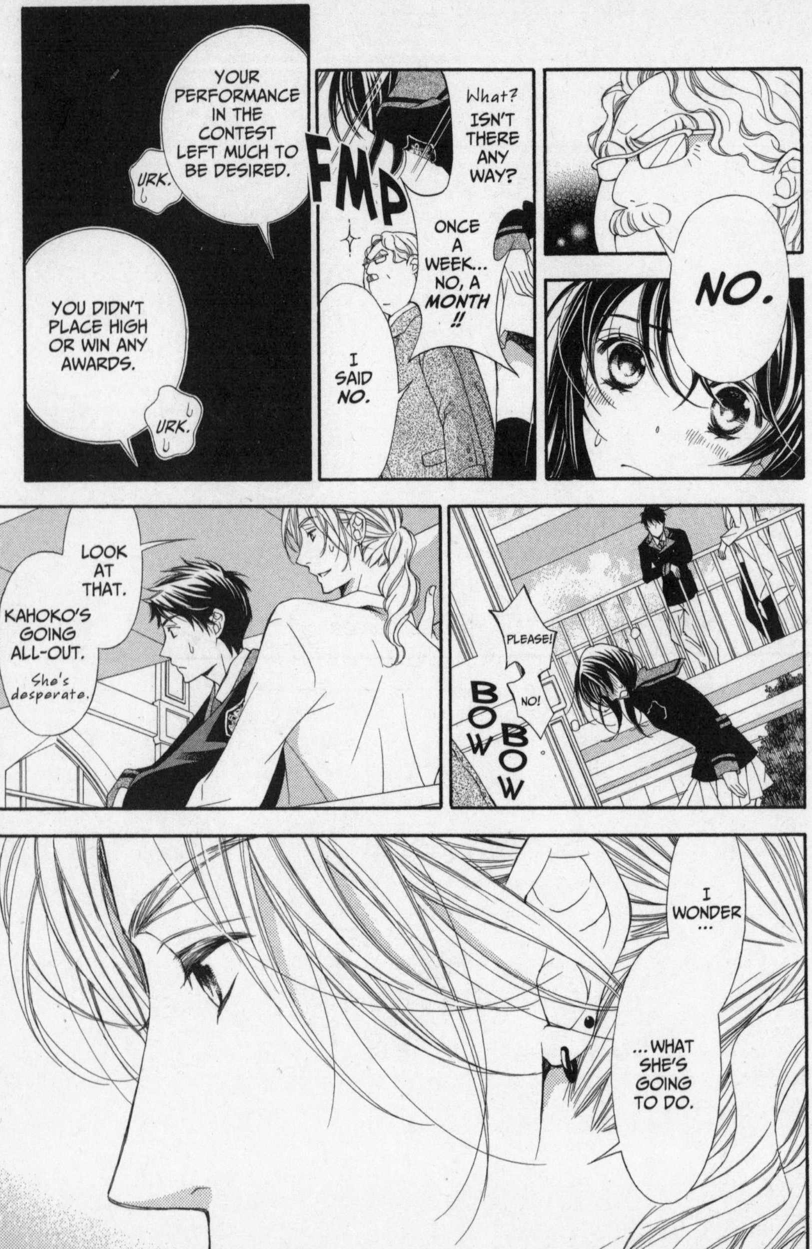
NO.
What?
ISN'T THERE ANY WAY?
FMP
ONCE A WEEK... NO, A MONTH!!
I SAID NO.
YOUR PERFORMANCE IN THE CONTEST LEFT MUCH TO BE DESIRED.
URK.
YOU DIDN'T PLACE HIGH OR WIN ANY AWARDS.
URK.
PLEASE!
NO!
BOW
BOW
LOOK AT THAT.
KAHOKO'S GOING ALL-OUT.
She's desperate.
I WONDER...
...WHAT SHE'S GOING TO DO.

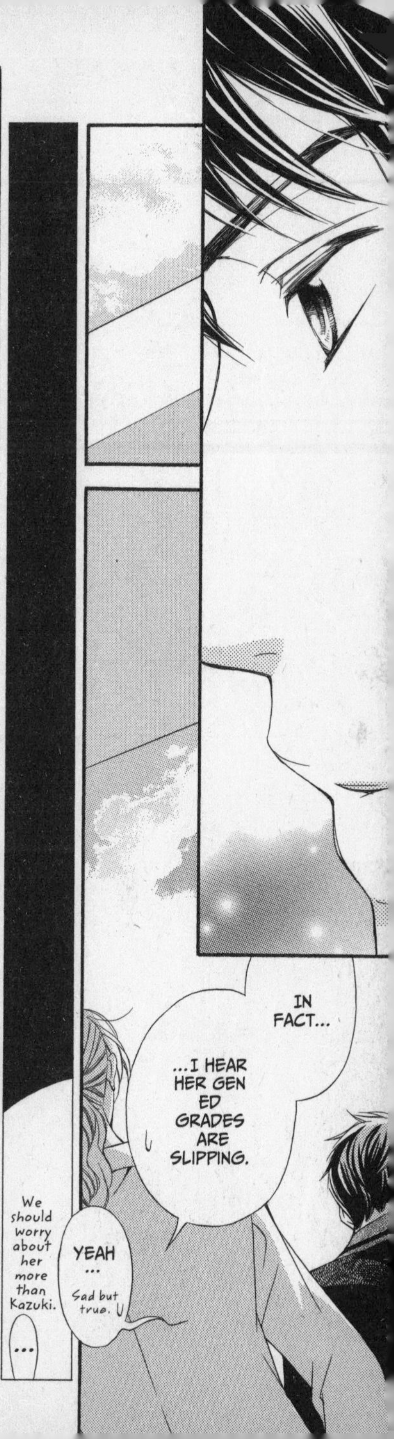
IN FACT...
...I HEAR HER GEN ED GRADES ARE SLIPPING.
YEAH... Sad but true.
We should worry about her more than Kazuki.
...

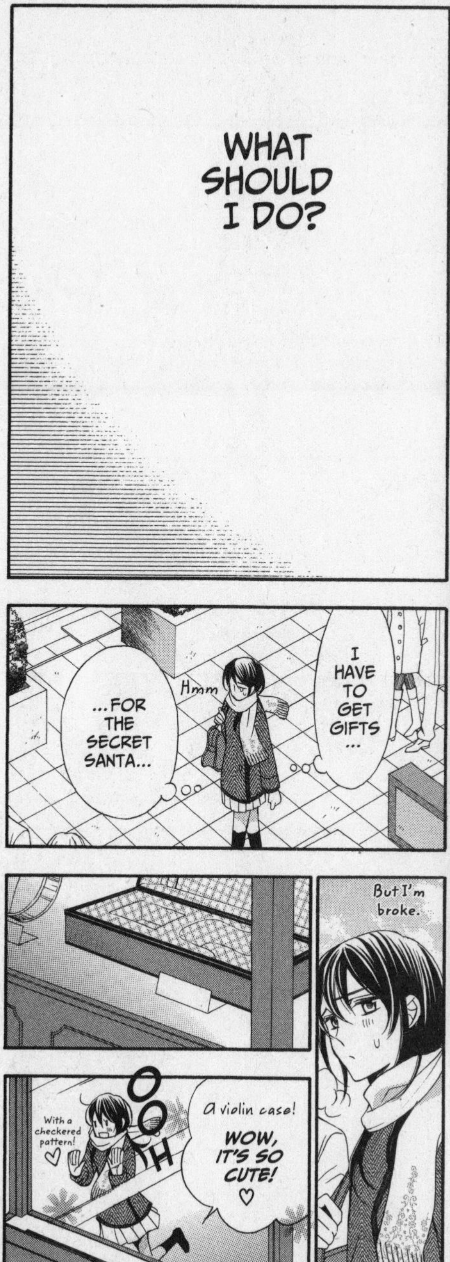
WHAT SHOULD I DO?
I HAVE TO GET GIFTS...
Hmm
...FOR THE SECRET SANTA...
But I'm broke.
A violin case! WOW, IT'S SO CUTE!
OOH
With a checkered pattern!

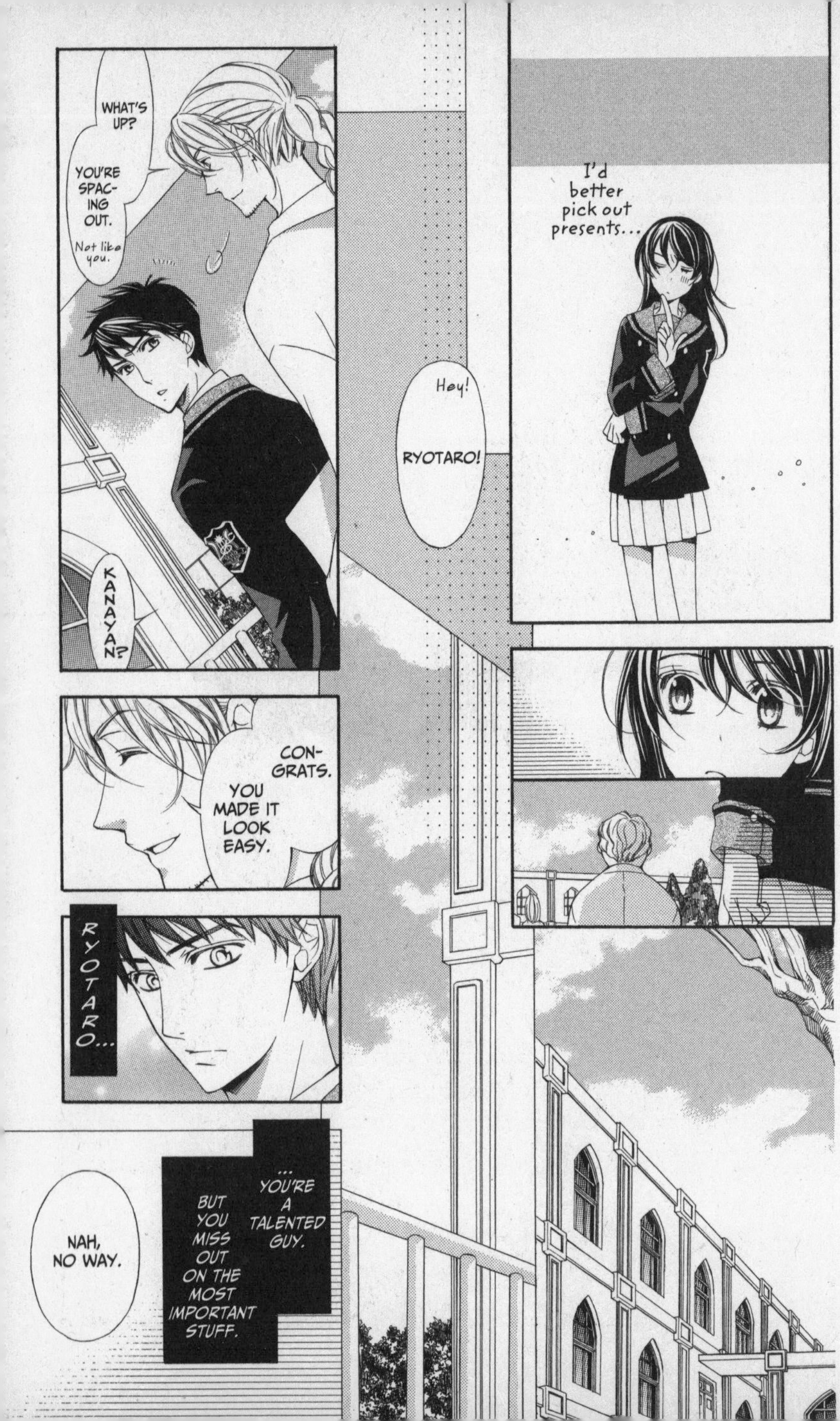
I'd better pick out presents...
Hey!
RYOTARO!
WHAT'S UP?
YOU'RE SPACING OUT.
Not like you.
KANAYAN?
CON-GRATS.
YOU MADE IT LOOK EASY.
RYOTARO...
...YOU'RE A TALENTED GUY.
BUT YOU MISS OUT ON THE MOST IMPORTANT STUFF.
NAH, NO WAY.

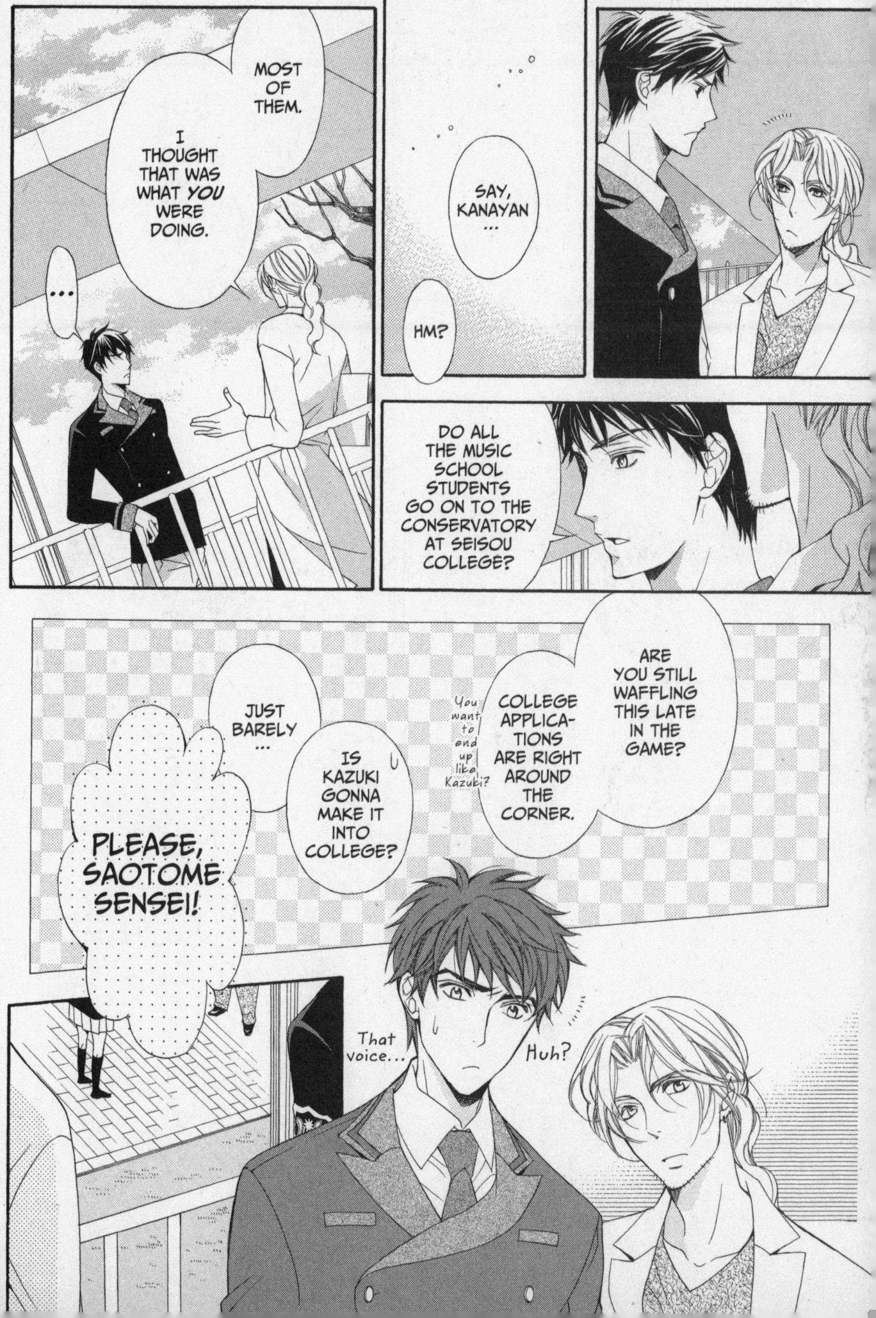
SAY, KANAYAN...
HM?
DO ALL THE MUSIC SCHOOL STUDENTS GO ON TO THE CONSERVATORY AT SEISOU COLLEGE?
MOST OF THEM.
I THOUGHT THAT WAS WHAT *YOU* WERE DOING.
...
ARE YOU STILL WAFFLING THIS LATE IN THE GAME?
COLLEGE APPLICA-TIONS ARE RIGHT AROUND THE CORNER.
You want to end up like Kazuki?
IS KAZUKI GONNA MAKE IT INTO COLLEGE?
JUST BARELY...
PLEASE, SAOTOME SENSEI!
Huh?
That voice...

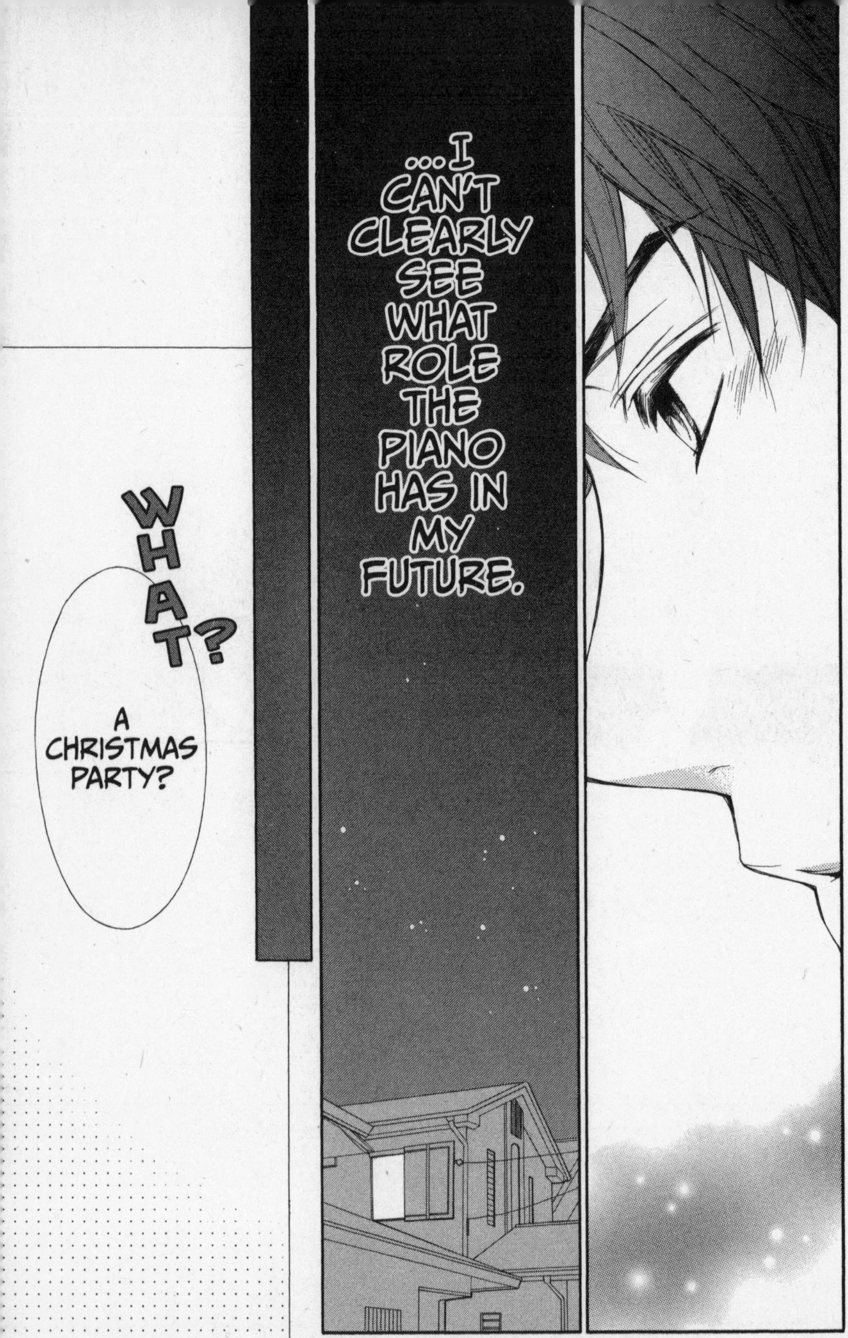
...I CAN'T CLEARLY SEE WHAT ROLE THE PIANO HAS IN MY FUTURE.
WHAT?
A CHRISTMAS PARTY?

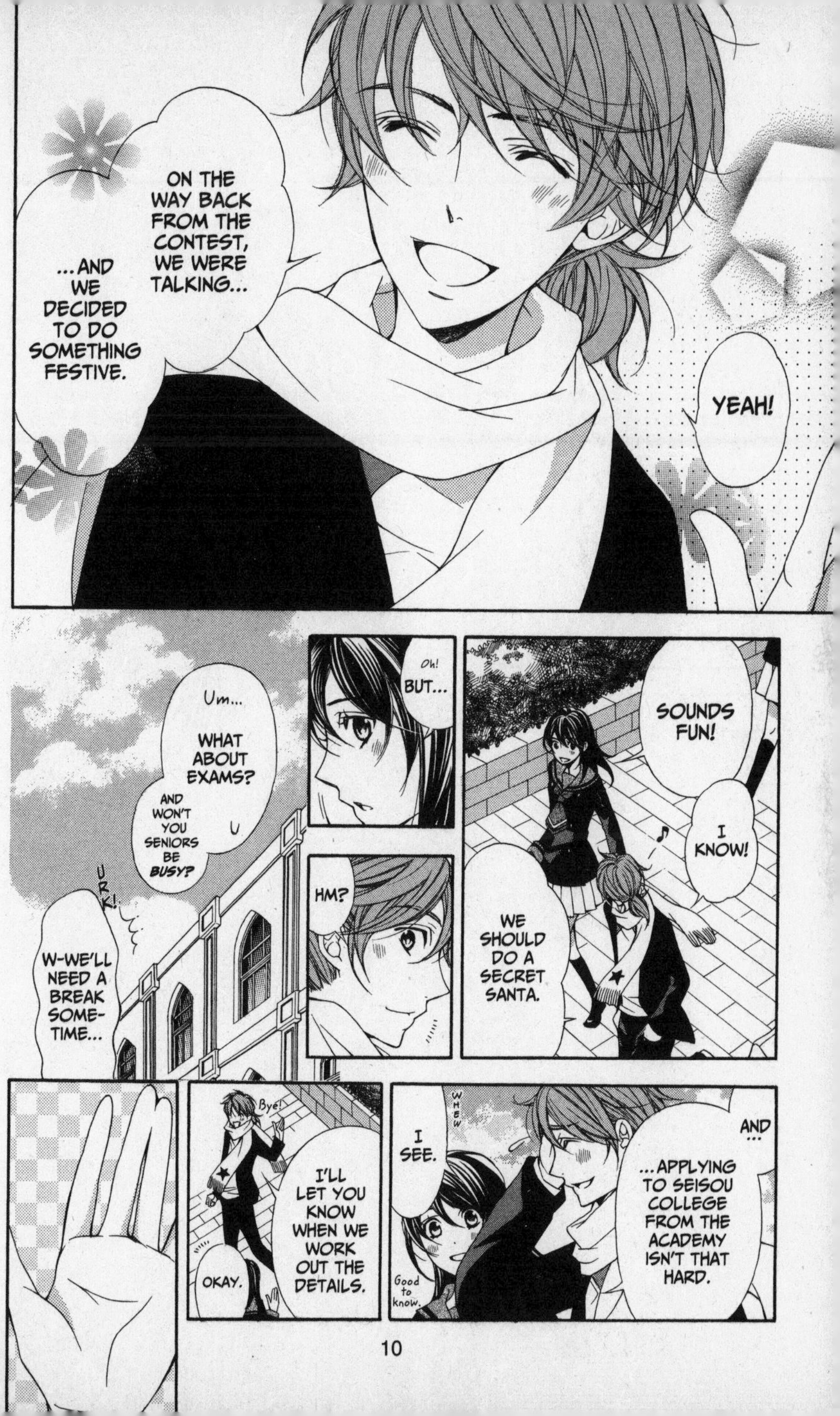
ON THE WAY BACK FROM THE CONTEST, WE WERE TALKING...
...AND WE DECIDED TO DO SOMETHING FESTIVE.
YEAH!
SOUNDS FUN!
I KNOW!
WE SHOULD DO A SECRET SANTA.
Oh! BUT...
HM?
Um...
WHAT ABOUT EXAMS?
AND WON'T YOU SENIORS BE BUSY?
URK!
W-WE'LL NEED A BREAK SOME-TIME...
AND...
...APPLYING TO SEISOU COLLEGE FROM THE ACADEMY ISN'T THAT HARD.
WHEW
I SEE.
Good to know.
Bye!
I'LL LET YOU KNOW WHEN WE WORK OUT THE DETAILS.
OKAY.

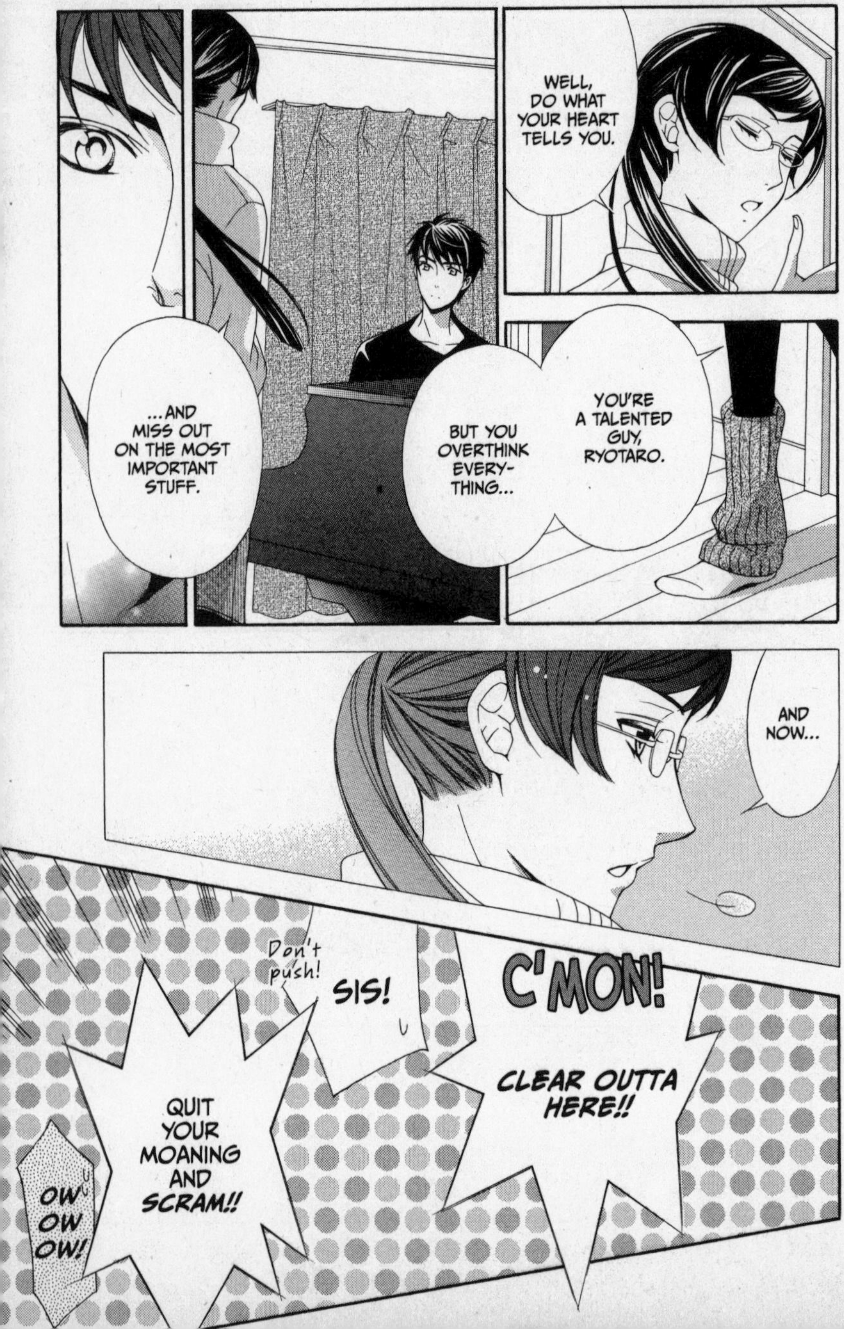
WELL, DO WHAT YOUR HEART TELLS YOU.
YOU'RE A TALENTED GUY, RYOTARO.
BUT YOU OVERTHINK EVERY-THING...
...AND MISS OUT ON THE MOST IMPORTANT STUFF.
AND NOW...
C'MON!
SIS!
Don't push!
CLEAR OUTTA HERE!!
QUIT YOUR MOANING AND SCRAM!!
OW OW OW!

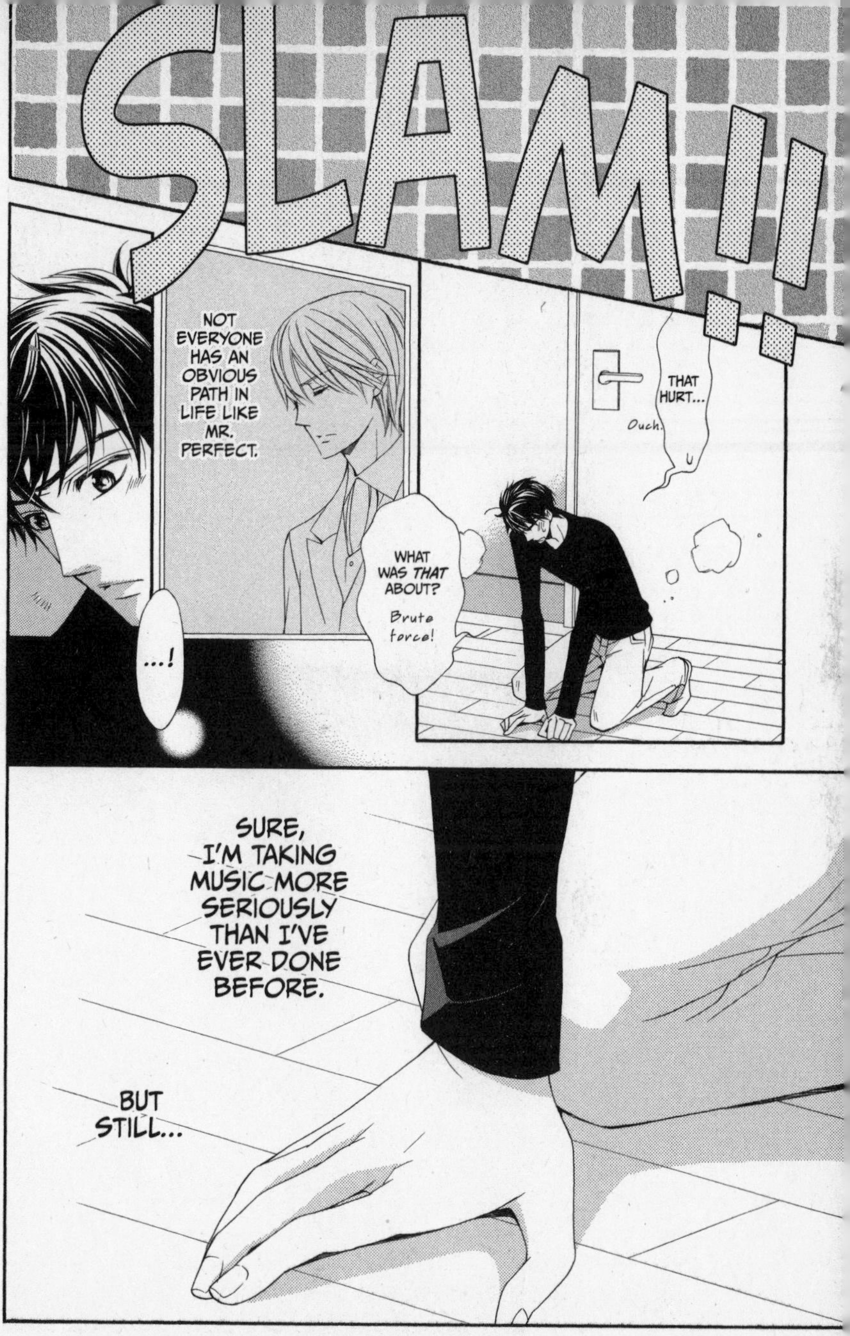
SLAM!!!
THAT HURT... Ouch.
WHAT WAS THAT ABOUT? Brute force!
NOT EVERYONE HAS AN OBVIOUS PATH IN LIFE LIKE MR. PERFECT.
...!
SURE, I'M TAKING MUSIC MORE SERIOUSLY THAN I'VE EVER DONE BEFORE.
BUT STILL...

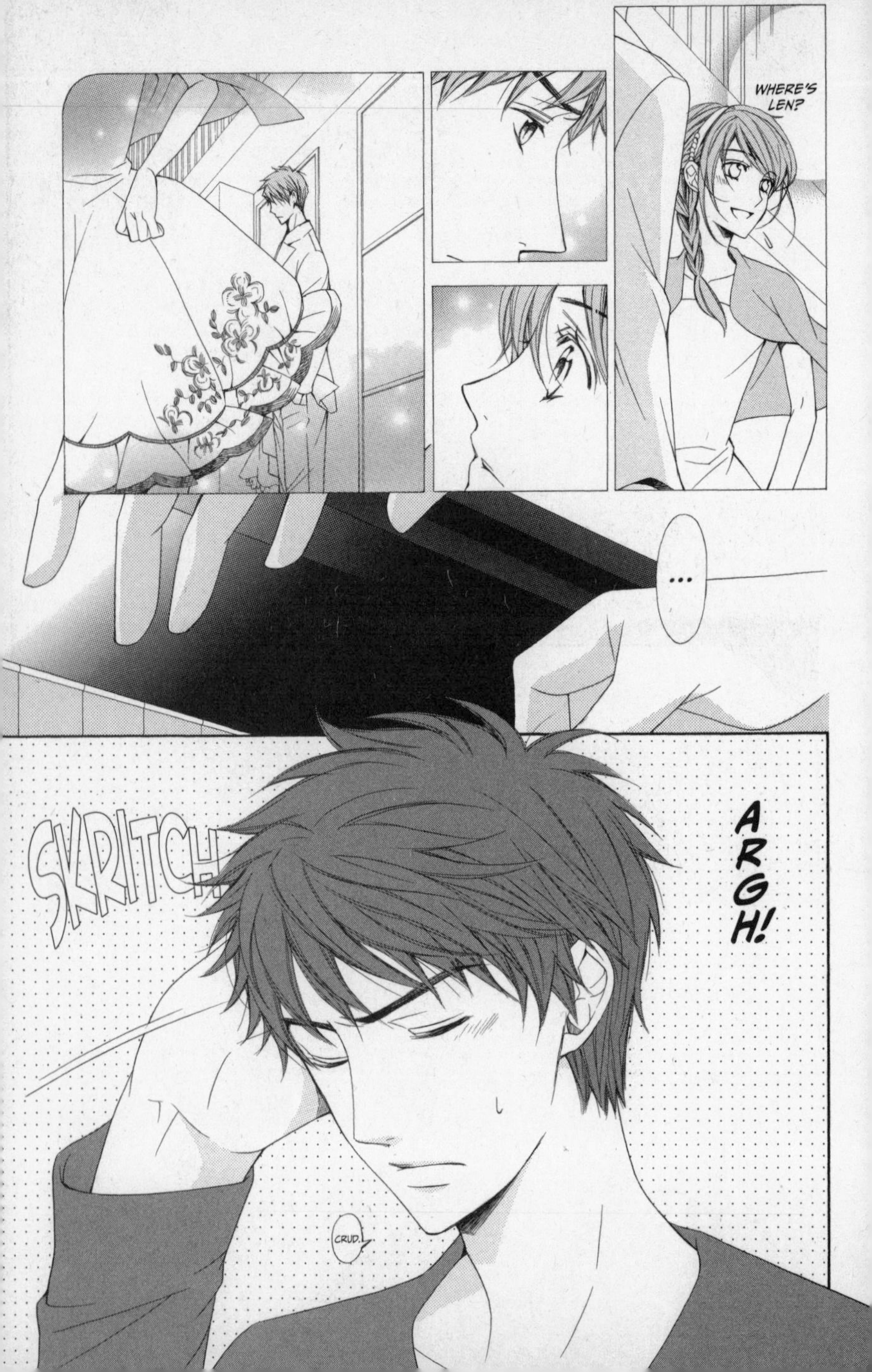
WHERE'S LEN?
...
ARGH!
SKRITCH
CRUD.

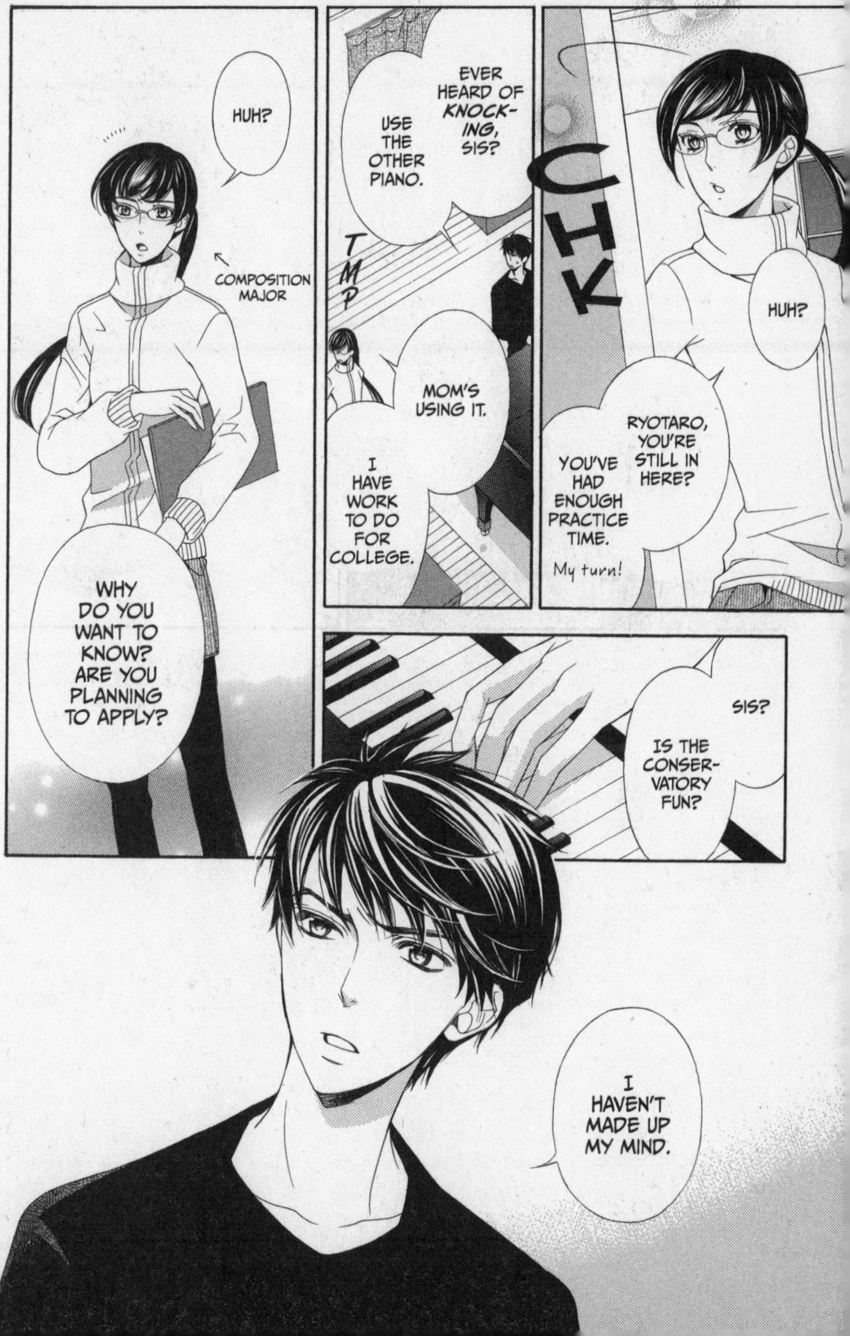
CHK
HUH?
RYOTARO, YOU'RE STILL IN HERE?
YOU'VE HAD ENOUGH PRACTICE TIME.
My turn!
EVER HEARD OF KNOCKING, SIS?
USE THE OTHER PIANO.
TMP
MOM'S USING IT.
I HAVE WORK TO DO FOR COLLEGE.
SIS?
IS THE CONSERVATORY FUN?
HUH?
COMPOSITION MAJOR
WHY DO YOU WANT TO KNOW? ARE YOU PLANNING TO APPLY?
I HAVEN'T MADE UP MY MIND.

La Corda d'Oro

MEASURE 71

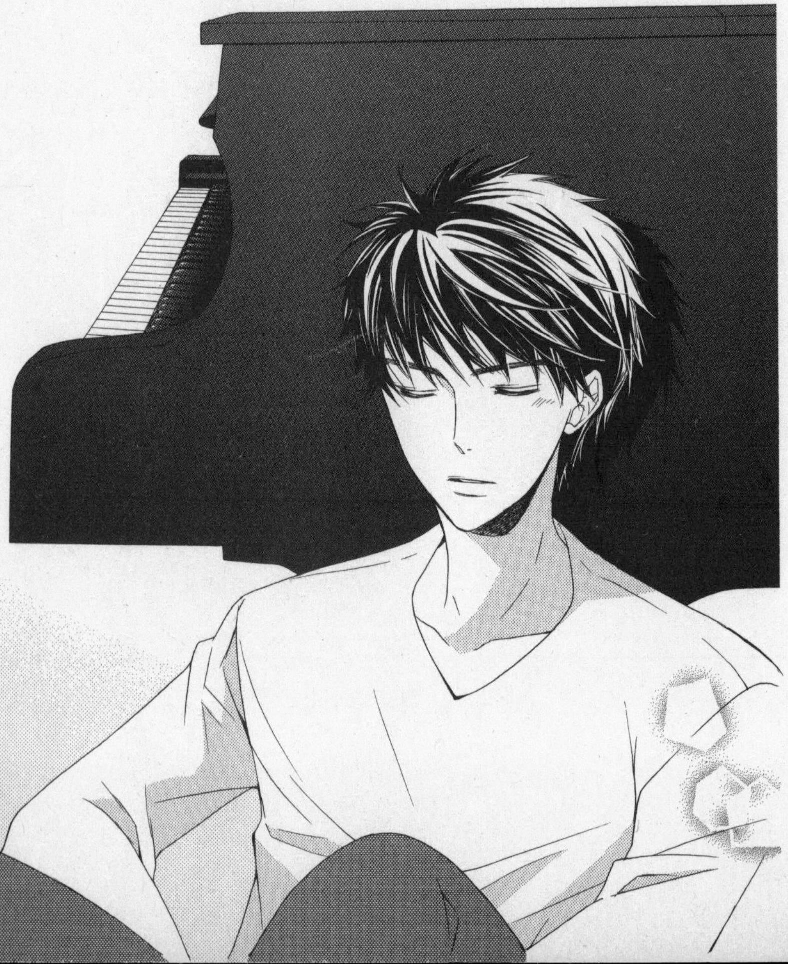

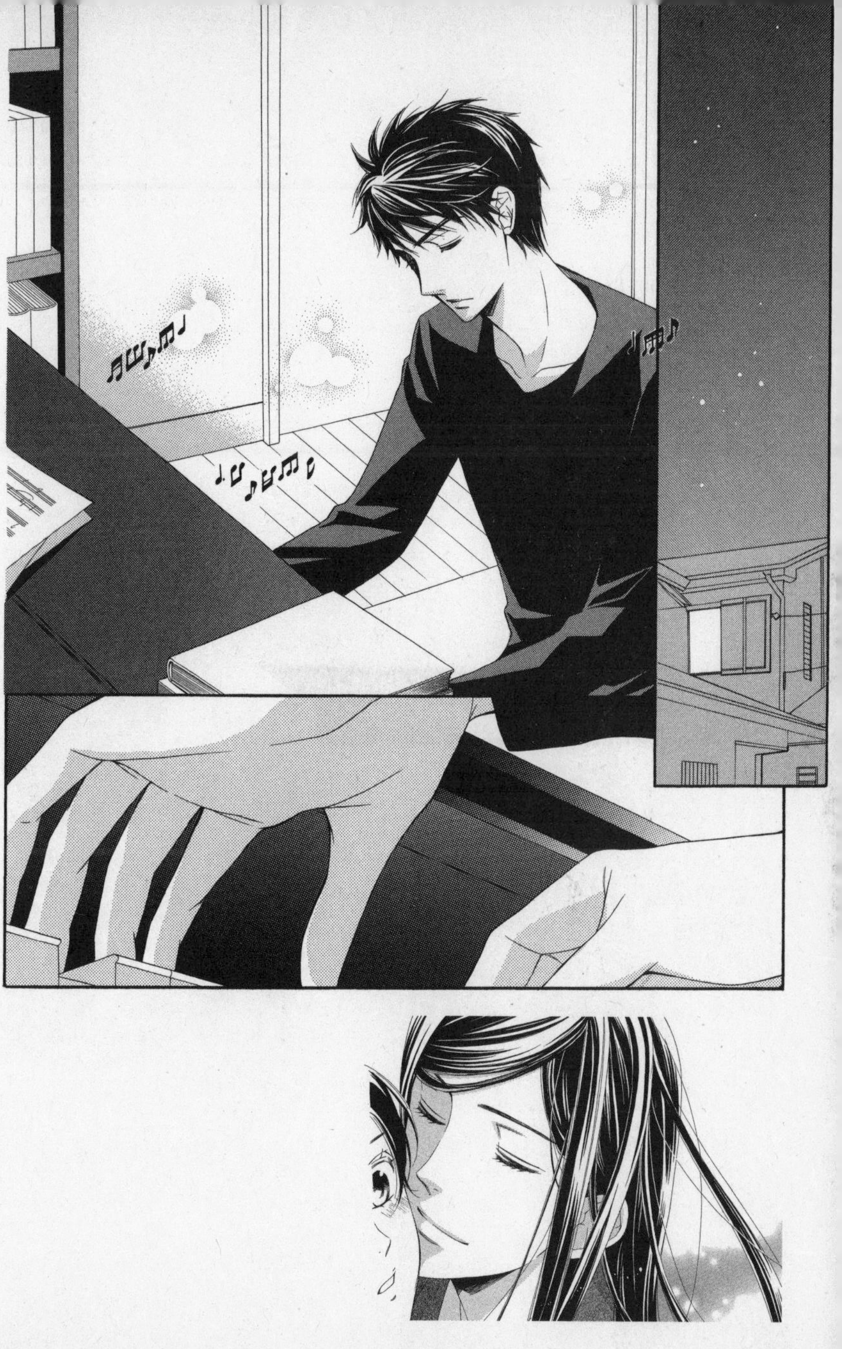

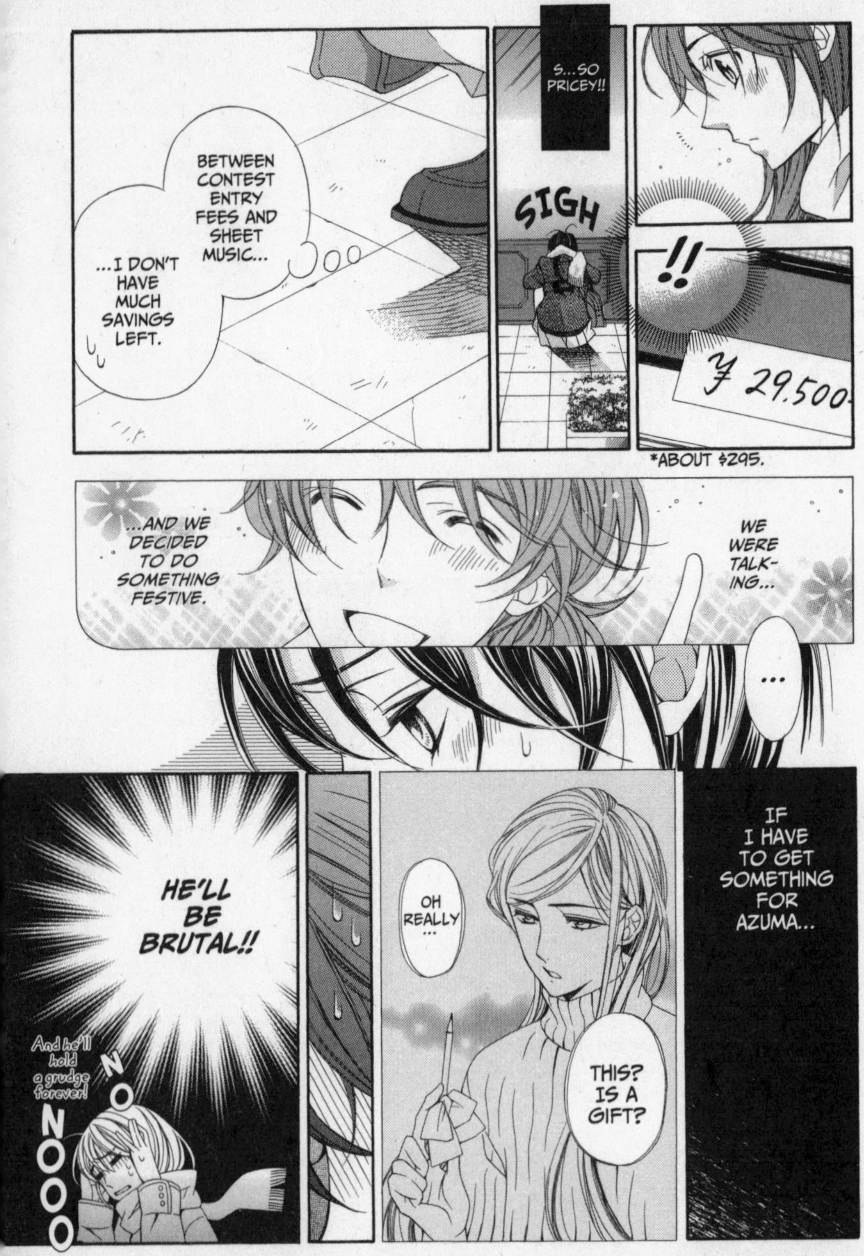
!!
¥ 29.500-
S...SO PRICEY!!
SIGH
BETWEEN CONTEST ENTRY FEES AND SHEET MUSIC...
...I DON'T HAVE MUCH SAVINGS LEFT.
*ABOUT $295.
WE WERE TALKING...
...AND WE DECIDED TO DO SOMETHING FESTIVE.
...
IF I HAVE TO GET SOMETHING FOR AZUMA...
THIS? IS A GIFT?
OH REALLY...
HE'LL BE BRUTAL!!
And he'll hold a grudge forever!
NOOOOO

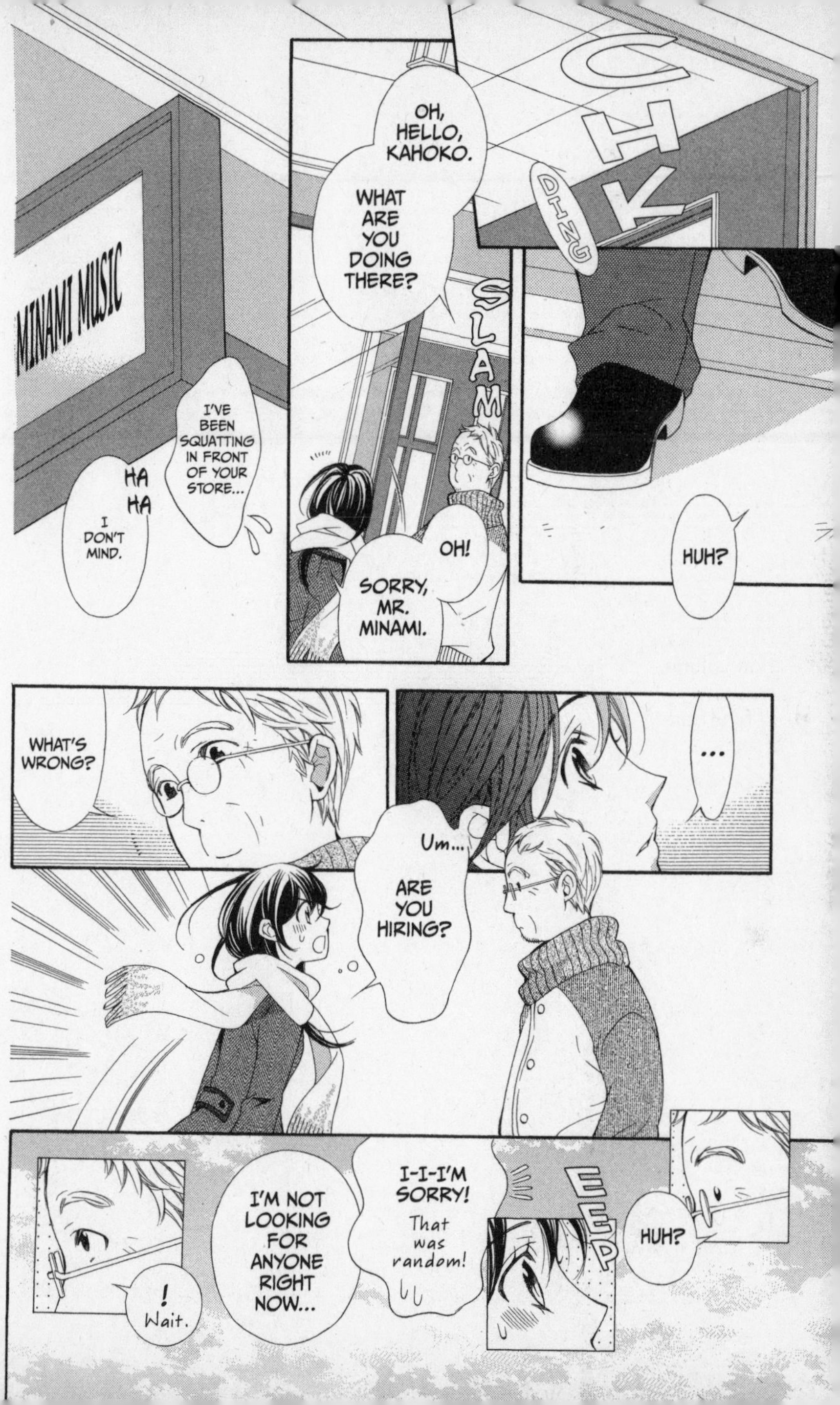
CHK
DING
HUH?
OH, HELLO, KAHOKO.
WHAT ARE YOU DOING THERE?
SLAM
OH!
SORRY, MR. MINAMI.
MINAMI MUSIC
I'VE BEEN SQUATTING IN FRONT OF YOUR STORE...
HA HA
I DON'T MIND.
...
WHAT'S WRONG?
Um...
ARE YOU HIRING?
HUH?
EEP
I-I-I'M SORRY!
That was random!
I'M NOT LOOKING FOR ANYONE RIGHT NOW...
!
Wait.

Hello!
It's been a while!
It's me, Kure.
Thank you so much for picking up the final volume of *La Corda d'Oro*.

I decided to use the columns in this volume to show off "ultimate date outfits" suggested by the readers of *LaLa* magazine.

I hope you enjoy them.

Yuki Kure

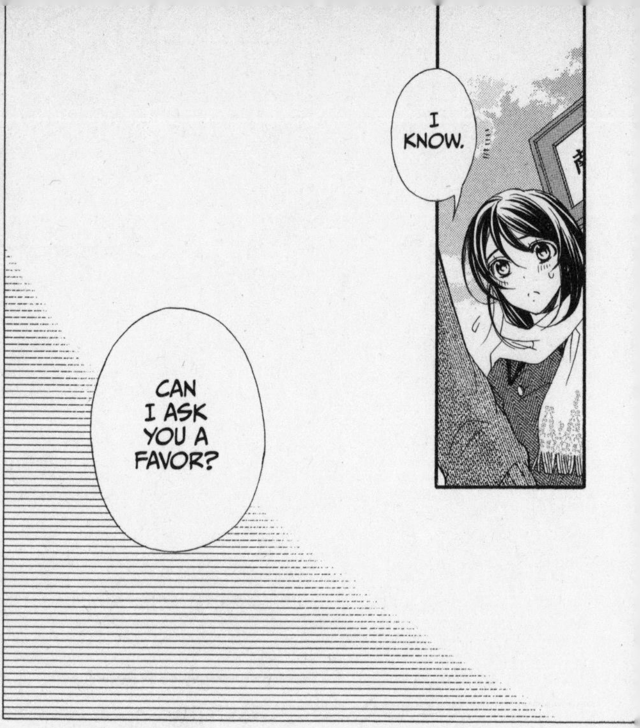

I KNOW.
CAN I ASK YOU A FAVOR?

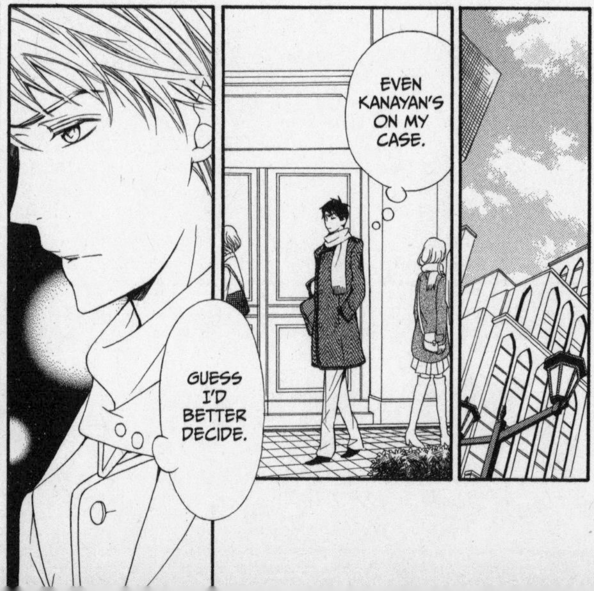

EVEN KANAYAN'S ON MY CASE.
GUESS I'D BETTER DECIDE.

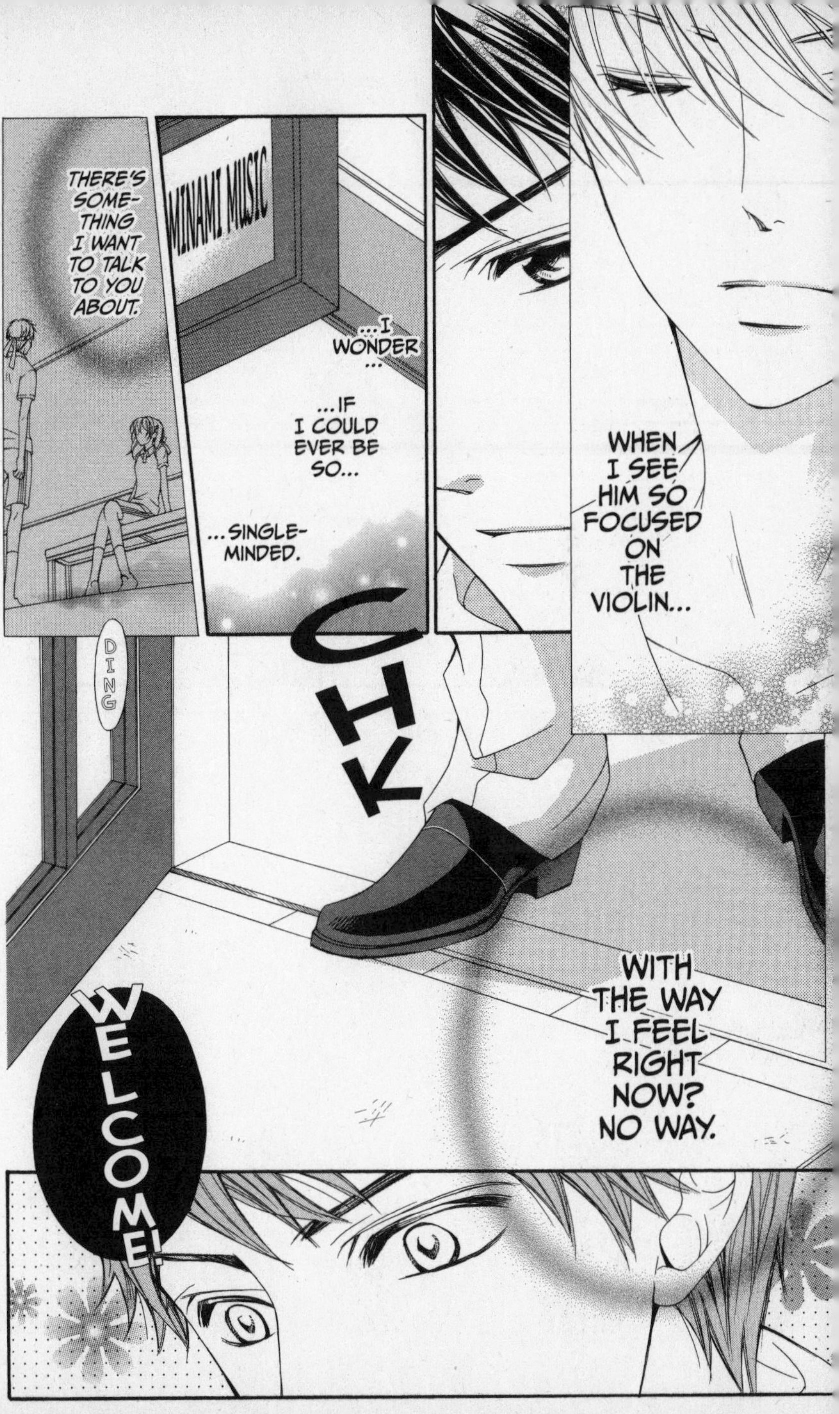
WHEN I SEE HIM SO FOCUSED ON THE VIOLIN...
...I WONDER...
...IF I COULD EVER BE SO...
...SINGLE-MINDED.
MINAMI MUSIC
THERE'S SOMETHING I WANT TO TALK TO YOU ABOUT.
WITH THE WAY I FEEL RIGHT NOW? NO WAY.
CHK
DING
WELCOME!

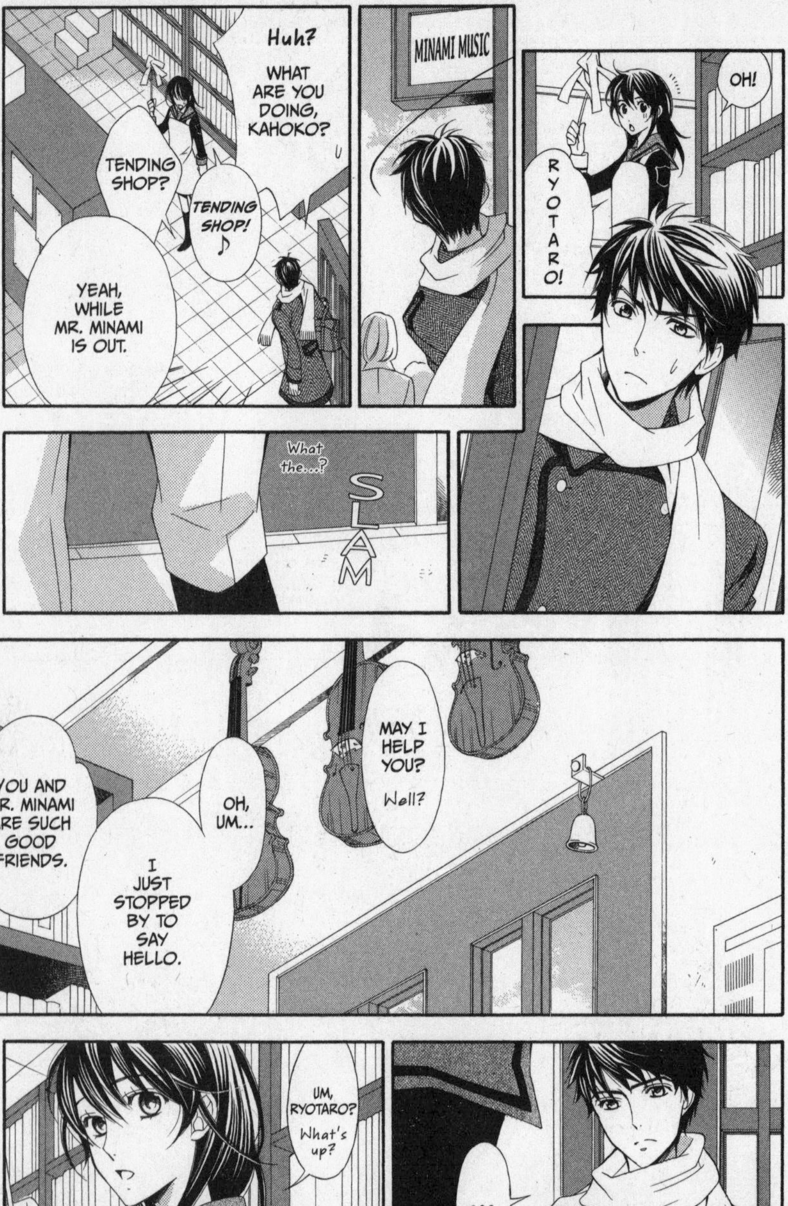
OH!
RYOTARO!
MINAMI MUSIC
Huh?
WHAT ARE YOU DOING, KAHOKO?
TENDING SHOP! ♪
TENDING SHOP?
YEAH, WHILE MR. MINAMI IS OUT.
What the...?
SLAM
MAY I HELP YOU?
Well?
OH, UM...
I JUST STOPPED BY TO SAY HELLO.
YOU AND MR. MINAMI ARE SUCH GOOD FRIENDS.
...
UM, RYOTARO?
What's up?

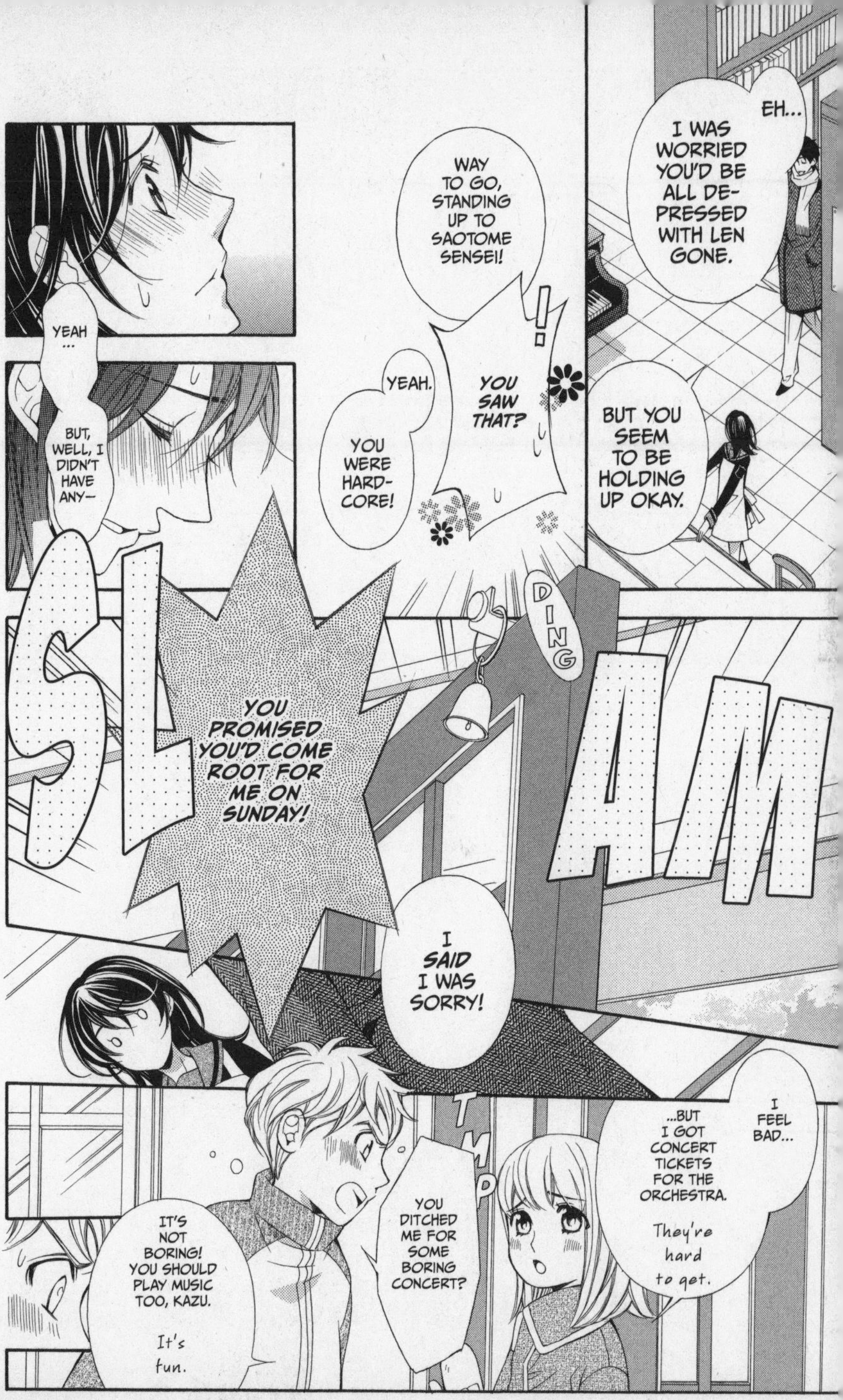
EH...
I WAS WORRIED YOU'D BE ALL DE-PRESSED WITH LEN GONE.
BUT YOU SEEM TO BE HOLDING UP OKAY.
WAY TO GO, STANDING UP TO SAOTOME SENSEI!
!
YOU SAW THAT?
YEAH.
YOU WERE HARD-CORE!
YEAH ...
BUT, WELL, I DIDN'T HAVE ANY—
DING
SLAM
YOU PROMISED YOU'D COME ROOT FOR ME ON SUNDAY!
I SAID I WAS SORRY!
I FEEL BAD...
...BUT I GOT CONCERT TICKETS FOR THE ORCHESTRA.
They're hard to get.
TMP
YOU DITCHED ME FOR SOME BORING CONCERT?
IT'S NOT BORING! YOU SHOULD PLAY MUSIC TOO, KAZU.
It's fun.

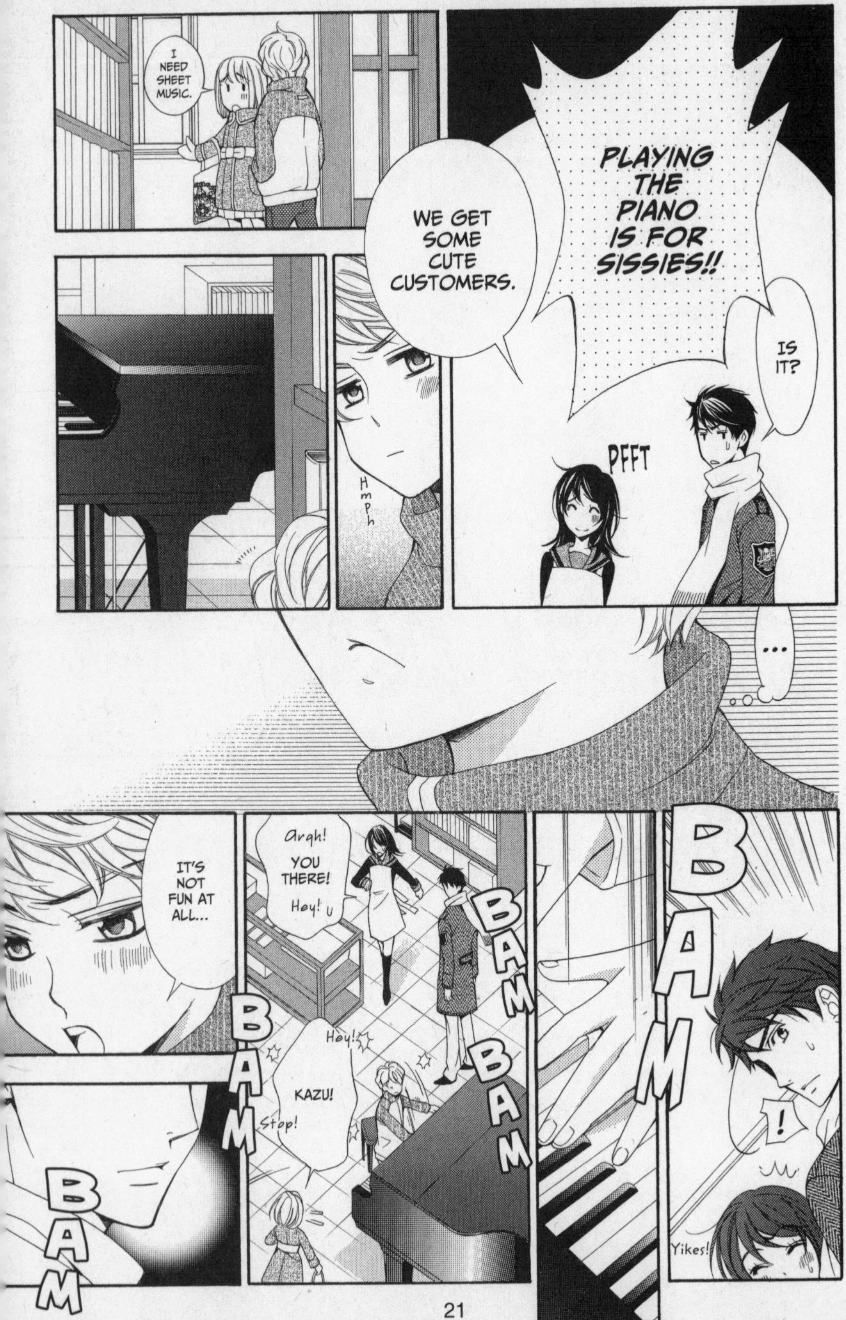
PLAYING THE PIANO IS FOR SISSIES!!
WE GET SOME CUTE CUSTOMERS.
I NEED SHEET MUSIC.
IS IT?
PFFT
Hmph
...
BAM
!
Yikes!
BAM
BAM
Argh!
YOU THERE!
Hey!
Hey!
KAZU!
Stop!
IT'S NOT FUN AT ALL...
BAM
BAM
BAM
BAM

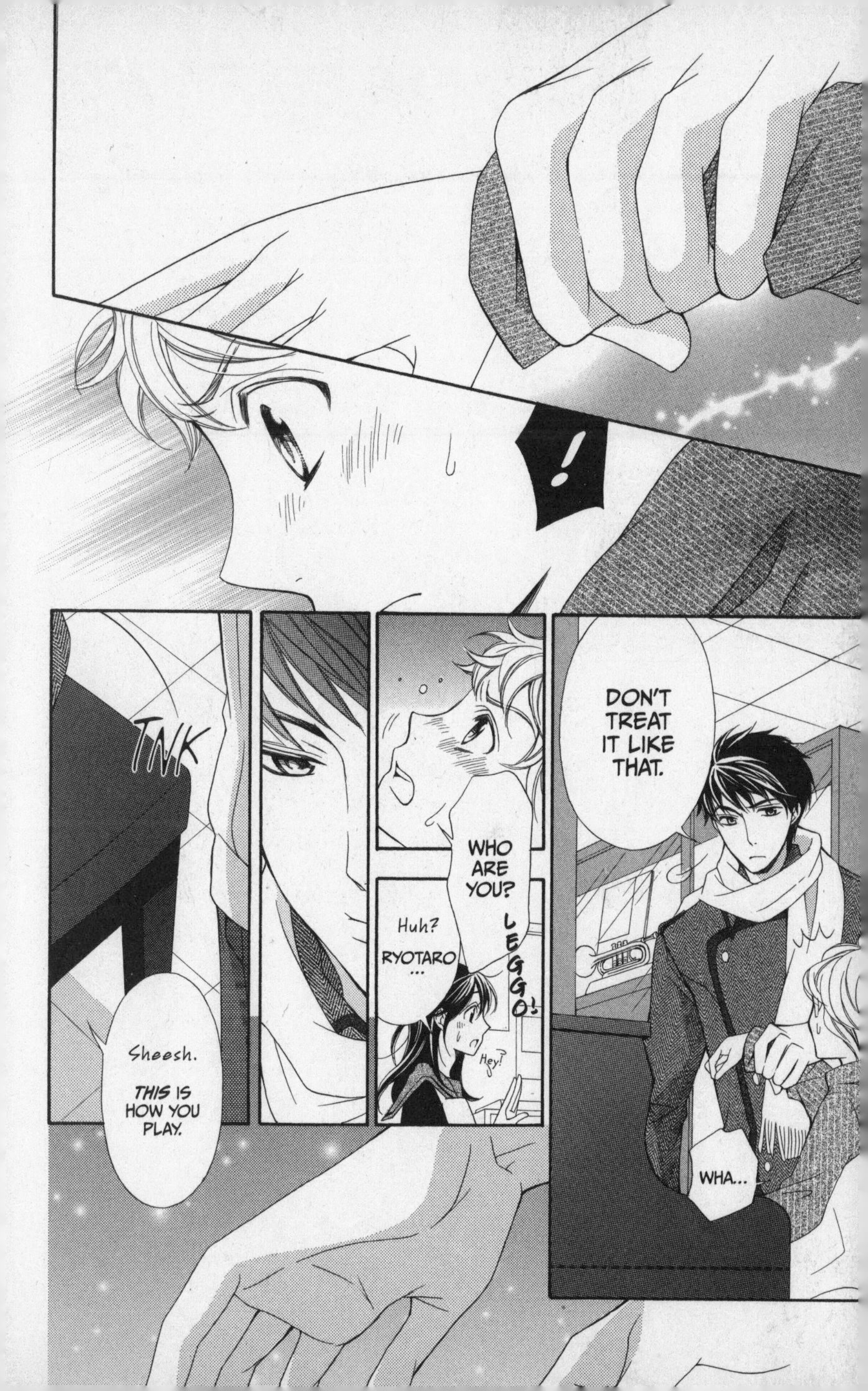
!
DON'T TREAT IT LIKE THAT.
WHA...
WHO ARE YOU?
LEGGO!
Huh?
RYOTARO ...
Hey!?
TNK
Sheesh.
THIS IS HOW YOU PLAY.

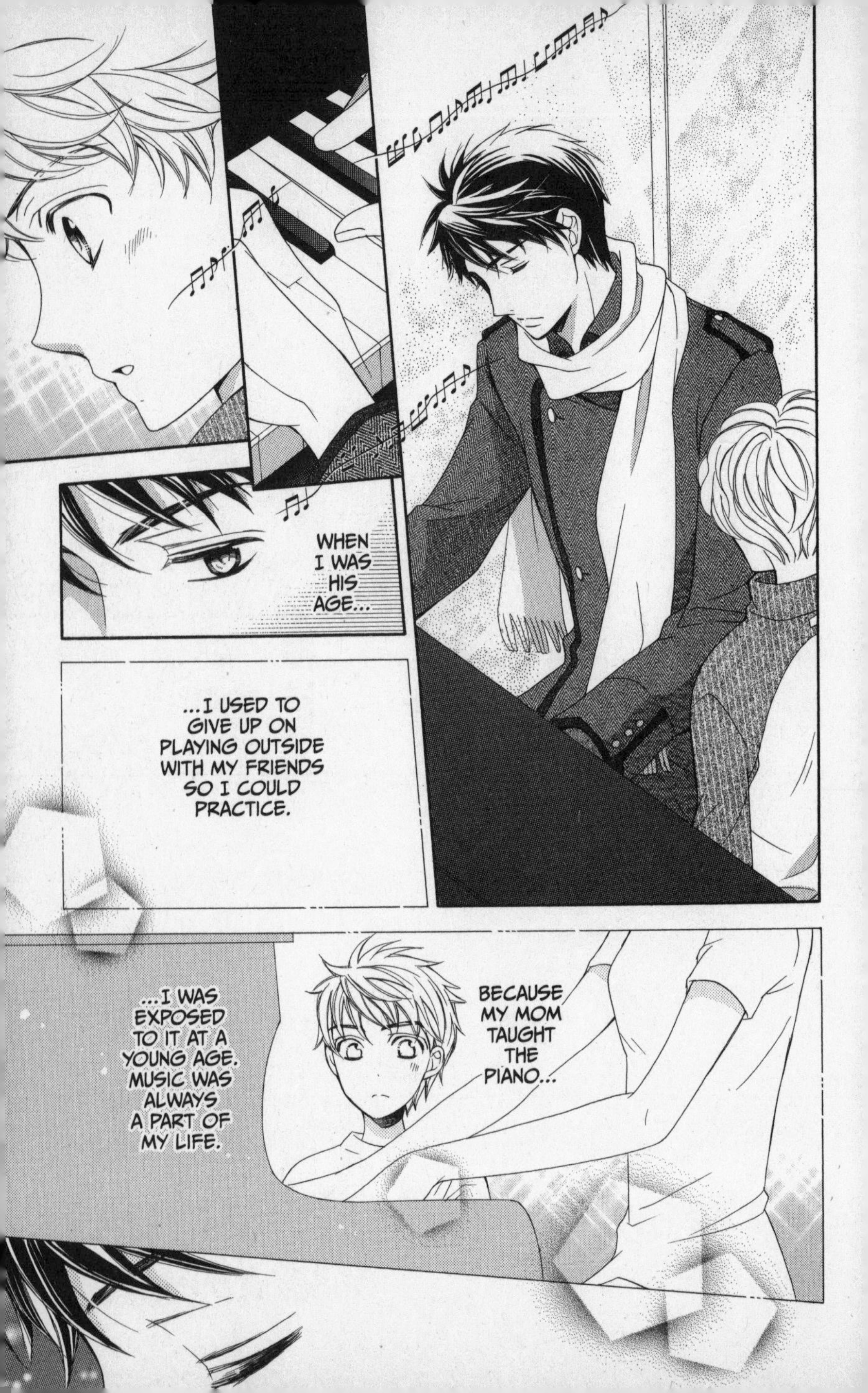
WHEN I WAS HIS AGE...
...I USED TO GIVE UP ON PLAYING OUTSIDE WITH MY FRIENDS SO I COULD PRACTICE.
BECAUSE MY MOM TAUGHT THE PIANO...
...I WAS EXPOSED TO IT AT A YOUNG AGE. MUSIC WAS ALWAYS A PART OF MY LIFE.

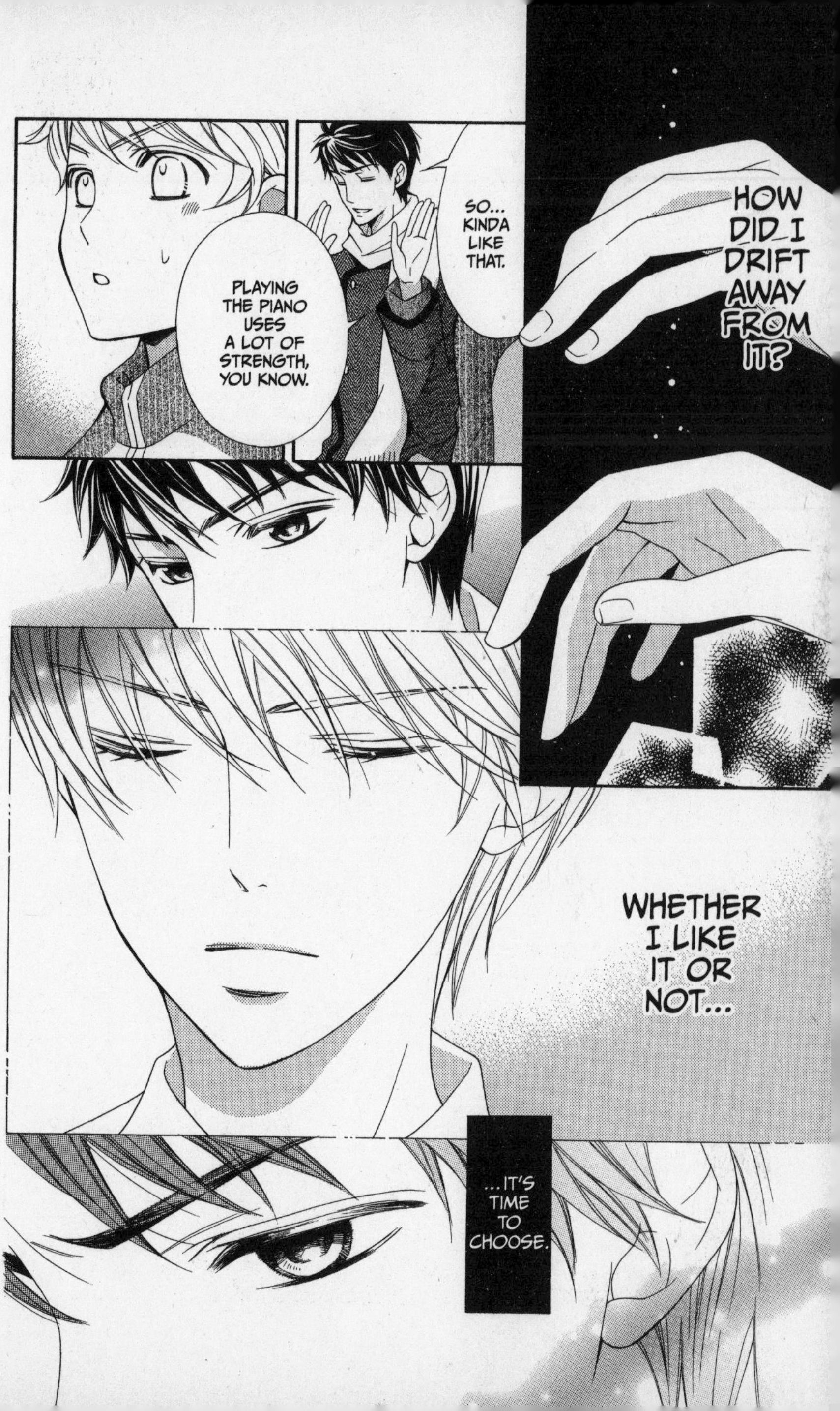
HOW DID I DRIFT AWAY FROM IT?
SO... KINDA LIKE THAT.
PLAYING THE PIANO USES A LOT OF STRENGTH, YOU KNOW.
WHETHER I LIKE IT OR NOT...
...IT'S TIME TO CHOOSE.

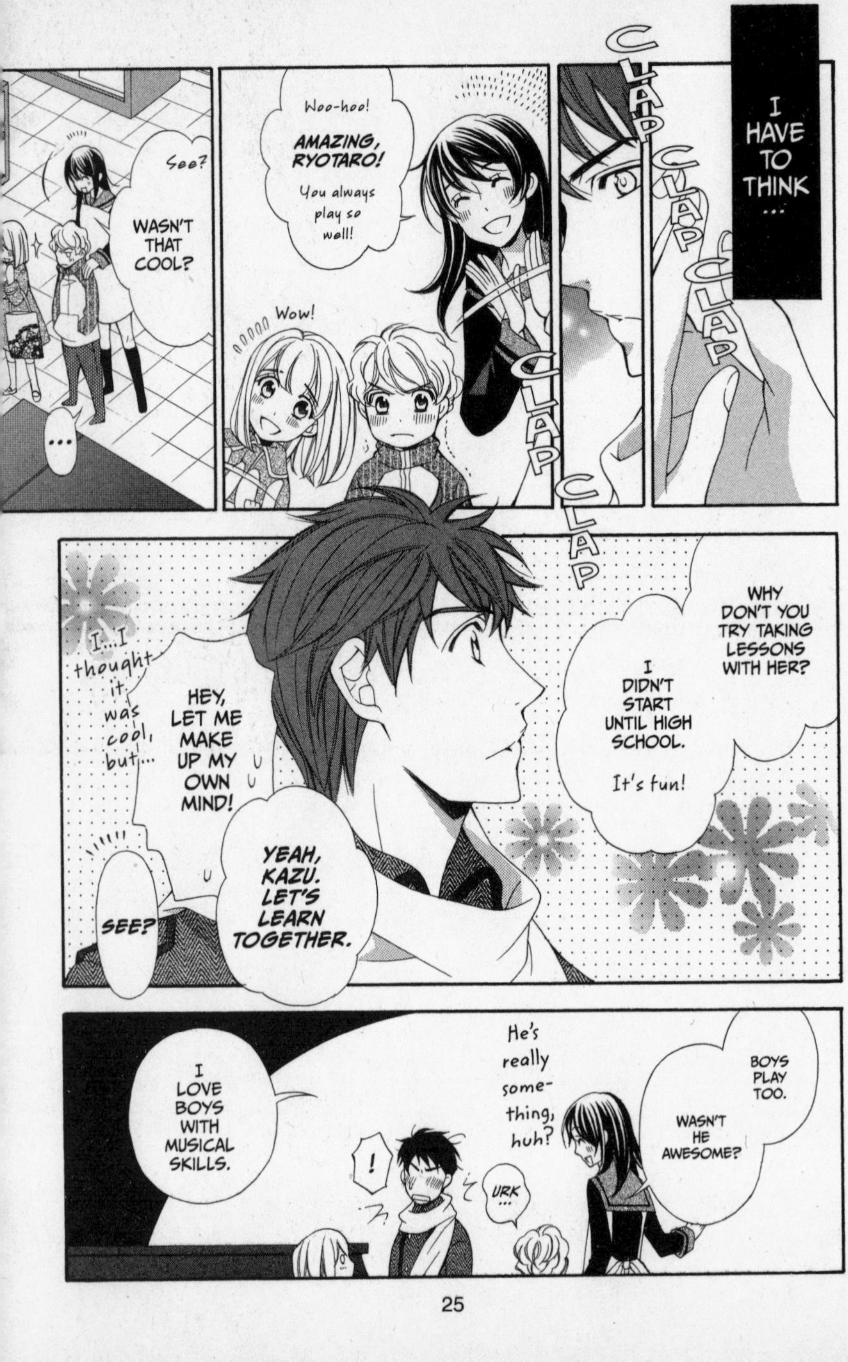
I HAVE TO THINK...
CLAP CLAP CLAP
CLAP CLAP CLAP
Woo-hoo! AMAZING, RYOTARO! You always play so well!
Wow!
See? WASN'T THAT COOL?
...
WHY DON'T YOU TRY TAKING LESSONS WITH HER?
I DIDN'T START UNTIL HIGH SCHOOL. It's fun!
YEAH, KAZU. LET'S LEARN TOGETHER.
HEY, LET ME MAKE UP MY OWN MIND!
I...I thought it was cool, but...
SEE?
BOYS PLAY TOO.
WASN'T HE AWESOME?
He's really some-thing, huh?
URK...
!
I LOVE BOYS WITH MUSICAL SKILLS.

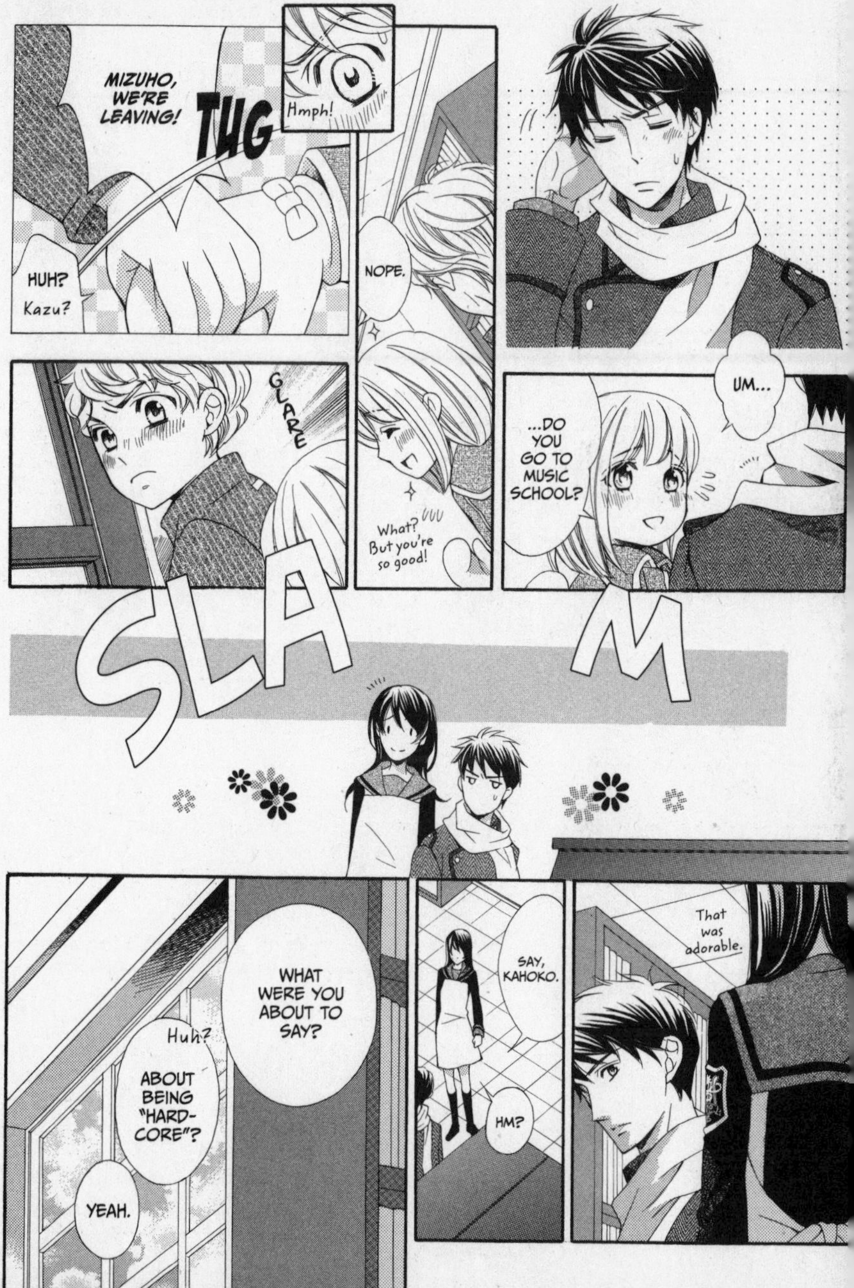
UM...
...DO YOU GO TO MUSIC SCHOOL?
Hmph!
NOPE.
What? But you're so good!
MIZUHO, WE'RE LEAVING!
TUG
HUH?
Kazu?
GLARE
SLAM
That was adorable.
SAY, KAHOKO.
HM?
WHAT WERE YOU ABOUT TO SAY?
Huh?
ABOUT BEING "HARD-CORE"?
YEAH.

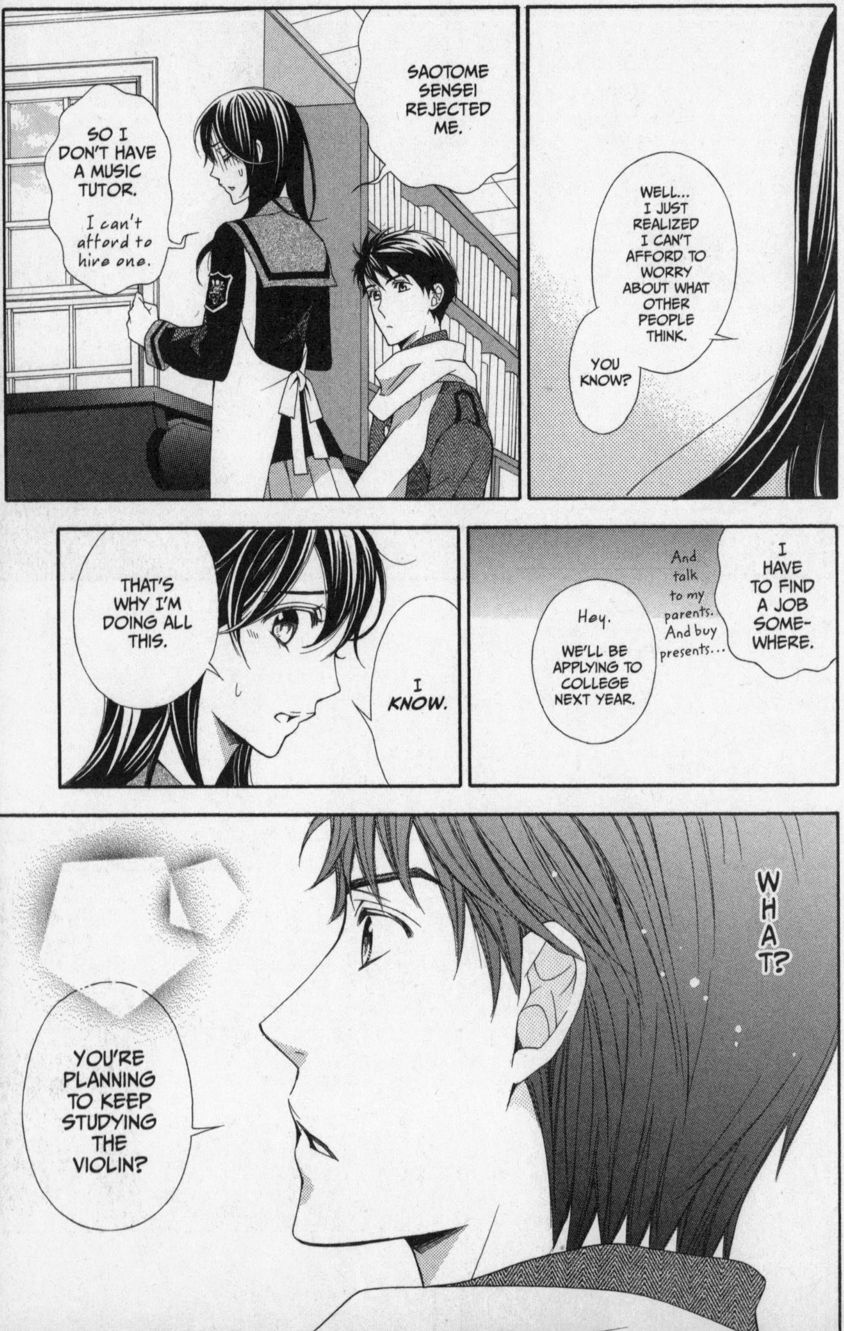
WELL... I JUST REALIZED I CAN'T AFFORD TO WORRY ABOUT WHAT OTHER PEOPLE THINK.
YOU KNOW?
SAOTOME SENSEI REJECTED ME.
SO I DON'T HAVE A MUSIC TUTOR.
I can't afford to hire one.
I HAVE TO FIND A JOB SOME-WHERE.
And talk to my parents. And buy presents...
Hey.
WE'LL BE APPLYING TO COLLEGE NEXT YEAR.
I KNOW.
THAT'S WHY I'M DOING ALL THIS.
WHAT?
YOU'RE PLANNING TO KEEP STUDYING THE VIOLIN?

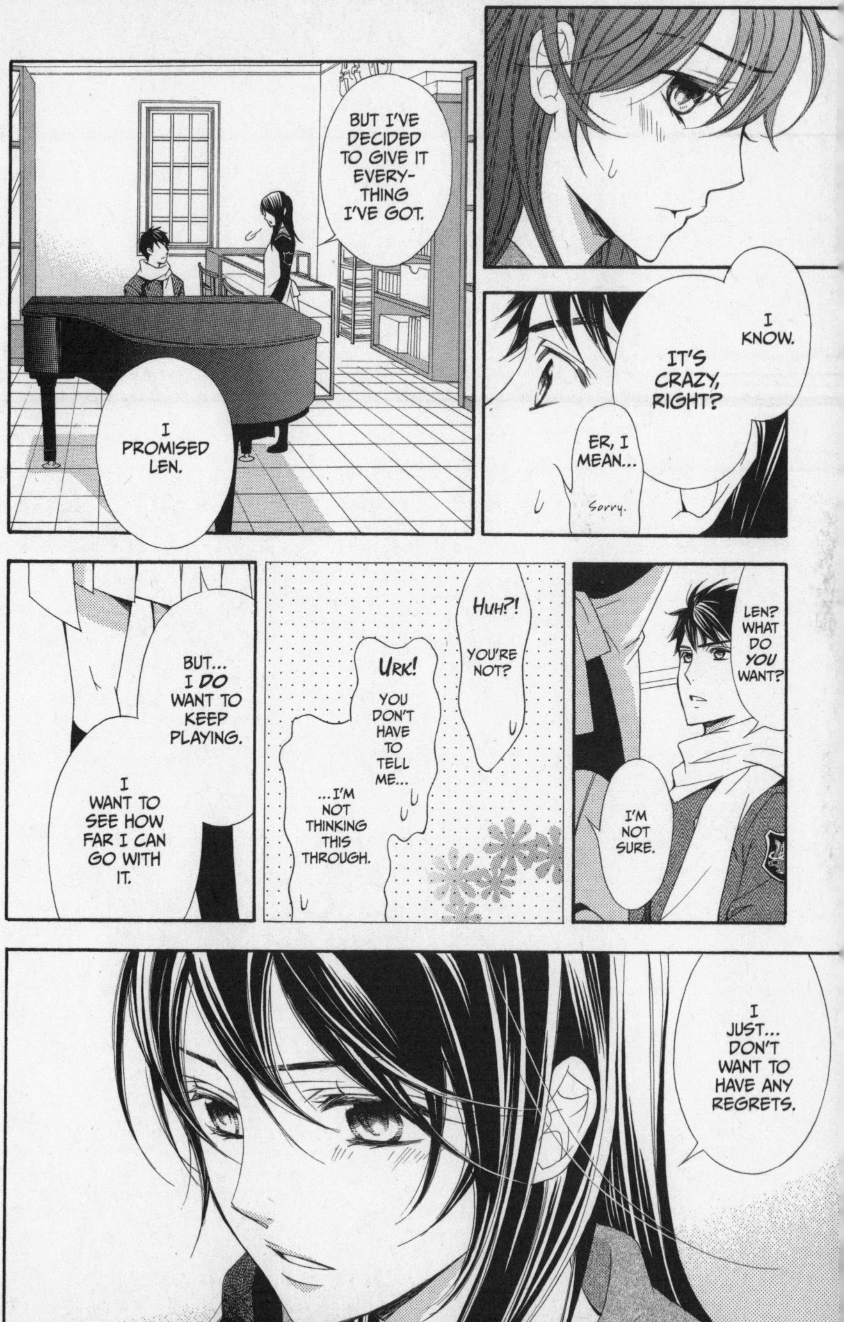
I KNOW.
IT'S CRAZY, RIGHT?
ER, I MEAN...
Sorry.
BUT I'VE DECIDED TO GIVE IT EVERYTHING I'VE GOT.
I PROMISED LEN.
LEN? WHAT DO *YOU* WANT?
I'M NOT SURE.
HUH?!
YOU'RE NOT?
URK!
YOU DON'T HAVE TO TELL ME...
...I'M NOT THINKING THIS THROUGH.
BUT... I *DO* WANT TO KEEP PLAYING.
I WANT TO SEE HOW FAR I CAN GO WITH IT.
I JUST... DON'T WANT TO HAVE ANY REGRETS.

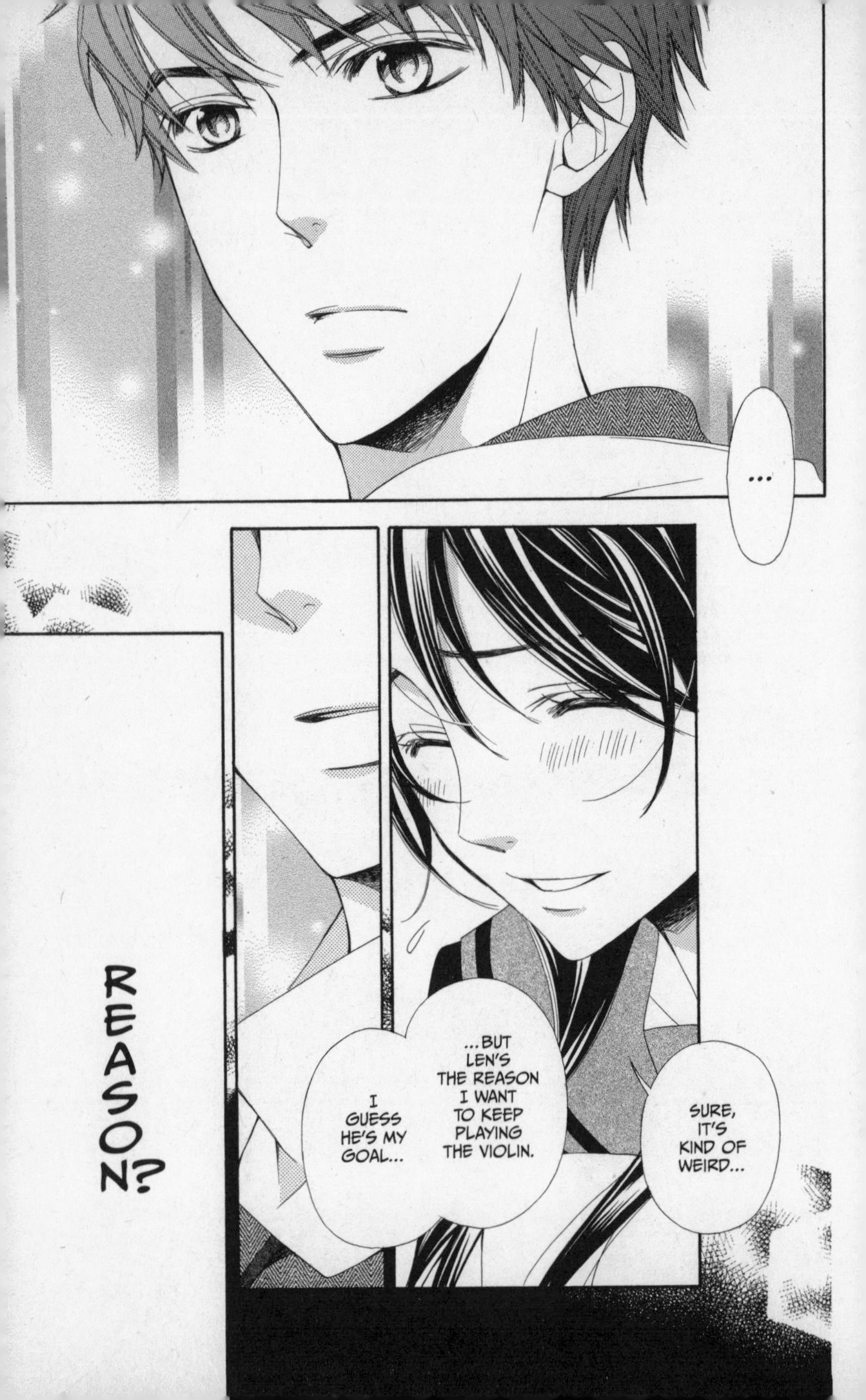
...
SURE, IT'S KIND OF WEIRD...
...BUT LEN'S THE REASON I WANT TO KEEP PLAYING THE VIOLIN.
I GUESS HE'S MY GOAL...
REASON?

WHAT'S MY REASON?
I KNOW, I KNOW.
I'LL NEVER HAVE THE TALENT...
HA HA
...TO GET ANYWHERE NEAR HIM.
KAHOKO...
...MY REASON IS YOU.

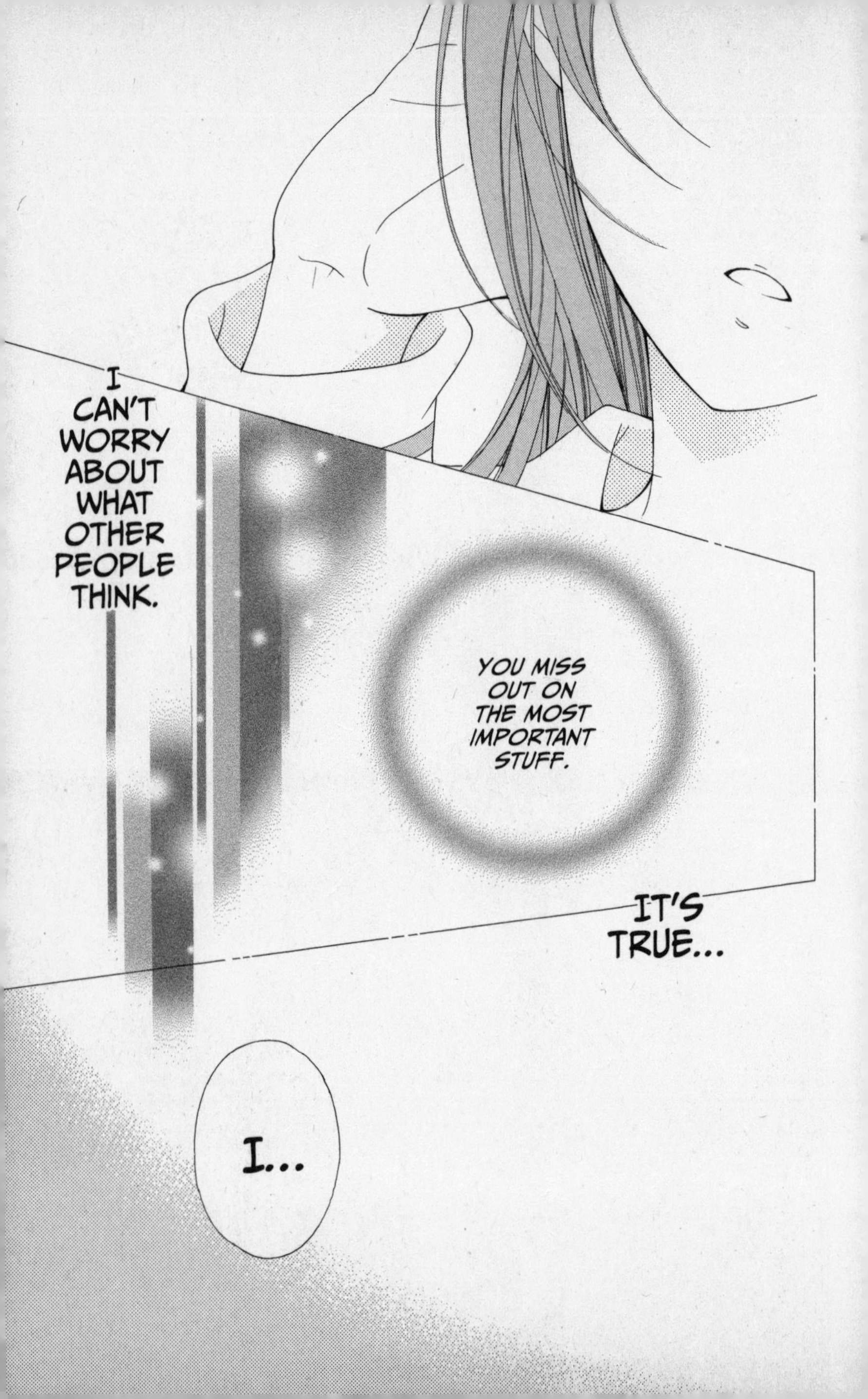
I CAN'T WORRY ABOUT WHAT OTHER PEOPLE THINK.
YOU MISS OUT ON THE MOST IMPORTANT STUFF.
IT'S TRUE...
I...

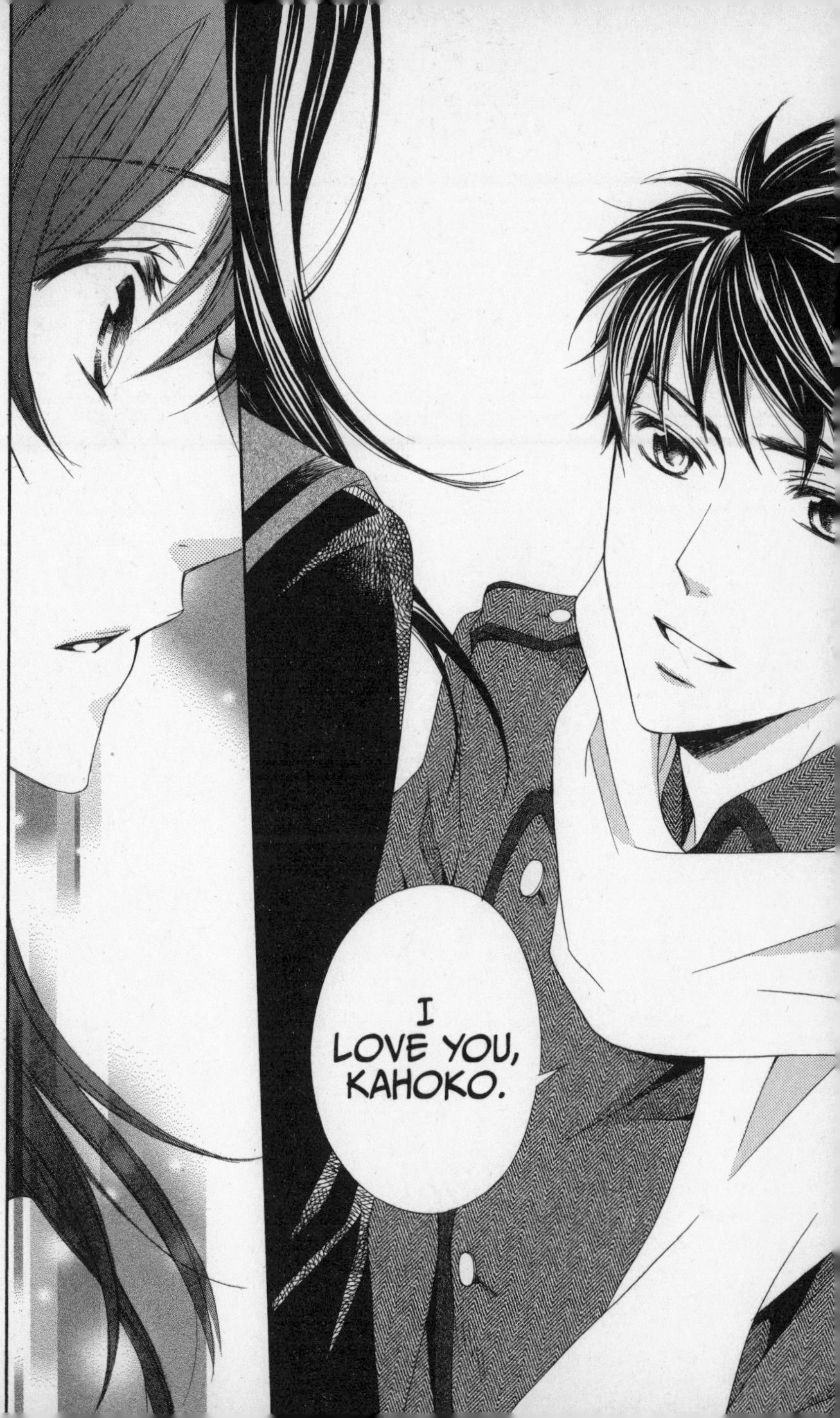
I LOVE YOU, KAHOKO.

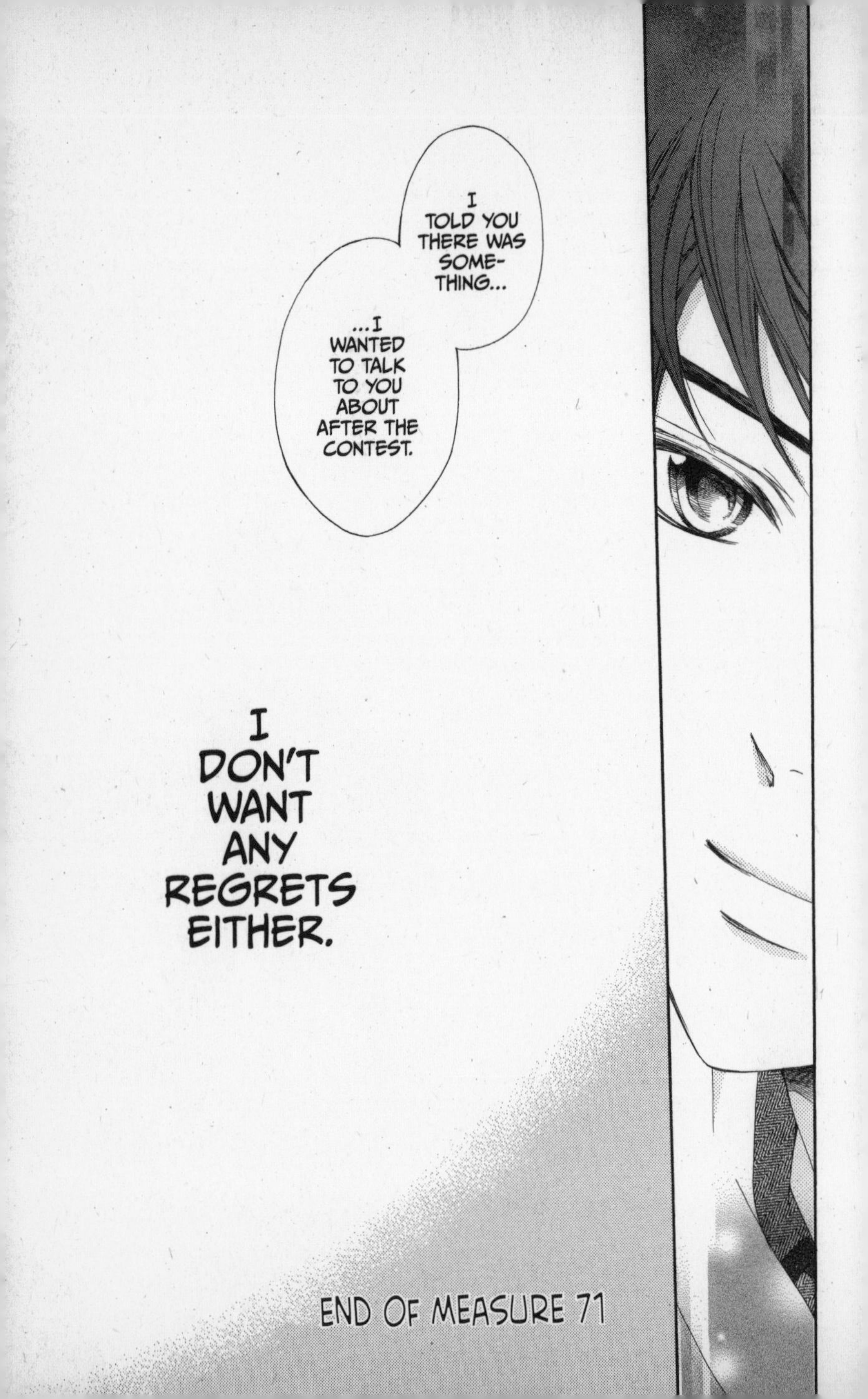
I TOLD YOU THERE WAS SOME-THING...
...I WANTED TO TALK TO YOU ABOUT AFTER THE CONTEST.
I DON'T WANT ANY REGRETS EITHER.
END OF MEASURE 71

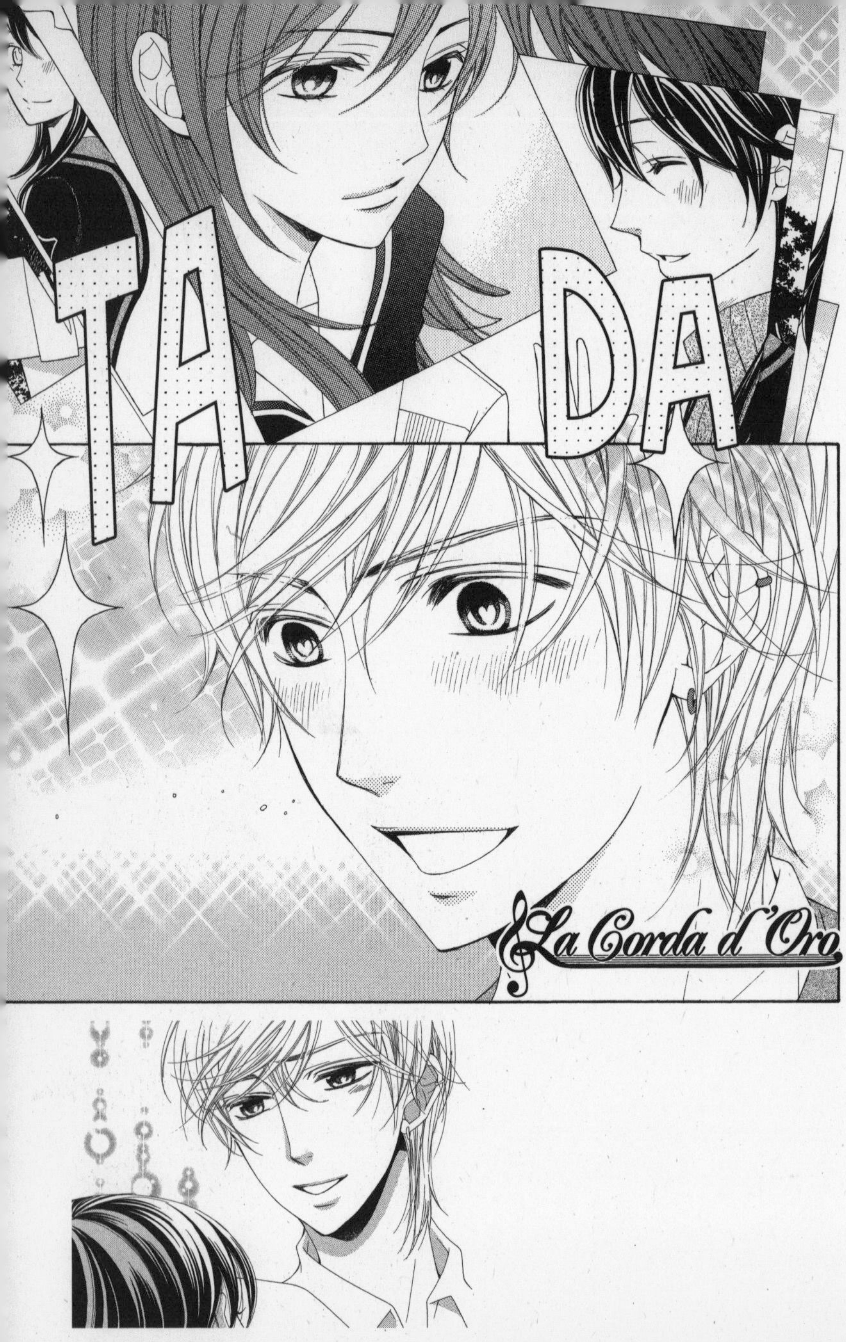
TA DA
La Corda d'Oro

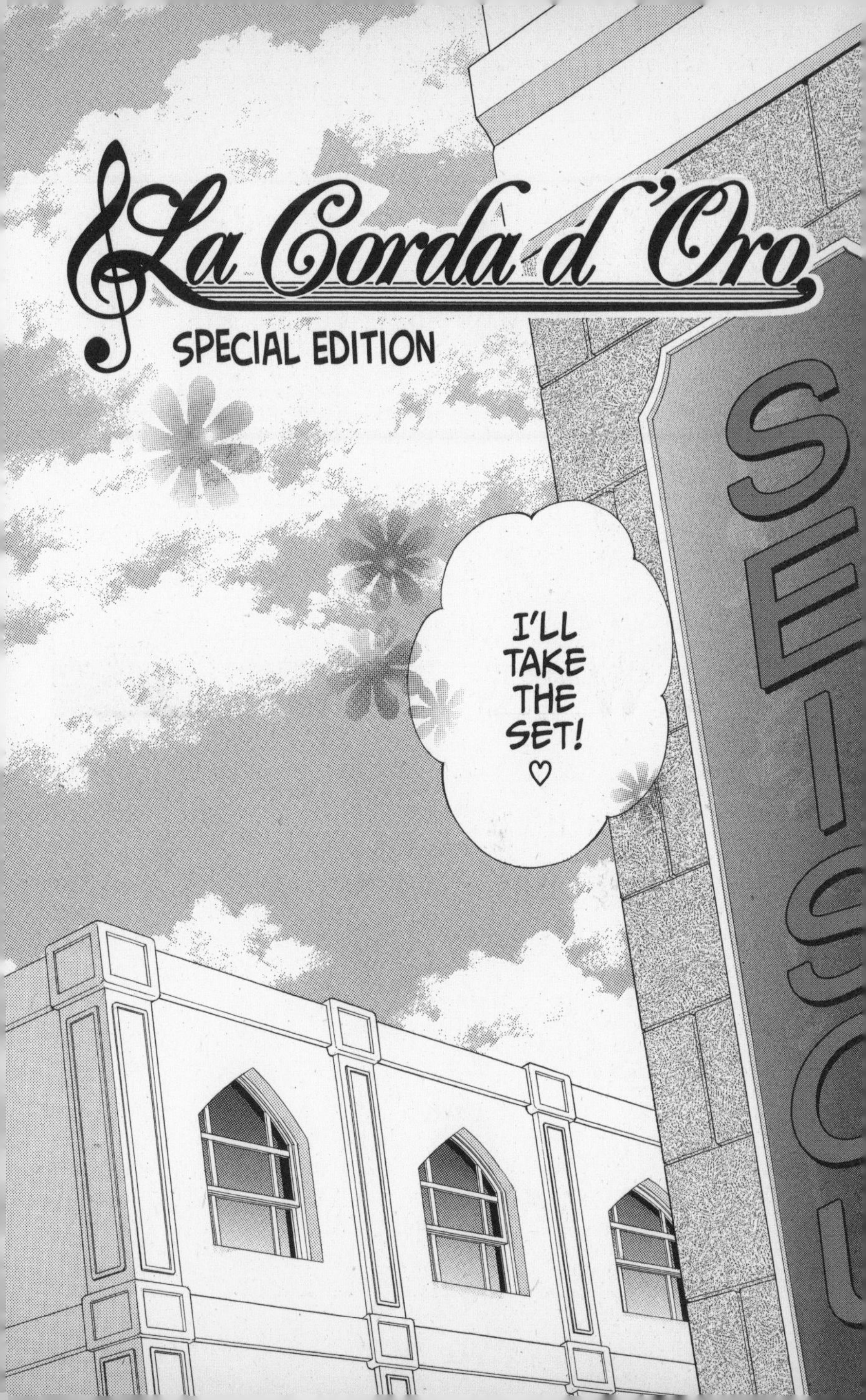
La Corda d'Oro
SPECIAL EDITION
I'LL TAKE THE SET! ♡
SEISO

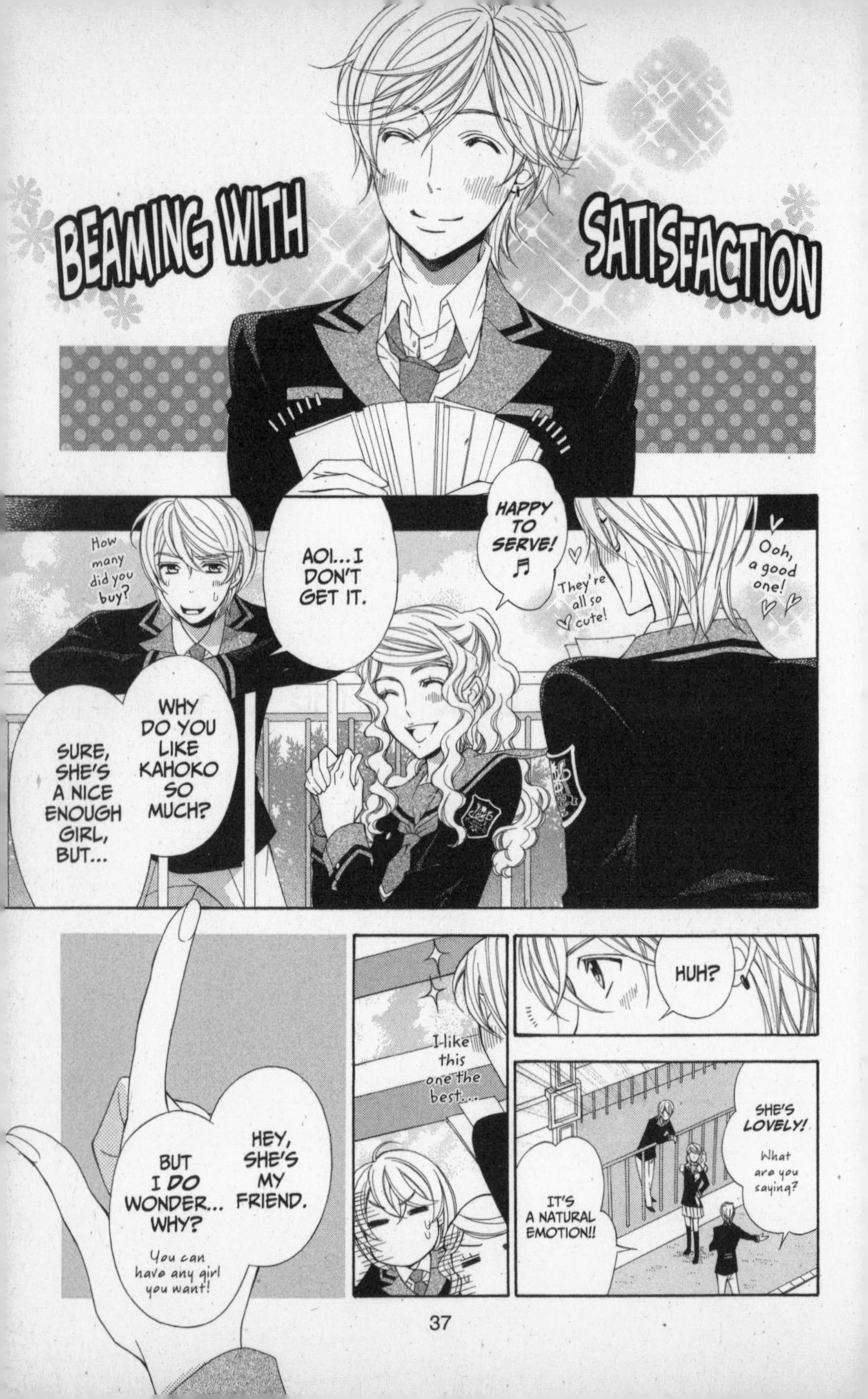
BEAMING WITH SATISFACTION
Ooh, a good one!
They're all so cute!
HAPPY TO SERVE! ♬
AOI...I DON'T GET IT.
How many did you buy?
WHY DO YOU LIKE KAHOKO SO MUCH?
SURE, SHE'S A NICE ENOUGH GIRL, BUT...
HUH?
SHE'S *LOVELY!*
What are you saying?
IT'S A NATURAL EMOTION!!
I like this one the best...
HEY, SHE'S MY FRIEND.
BUT I *DO* WONDER... WHY?
You can have any girl you want!

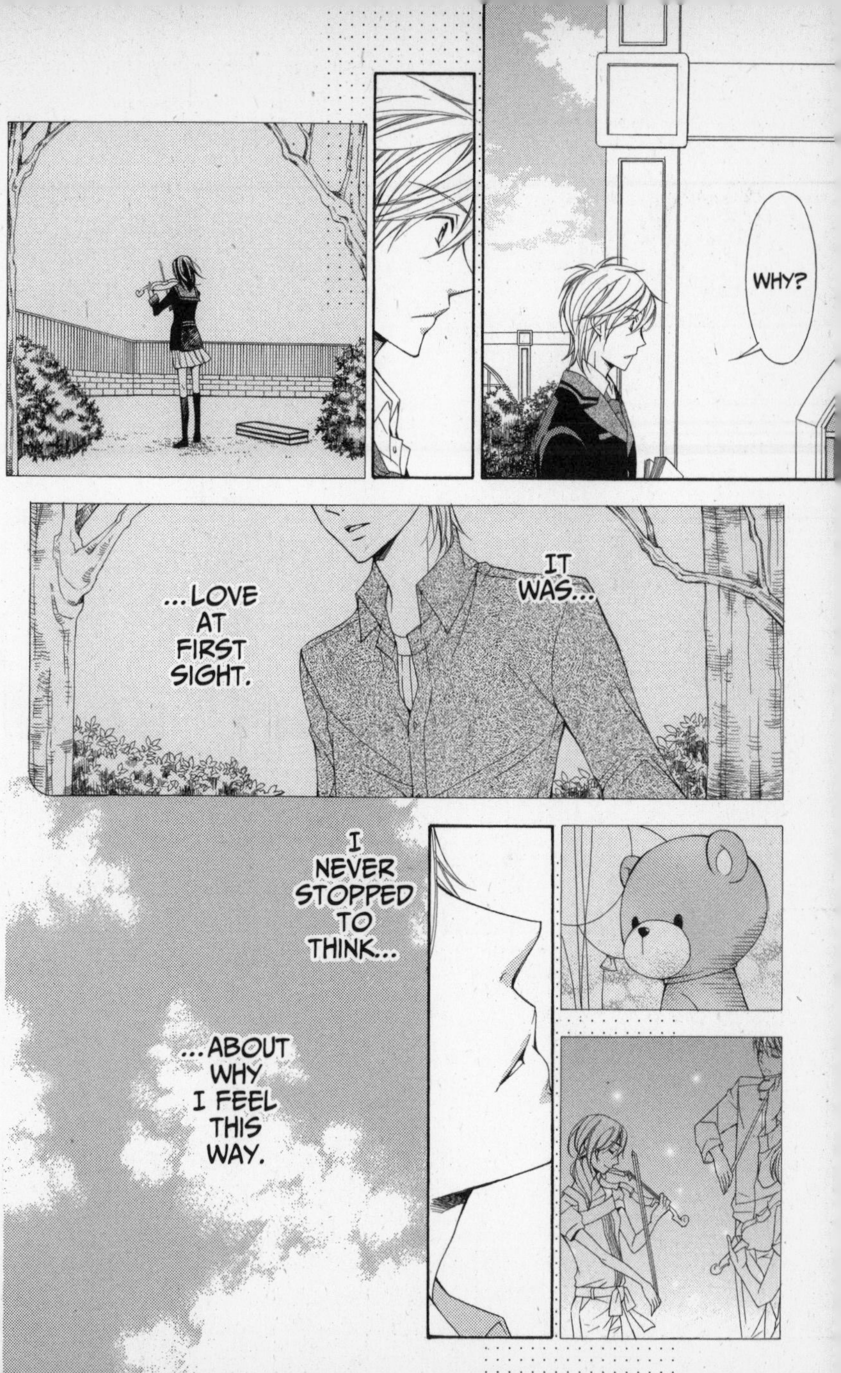
WHY?
IT WAS...
...LOVE AT FIRST SIGHT.
I NEVER STOPPED TO THINK...
...ABOUT WHY I FEEL THIS WAY.

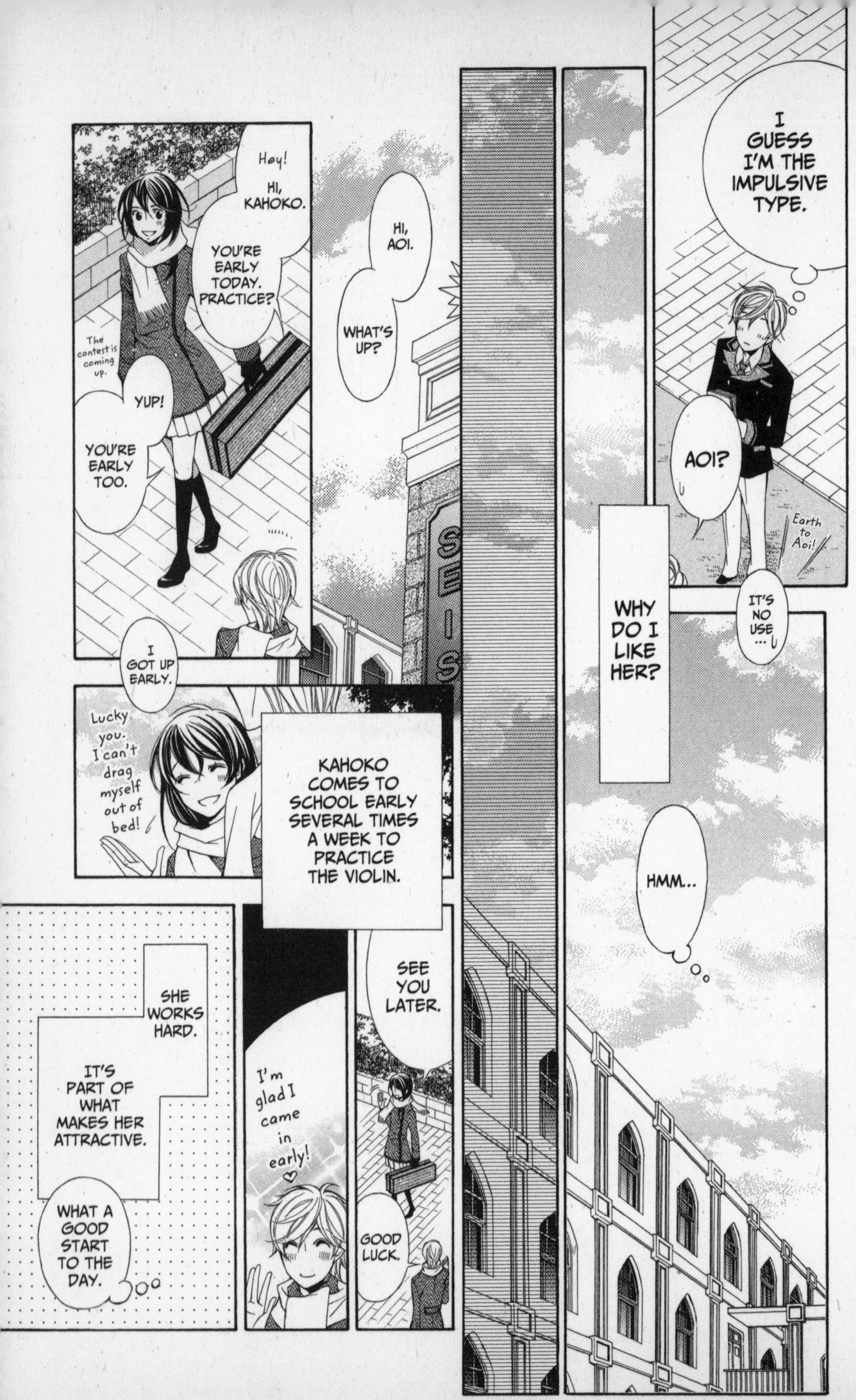
I GUESS I'M THE IMPULSIVE TYPE.
AOI?
Earth to Aoi!
IT'S NO USE...
WHY DO I LIKE HER?
HMM...
HI, AOI.
WHAT'S UP?
Hey!
HI, KAHOKO.
YOU'RE EARLY TODAY. PRACTICE?
The contest is coming up.
YUP!
YOU'RE EARLY TOO.
I GOT UP EARLY.
Lucky you. I can't drag myself out of bed!
KAHOKO COMES TO SCHOOL EARLY SEVERAL TIMES A WEEK TO PRACTICE THE VIOLIN.
SEE YOU LATER.
GOOD LUCK.
I'm glad I came in early!
SHE WORKS HARD.
IT'S PART OF WHAT MAKES HER ATTRACTIVE.
WHAT A GOOD START TO THE DAY.

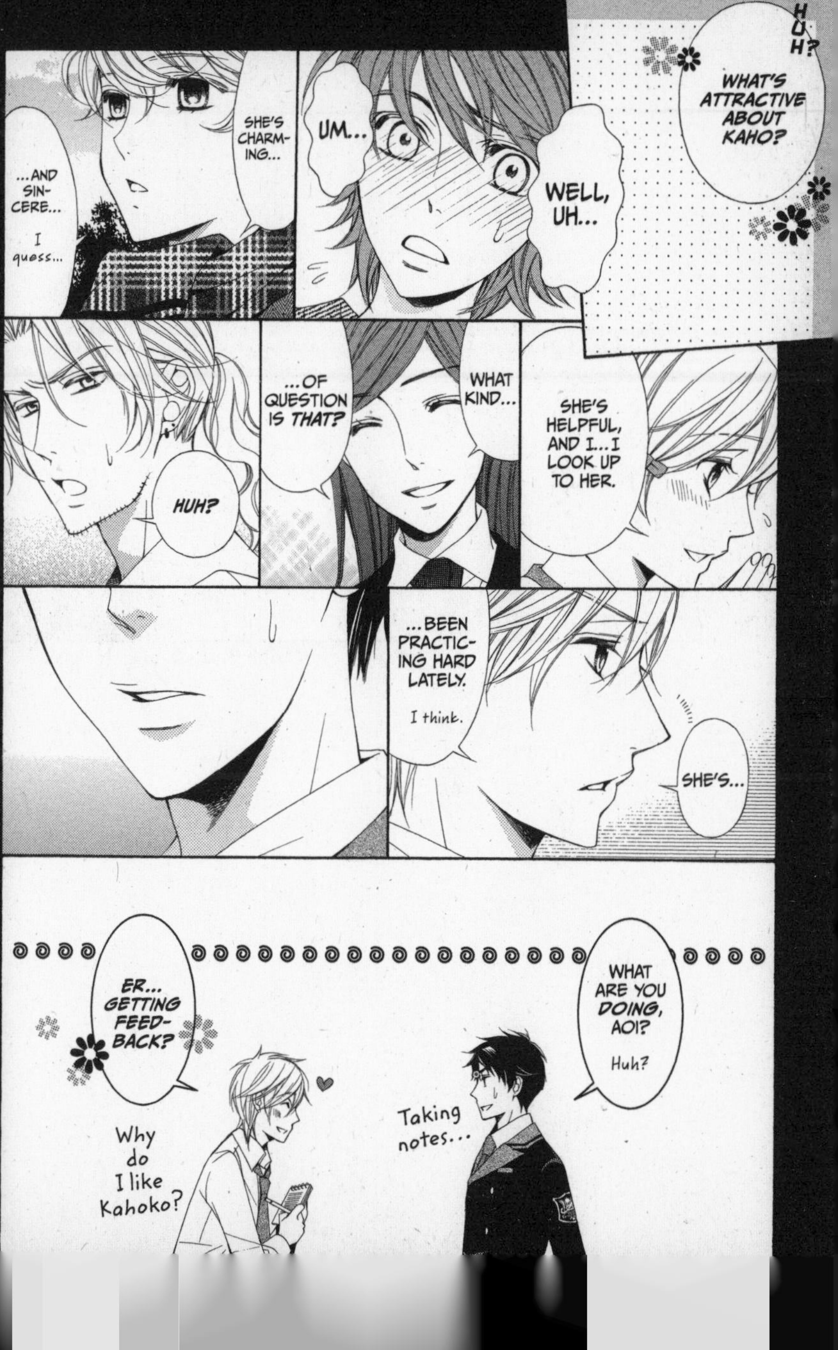
HUH?
WHAT'S ATTRACTIVE ABOUT KAHO?
WELL, UH...
UM...
SHE'S CHARMING...
...AND SINCERE...
I guess...
SHE'S HELPFUL, AND I...I LOOK UP TO HER.
WHAT KIND...
...OF QUESTION IS THAT?
HUH?
SHE'S...
...BEEN PRACTICING HARD LATELY.
I think.
WHAT ARE YOU DOING, AOI?
Huh?
Taking notes...
ER... GETTING FEEDBACK?
Why do I like Kahoko?

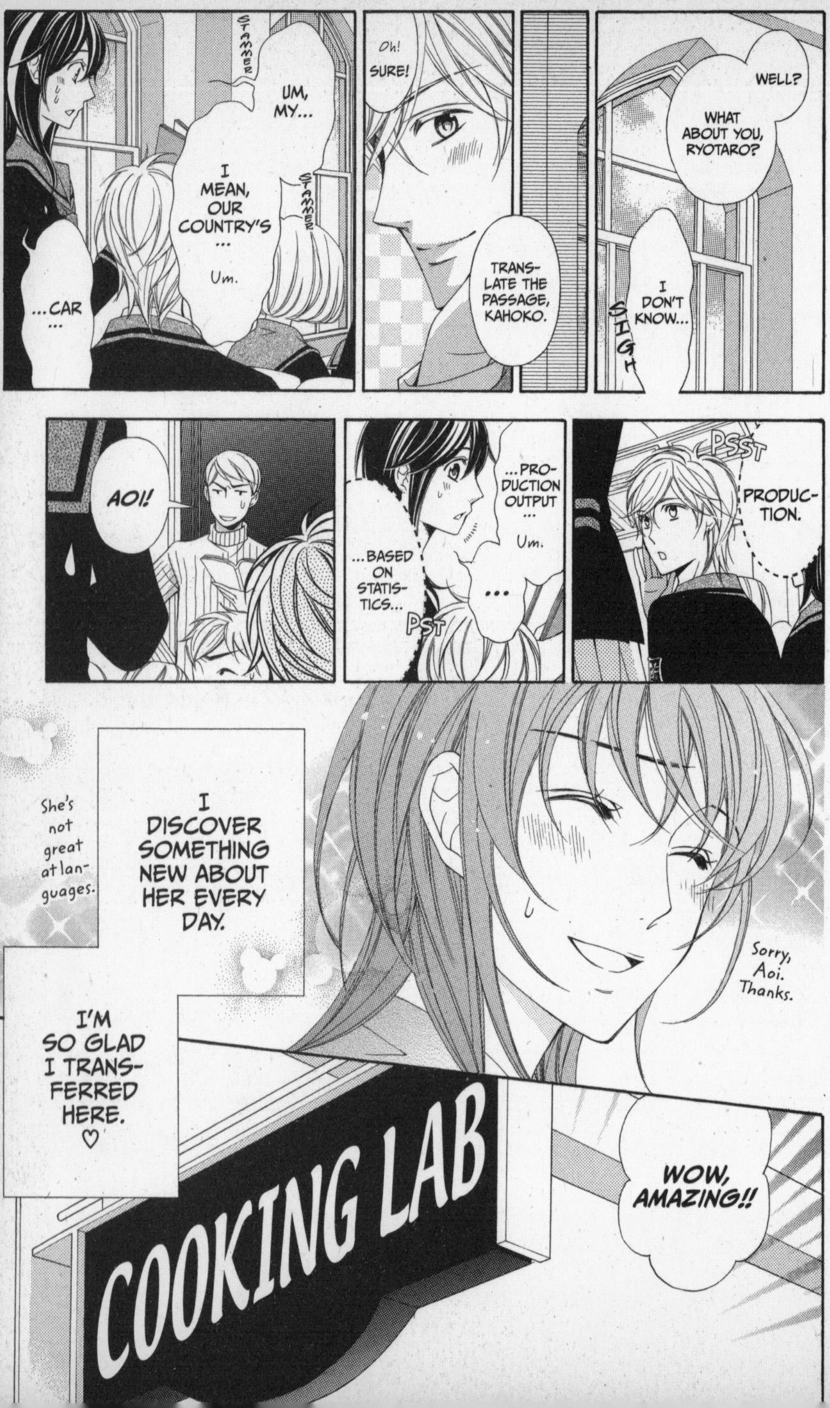
WELL? WHAT ABOUT YOU, RYOTARO?
I DON'T KNOW...
SIGH
TRANS-LATE THE PASSAGE, KAHOKO.
Oh! SURE!
STAMMER
UM, MY...
STAMMER
I MEAN, OUR COUNTRY'S ... Um.
...CAR ...
PSSST
PRODUC-TION.
...PRO-DUCTION OUTPUT ... Um.
...
...BASED ON STATIS-TICS...
PST
AOI!
Sorry, Aoi. Thanks.
I DISCOVER SOMETHING NEW ABOUT HER EVERY DAY.
She's not great at lan-guages.
I'M SO GLAD I TRANS-FERRED HERE. ♡
WOW, AMAZING!!
COOKING LAB

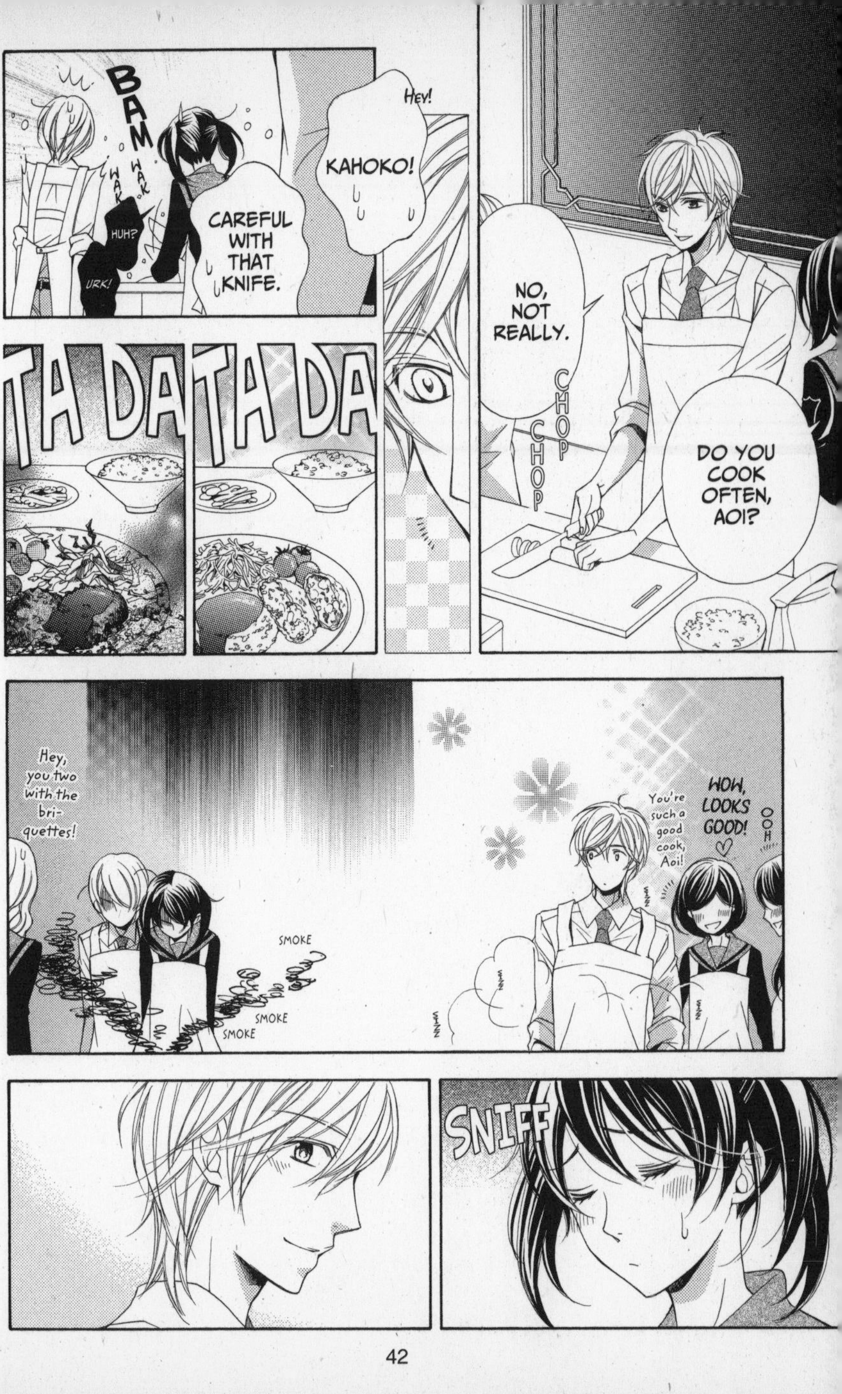
DO YOU COOK OFTEN, AOI?
NO, NOT REALLY.
CHOP CHOP
CHOP CHOP
Hey!
KAHOKO!
CAREFUL WITH THAT KNIFE.
BAM
WAK WAK
HUH?
URK!
TA DA
TA DA
WOW, LOOKS GOOD!
OOH
You're such a good cook, Aoi!
SIZZ
SIZZ
SIZZ
SIZZ
SMOKE
SMOKE
SMOKE
Hey, you two with the bri-quettes!
SNIFF

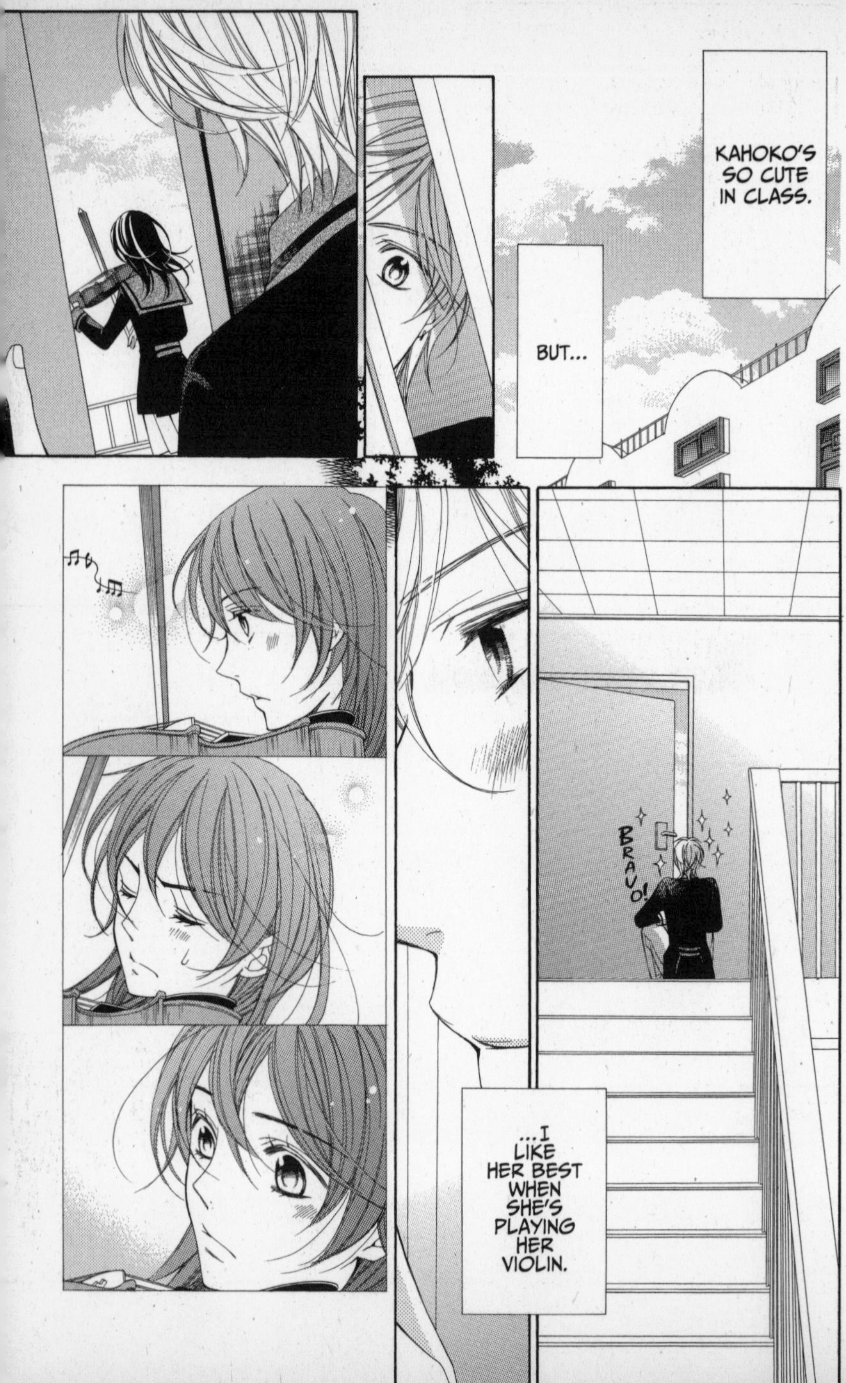
KAHOKO'S SO CUTE IN CLASS.
BUT...
BRAVO!
...I LIKE HER BEST WHEN SHE'S PLAYING HER VIOLIN.

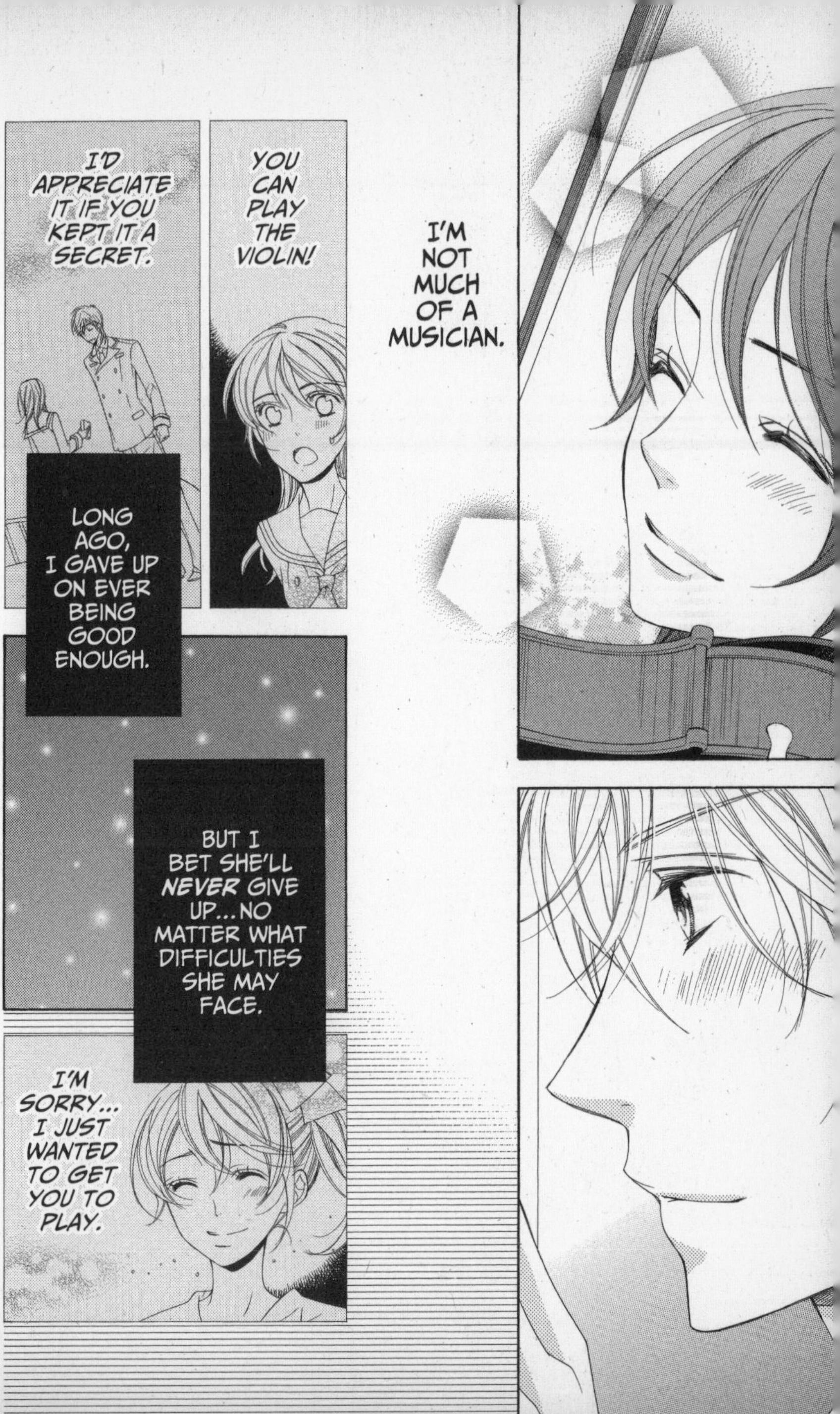
I'M NOT MUCH OF A MUSICIAN.
YOU CAN PLAY THE VIOLIN!
I'D APPRECIATE IT IF YOU KEPT IT A SECRET.
LONG AGO, I GAVE UP ON EVER BEING GOOD ENOUGH.
BUT I BET SHE'LL ***NEVER*** GIVE UP...NO MATTER WHAT DIFFICULTIES SHE MAY FACE.
I'M SORRY... I JUST WANTED TO GET YOU TO PLAY.

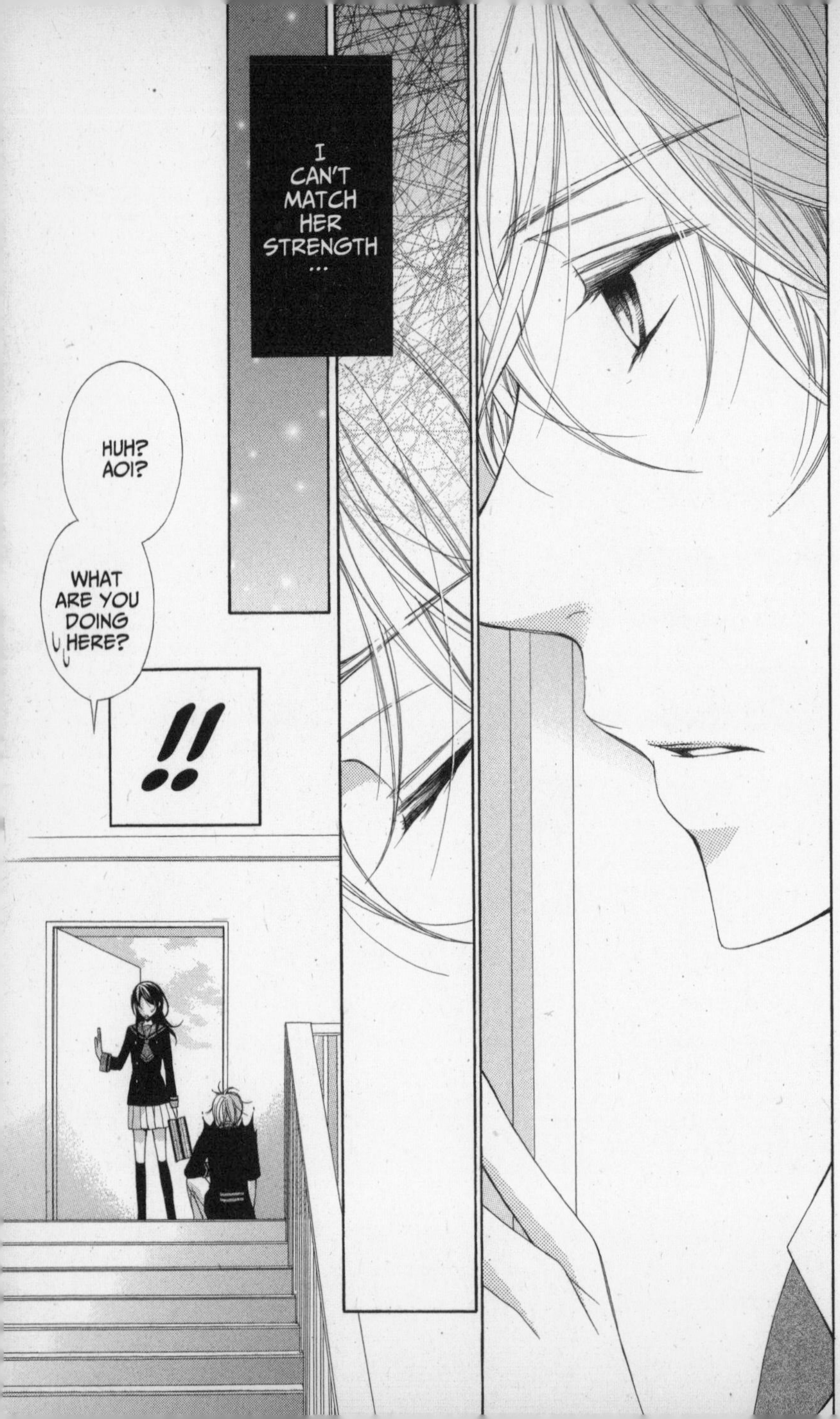
I CAN'T MATCH HER STRENGTH...
HUH? AOI?
WHAT ARE YOU DOING HERE?
!!

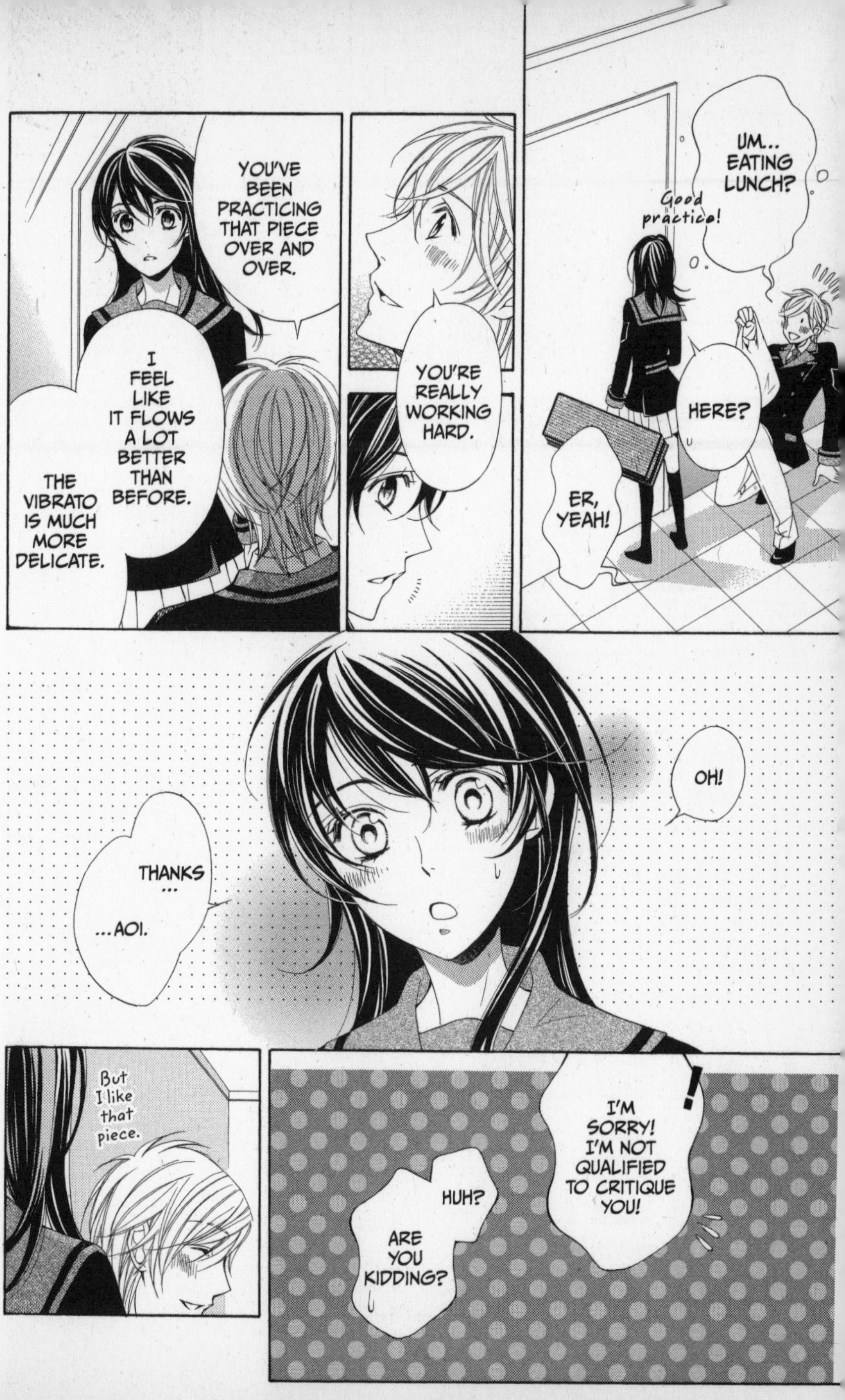
UM... EATING LUNCH?
Good practice!
HERE?
ER, YEAH!
YOU'RE REALLY WORKING HARD.
YOU'VE BEEN PRACTICING THAT PIECE OVER AND OVER.
I FEEL LIKE IT FLOWS A LOT BETTER THAN BEFORE.
THE VIBRATO IS MUCH MORE DELICATE.
OH!
THANKS...
...AOI.
I'M SORRY! I'M NOT QUALIFIED TO CRITIQUE YOU!
HUH?
ARE YOU KIDDING?
But I like that piece.

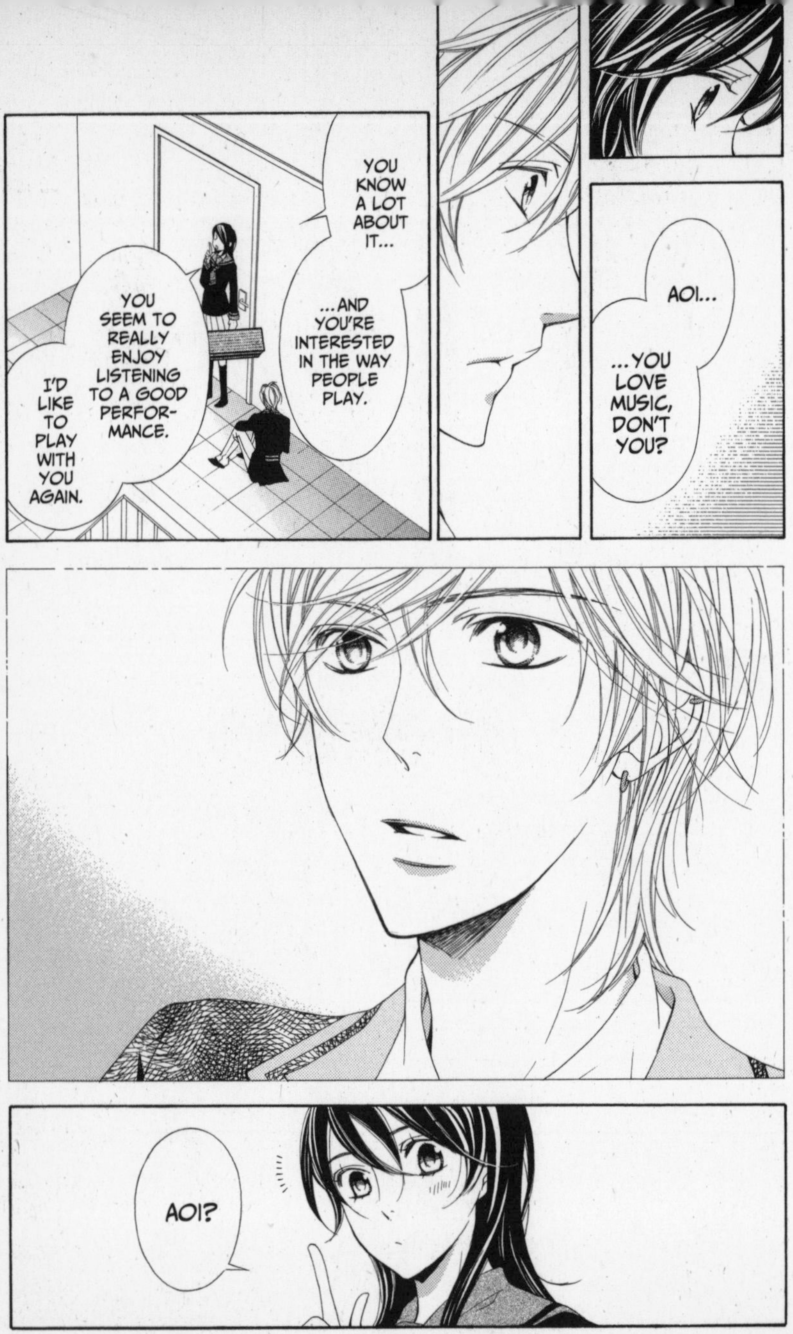
AOI... ...YOU LOVE MUSIC, DON'T YOU?
YOU KNOW A LOT ABOUT IT...
...AND YOU'RE INTERESTED IN THE WAY PEOPLE PLAY.
YOU SEEM TO REALLY ENJOY LISTENING TO A GOOD PERFORMANCE.
I'D LIKE TO PLAY WITH YOU AGAIN.
AOI?

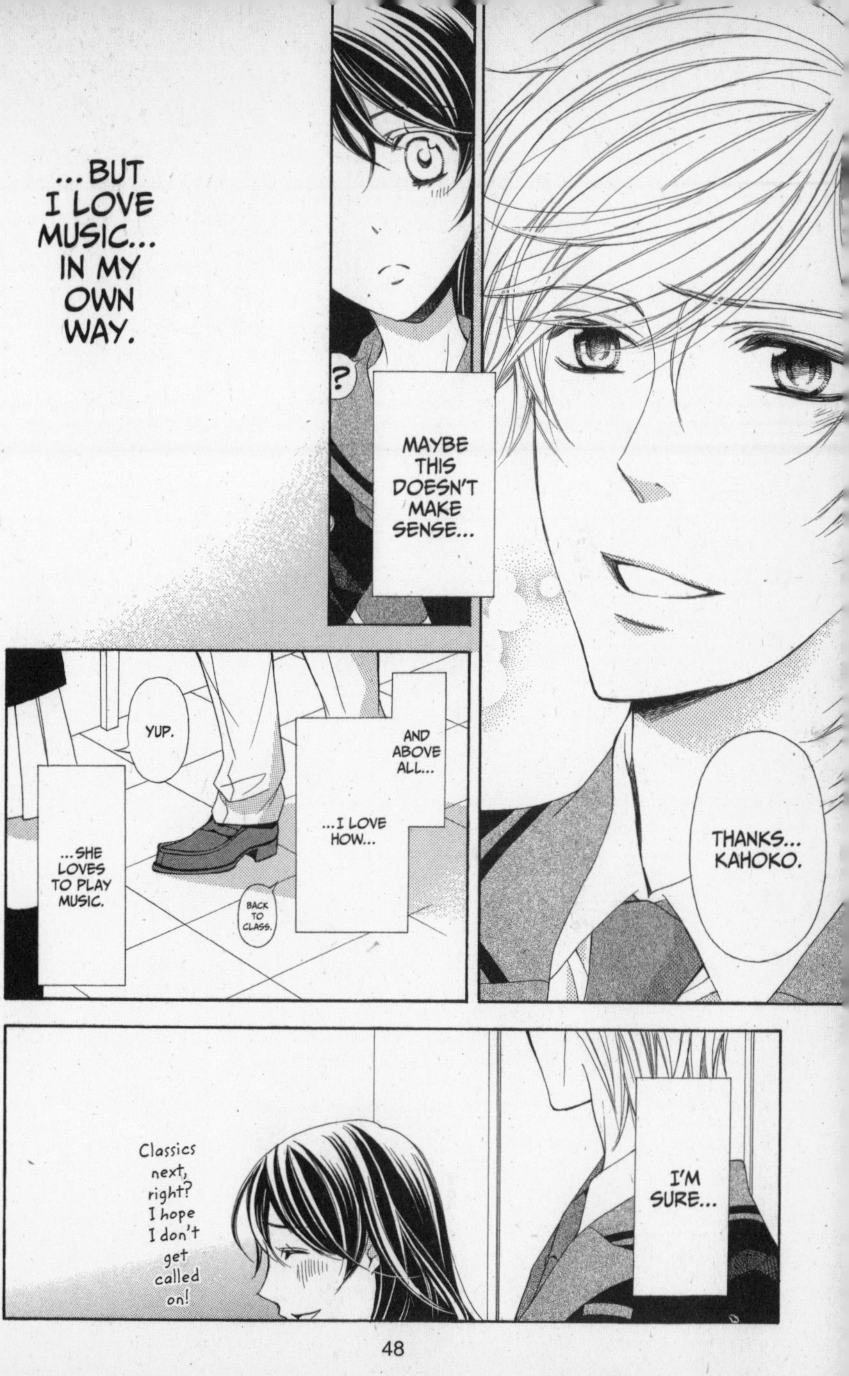
?
MAYBE THIS DOESN'T MAKE SENSE...
...BUT I LOVE MUSIC... IN MY OWN WAY.
THANKS... KAHOKO.
YUP.
AND ABOVE ALL...
...I LOVE HOW...
BACK TO CLASS.
...SHE LOVES TO PLAY MUSIC.
I'M SURE...
Classics next, right? I hope I don't get called on!

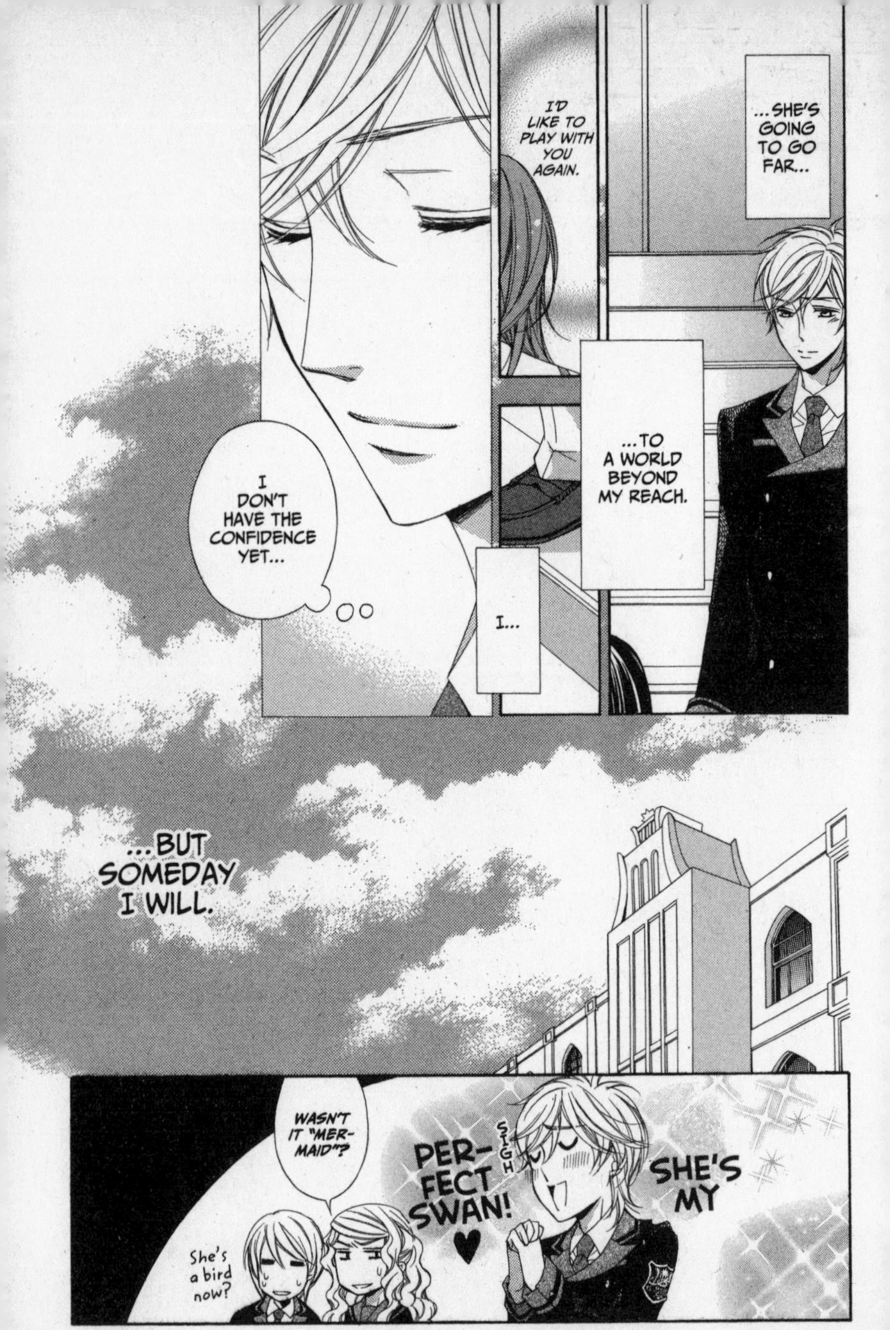
...SHE'S GOING TO GO FAR...
...TO A WORLD BEYOND MY REACH.
I'D LIKE TO PLAY WITH YOU AGAIN.
I...
I DON'T HAVE THE CONFIDENCE YET...
...BUT SOMEDAY I WILL.
SHE'S MY
PER-FECT SWAN!
SIGH
WASN'T IT "MER-MAID"?
She's a bird now?

End of Special Edition

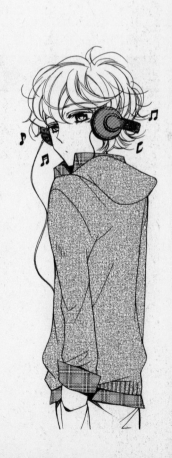

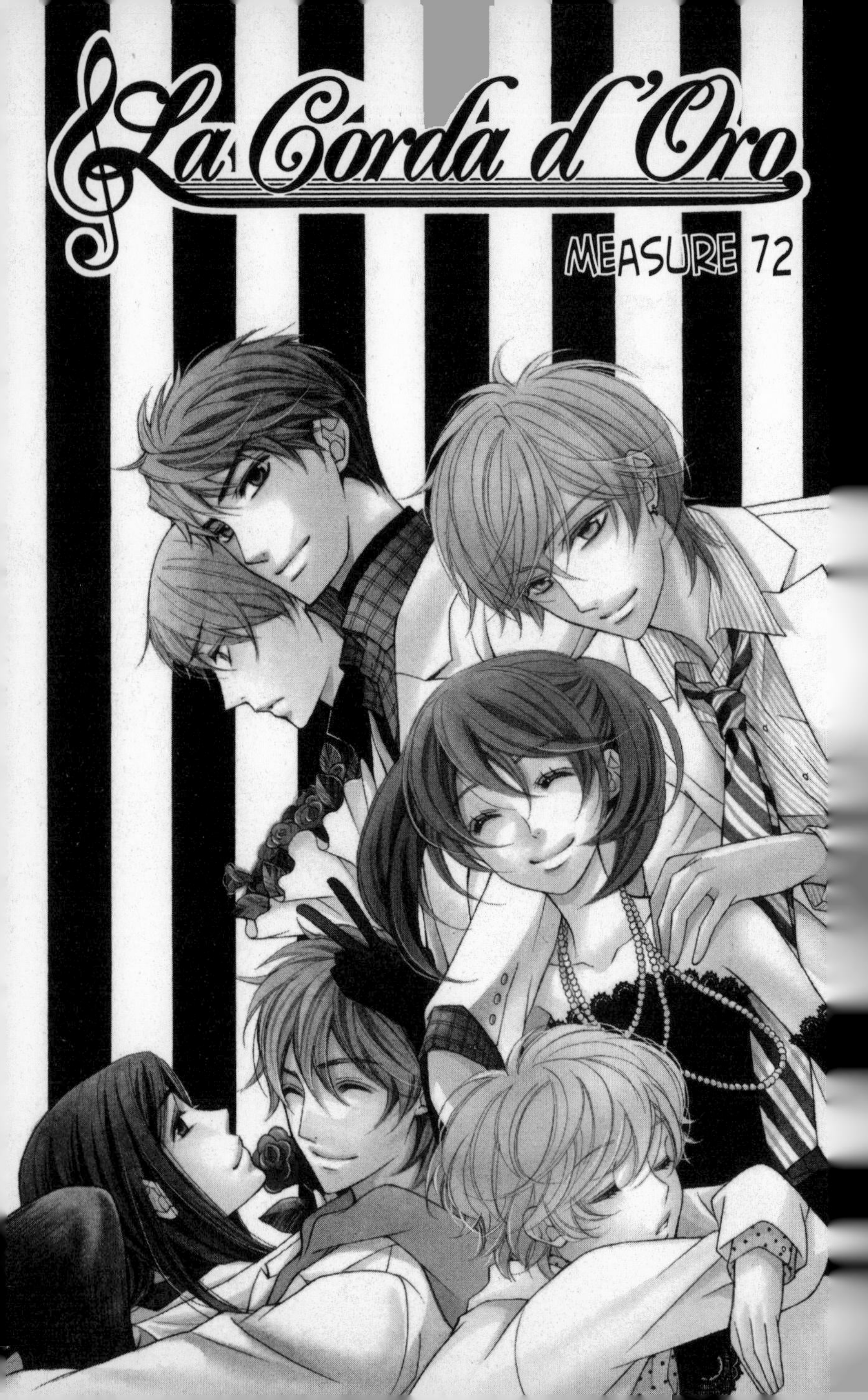
La Corda d'Oro
MEASURE 72

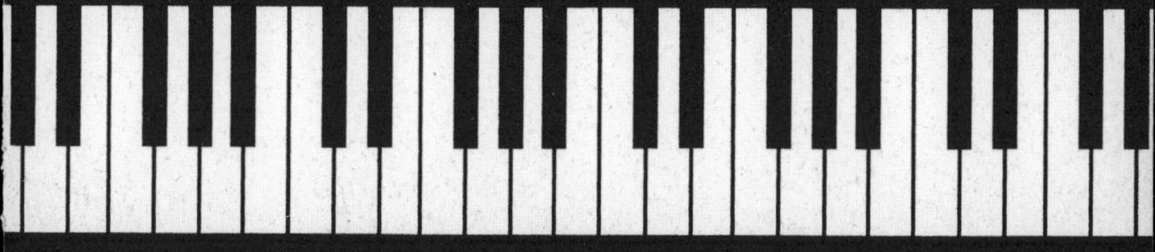

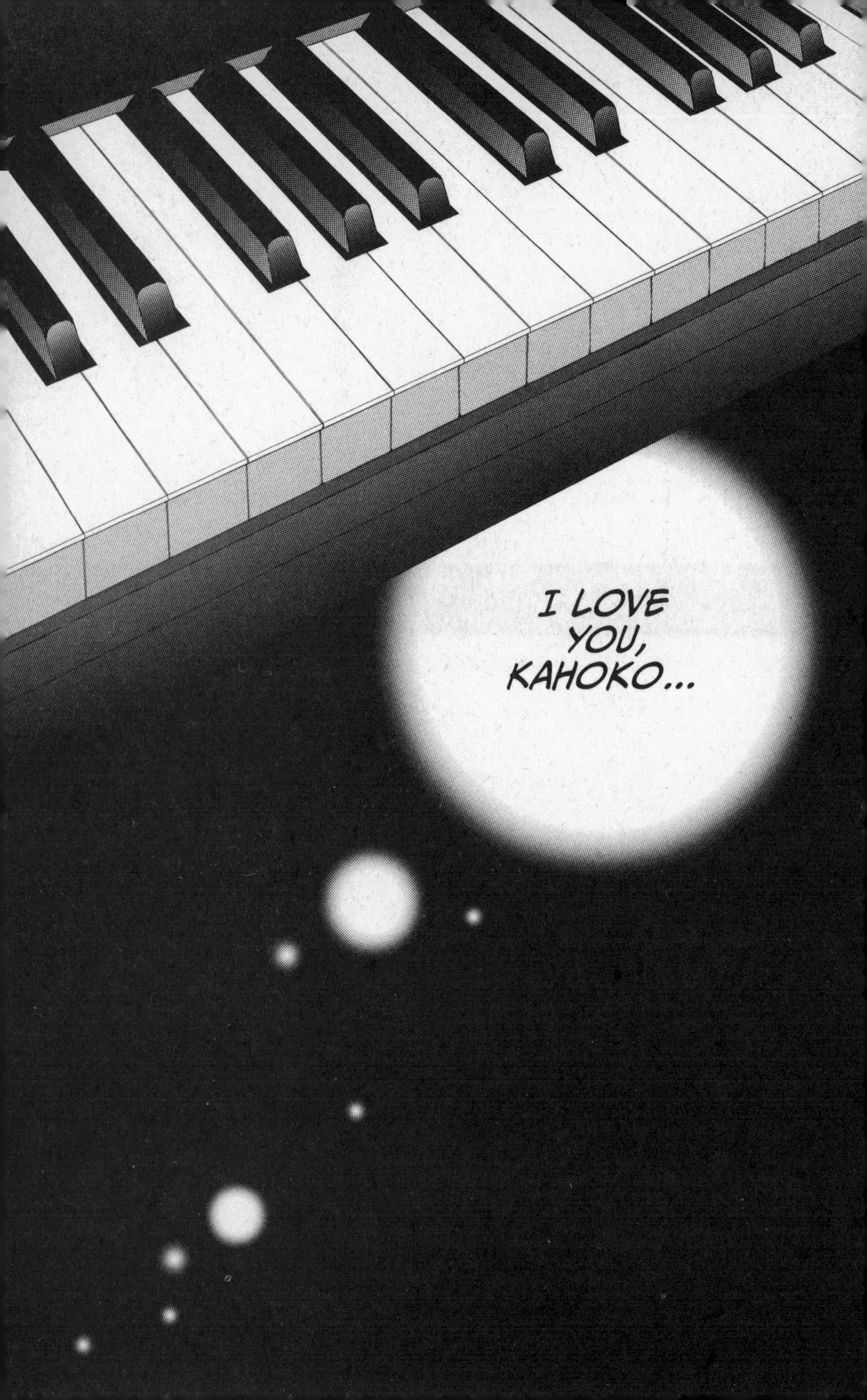
I LOVE YOU, KAHOKO...

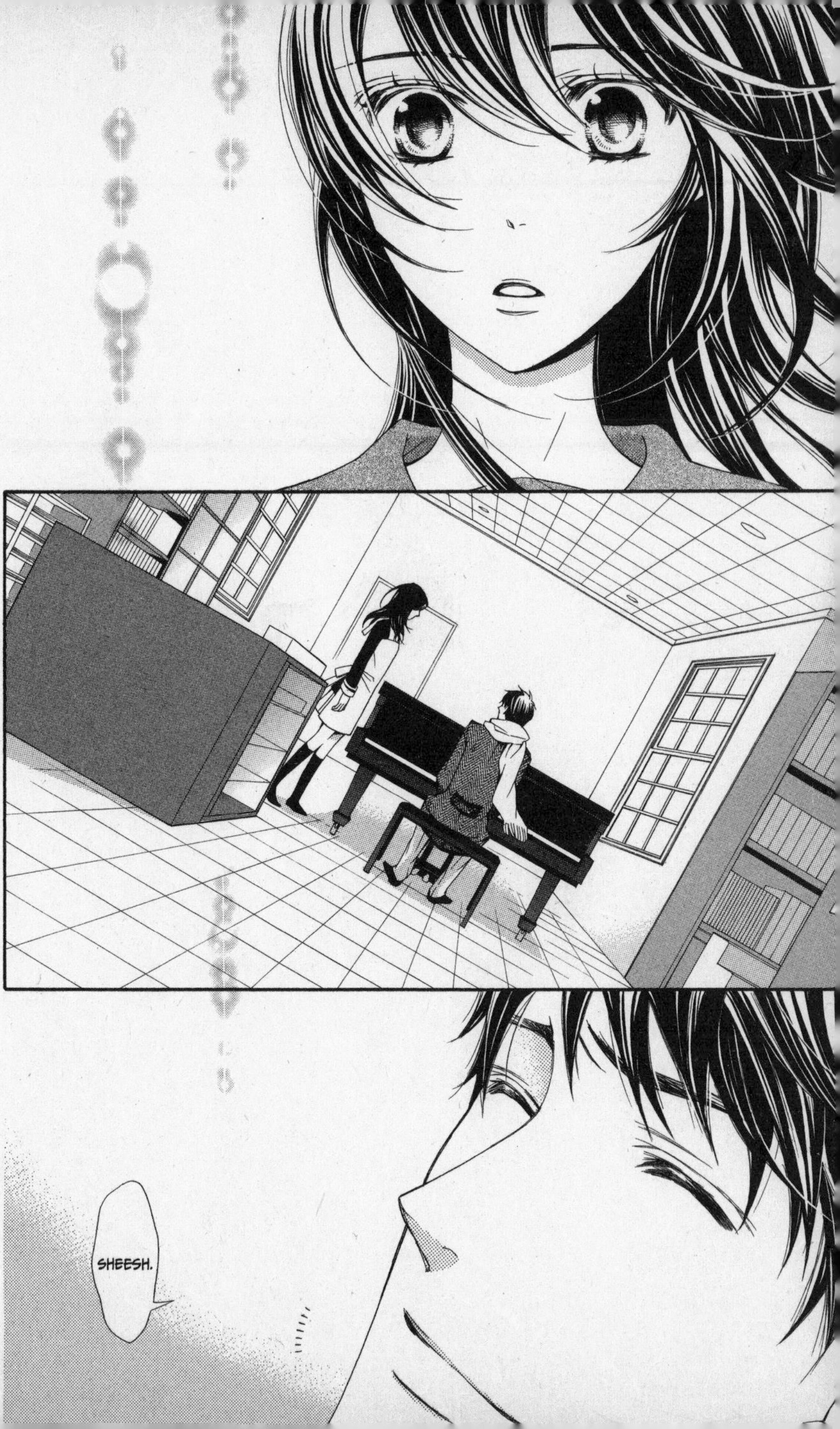
SHEESH.

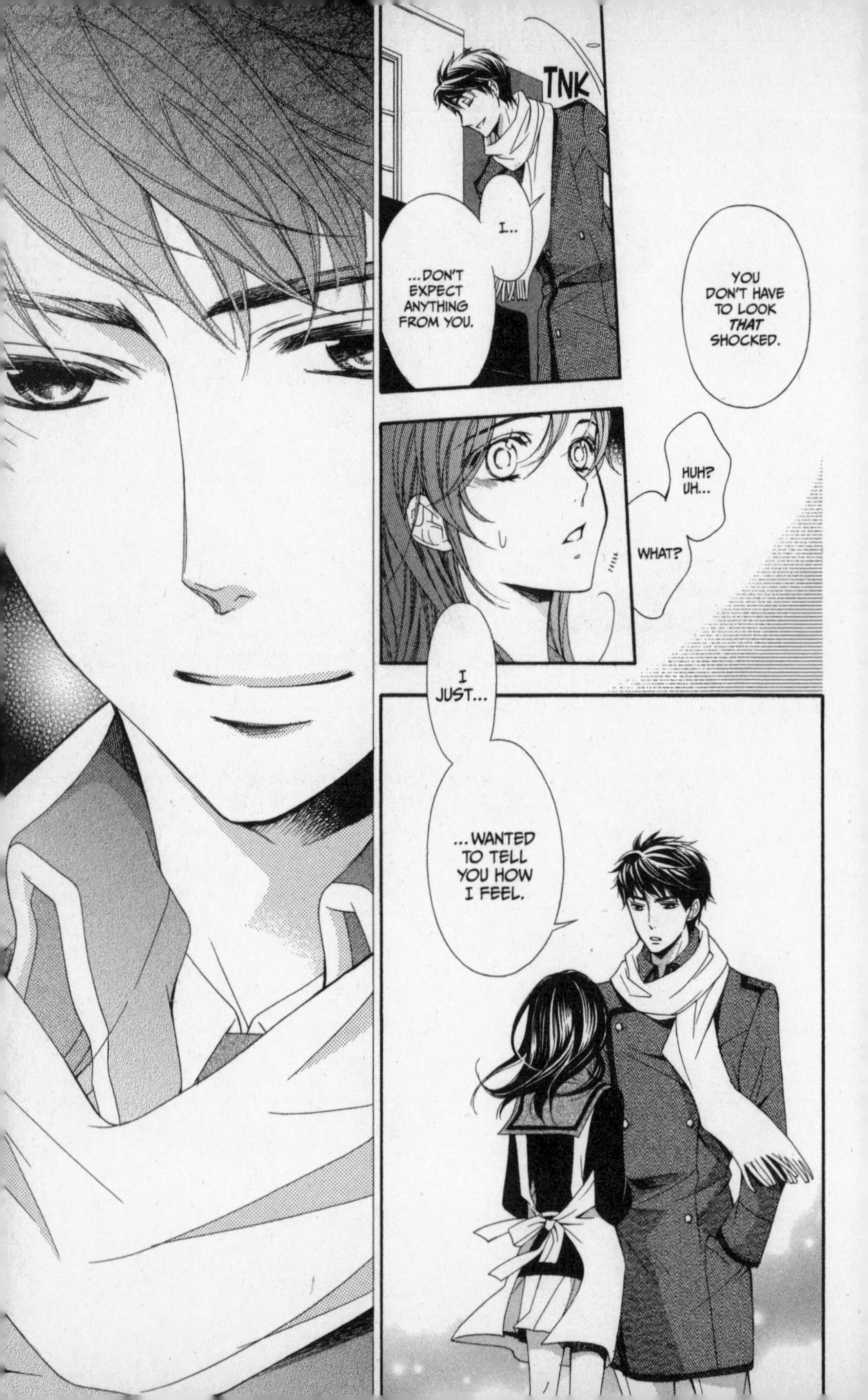
TNK
YOU DON'T HAVE TO LOOK *THAT* SHOCKED.
I...
...DON'T EXPECT ANYTHING FROM YOU.
HUH? UH...
WHAT?
I JUST...
...WANTED TO TELL YOU HOW I FEEL.

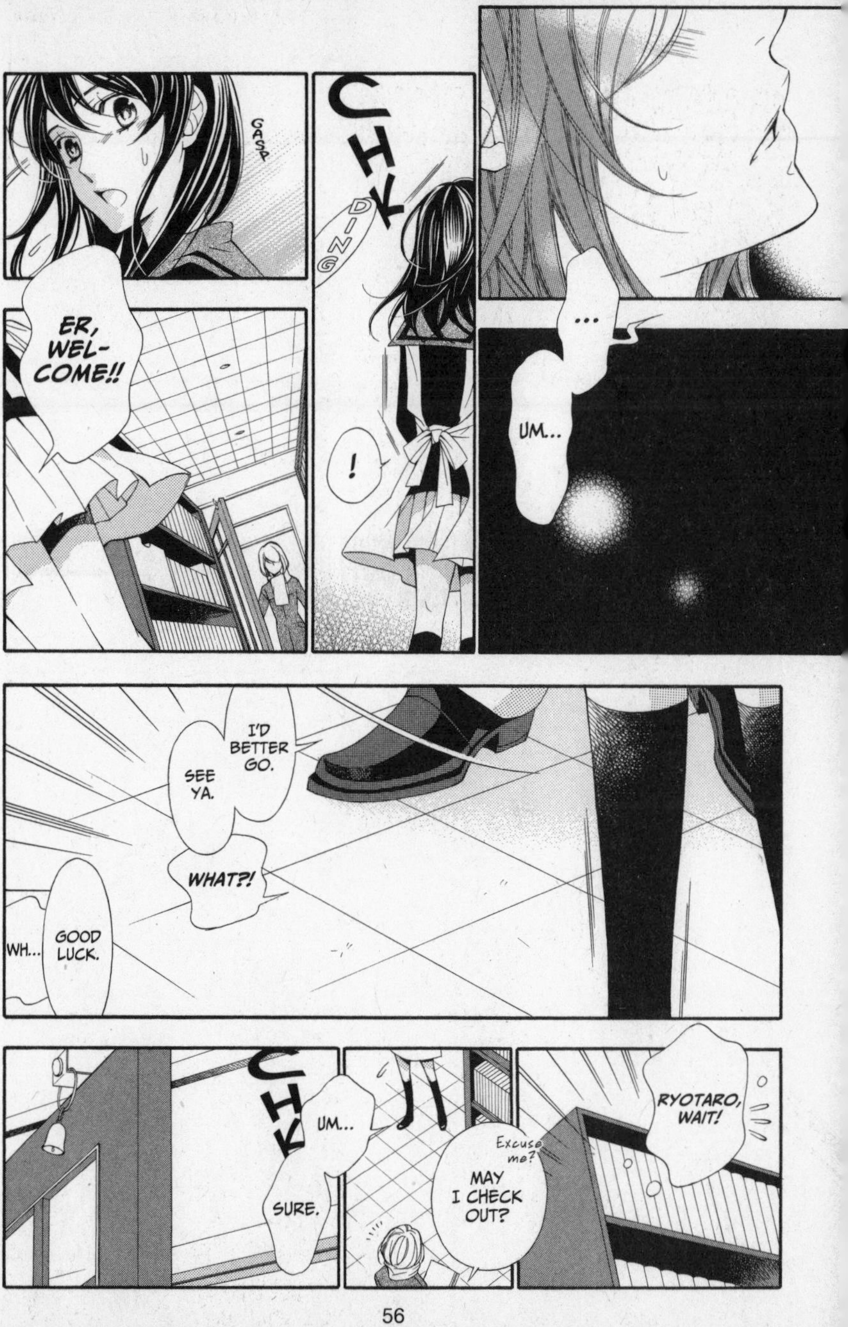
...
UM...
CHK
DING
!
GASP
ER, WEL-COME!!
I'D BETTER GO.
SEE YA.
WHAT?!
GOOD LUCK.
WH...
RYOTARO, WAIT!
Excuse me?
MAY I CHECK OUT?
CHK
UM...
SURE.

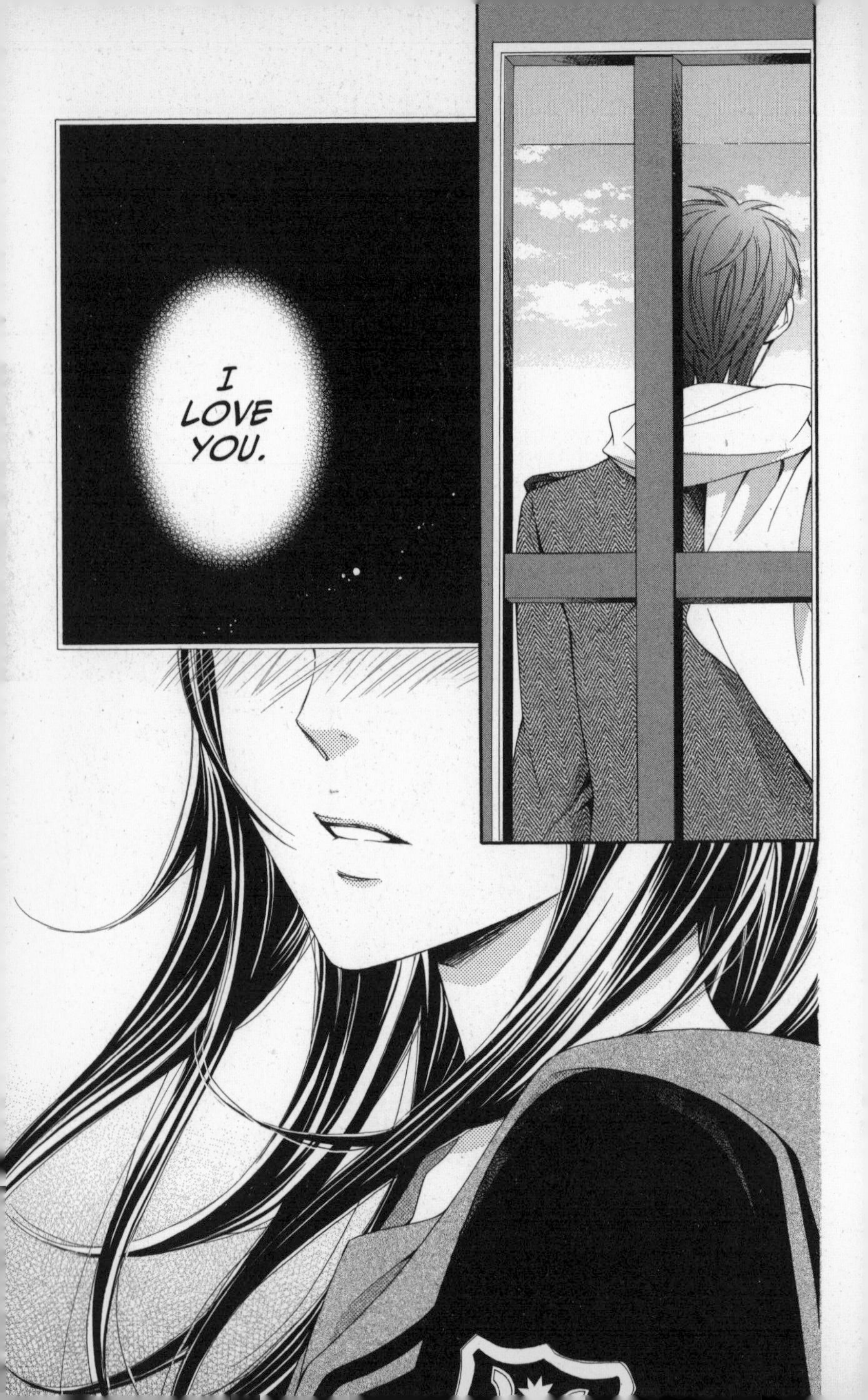
I LOVE YOU.

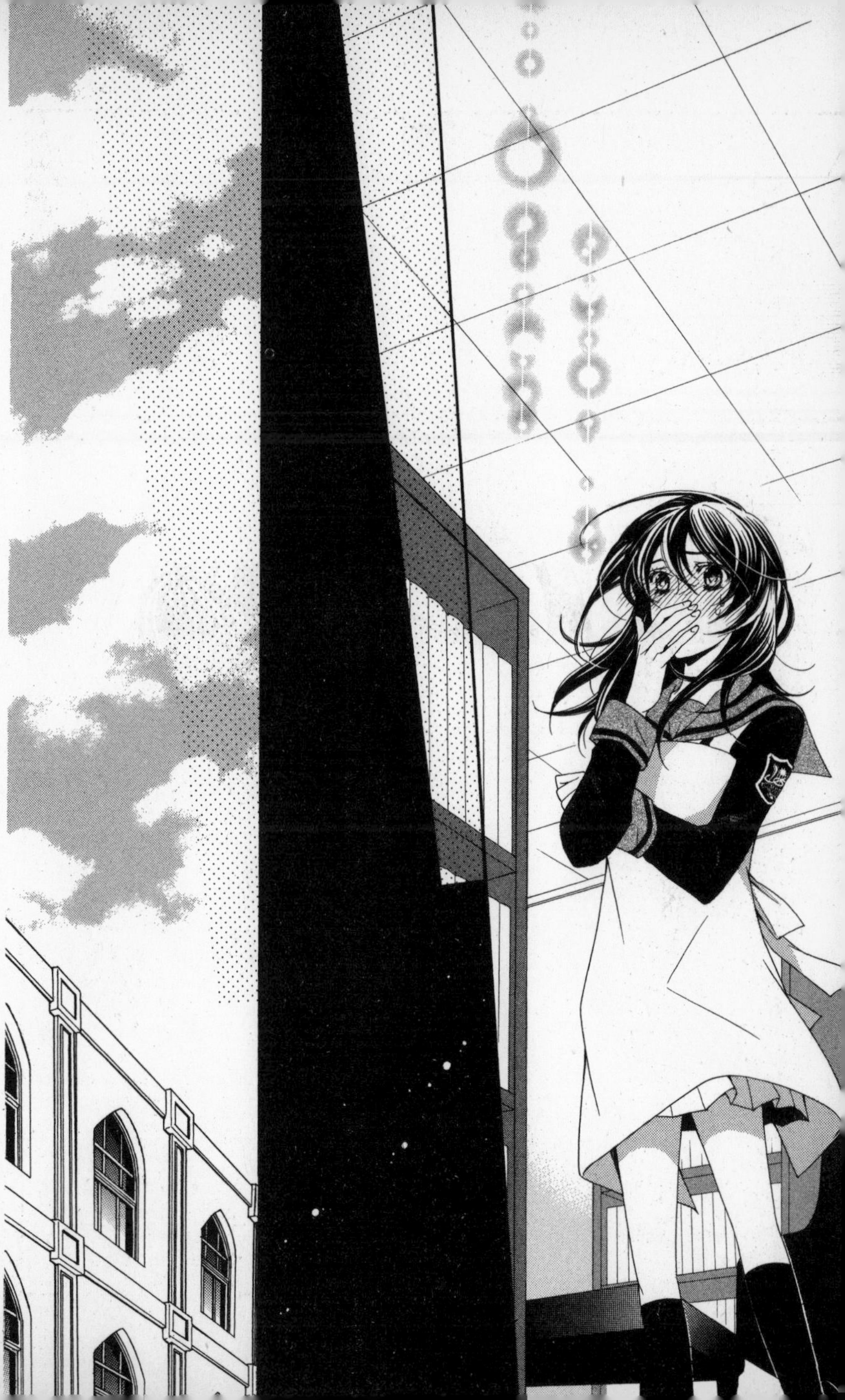

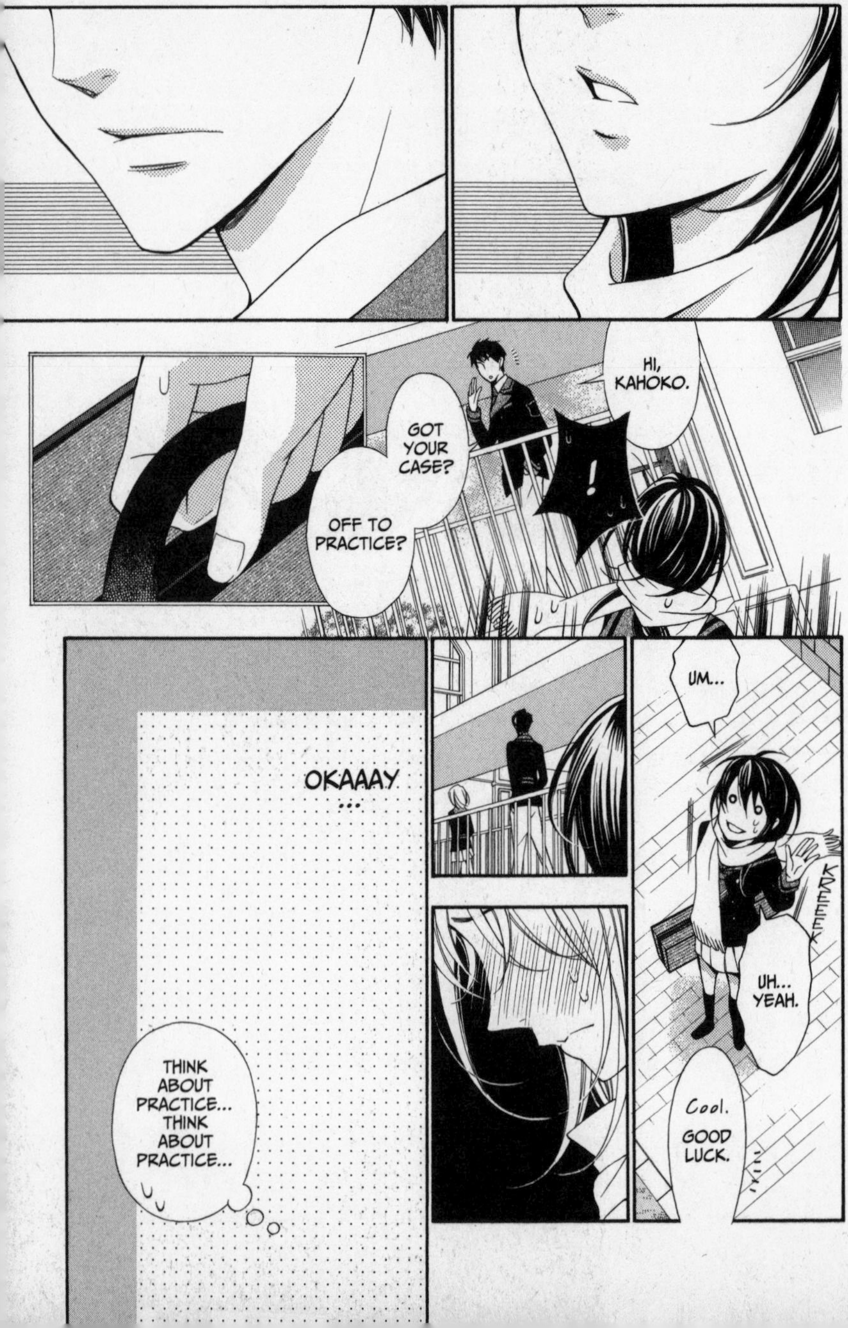
HI, KAHOKO.
GOT YOUR CASE?
OFF TO PRACTICE?
UM...
KREEEK
UH... YEAH.
Cool. GOOD LUCK.
OKAAAY ...
THINK ABOUT PRACTICE... THINK ABOUT PRACTICE...

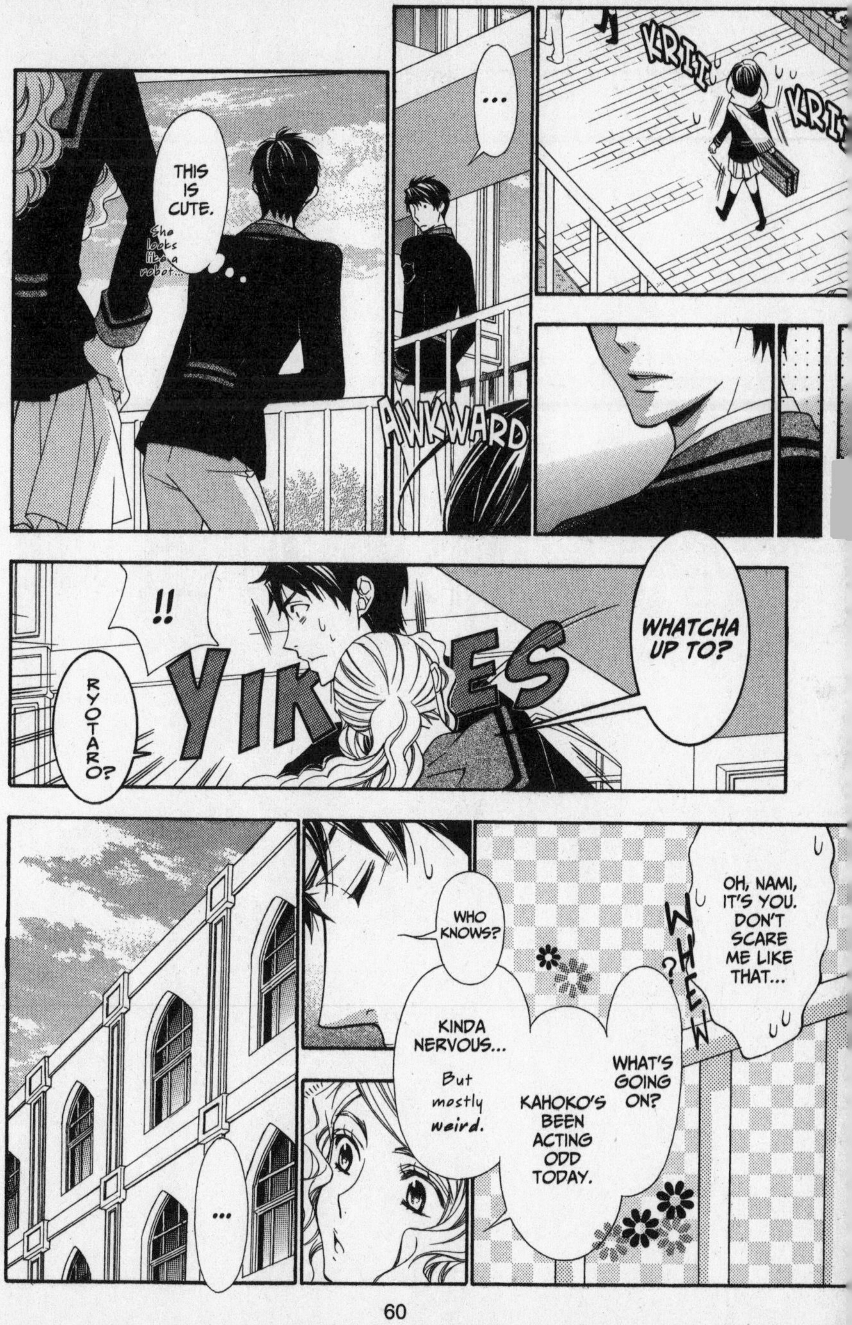
KRII
KRII
...
AWKWARD
THIS IS CUTE.
She looks like a robot...
WHATCHA UP TO?
YIKES
!!
RYOTARO?
OH, NAMI, IT'S YOU. DON'T SCARE ME LIKE THAT...
WHEW
?
WHAT'S GOING ON?
KAHOKO'S BEEN ACTING ODD TODAY.
WHO KNOWS?
KINDA NERVOUS...
But mostly weird.
...

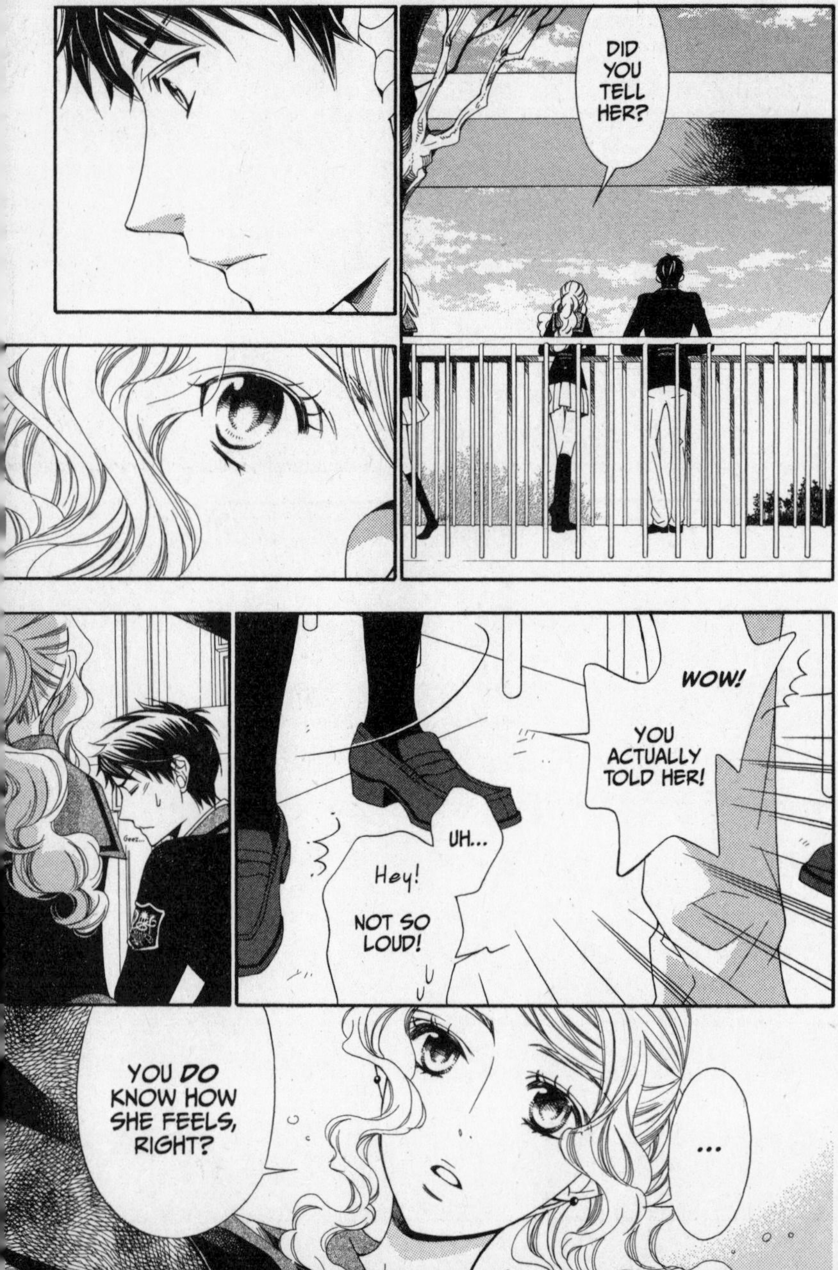
DID YOU TELL HER?
WOW!
YOU ACTUALLY TOLD HER!
UH...
Hey!
NOT SO LOUD!
Geez...
YOU DO KNOW HOW SHE FEELS, RIGHT?
...

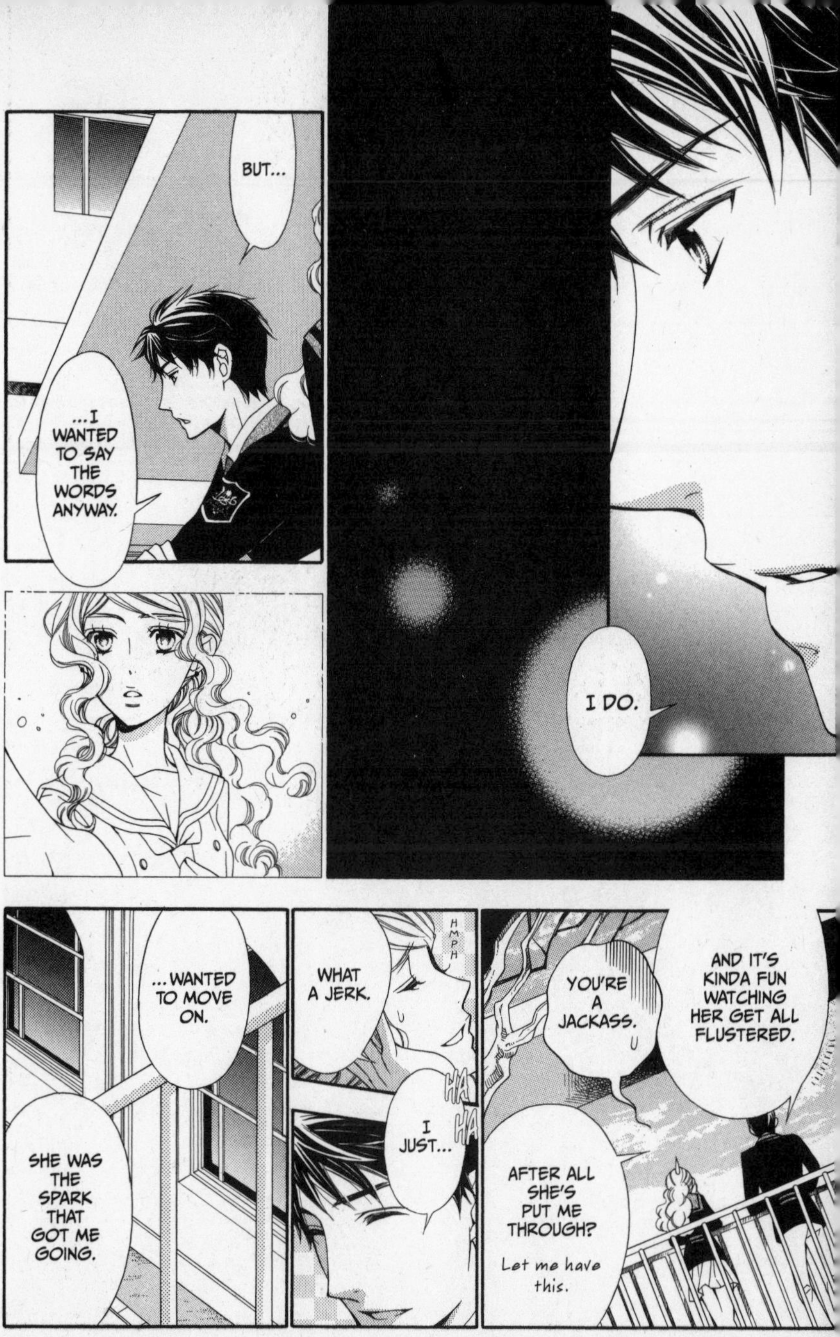
I DO.
BUT...
...I WANTED TO SAY THE WORDS ANYWAY.
AND IT'S KINDA FUN WATCHING HER GET ALL FLUSTERED.
YOU'RE A JACKASS.
AFTER ALL SHE'S PUT ME THROUGH?
Let me have this.
HMPH
WHAT A JERK.
HA HA
I JUST...
...WANTED TO MOVE ON.
SHE WAS THE SPARK THAT GOT ME GOING.

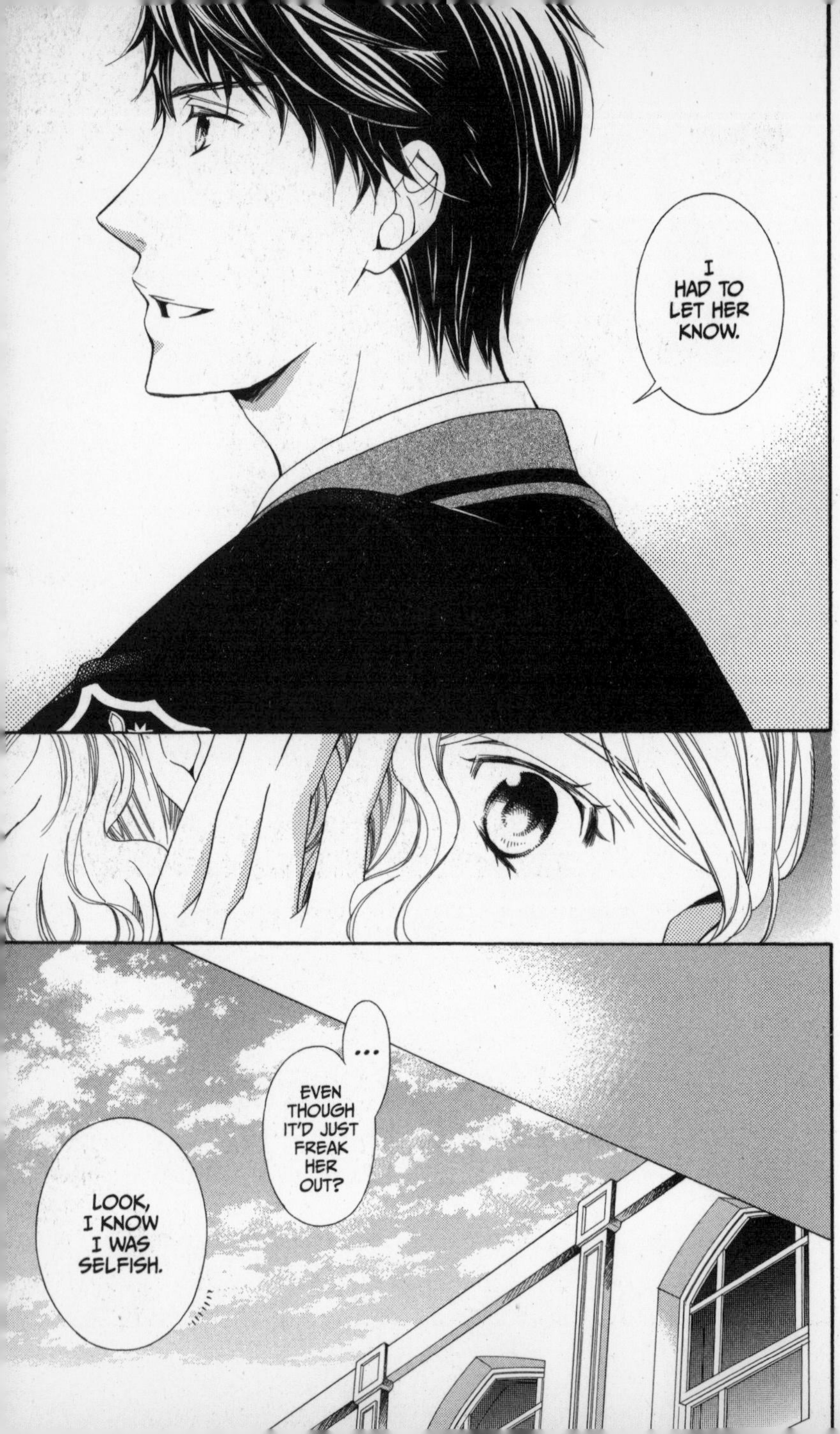
I HAD TO LET HER KNOW.
...
EVEN THOUGH IT'D JUST FREAK HER OUT?
LOOK, I KNOW I WAS SELFISH.

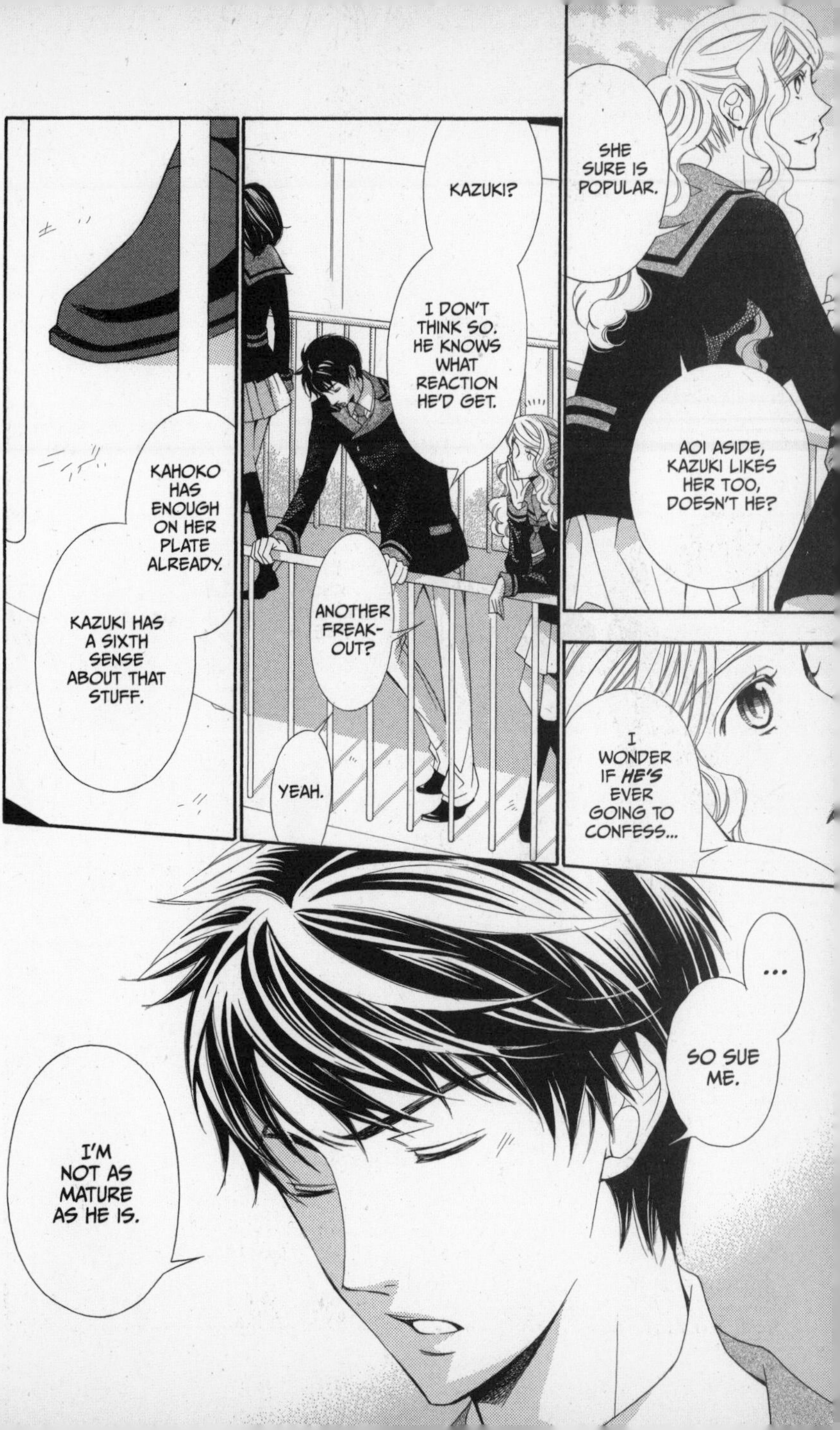
SHE SURE IS POPULAR.
AOI ASIDE, KAZUKI LIKES HER TOO, DOESN'T HE?
I WONDER IF *HE'S* EVER GOING TO CONFESS...
KAZUKI?
I DON'T THINK SO. HE KNOWS WHAT REACTION HE'D GET.
ANOTHER FREAK-OUT?
YEAH.
KAHOKO HAS ENOUGH ON HER PLATE ALREADY.
KAZUKI HAS A SIXTH SENSE ABOUT THAT STUFF.
...
SO SUE ME.
I'M NOT AS MATURE AS HE IS.

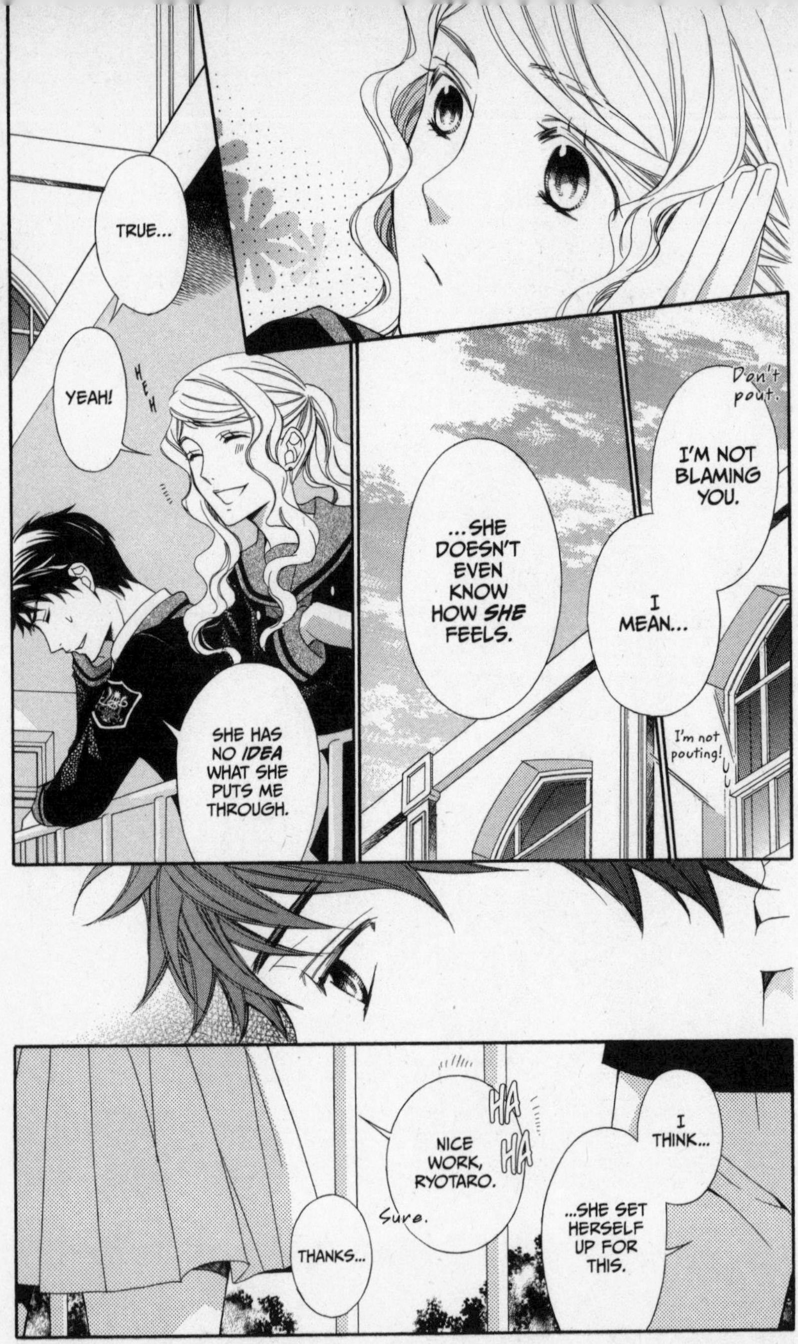
TRUE...
Don't pout.
I'M NOT BLAMING YOU.
I MEAN...
I'm not pouting!
...SHE DOESN'T EVEN KNOW HOW *SHE* FEELS.
YEAH!
HEH
SHE HAS NO *IDEA* WHAT SHE PUTS ME THROUGH.
I THINK...
...SHE SET HERSELF UP FOR THIS.
HA HA
NICE WORK, RYOTARO.
Sure.
THANKS...

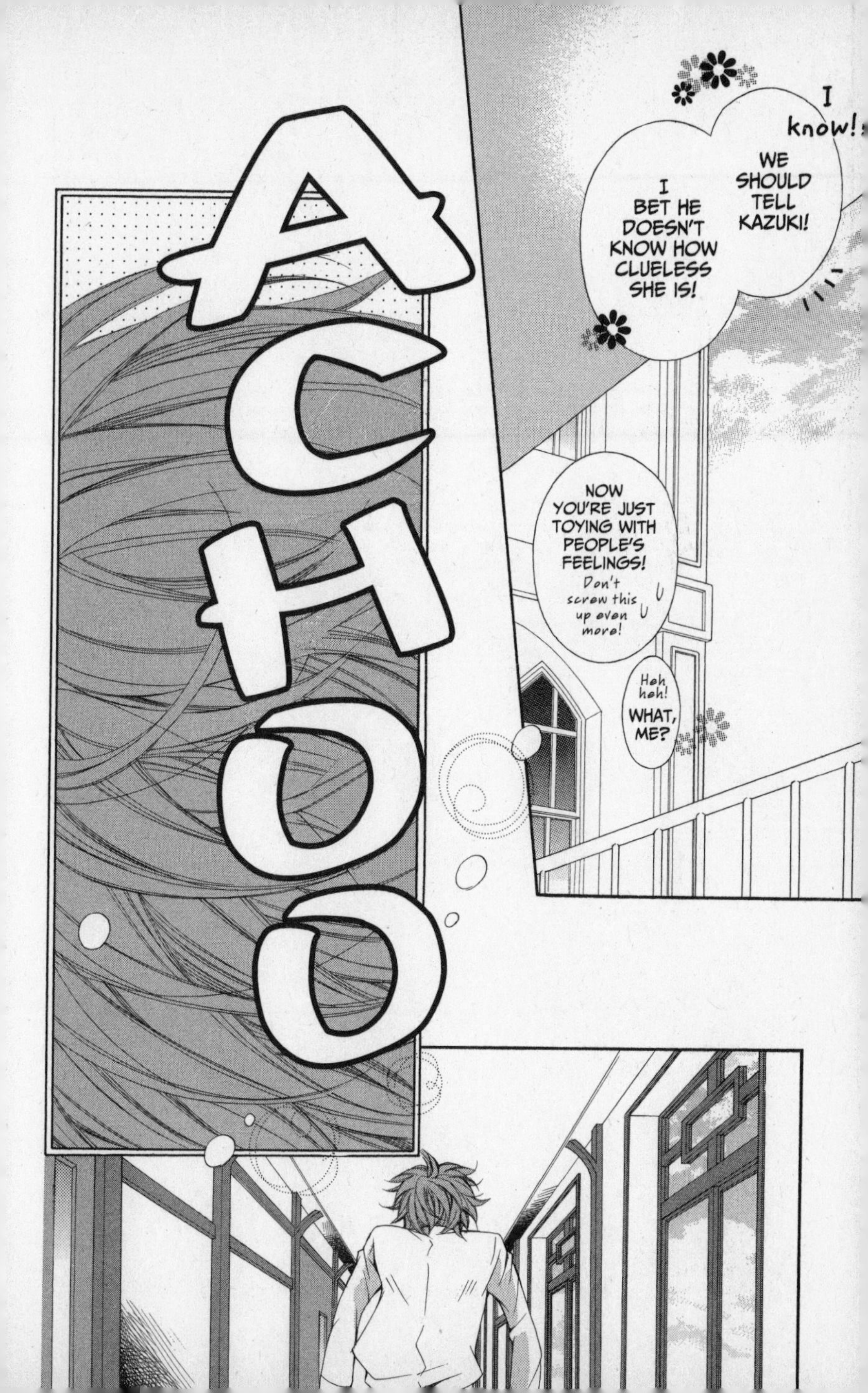
I know!!
WE SHOULD TELL KAZUKI!
I BET HE DOESN'T KNOW HOW CLUELESS SHE IS!
NOW YOU'RE JUST TOYING WITH PEOPLE'S FEELINGS!
Don't screw this up even more!
Heh heh!
WHAT, ME?
ACHOO

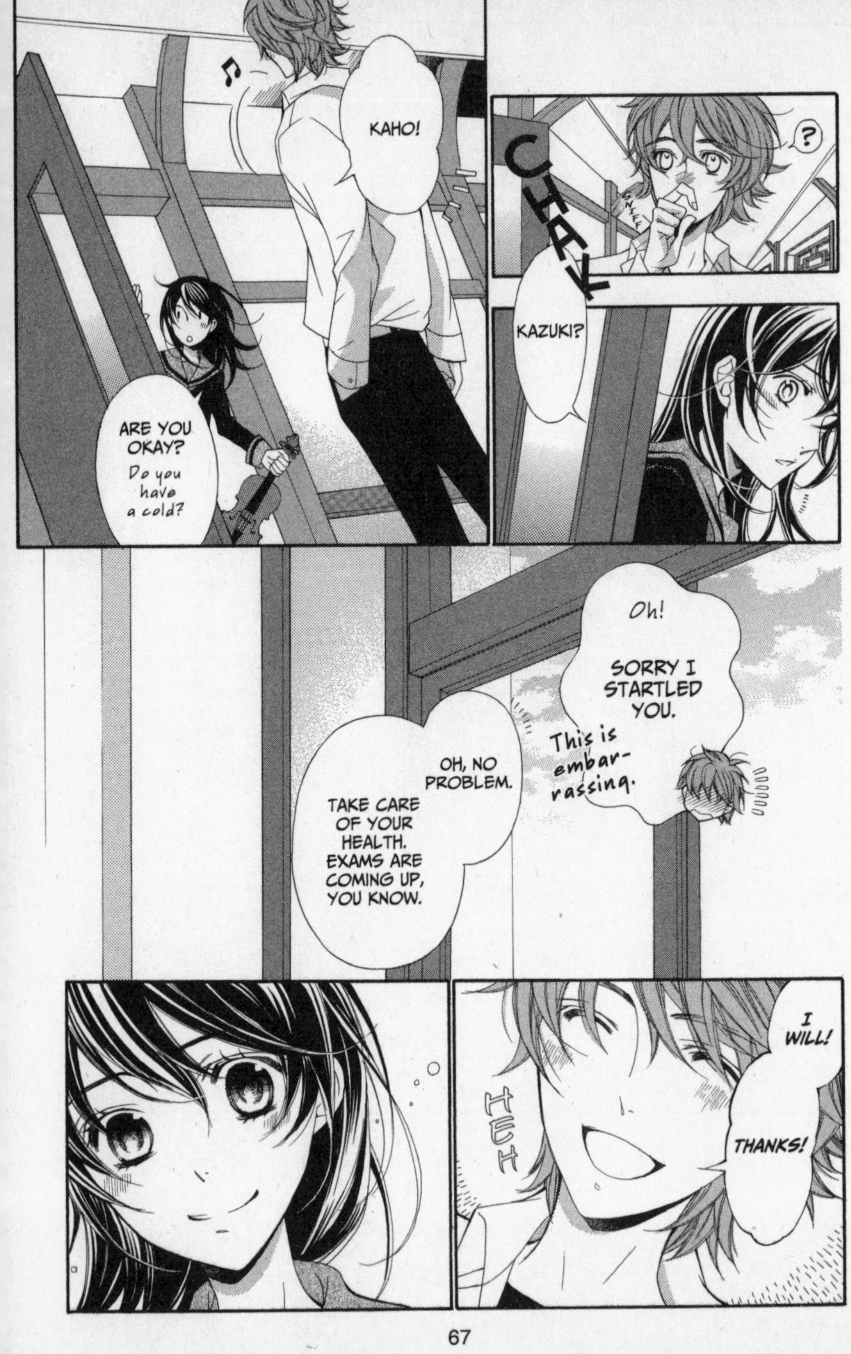
?
SNIFF
CHAK
KAZUKI?
♪
KAHO!
ARE YOU OKAY? Do you have a cold?
Oh!
SORRY I STARTLED YOU.
This is embarrassing.
OH, NO PROBLEM.
TAKE CARE OF YOUR HEALTH. EXAMS ARE COMING UP, YOU KNOW.
I WILL!
THANKS!
HEH

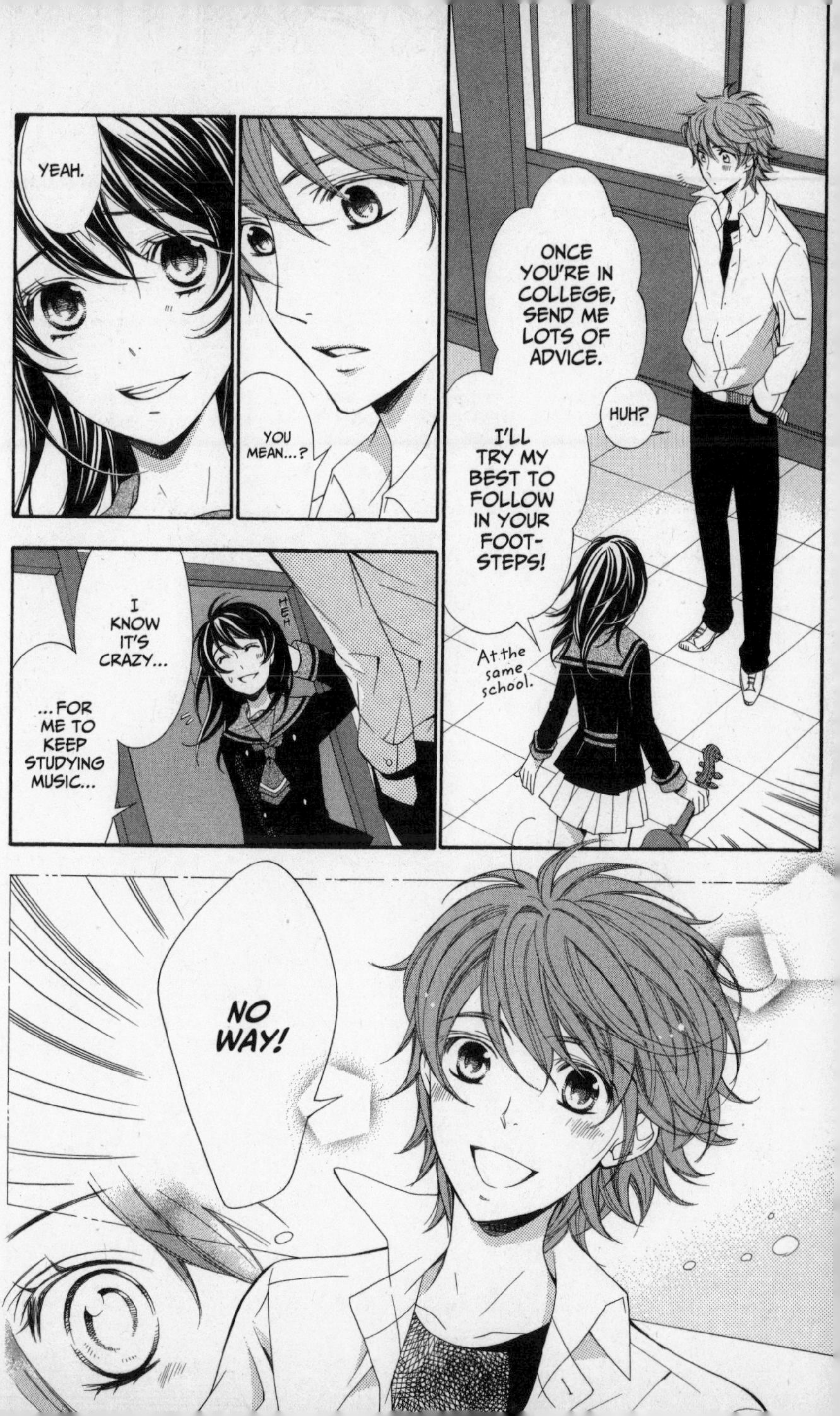
ONCE YOU'RE IN COLLEGE, SEND ME LOTS OF ADVICE.
HUH?
I'LL TRY MY BEST TO FOLLOW IN YOUR FOOT-STEPS!
At the same school.
YOU MEAN...?
YEAH.
I KNOW IT'S CRAZY...
...FOR ME TO KEEP STUDYING MUSIC...
HEH
NO WAY!

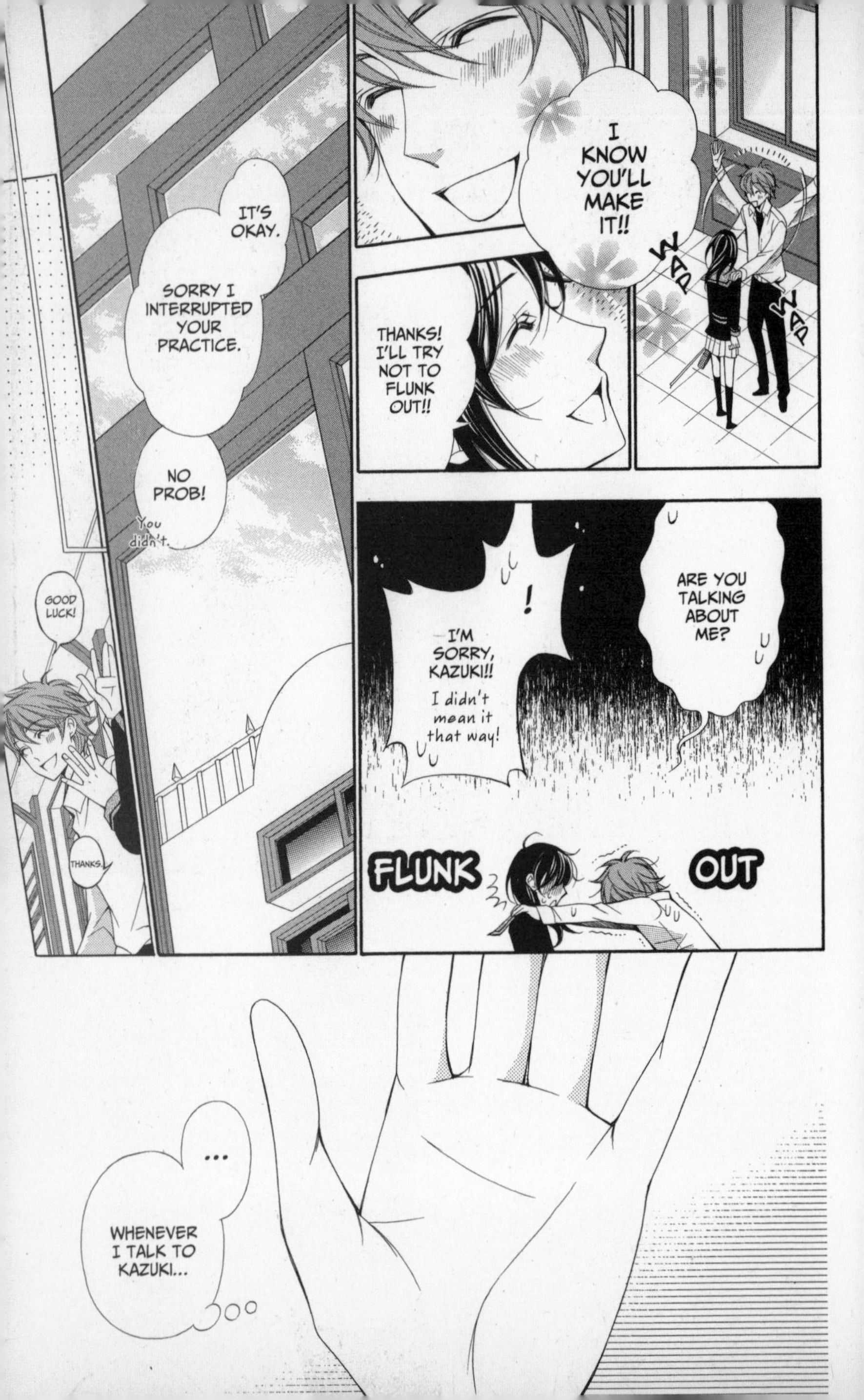
WAP
WAP
I KNOW YOU'LL MAKE IT!!
THANKS! I'LL TRY NOT TO FLUNK OUT!!
ARE YOU TALKING ABOUT ME?
!
I'M SORRY, KAZUKI!! I didn't mean it that way!
FLUNK OUT
IT'S OKAY.
SORRY I INTERRUPTED YOUR PRACTICE.
NO PROB!
You didn't.
GOOD LUCK!
THANKS.
...
WHENEVER I TALK TO KAZUKI...

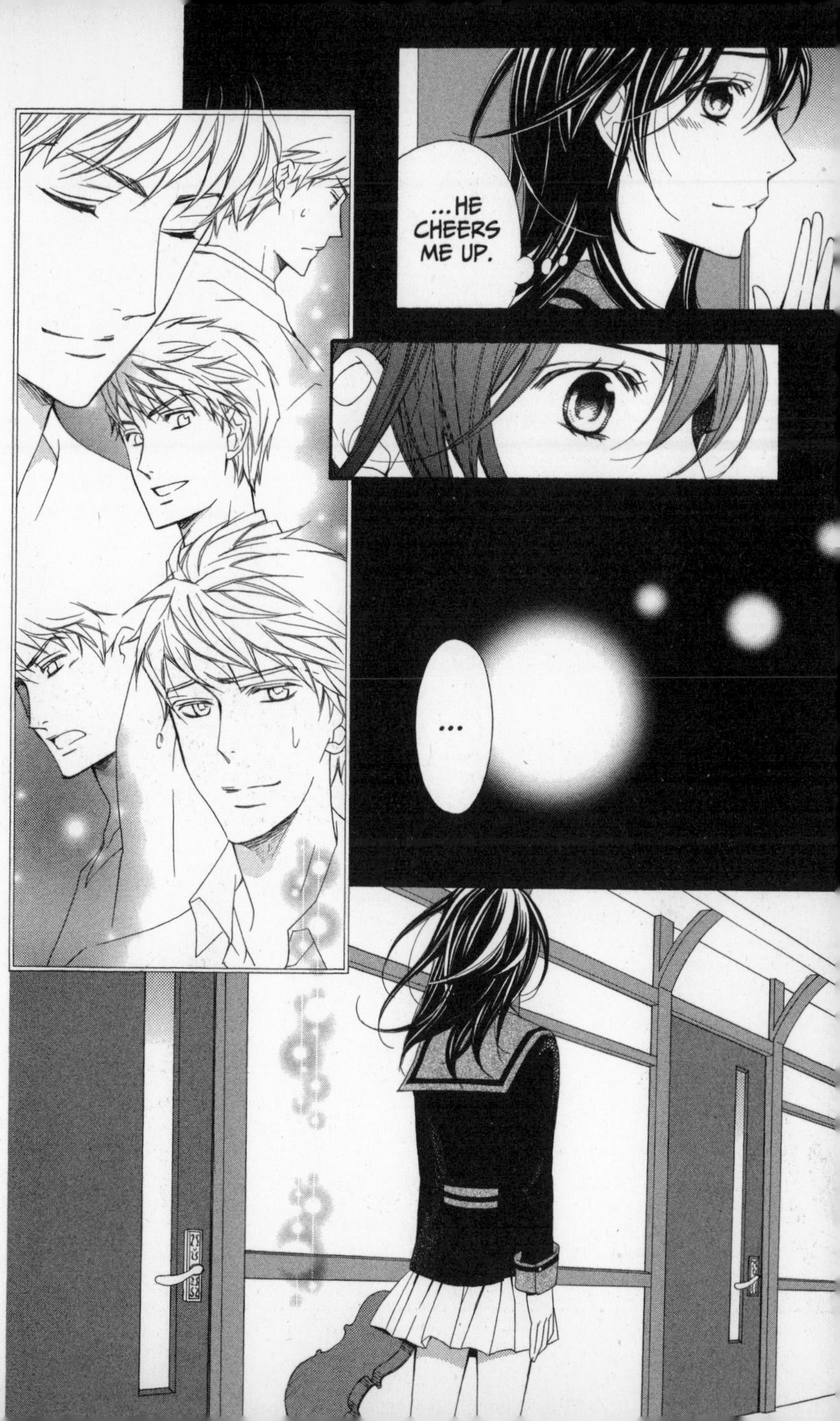
...HE CHEERS ME UP.
...

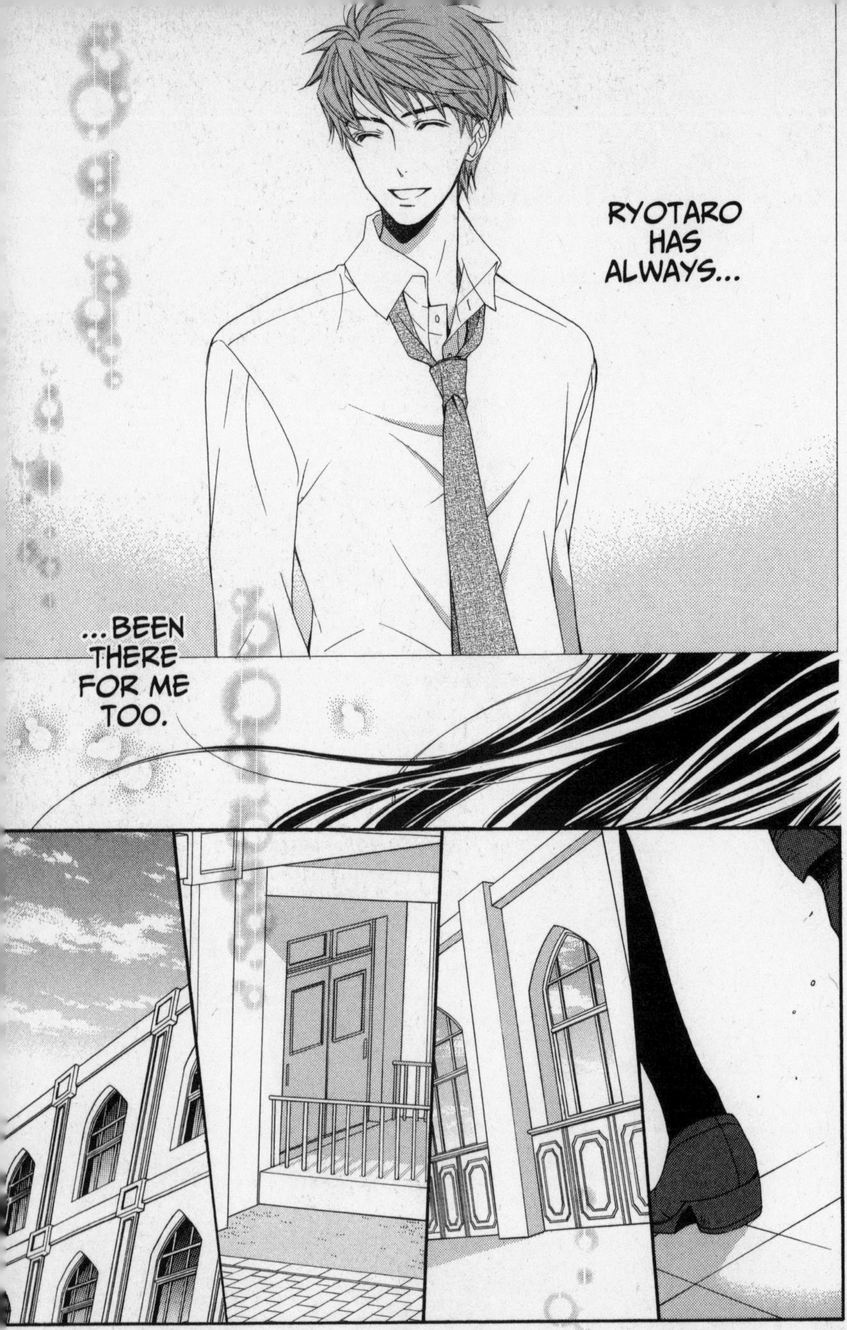
RYOTARO HAS ALWAYS...
...BEEN THERE FOR ME TOO.

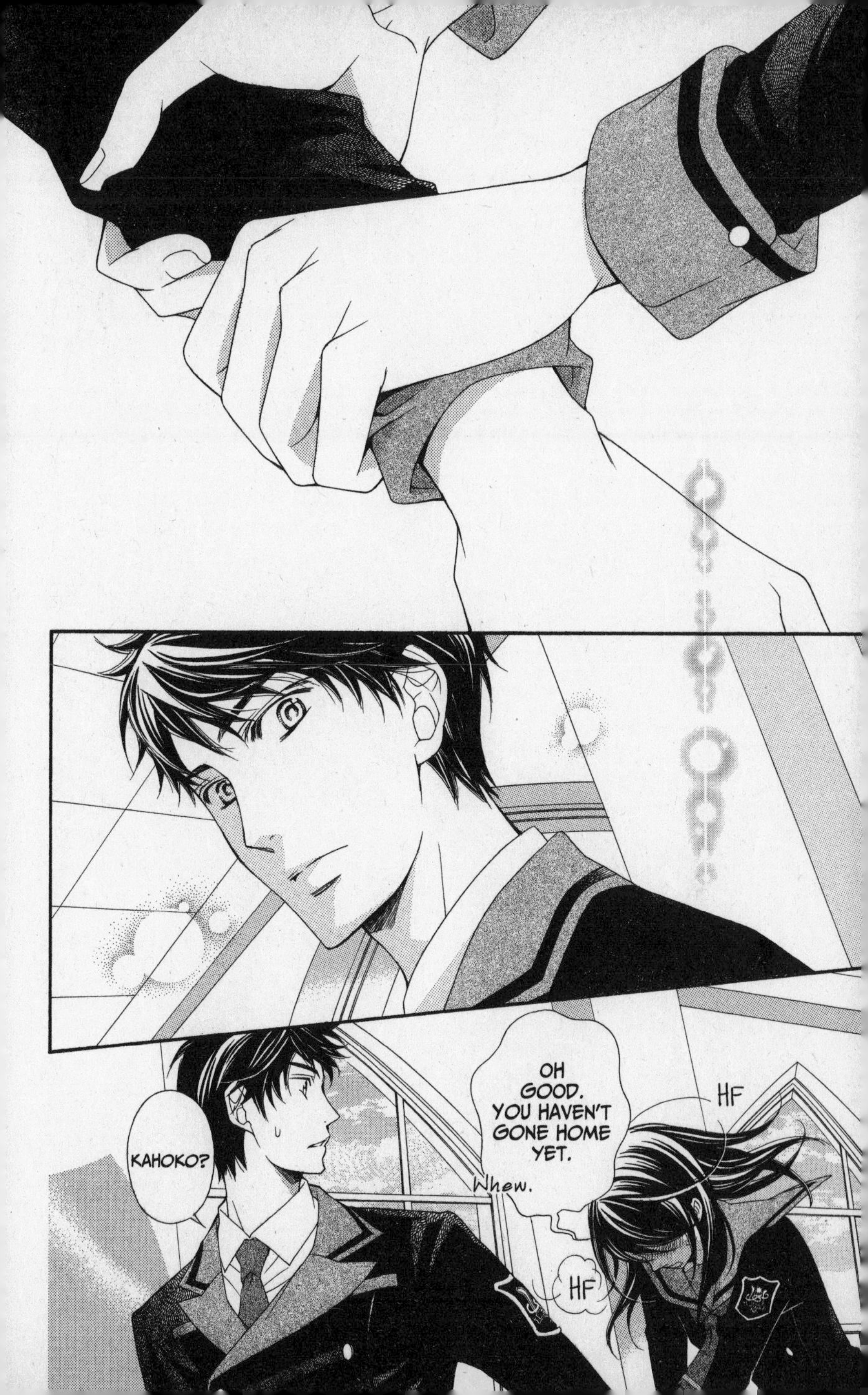
HF
OH GOOD. YOU HAVEN'T GONE HOME YET.
Whew.
HF
KAHOKO?

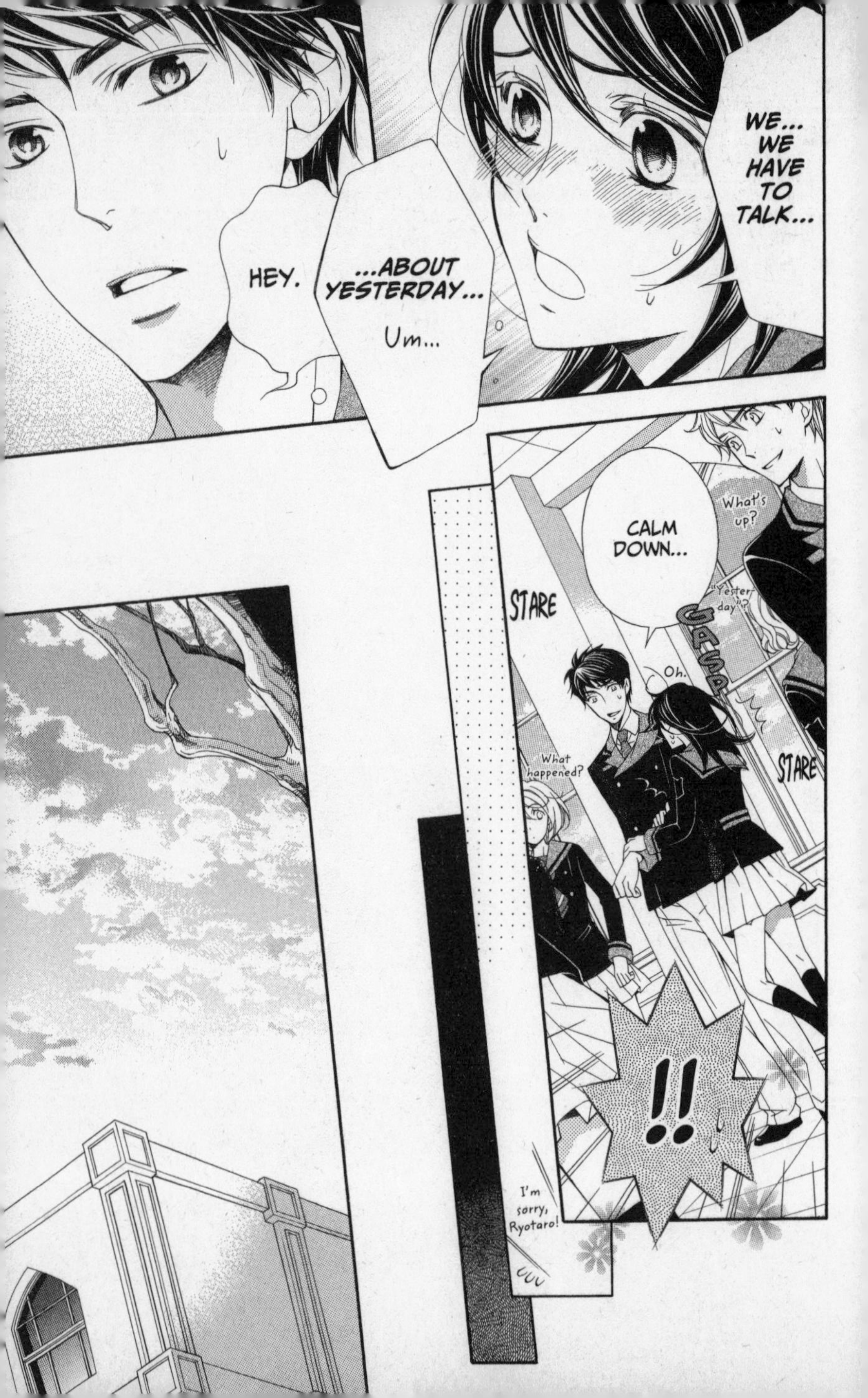

WE... WE HAVE TO TALK...
...ABOUT YESTERDAY...
Um...
HEY.
What's up?
CALM DOWN...
"Yesterday"?
GASP
STARE
Oh.
STARE
What happened?
!!
I'm sorry, Ryotaro!

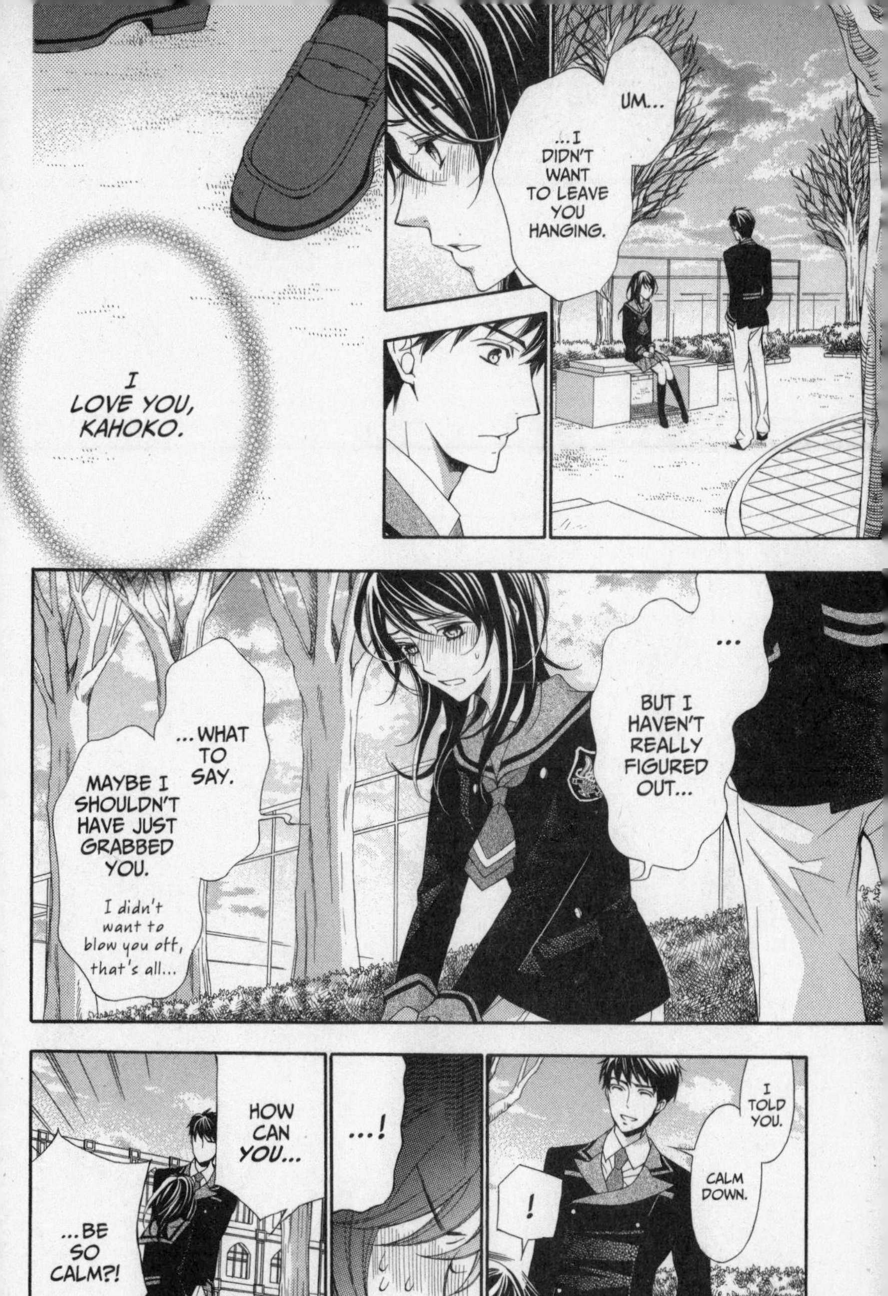
UM...
...I DIDN'T WANT TO LEAVE YOU HANGING.
I LOVE YOU, KAHOKO.
...
BUT I HAVEN'T REALLY FIGURED OUT...
...WHAT TO SAY.
MAYBE I SHOULDN'T HAVE JUST GRABBED YOU.
I didn't want to blow you off, that's all...
I TOLD YOU.
CALM DOWN.
!
...!
HOW CAN YOU...
...BE SO CALM?!

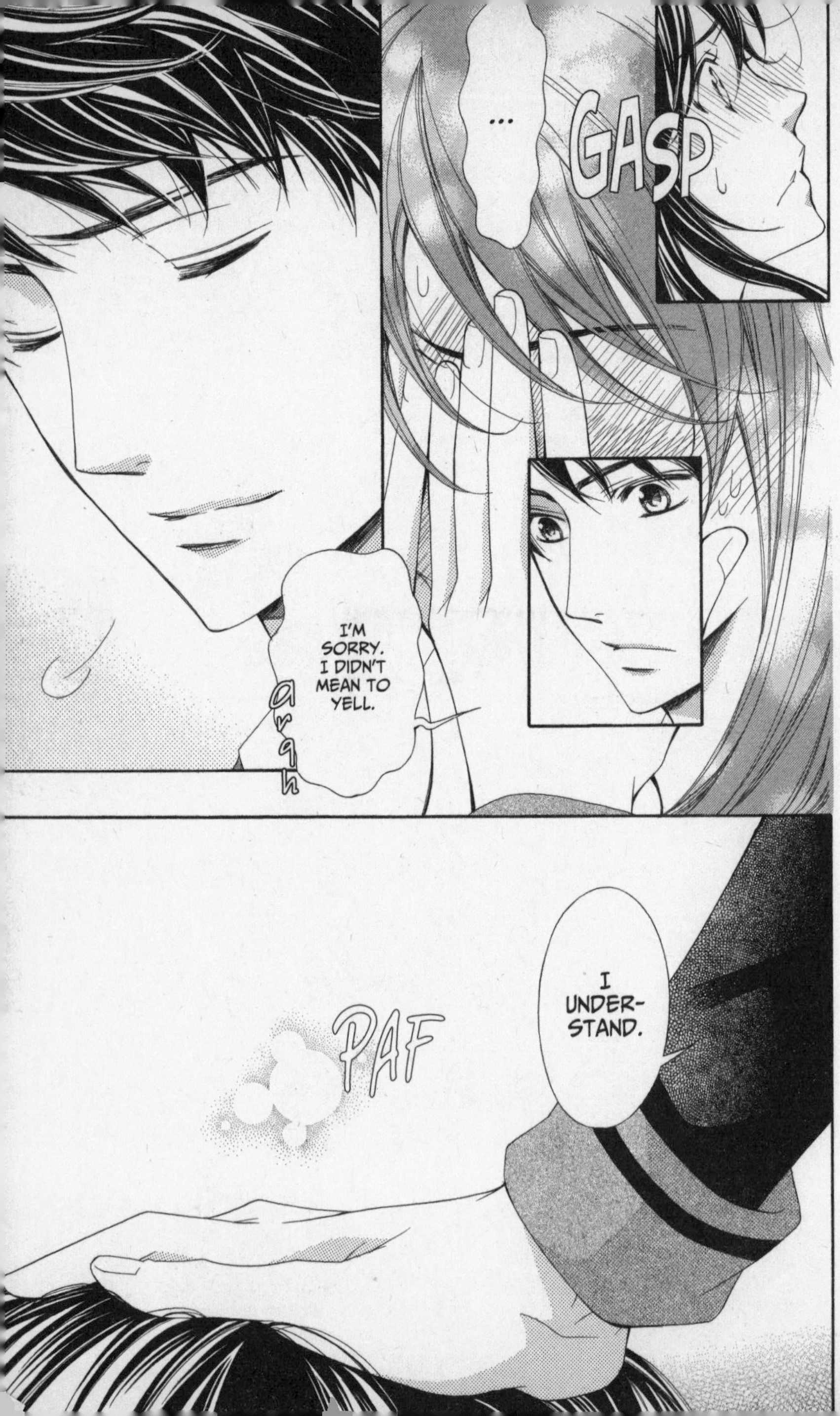
GASP
...
I'M SORRY. I DIDN'T MEAN TO YELL.
Argh
I UNDER-STAND.
PAF

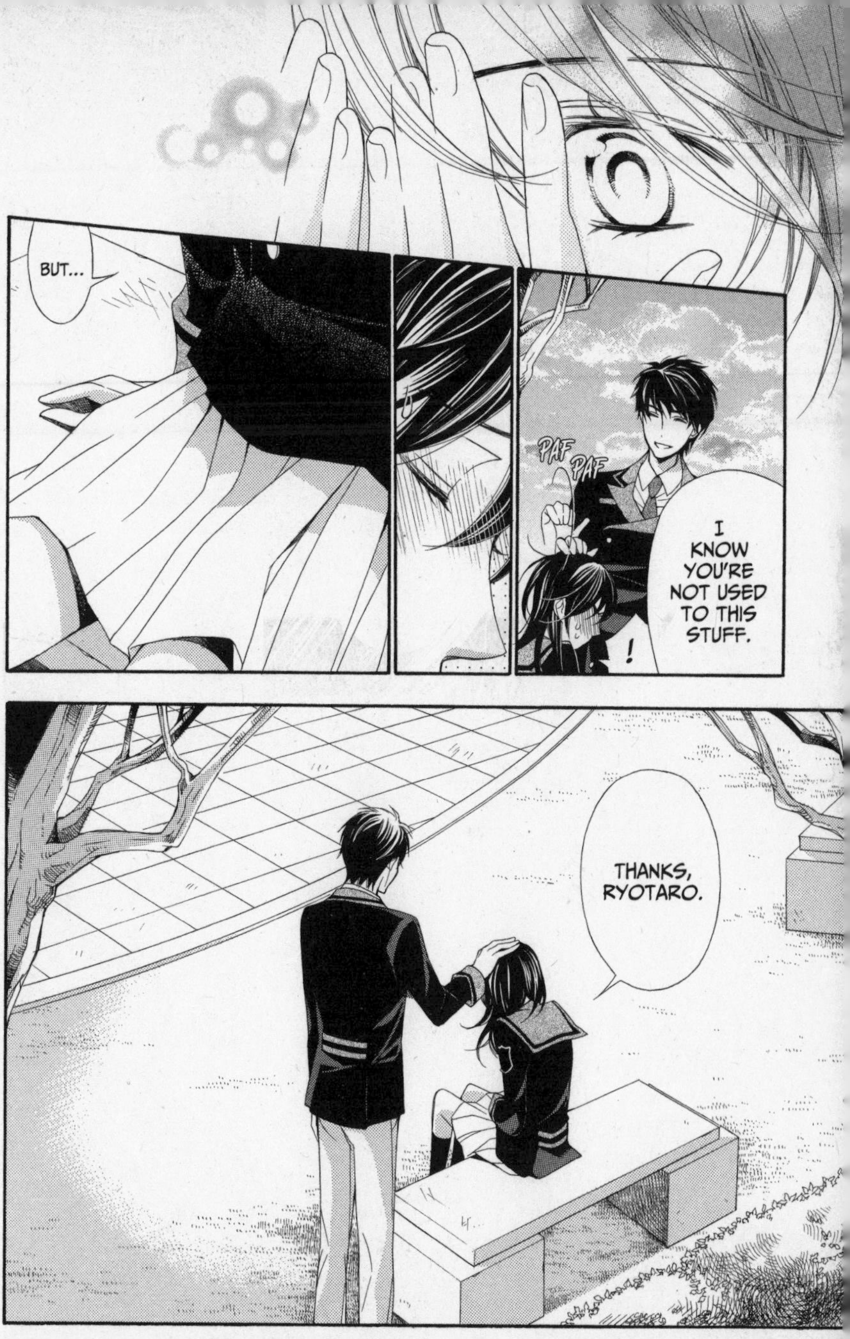
PAF PAF
I KNOW YOU'RE NOT USED TO THIS STUFF.
!
BUT...
THANKS, RYOTARO.

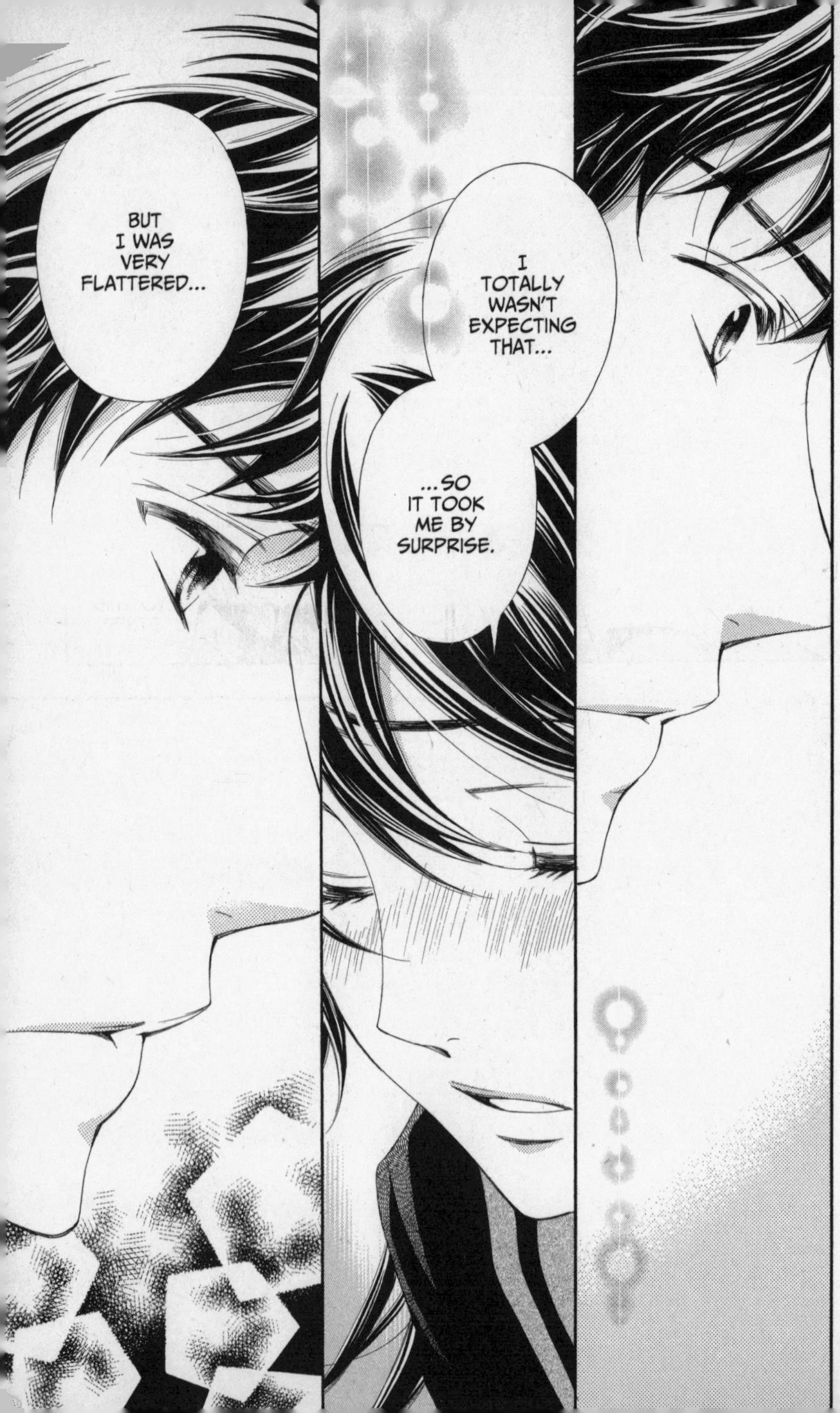
I TOTALLY WASN'T EXPECTING THAT...
...SO IT TOOK ME BY SURPRISE.
BUT I WAS VERY FLATTERED...

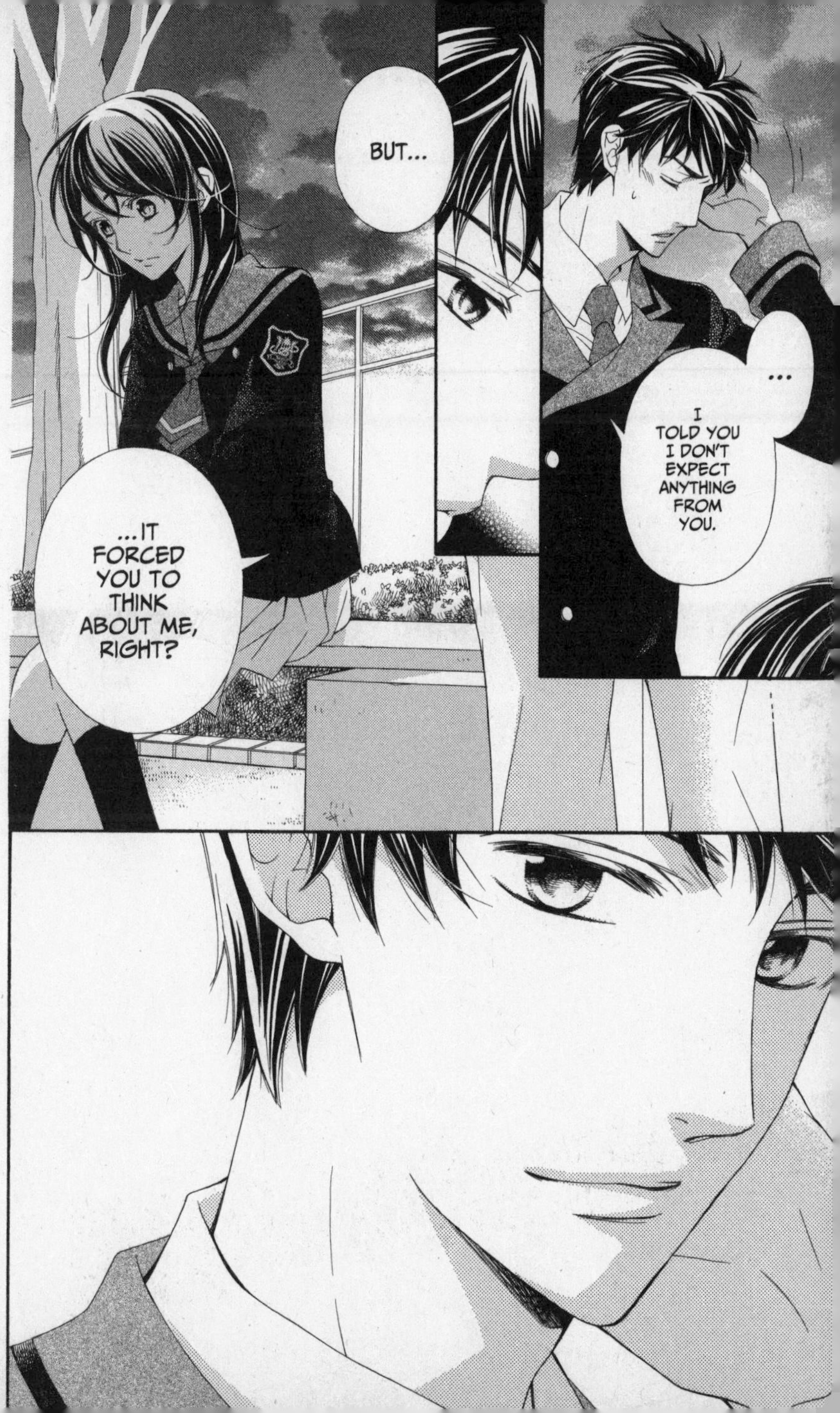
...
I TOLD YOU I DON'T EXPECT ANYTHING FROM YOU.
BUT...
...IT FORCED YOU TO THINK ABOUT ME, RIGHT?

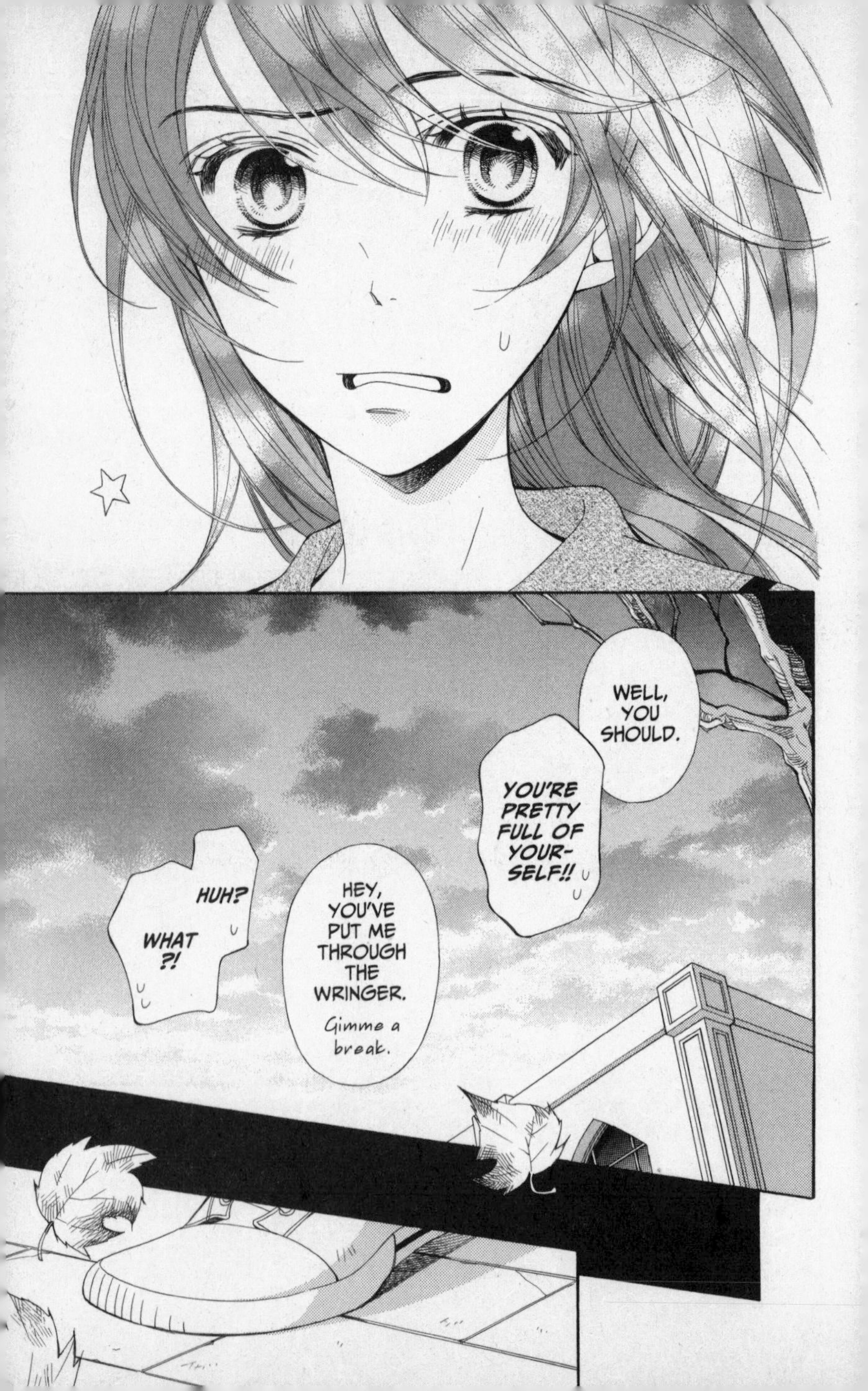
WELL, YOU SHOULD.
YOU'RE PRETTY FULL OF YOUR-SELF!!
HEY, YOU'VE PUT ME THROUGH THE WRINGER.
Gimme a break.
HUH?
WHAT ?!

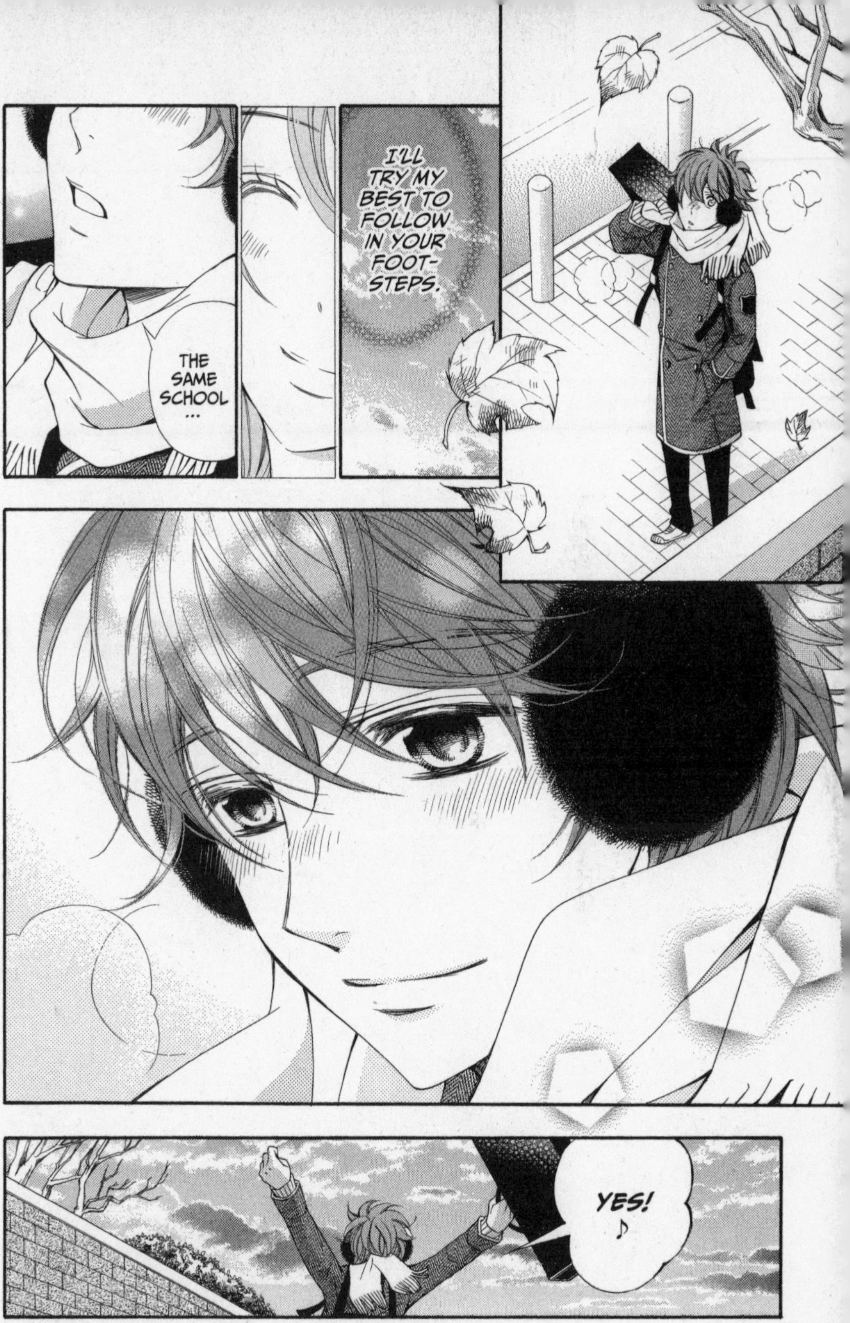
I'LL TRY MY BEST TO FOLLOW IN YOUR FOOT-STEPS.
THE SAME SCHOOL ...
YES! ♪

There were so many cute or cool outfits, it was tough to choose which to draw.

I picked some that had music as a motif.
← Kazuki's next.

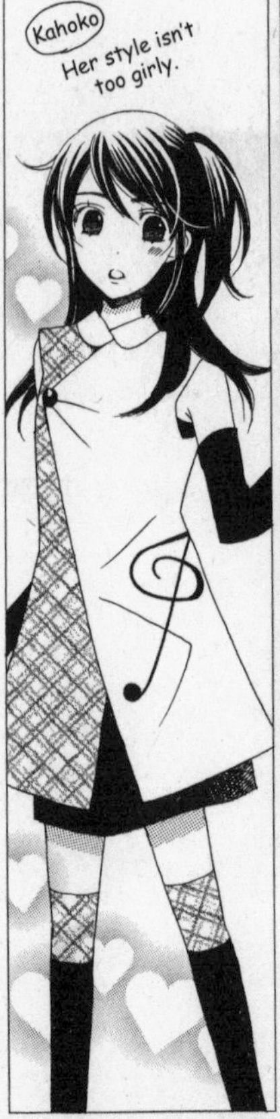
Kahoko
Her style isn't too girly.

BY BLACK KITTY FROM KOCHI

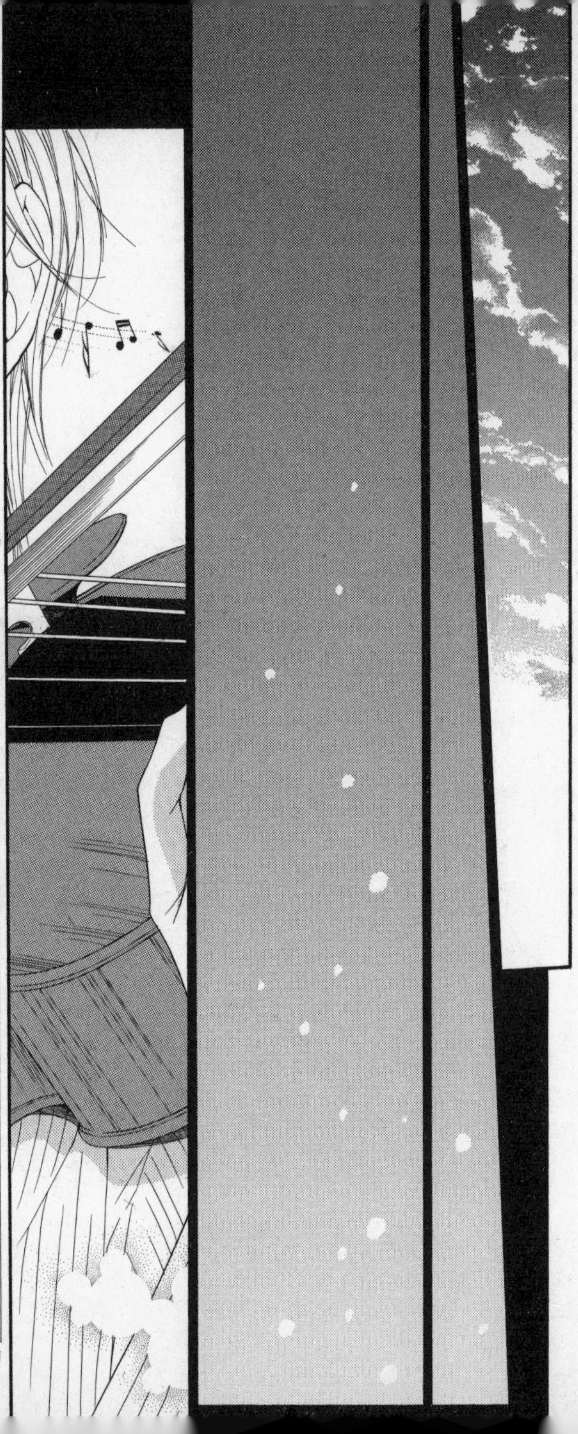

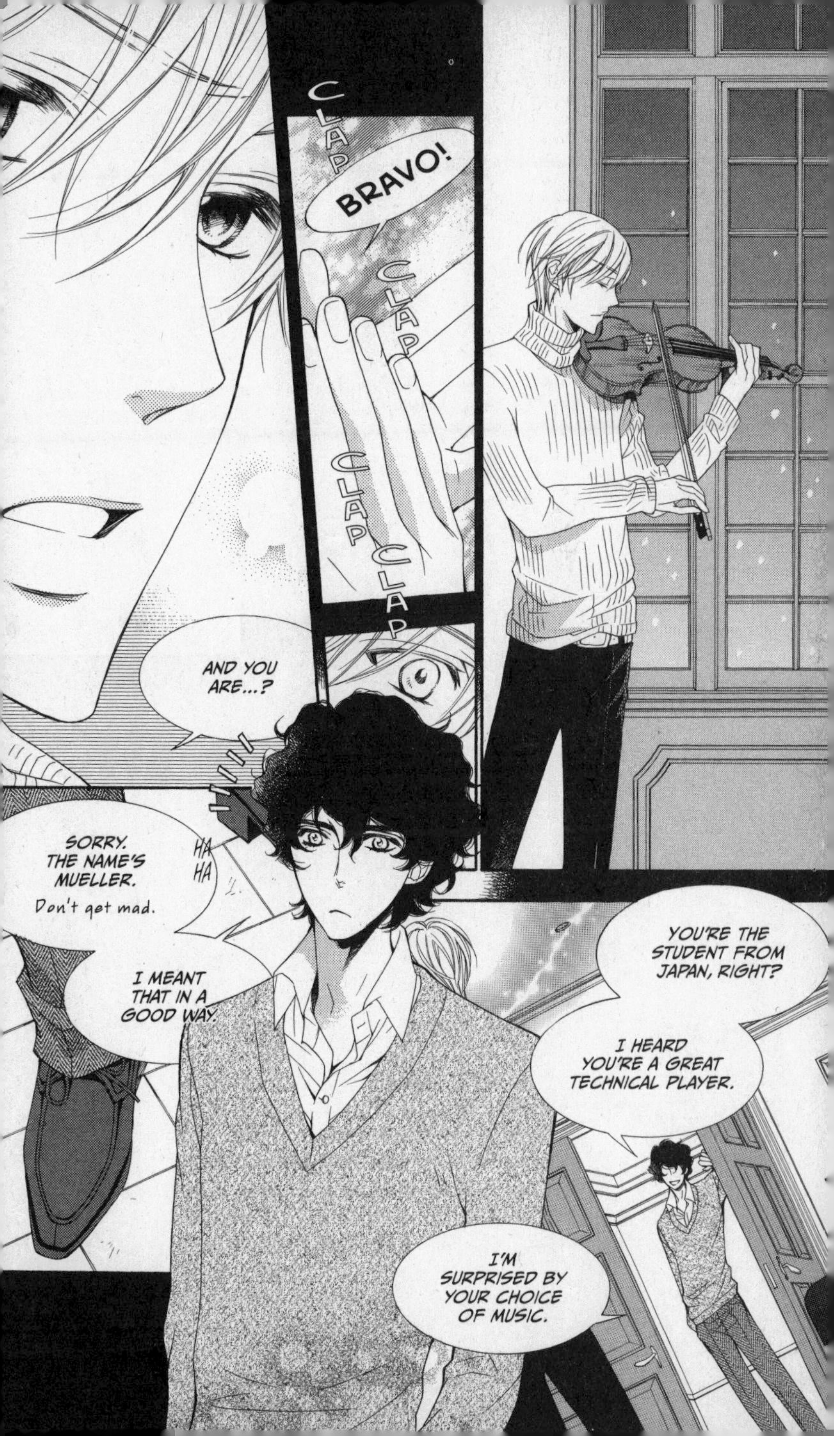
CLAP
CLAP
BRAVO!
CLAP
CLAP
YOU'RE THE STUDENT FROM JAPAN, RIGHT?
I HEARD YOU'RE A GREAT TECHNICAL PLAYER.
I'M SURPRISED BY YOUR CHOICE OF MUSIC.
AND YOU ARE...?
SORRY. THE NAME'S MUELLER.
HA HA
Don't get mad.
I MEANT THAT IN A GOOD WAY.

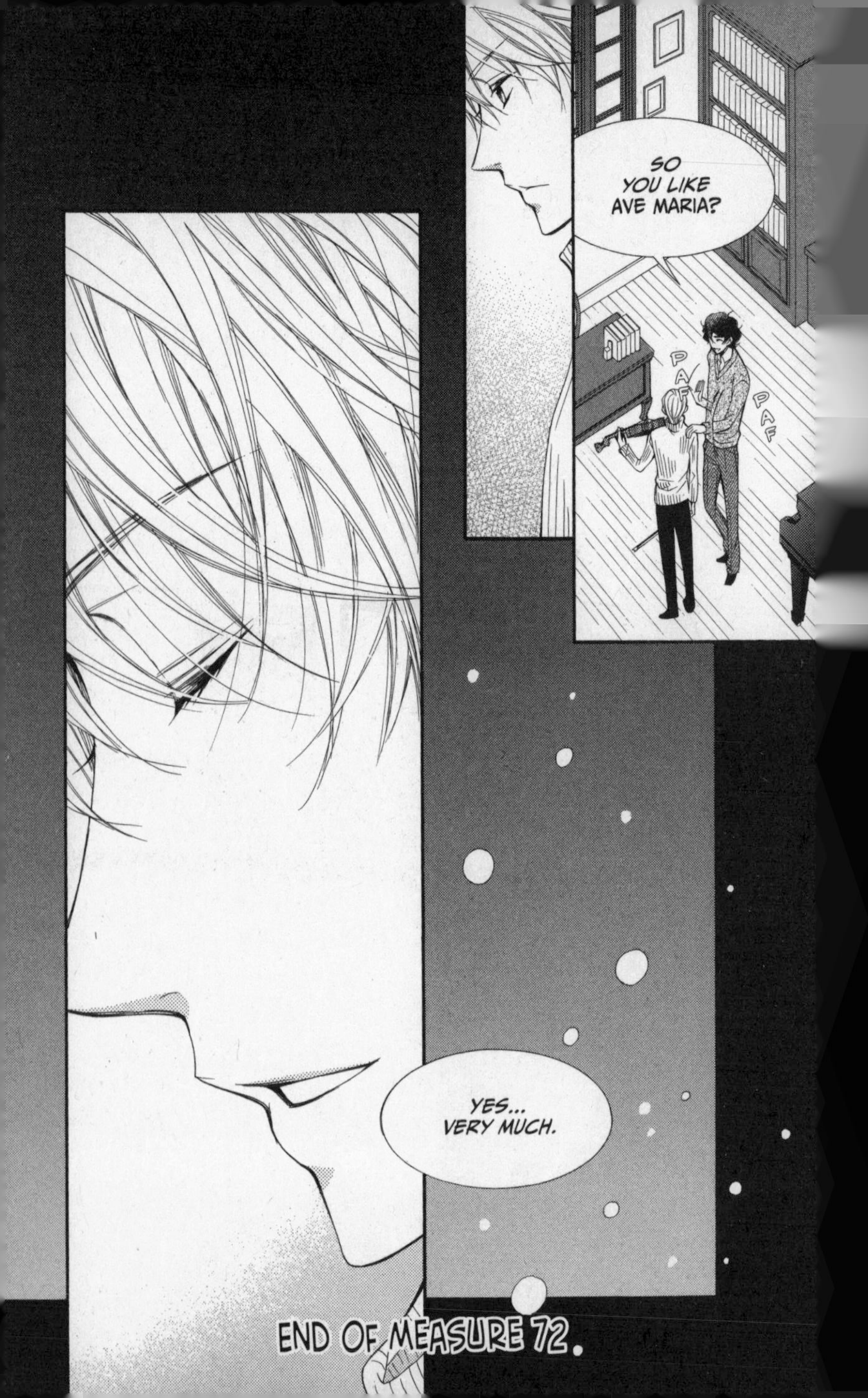
SO YOU LIKE AVE MARIA?
PAF
PAF
YES... VERY MUCH.
END OF MEASURE 72

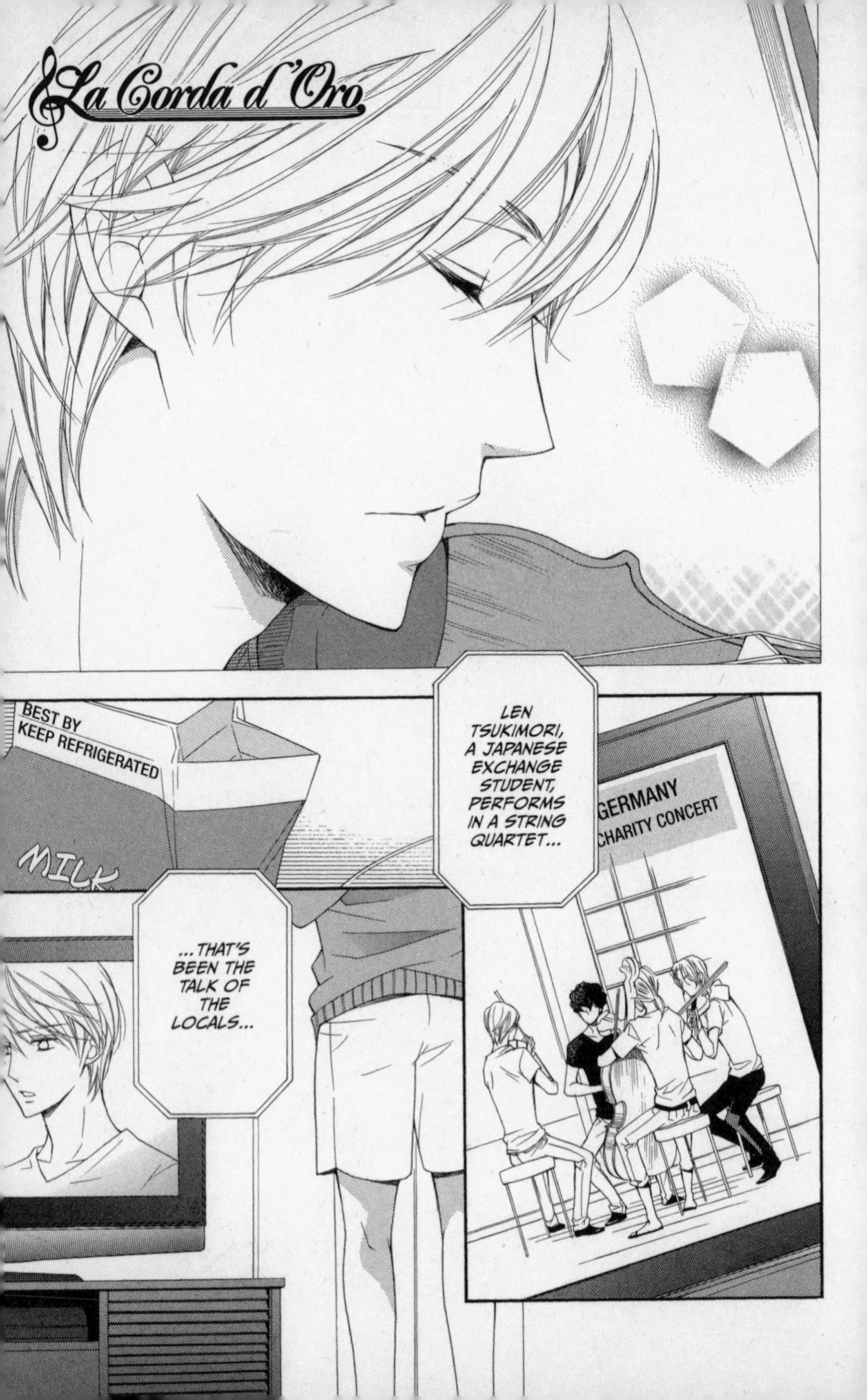
La Corda d'Oro
BEST BY
KEEP REFRIGERATED
MILK
GERMANY
CHARITY CONCERT
LEN TSUKIMORI, A JAPANESE EXCHANGE STUDENT, PERFORMS IN A STRING QUARTET...
...THAT'S BEEN THE TALK OF THE LOCALS...

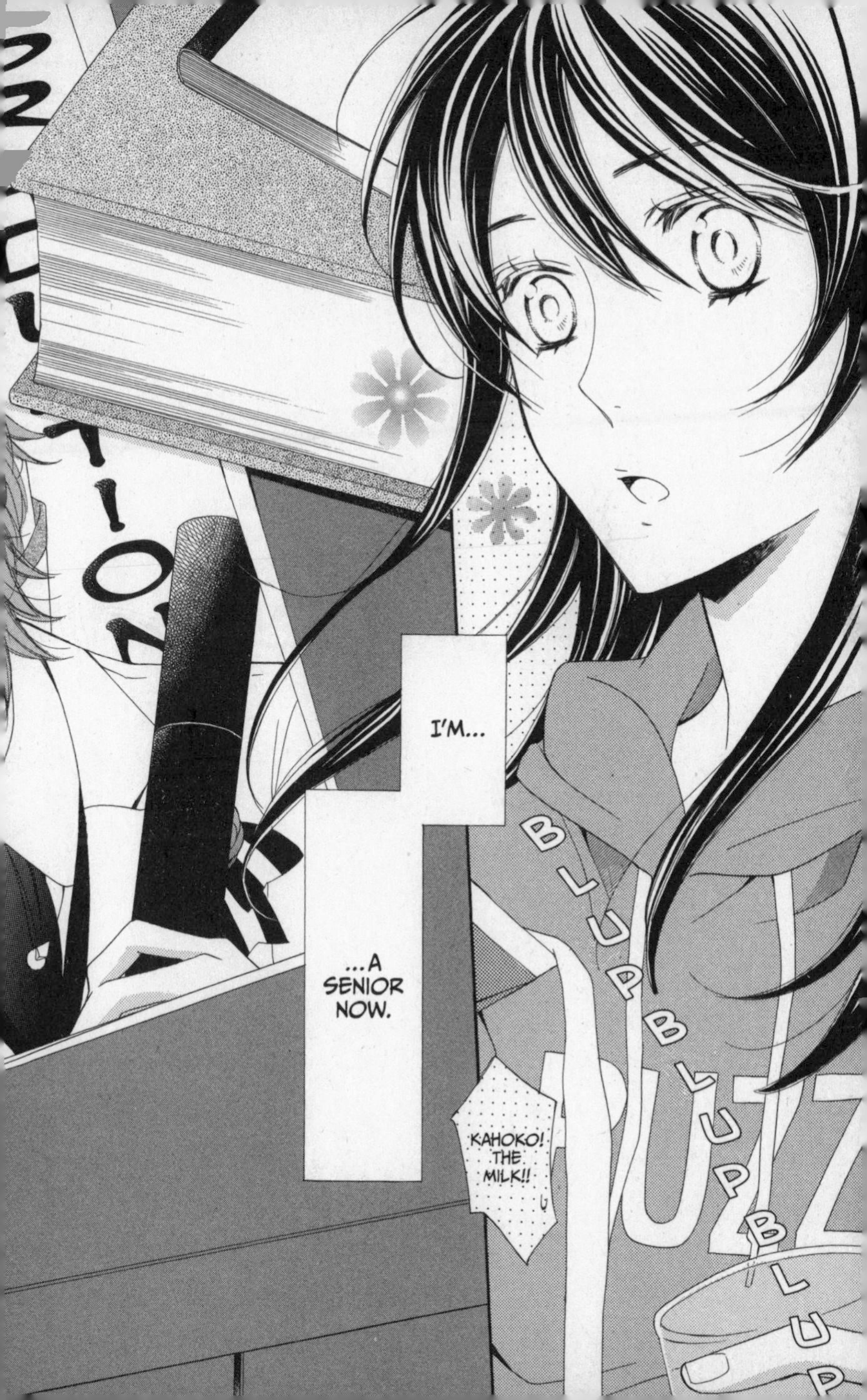
I'M...
...A SENIOR NOW.
KAHOKO! THE MILK!!
BLUP BLUP BLUP BLUP

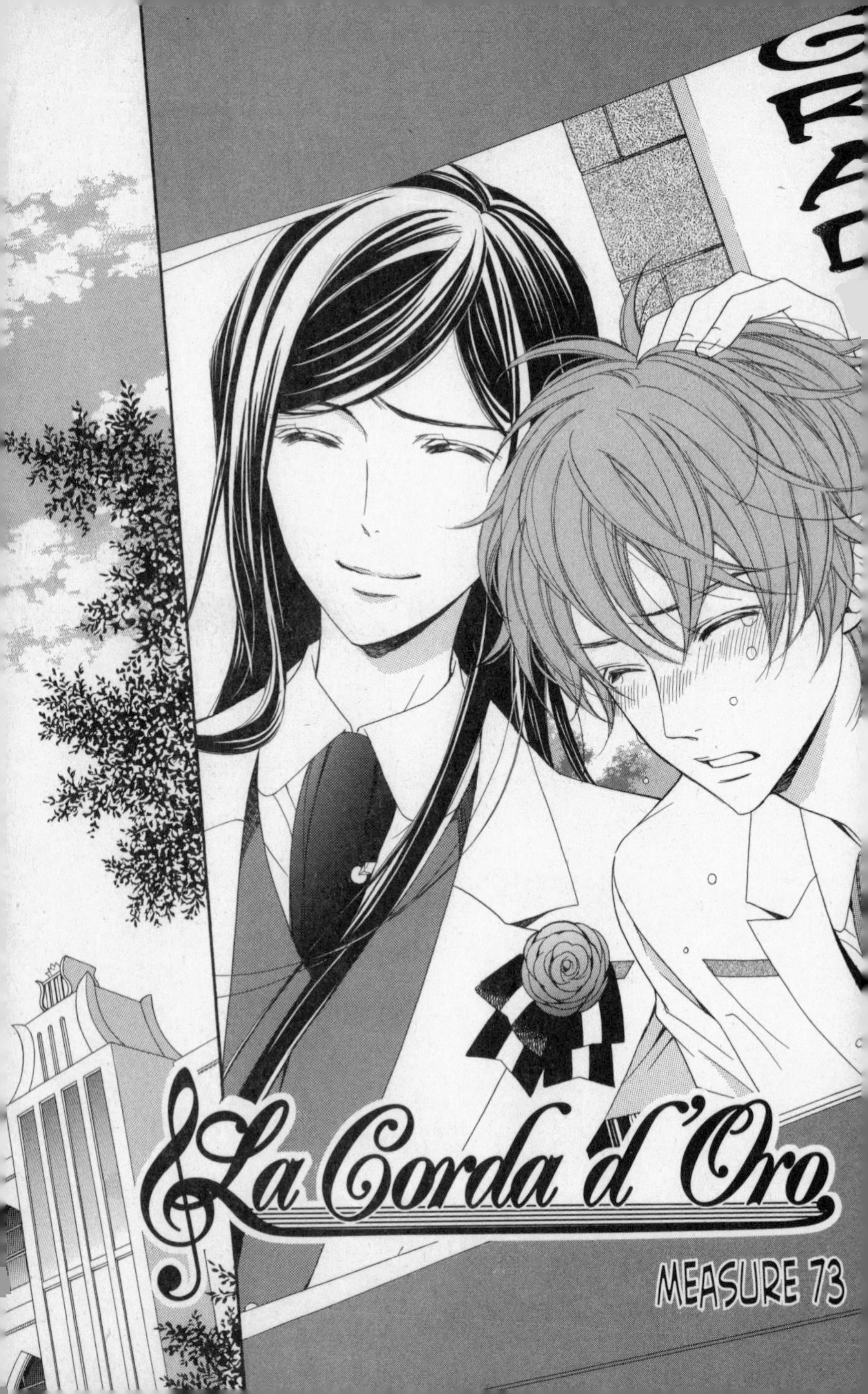
GRAD
La Corda d'Oro
MEASURE 73

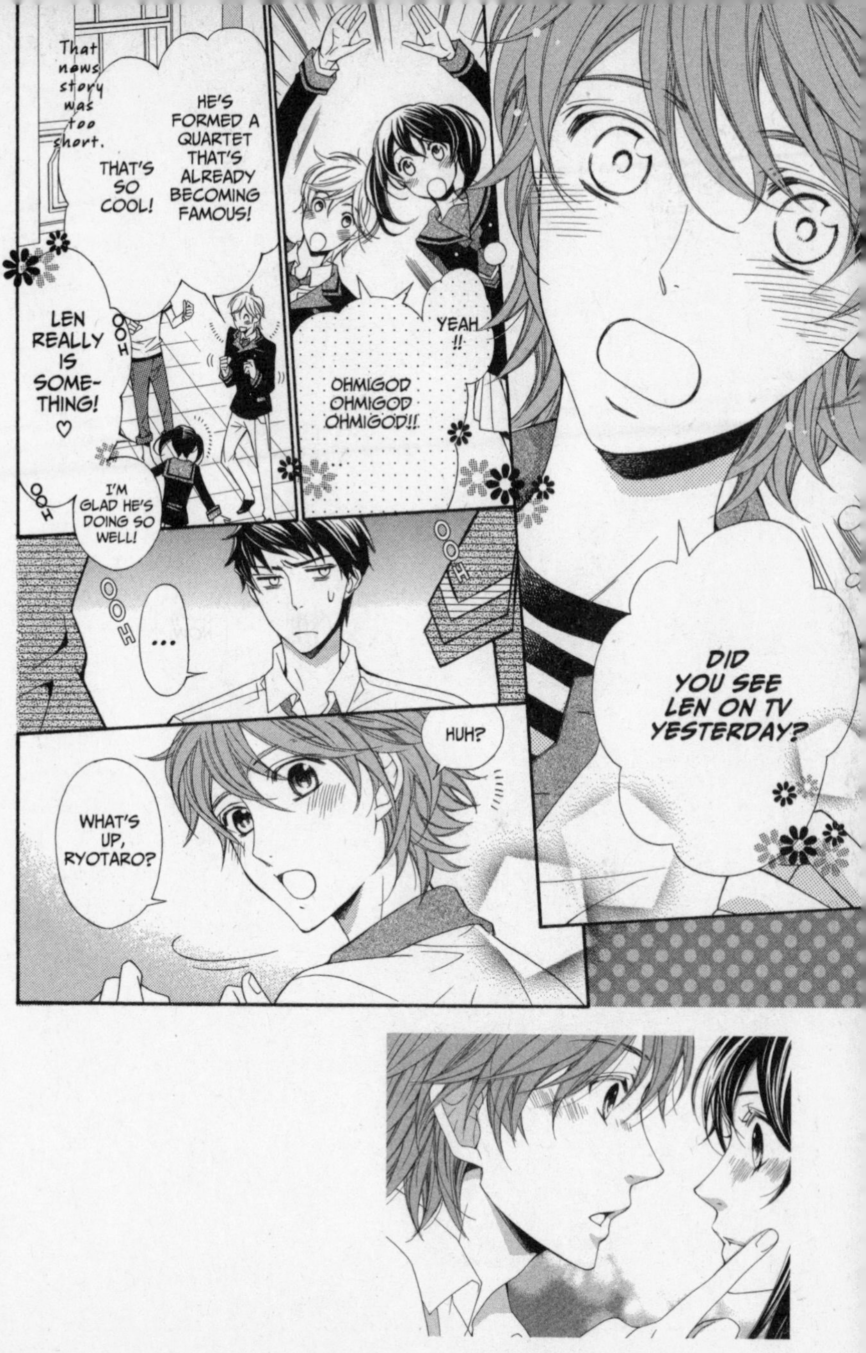
DID YOU SEE LEN ON TV YESTERDAY?
YEAH!!
OHMIGOD OHMIGOD OHMIGOD!!
HE'S FORMED A QUARTET THAT'S ALREADY BECOMING FAMOUS!
That news story was too short.
THAT'S SO COOL!
LEN REALLY IS SOMETHING! ♡
OOH
I'M GLAD HE'S DOING SO WELL!
OOH
OOH
OOH
...
HUH?
WHAT'S UP, RYOTARO?

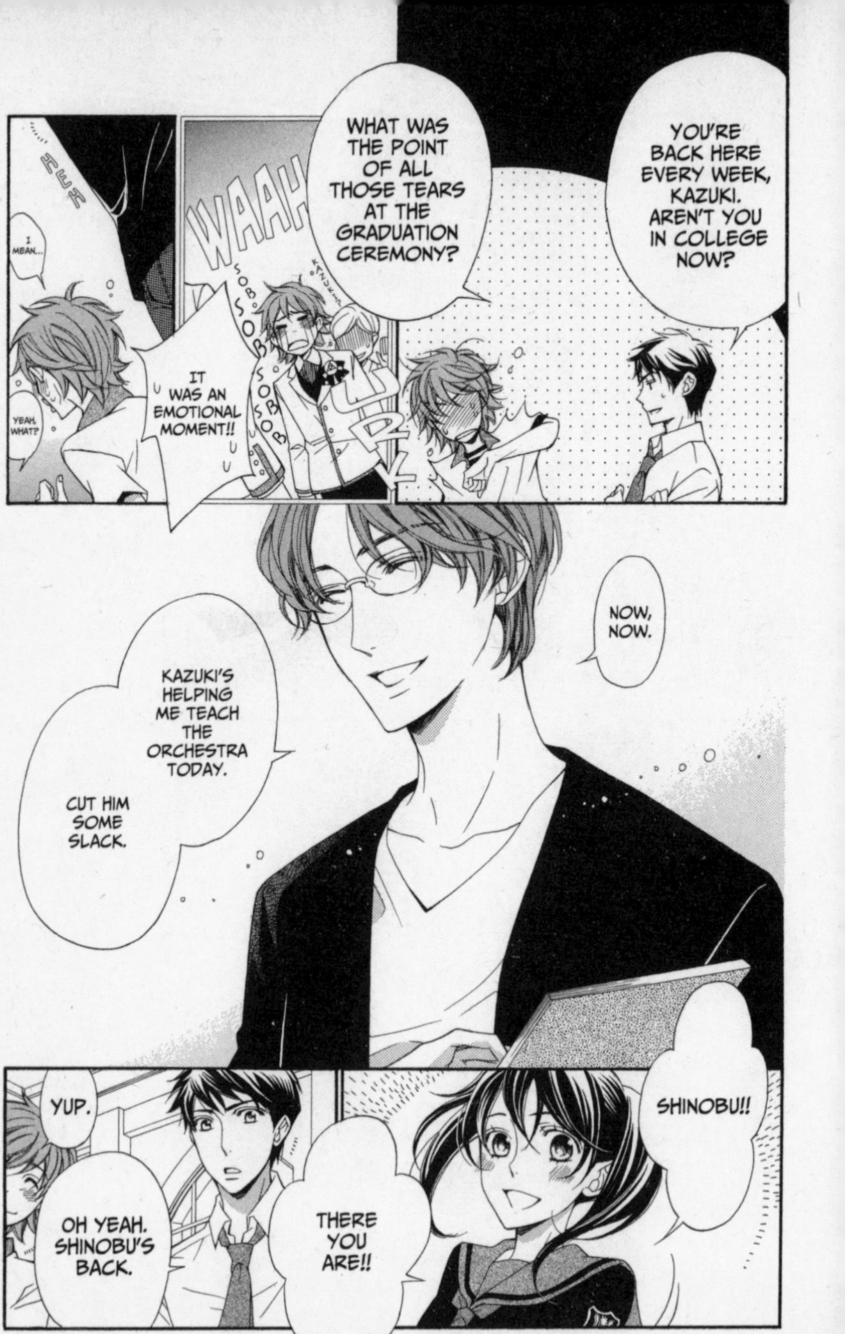
YOU'RE BACK HERE EVERY WEEK, KAZUKI. AREN'T YOU IN COLLEGE NOW?
WHAT WAS THE POINT OF ALL THOSE TEARS AT THE GRADUATION CEREMONY?
URK
WAAH
SOB SOB
SOB SOB
IT WAS AN EMOTIONAL MOMENT!!
I MEAN...
YEAH, WHAT?
NOW, NOW.
KAZUKI'S HELPING ME TEACH THE ORCHESTRA TODAY.
CUT HIM SOME SLACK.
SHINOBU!!
THERE YOU ARE!!
YUP.
OH YEAH. SHINOBU'S BACK.

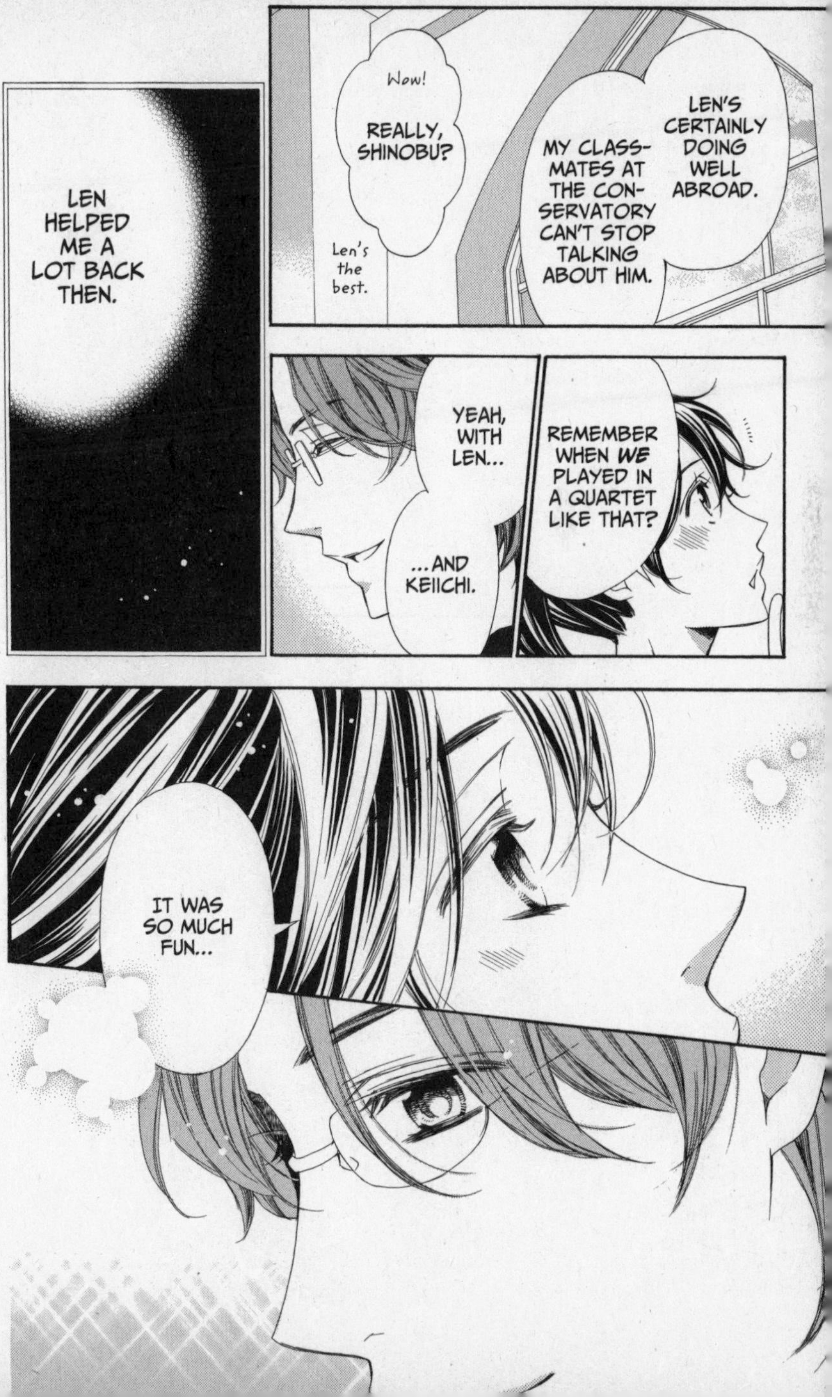
LEN'S CERTAINLY DOING WELL ABROAD.
MY CLASS-MATES AT THE CON-SERVATORY CAN'T STOP TALKING ABOUT HIM.
Wow!
REALLY, SHINOBU?
Len's the best.
REMEMBER WHEN *WE* PLAYED IN A QUARTET LIKE THAT?
YEAH, WITH LEN...
...AND KEIICHI.
LEN HELPED ME A LOT BACK THEN.
IT WAS SO MUCH FUN...

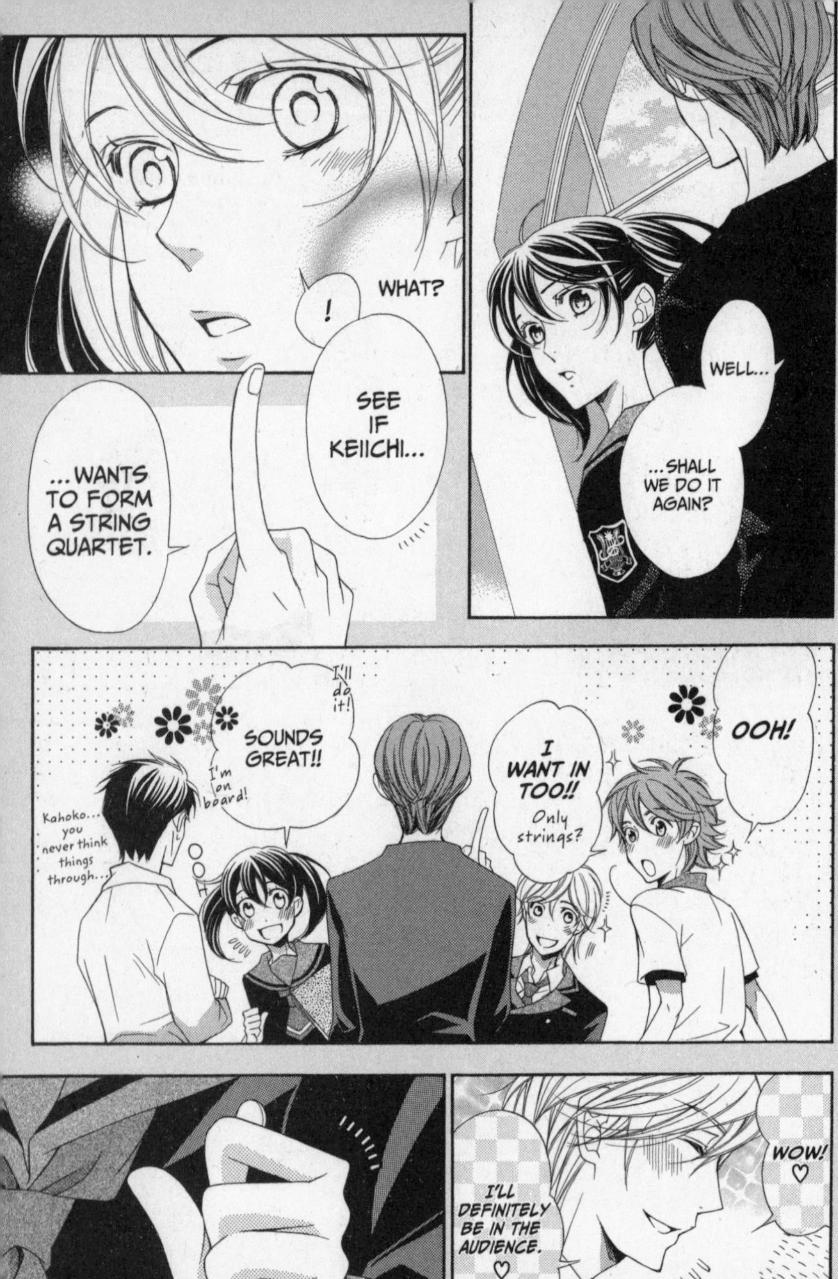
WELL...
...SHALL WE DO IT AGAIN?
WHAT?
!
SEE IF KEIICHI...
...WANTS TO FORM A STRING QUARTET.
OOH!
I WANT IN TOO!!
Only strings?
SOUNDS GREAT!!
I'll do it!
I'm on board!
Kahoko... you never think things through...
WOW! ♥
I'LL DEFINITELY BE IN THE AUDIENCE. ♥

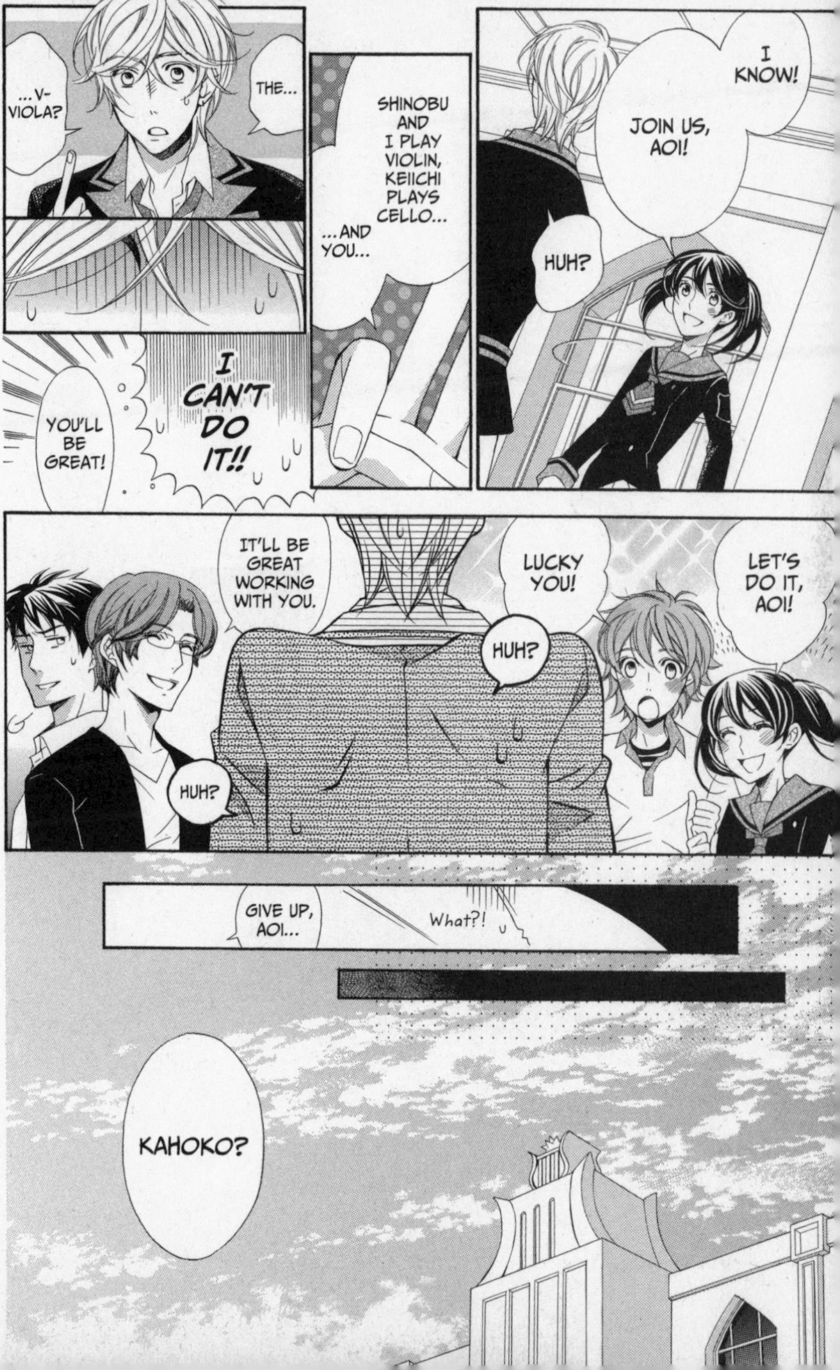
I KNOW!
JOIN US, AOI!
HUH?
SHINOBU AND I PLAY VIOLIN, KEIICHI PLAYS CELLO...
...AND YOU...
THE...
...V-VIOLA?
I CAN'T DO IT!!
YOU'LL BE GREAT!
LET'S DO IT, AOI!
LUCKY YOU!
HUH?
IT'LL BE GREAT WORKING WITH YOU.
HUH?
What?!
GIVE UP, AOI...
KAHOKO?

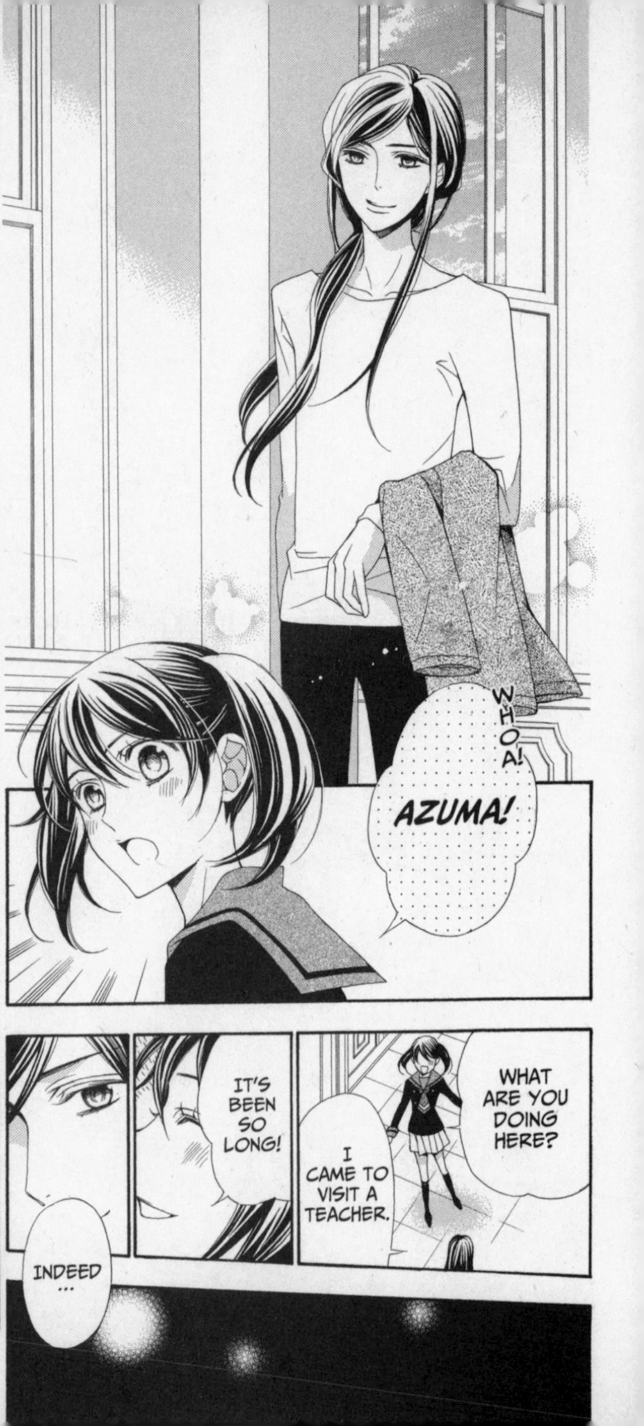
WHOA!
AZUMA!
WHAT ARE YOU DOING HERE?
I CAME TO VISIT A TEACHER.
IT'S BEEN SO LONG!
INDEED...

Readers also submitted lines the guys could say that would sweep them off their feet. For Kazuki: "I promise I'll make you happy!"

↑ He would totally say something like that!!

← Ryotaro's next.

The sunflower on the lapel is very much his style! ♡

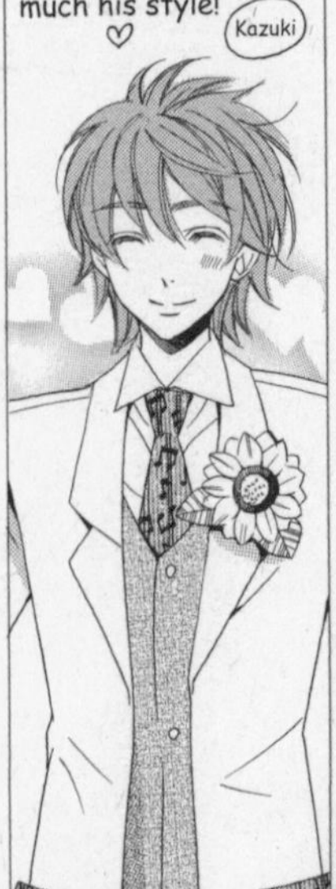
Kazuki

BY ITSUKI FROM MIYAGI

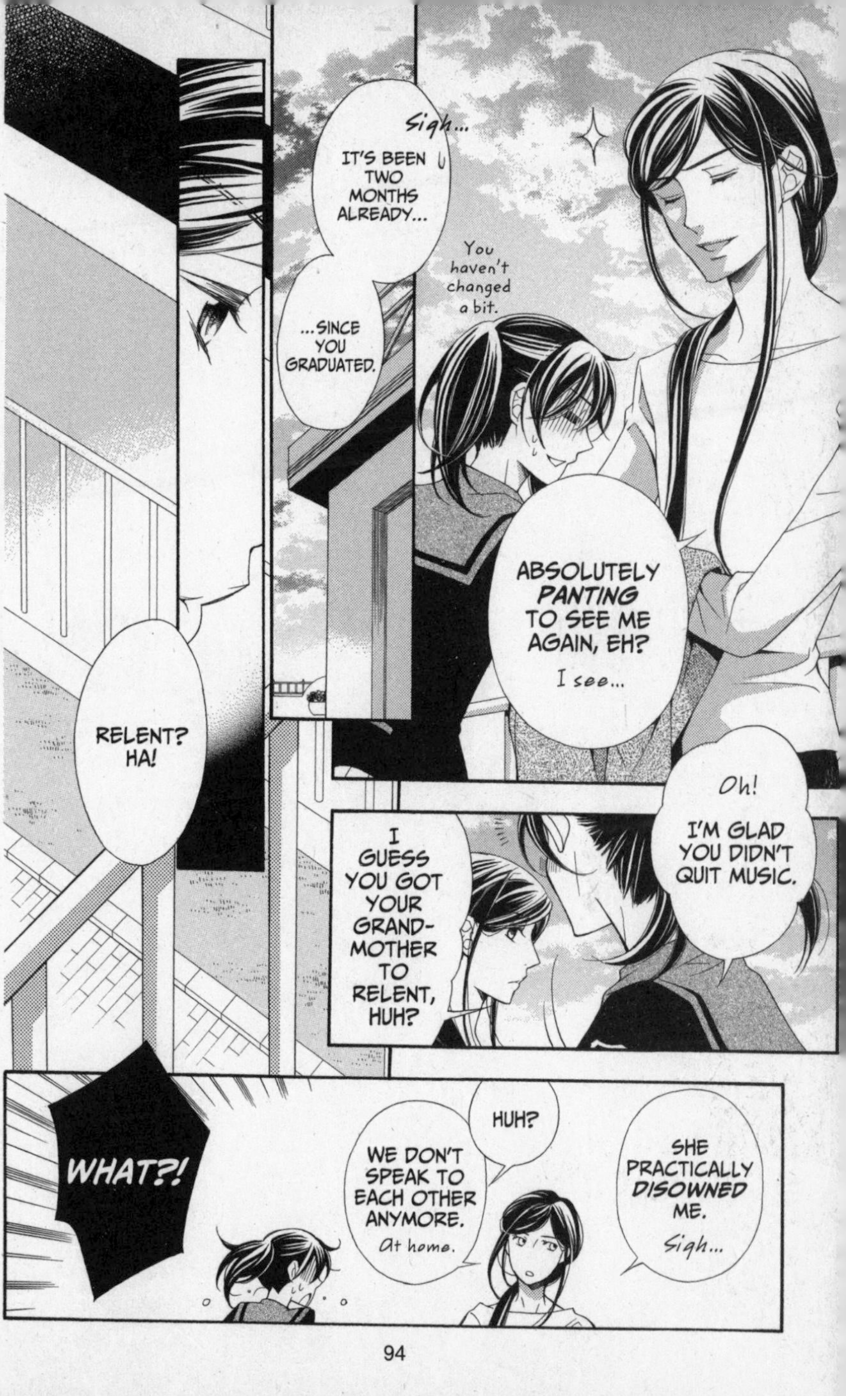
Sigh...
IT'S BEEN TWO MONTHS ALREADY...
...SINCE YOU GRADUATED.
You haven't changed a bit.
ABSOLUTELY PANTING TO SEE ME AGAIN, EH?
I see...
Oh!
I'M GLAD YOU DIDN'T QUIT MUSIC.
I GUESS YOU GOT YOUR GRAND-MOTHER TO RELENT, HUH?
RELENT? HA!
SHE PRACTICALLY DISOWNED ME.
Sigh...
WE DON'T SPEAK TO EACH OTHER ANYMORE.
At home.
HUH?
WHAT?!

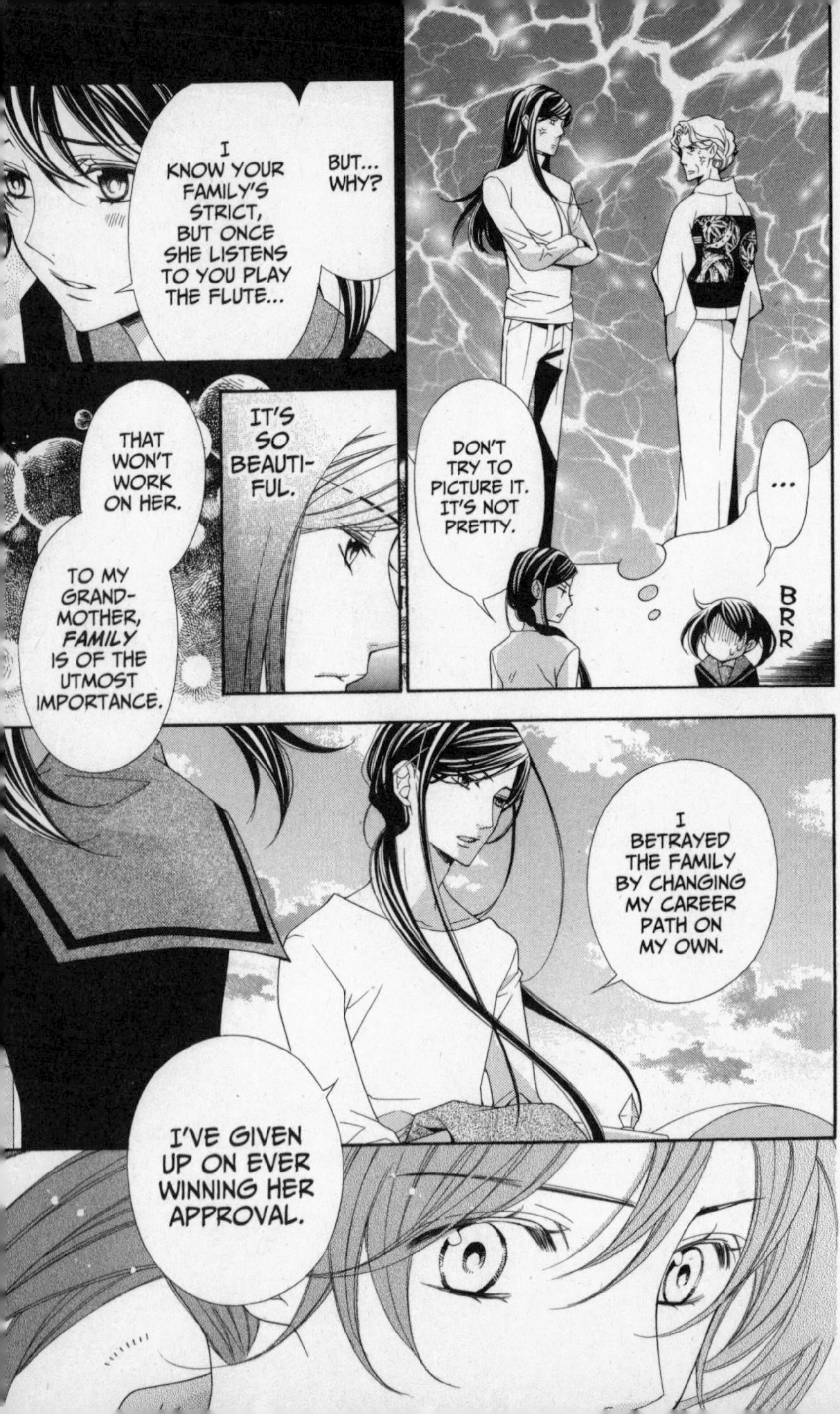
BUT... WHY?
I KNOW YOUR FAMILY'S STRICT, BUT ONCE SHE LISTENS TO YOU PLAY THE FLUTE...
IT'S SO BEAUTI-FUL.
THAT WON'T WORK ON HER.
TO MY GRAND-MOTHER, *FAMILY* IS OF THE UTMOST IMPORTANCE.
...
BRR
DON'T TRY TO PICTURE IT. IT'S NOT PRETTY.
I BETRAYED THE FAMILY BY CHANGING MY CAREER PATH ON MY OWN.
I'VE GIVEN UP ON EVER WINNING HER APPROVAL.

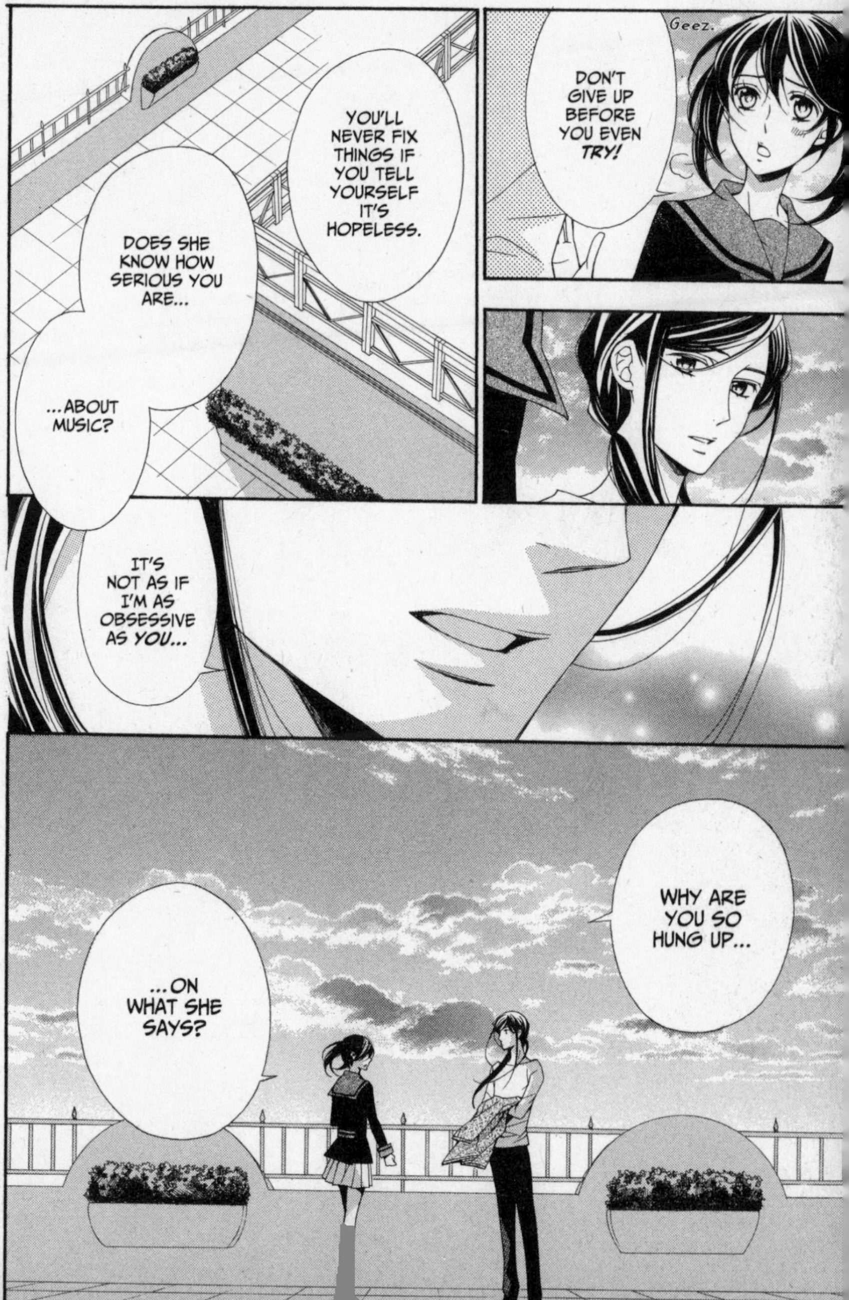
Geez.
DON'T GIVE UP BEFORE YOU EVEN *TRY!*
YOU'LL NEVER FIX THINGS IF YOU TELL YOURSELF IT'S HOPELESS.
DOES SHE KNOW HOW SERIOUS YOU ARE...
...ABOUT MUSIC?
IT'S NOT AS IF I'M AS OBSESSIVE AS *YOU...*
WHY ARE YOU SO HUNG UP...
...ON WHAT SHE SAYS?

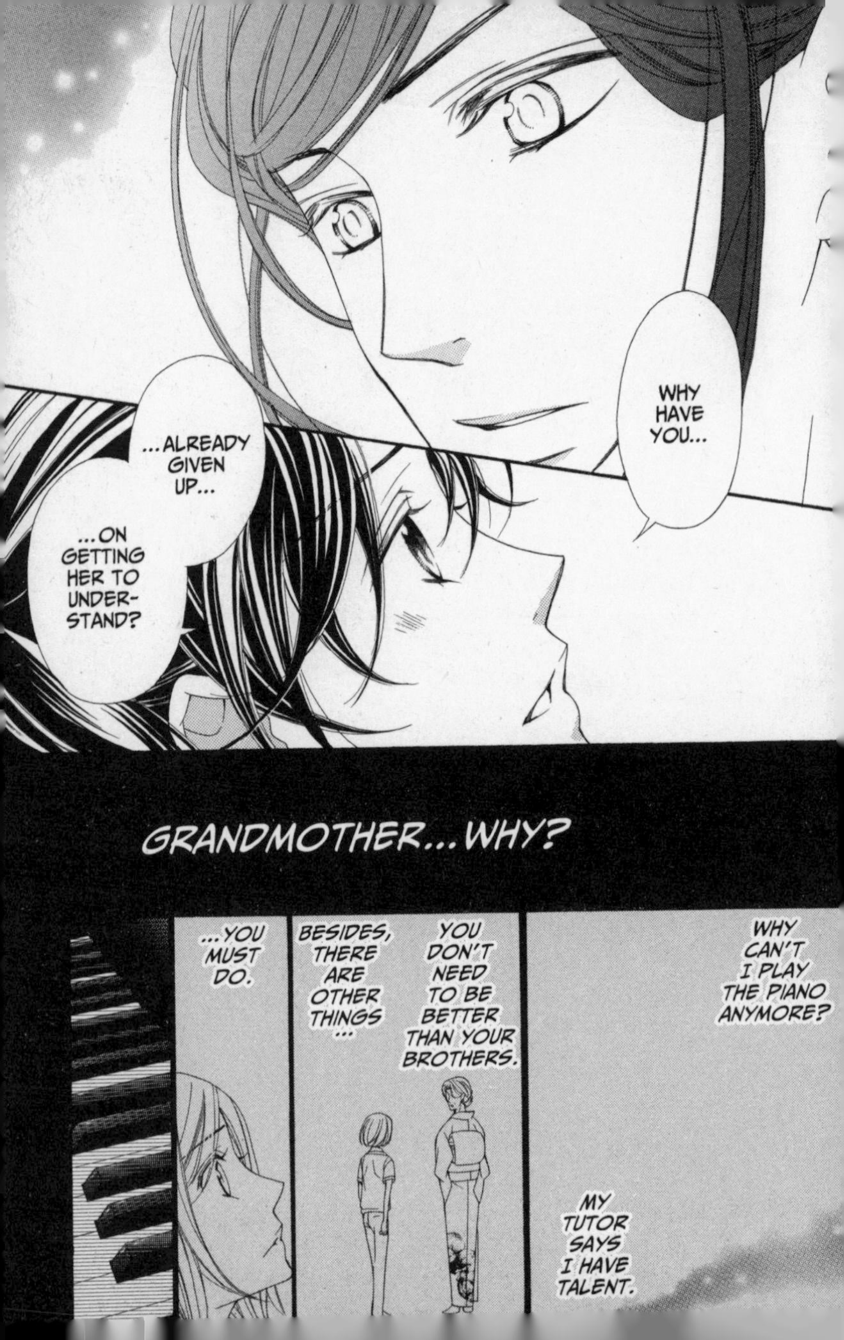
WHY HAVE YOU...
...ALREADY GIVEN UP...
...ON GETTING HER TO UNDER-STAND?
GRANDMOTHER...WHY?
WHY CAN'T I PLAY THE PIANO ANYMORE?
MY TUTOR SAYS I HAVE TALENT.
YOU DON'T NEED TO BE BETTER THAN YOUR BROTHERS.
BESIDES, THERE ARE OTHER THINGS...
...YOU MUST DO.

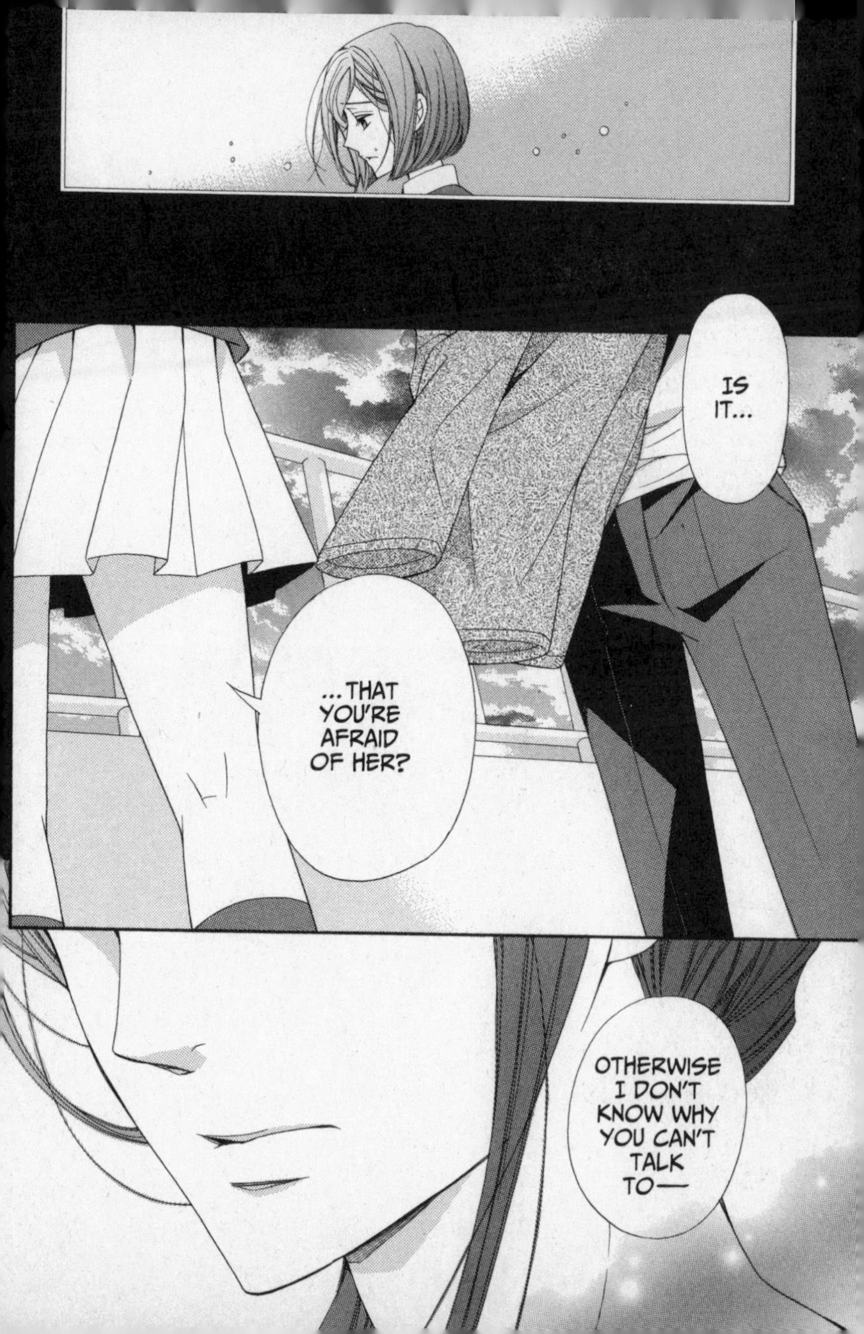
IS IT...
...THAT YOU'RE AFRAID OF HER?
OTHERWISE I DON'T KNOW WHY YOU CAN'T TALK TO—

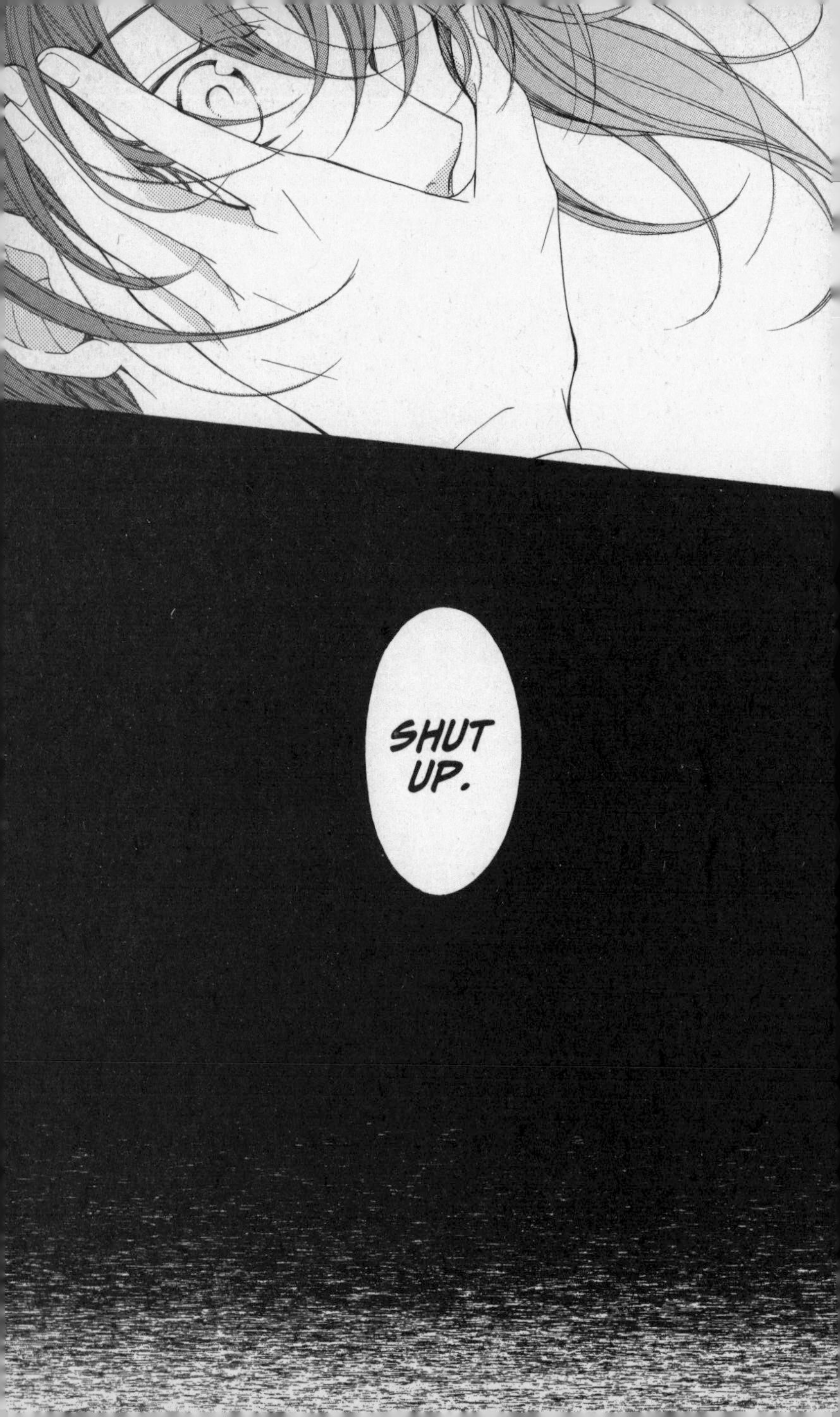
SHUT UP.

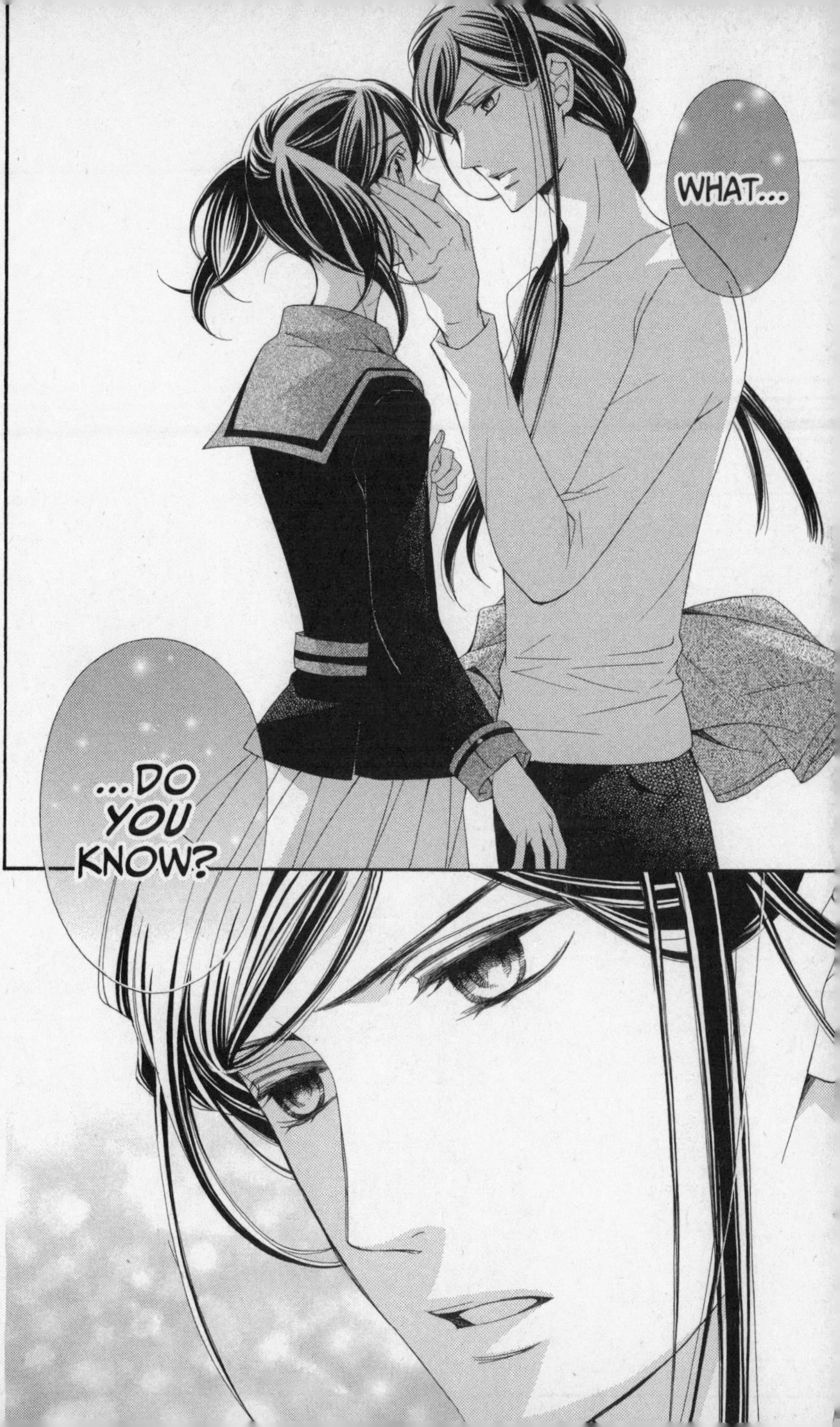
WHAT...
...DO YOU KNOW?

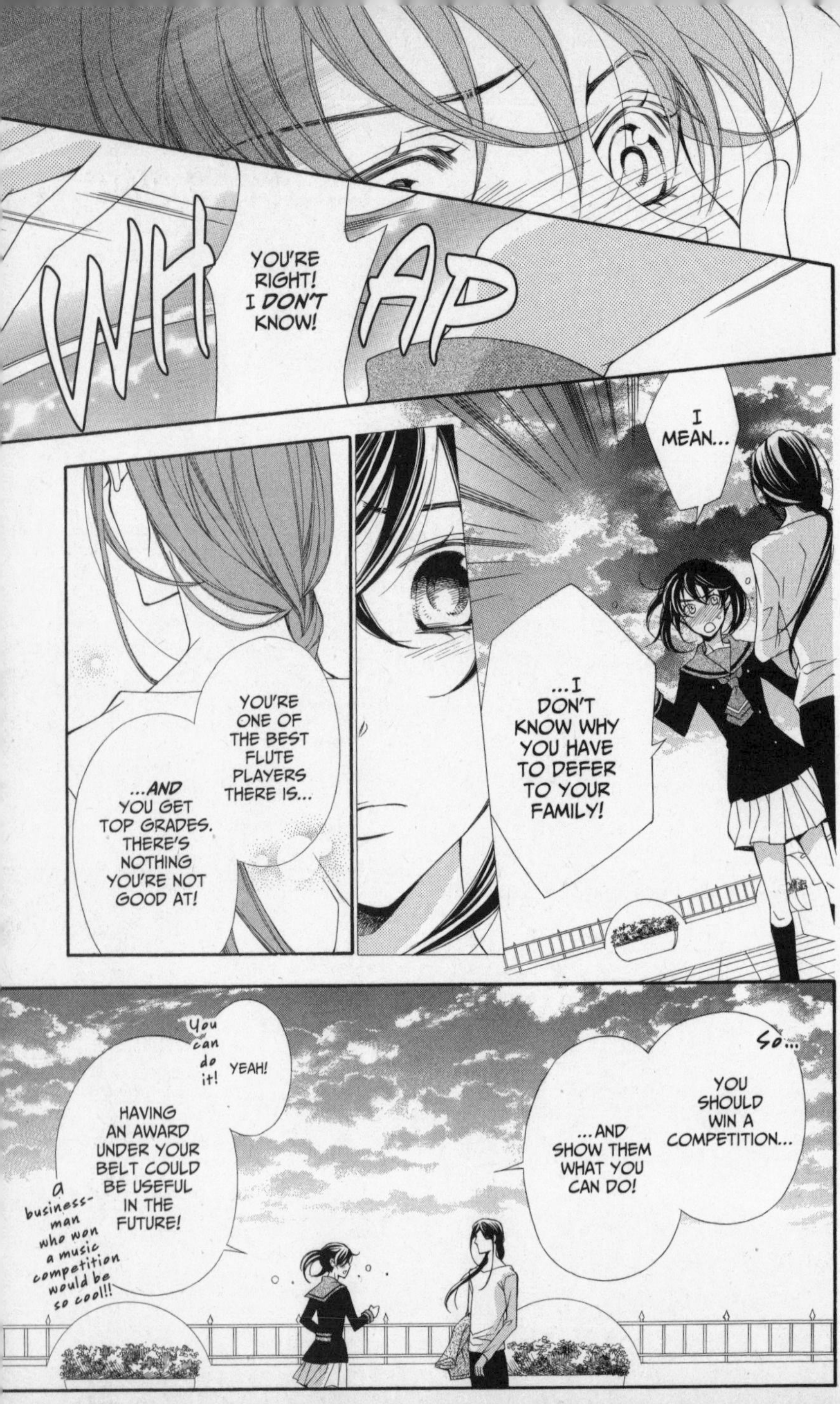
WHAP
YOU'RE RIGHT! I DON'T KNOW!
I MEAN...
...I DON'T KNOW WHY YOU HAVE TO DEFER TO YOUR FAMILY!
YOU'RE ONE OF THE BEST FLUTE PLAYERS THERE IS...
...AND YOU GET TOP GRADES. THERE'S NOTHING YOU'RE NOT GOOD AT!
So...
YOU SHOULD WIN A COMPETITION...
...AND SHOW THEM WHAT YOU CAN DO!
YEAH!
You can do it!
HAVING AN AWARD UNDER YOUR BELT COULD BE USEFUL IN THE FUTURE!
a business-man who won a music competition would be so cool!!!

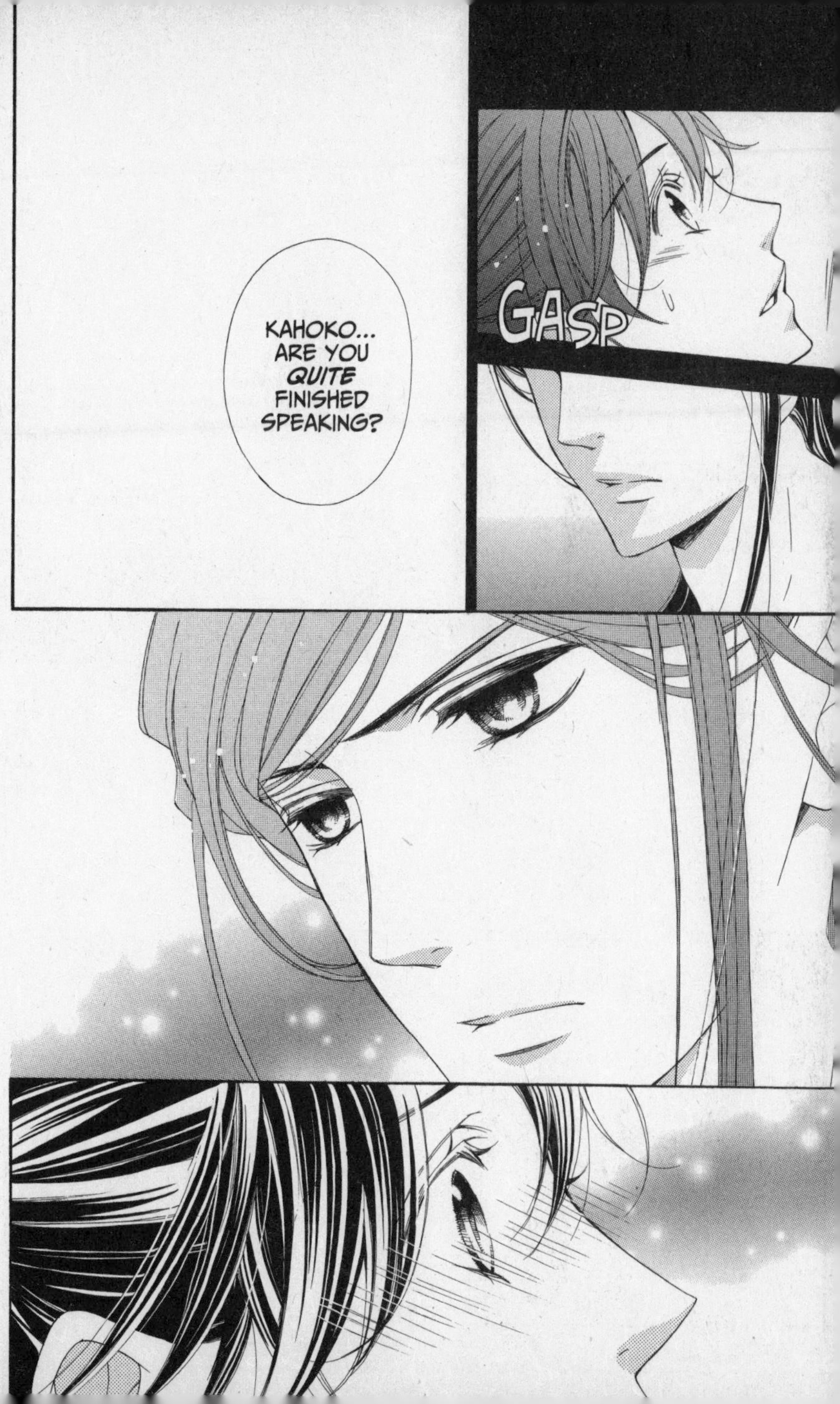
GASP
KAHOKO... ARE YOU *QUITE* FINISHED SPEAKING?

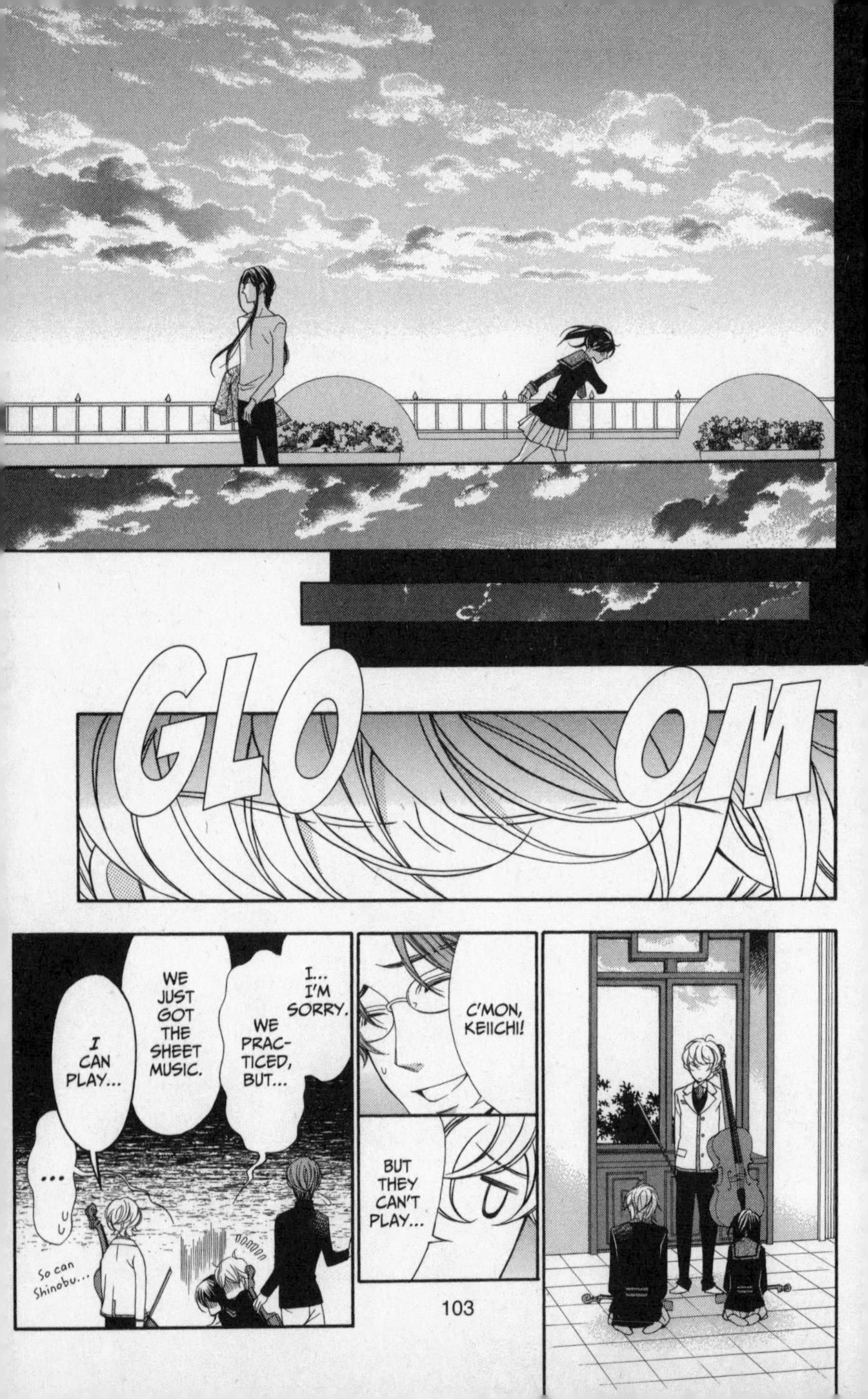
GLOOM
C'MON, KEIICHI!
BUT THEY CAN'T PLAY...
I... I'M SORRY.
WE PRACTICED, BUT...
WE JUST GOT THE SHEET MUSIC.
I CAN PLAY...
...
So can Shinobu...

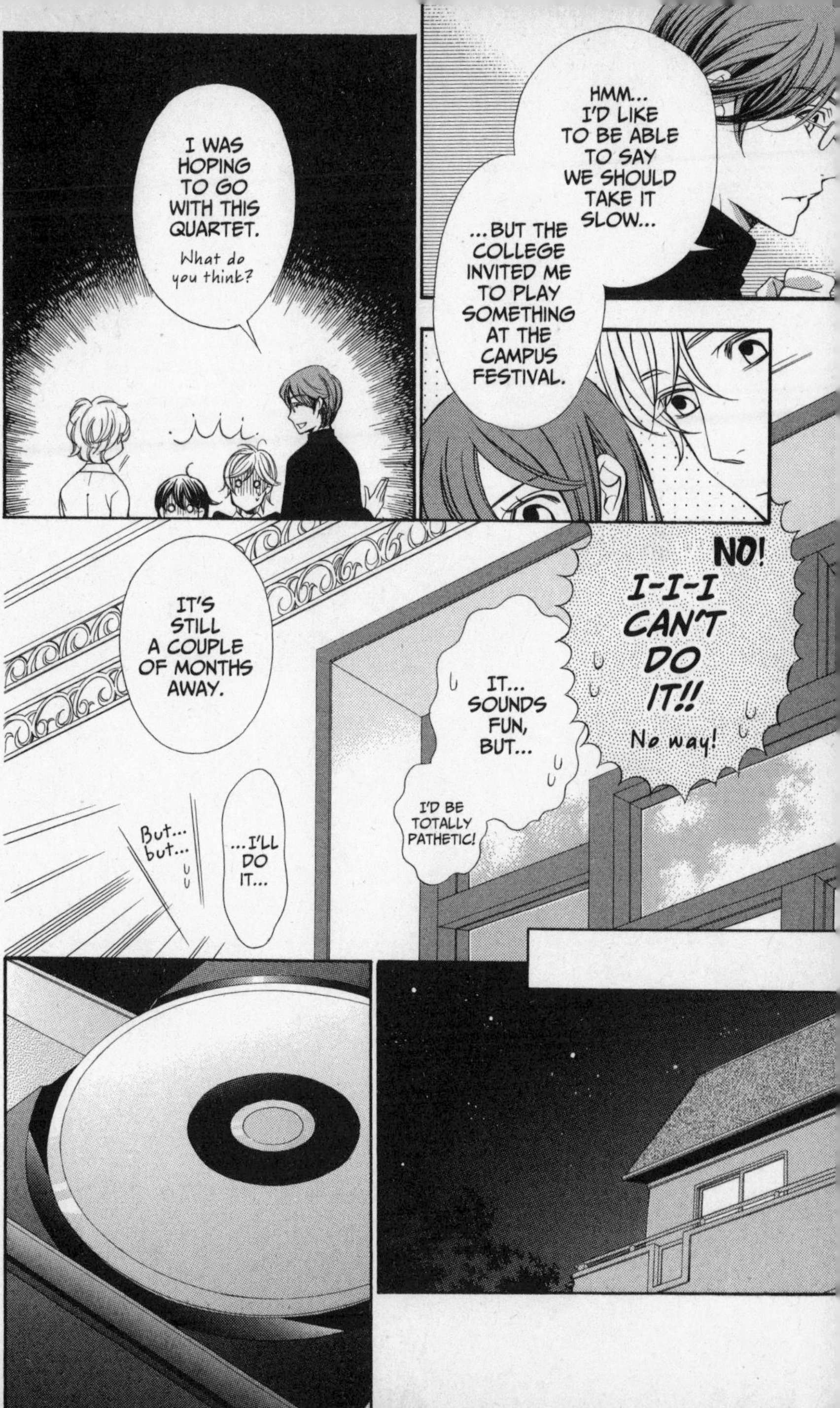
HMM... I'D LIKE TO BE ABLE TO SAY WE SHOULD TAKE IT SLOW...
...BUT THE COLLEGE INVITED ME TO PLAY SOMETHING AT THE CAMPUS FESTIVAL.
I WAS HOPING TO GO WITH THIS QUARTET.
What do you think?
NO!
I-I-I CAN'T DO IT!!
No way!
IT... SOUNDS FUN, BUT...
I'D BE TOTALLY PATHETIC!
IT'S STILL A COUPLE OF MONTHS AWAY.
...I'LL DO IT...
But... but...

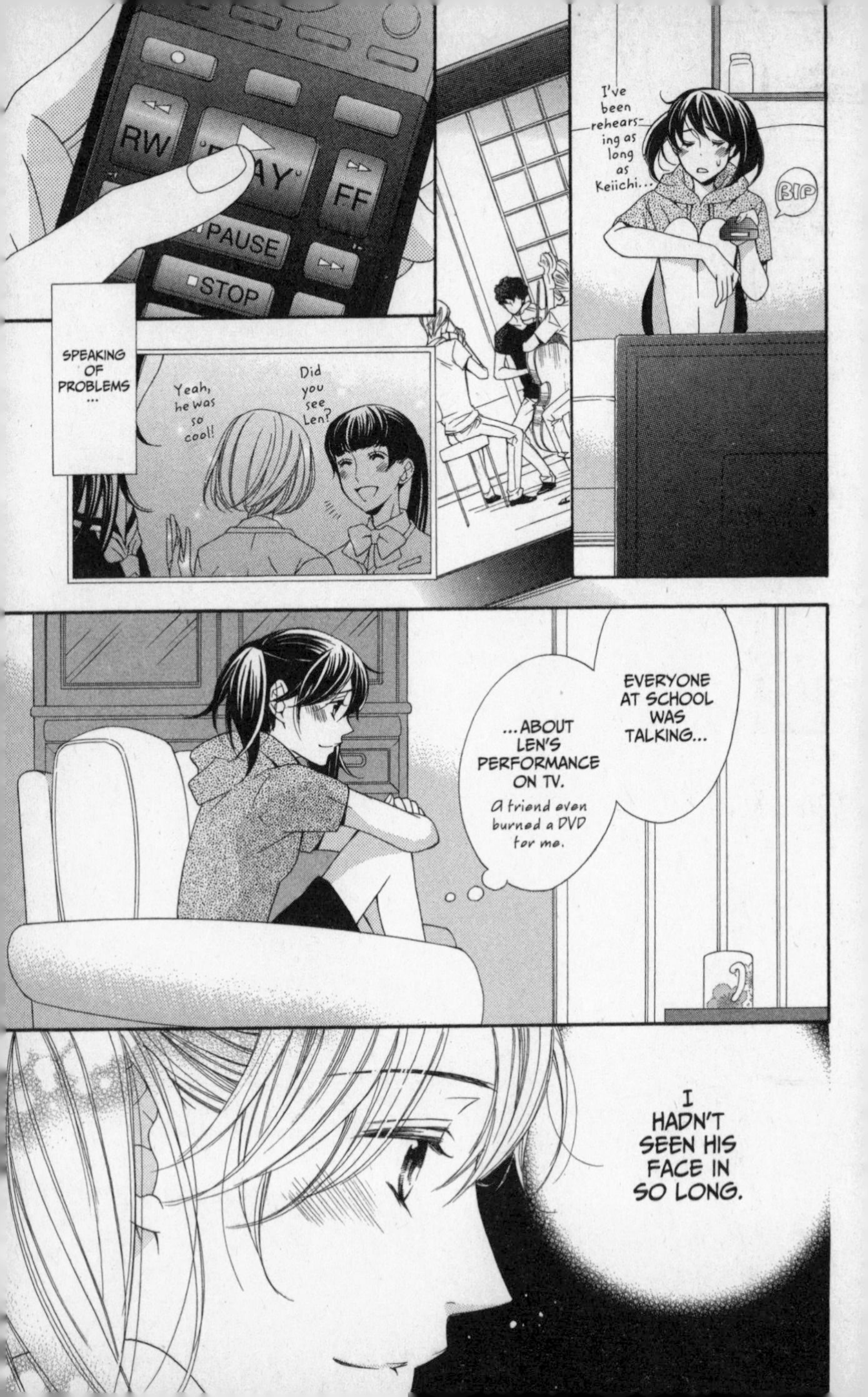
I've been rehearsing as long as Keiichi...
BIP
RW
FF
PAUSE
STOP
SPEAKING OF PROBLEMS...
Did you see Len?
Yeah, he was so cool!
EVERYONE AT SCHOOL WAS TALKING...
...ABOUT LEN'S PERFORMANCE ON TV.
A friend even burned a DVD for me.
I HADN'T SEEN HIS FACE IN SO LONG.

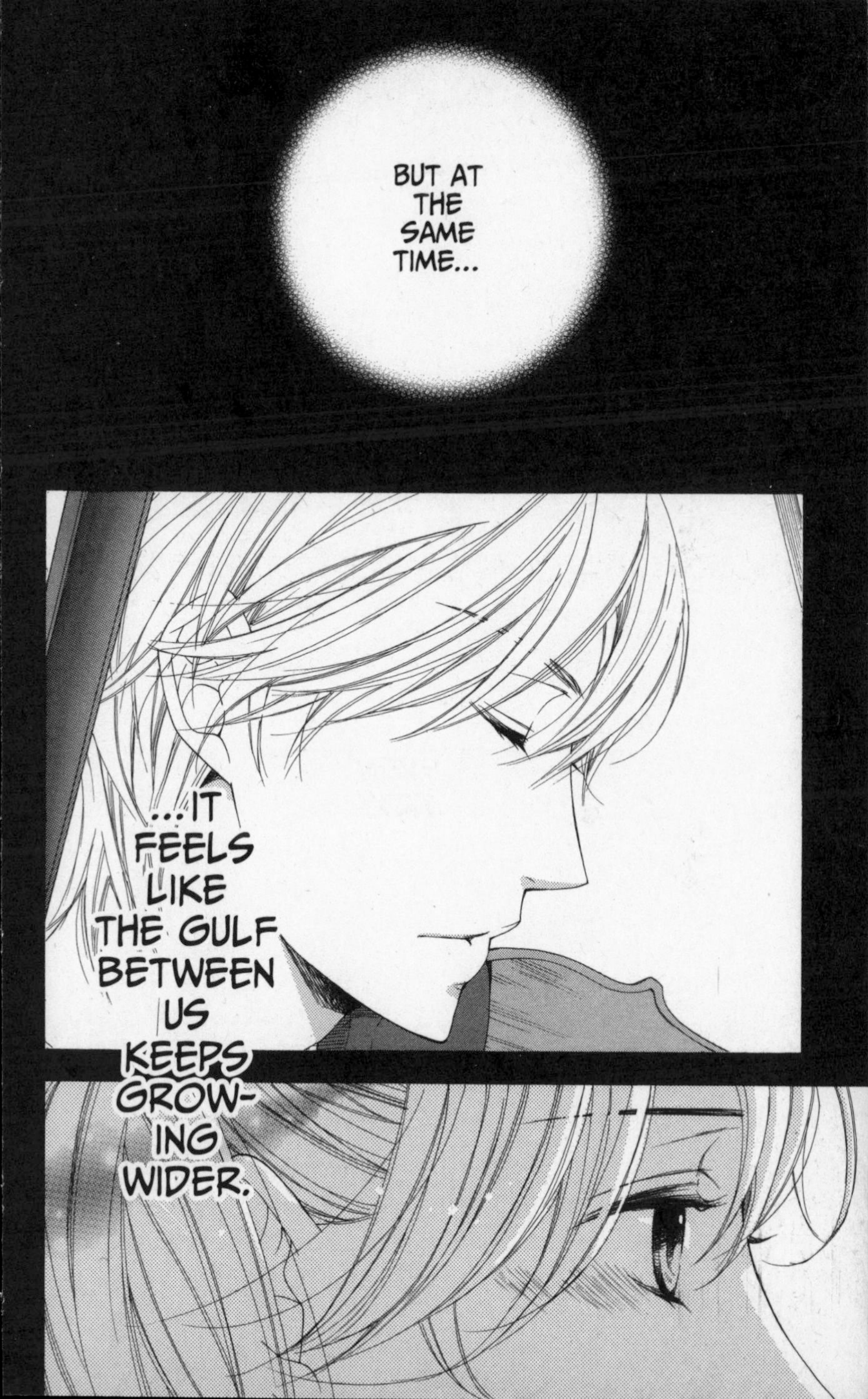
BUT AT THE SAME TIME...
...IT FEELS LIKE THE GULF BETWEEN US KEEPS GROW-ING WIDER.

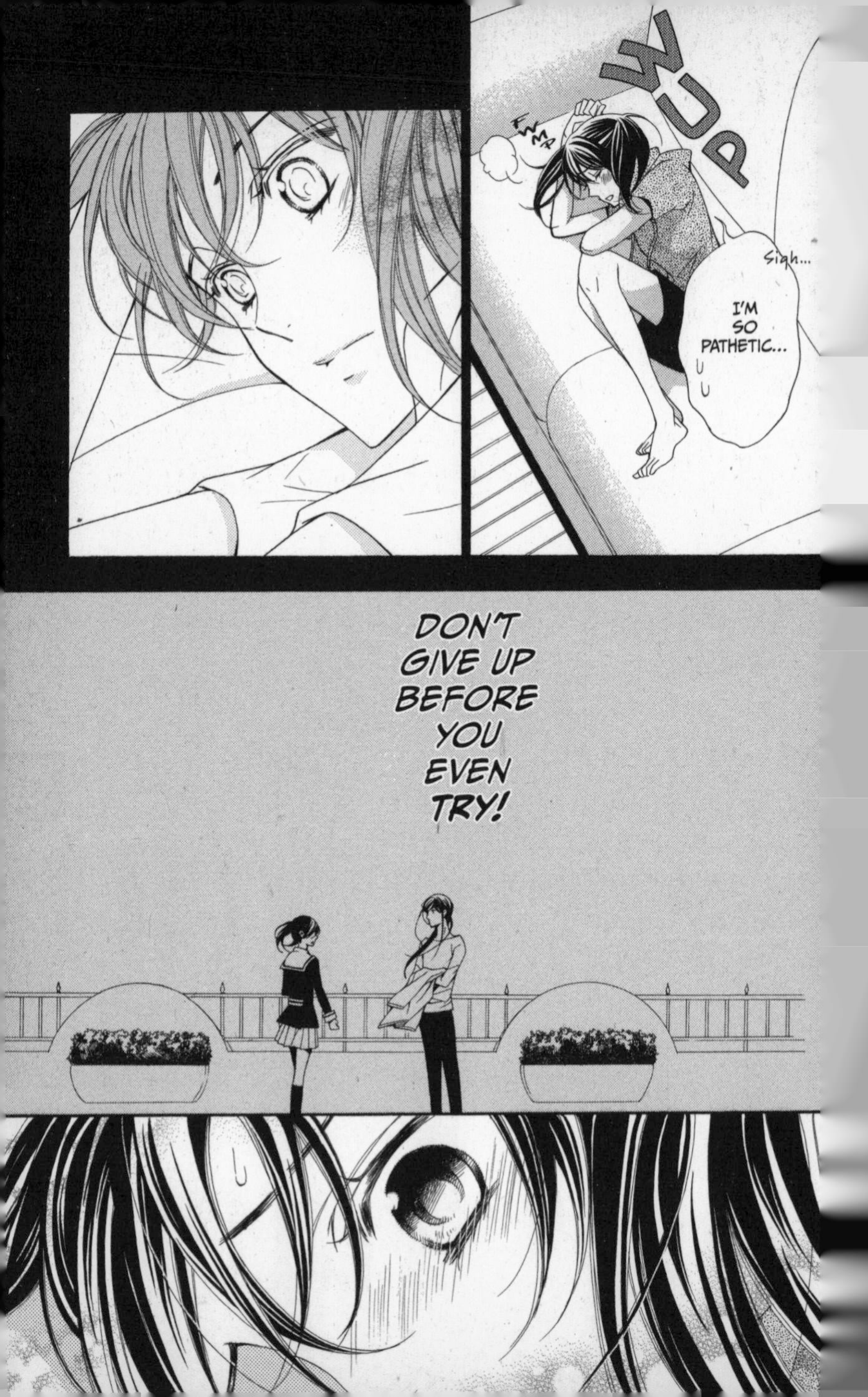
FLUMP
FWMP
Sigh...
I'M SO PATHETIC...
DON'T GIVE UP BEFORE YOU EVEN TRY!

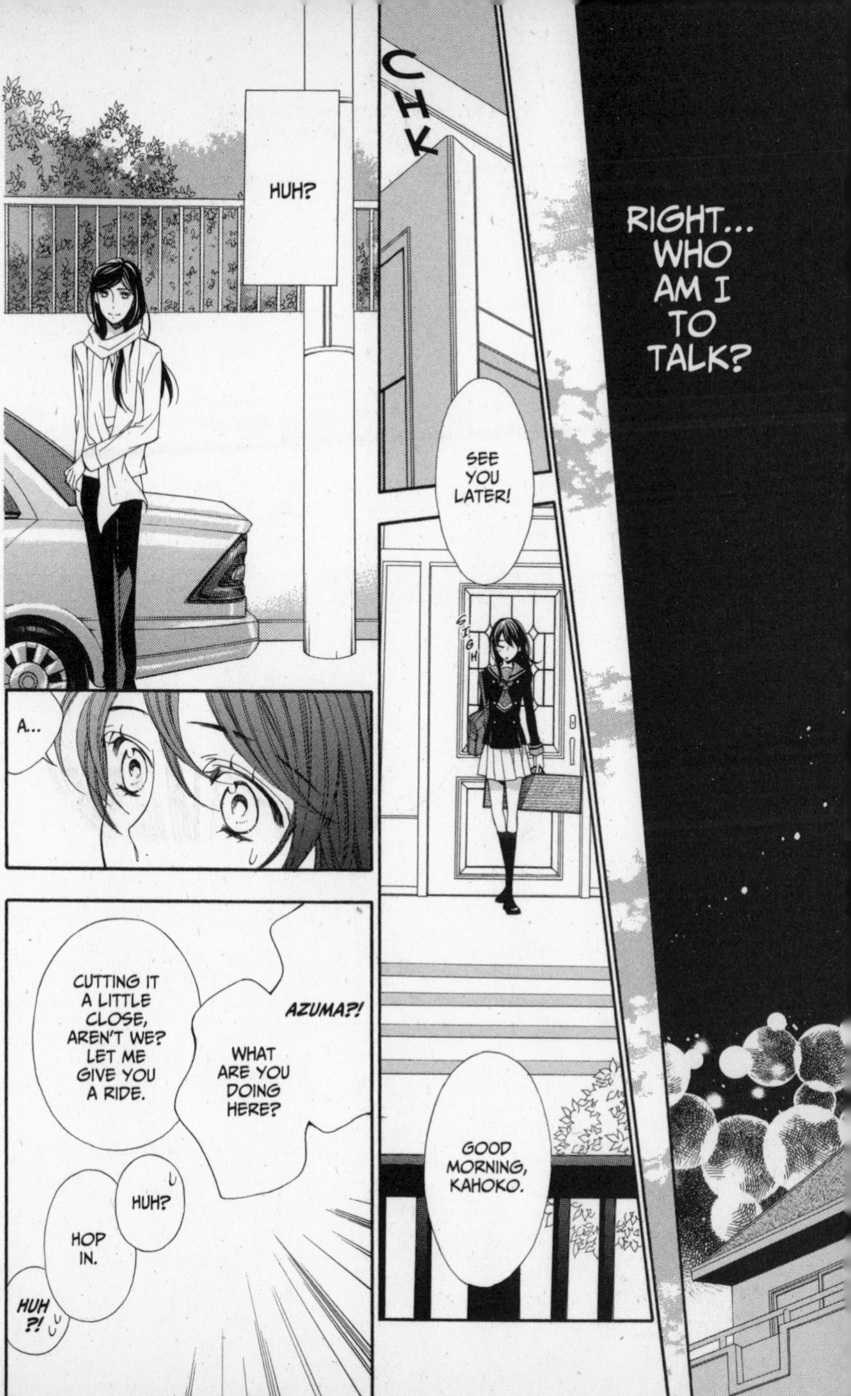
RIGHT... WHO AM I TO TALK?
CHK
SEE YOU LATER!
SIGH
GOOD MORNING, KAHOKO.
HUH?
A...
AZUMA?!
WHAT ARE YOU DOING HERE?
CUTTING IT A LITTLE CLOSE, AREN'T WE? LET ME GIVE YOU A RIDE.
HUH?
HOP IN.
HUH?!

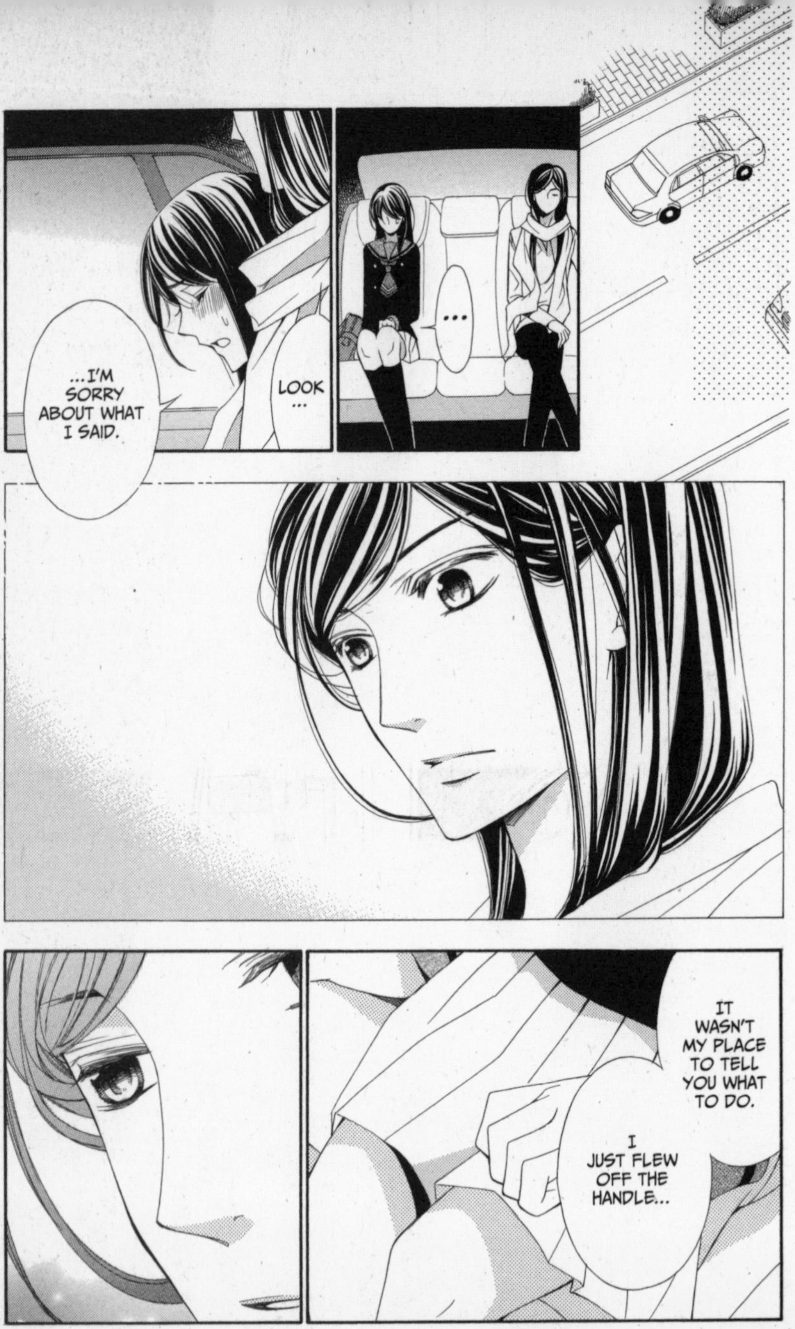
...
LOOK ...
...I'M SORRY ABOUT WHAT I SAID.
IT WASN'T MY PLACE TO TELL YOU WHAT TO DO.
I JUST FLEW OFF THE HANDLE...

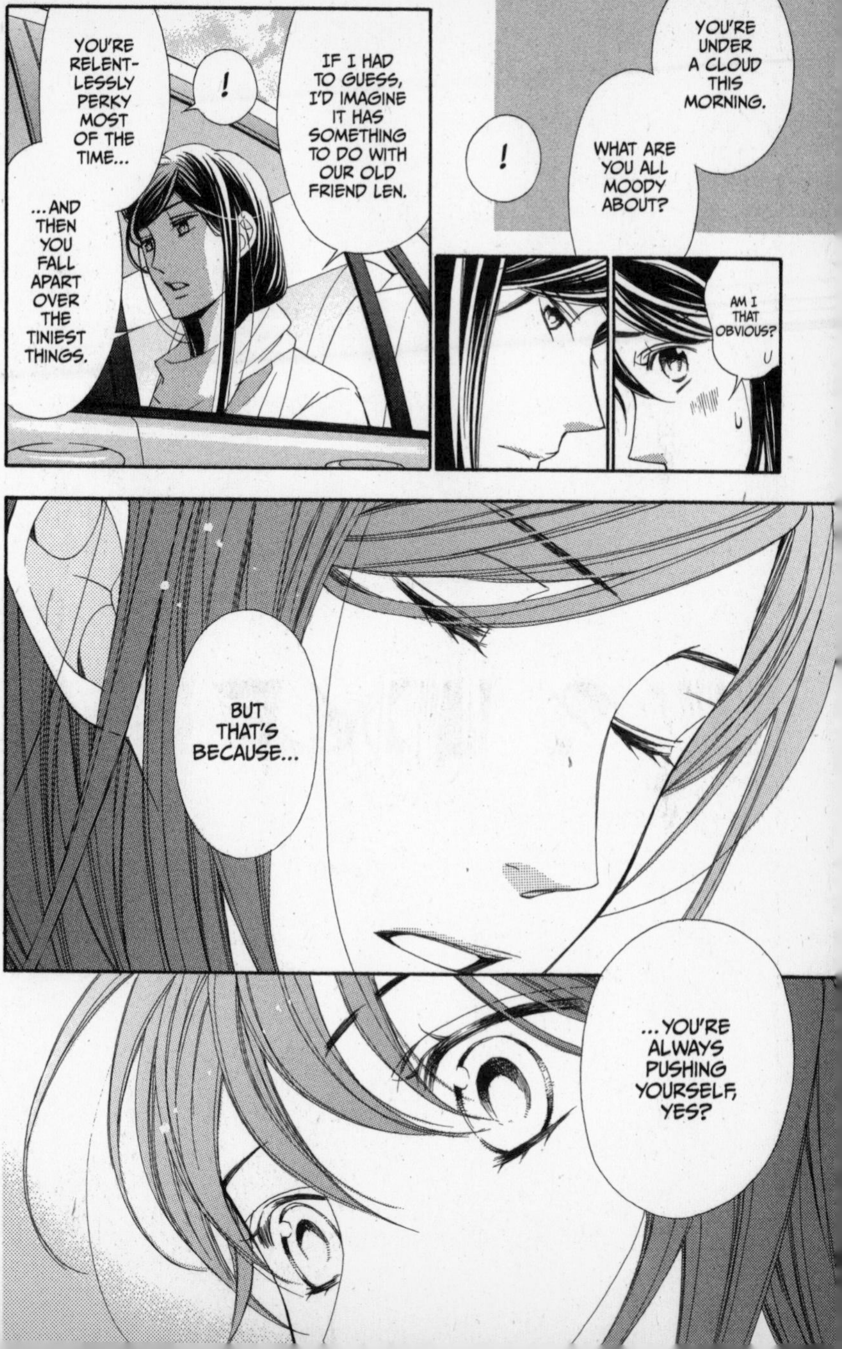
YOU'RE UNDER A CLOUD THIS MORNING.
WHAT ARE YOU ALL MOODY ABOUT?
!
AM I THAT OBVIOUS?
IF I HAD TO GUESS, I'D IMAGINE IT HAS SOMETHING TO DO WITH OUR OLD FRIEND LEN.
!
YOU'RE RELENT-LESSLY PERKY MOST OF THE TIME...
...AND THEN YOU FALL APART OVER THE TINIEST THINGS.
BUT THAT'S BECAUSE...
...YOU'RE ALWAYS PUSHING YOURSELF, YES?

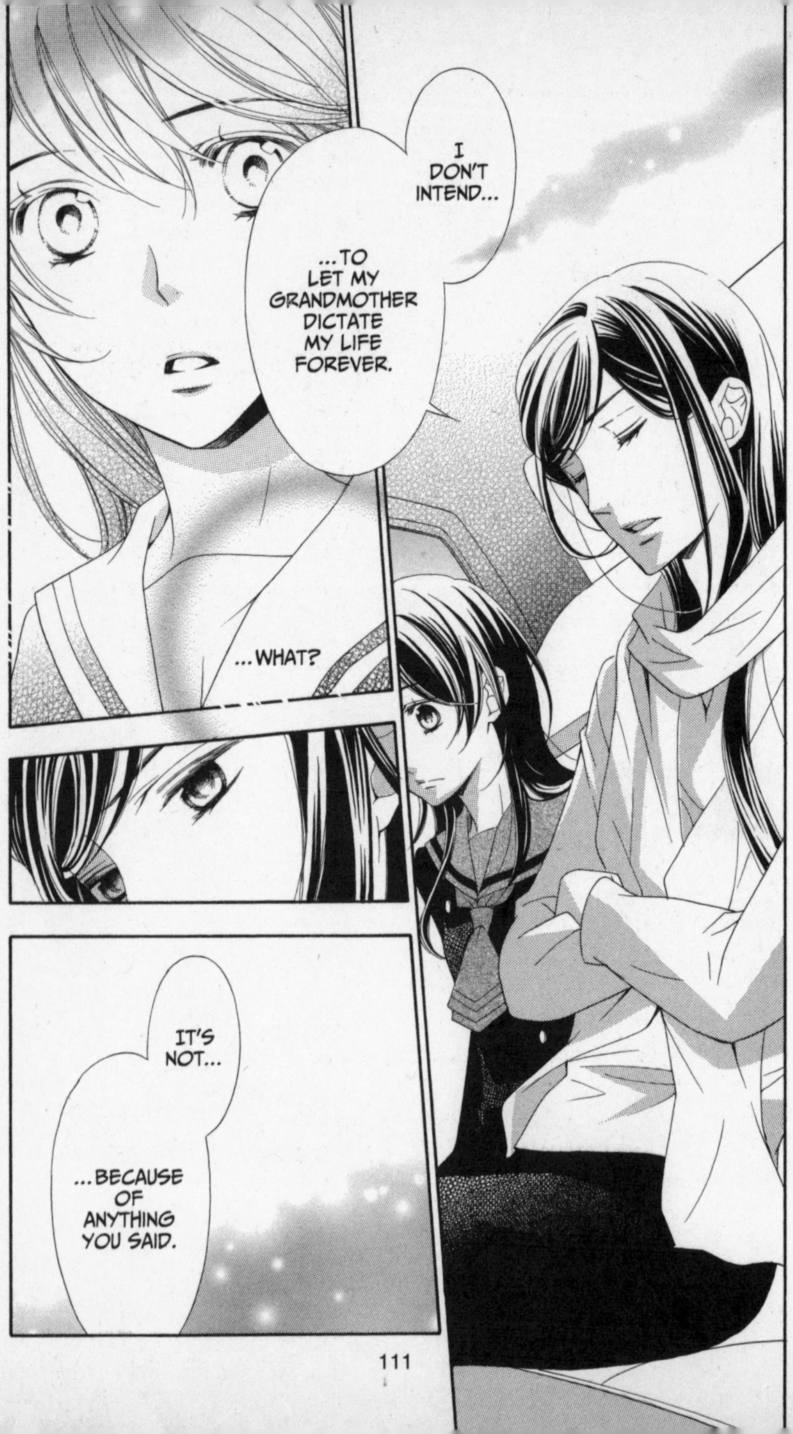
I DON'T INTEND...
...TO LET MY GRANDMOTHER DICTATE MY LIFE FOREVER.
...WHAT?
IT'S NOT...
...BECAUSE OF ANYTHING YOU SAID.

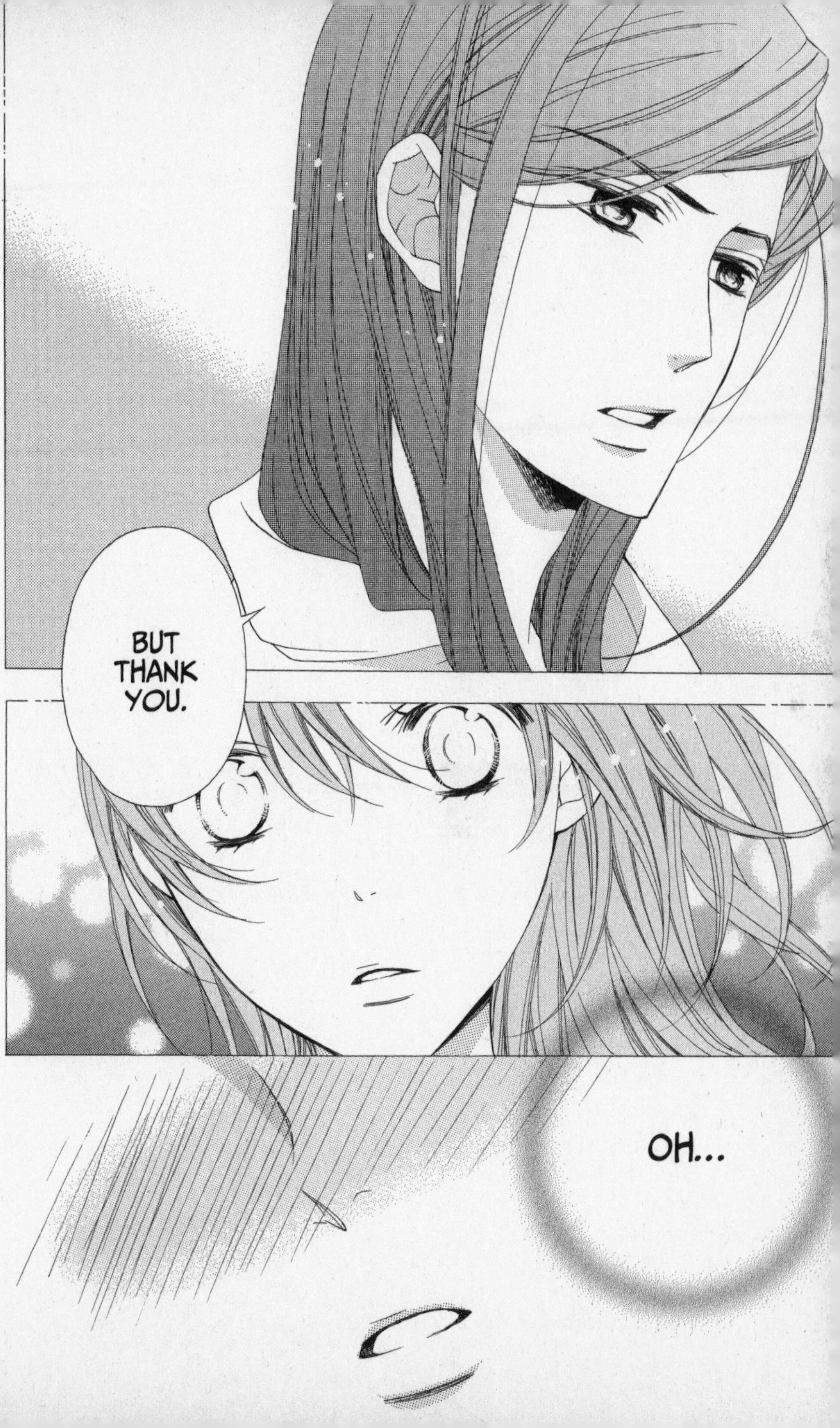
BUT THANK YOU.
OH...

I ADMIT...

...YOU *DID* GET ON MY NERVES.

HUH?

AAH
AAH

No way!

Azuma!

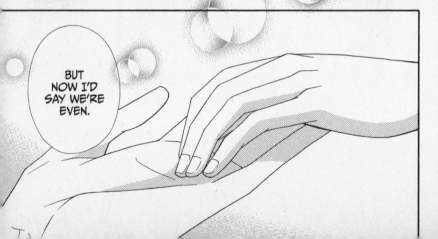

BUT NOW I'D SAY WE'RE EVEN.

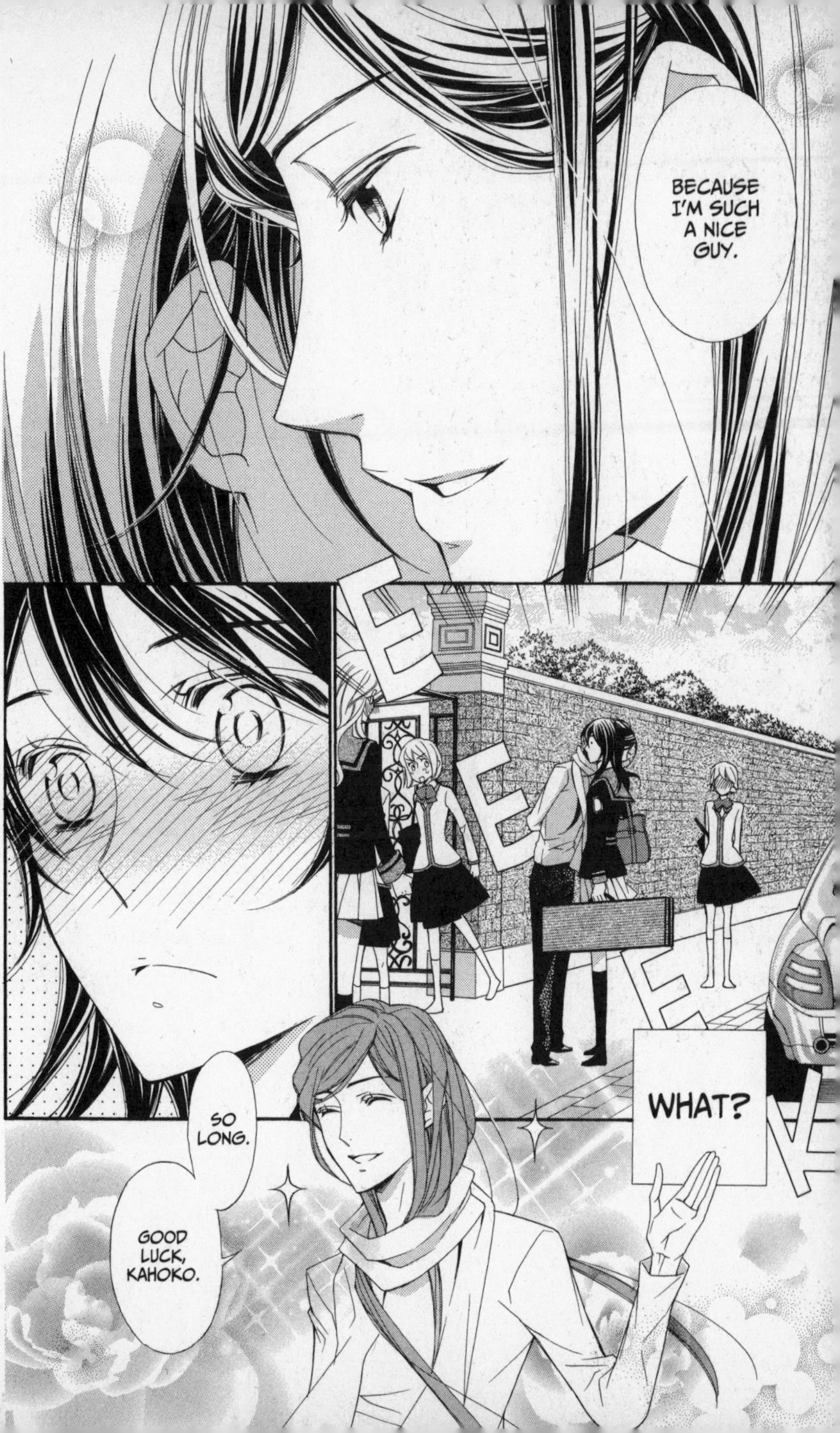
BECAUSE I'M SUCH A NICE GUY.
WHAT?
SO LONG.
GOOD LUCK, KAHOKO.

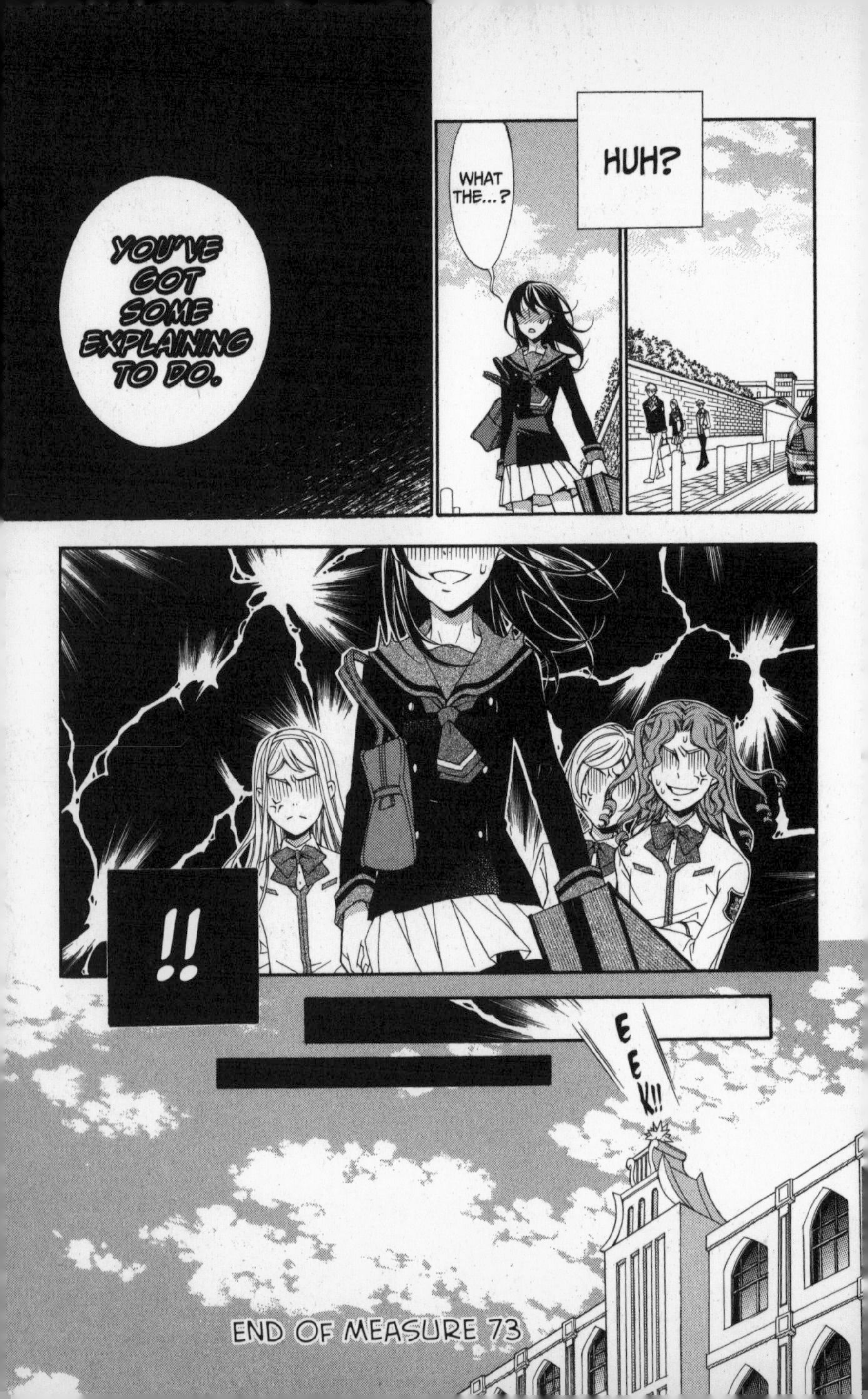
HUH?
WHAT THE...?
YOU'VE GOT SOME EXPLAINING TO DO.
!!
[redacted]
EEEK!!
END OF MEASURE 73

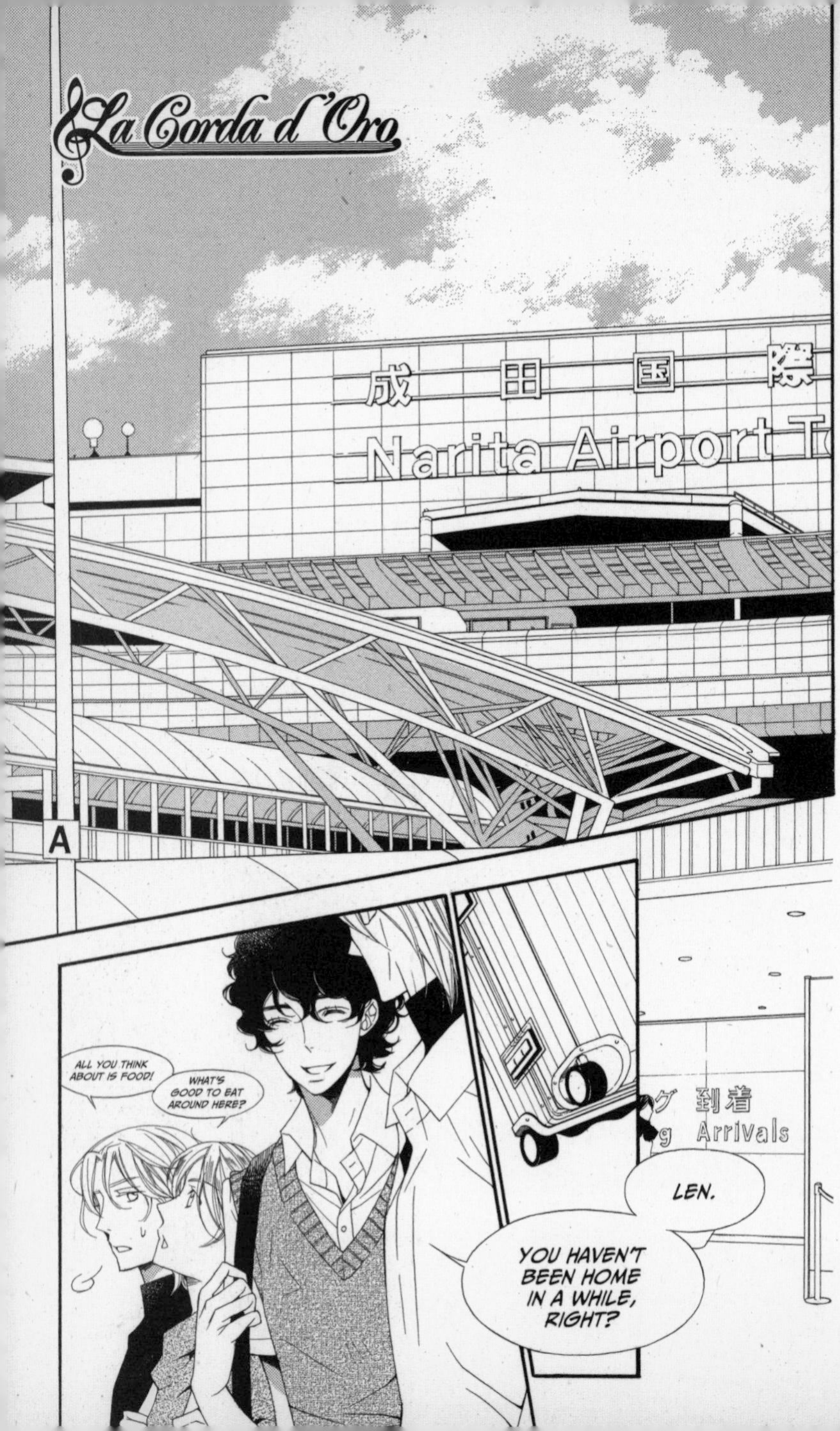
La Corda d'Oro
成田国際
Narita Airport
到着
Arrivals
LEN.
YOU HAVEN'T BEEN HOME IN A WHILE, RIGHT?
WHAT'S GOOD TO EAT AROUND HERE?
ALL YOU THINK ABOUT IS FOOD!

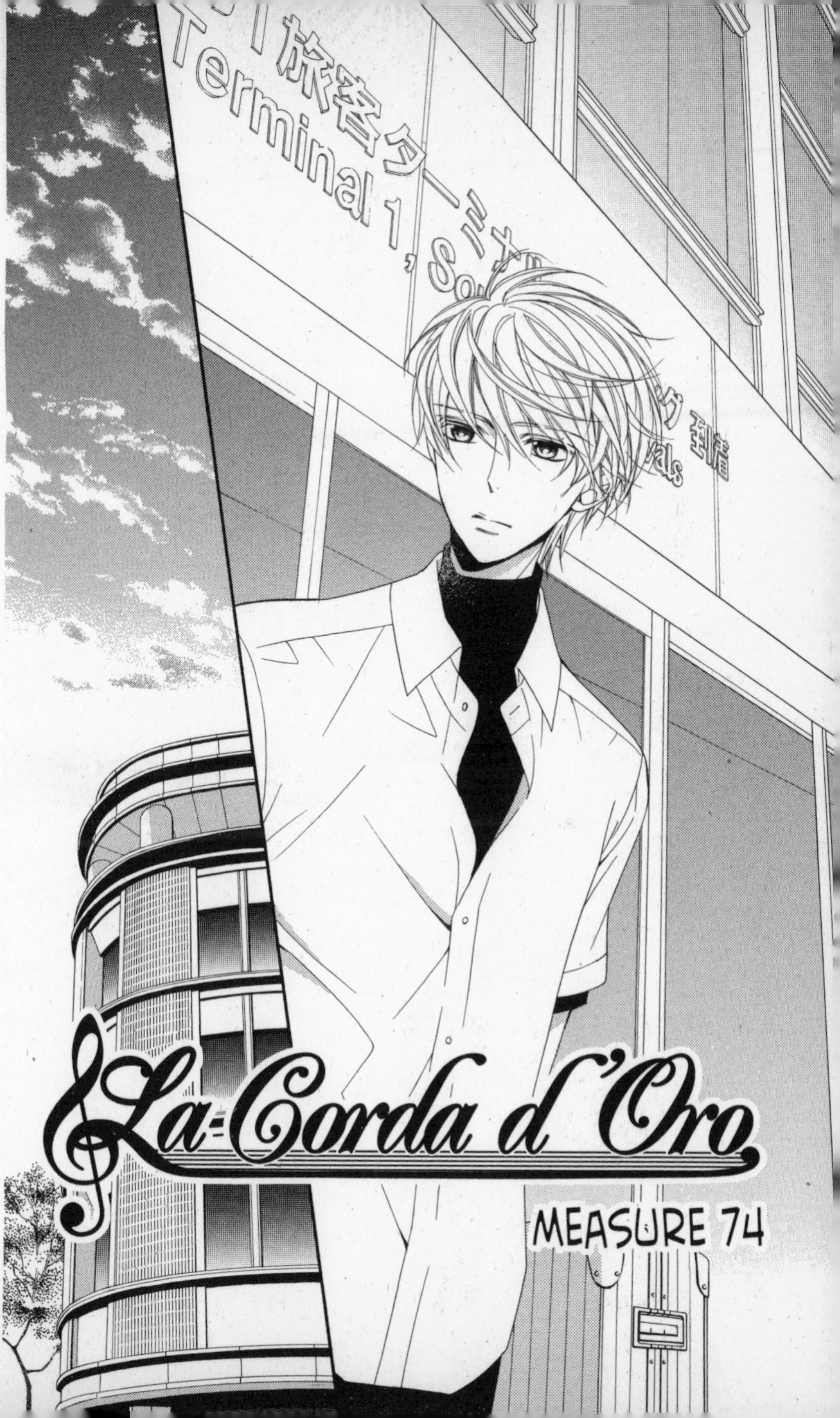
Terminal 1,
La Corda d'Oro
MEASURE 74

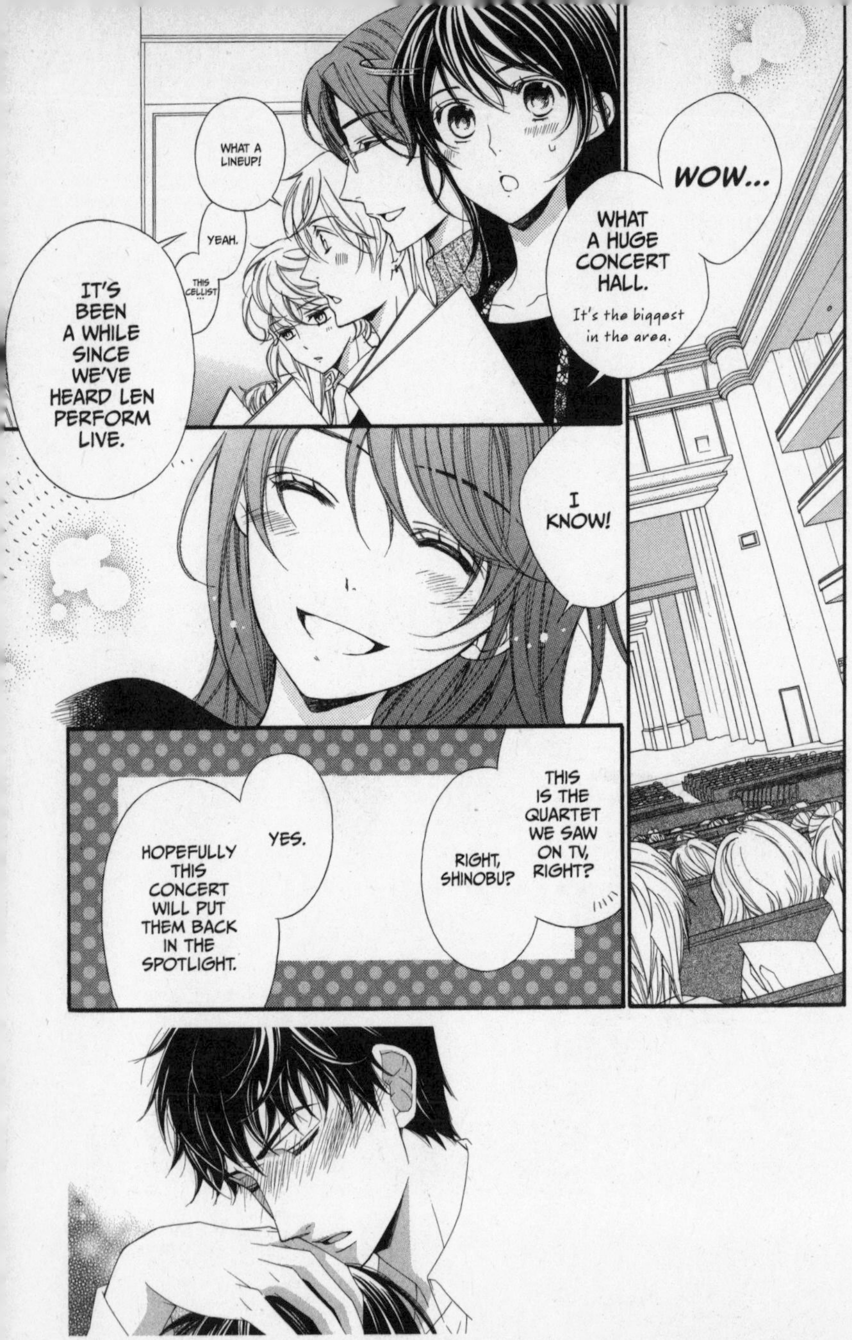
WOW...
WHAT A HUGE CONCERT HALL.
It's the biggest in the area.
WHAT A LINEUP!
YEAH.
THIS CELLIST...
IT'S BEEN A WHILE SINCE WE'VE HEARD LEN PERFORM LIVE.
I KNOW!
THIS IS THE QUARTET WE SAW ON TV, RIGHT?
RIGHT, SHINOBU?
YES.
HOPEFULLY THIS CONCERT WILL PUT THEM BACK IN THE SPOTLIGHT.

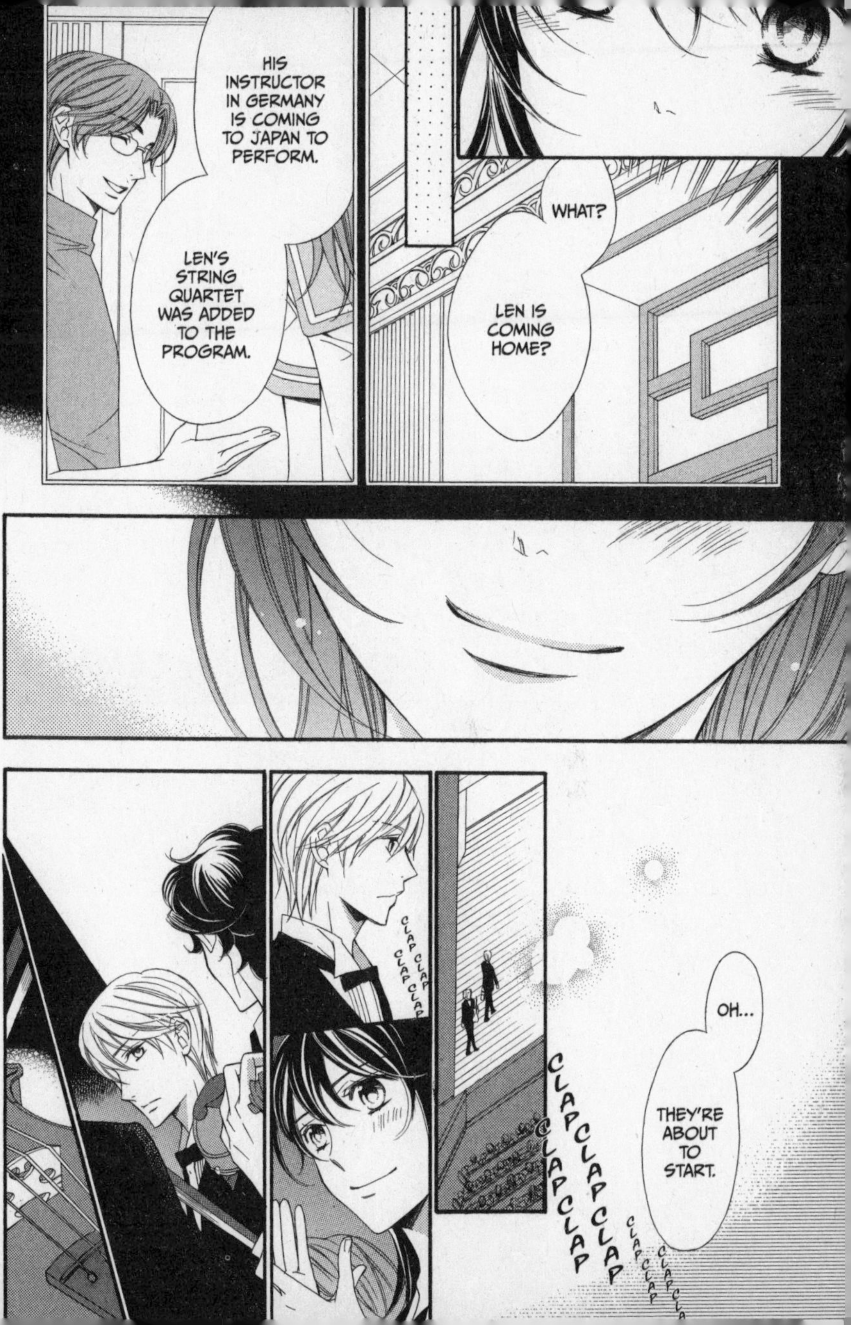
WHAT?
LEN IS COMING HOME?
HIS INSTRUCTOR IN GERMANY IS COMING TO JAPAN TO PERFORM.
LEN'S STRING QUARTET WAS ADDED TO THE PROGRAM.
OH...
THEY'RE ABOUT TO START.
CLAP CLAP CLAP CLA
CLAP CLAP CLAP CLAP
CLAP CLAP CLAP CLAP

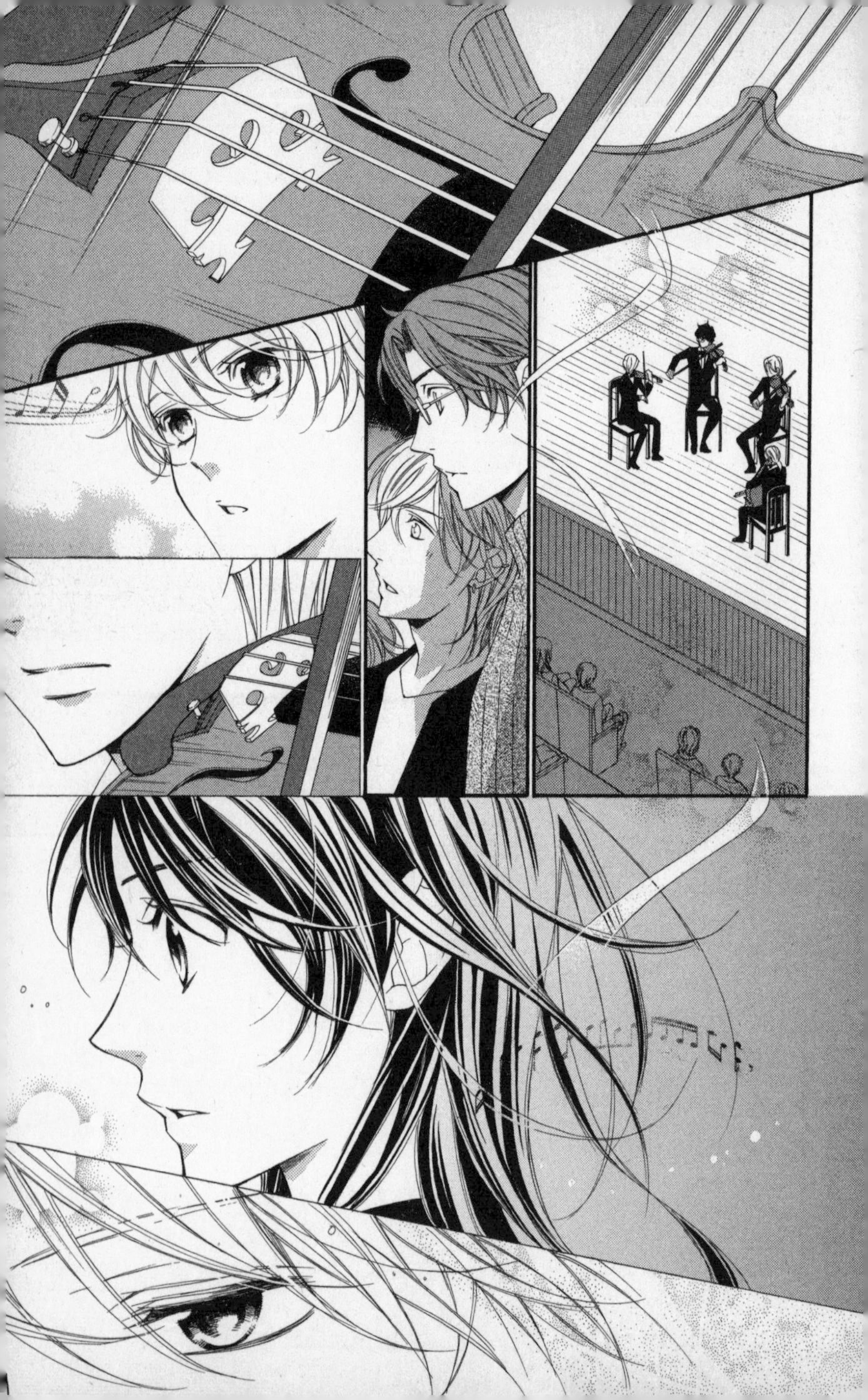

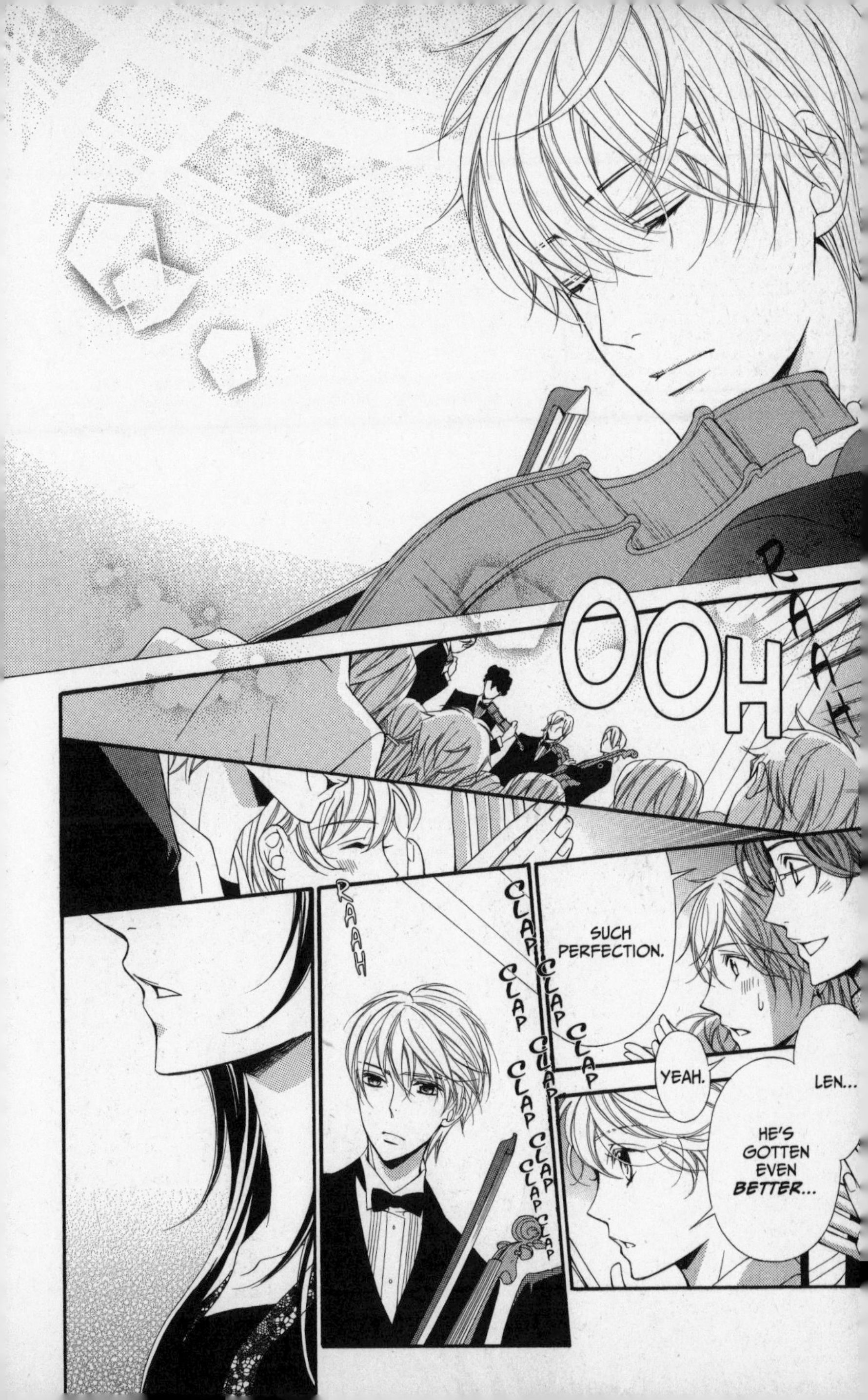
RAAH
OOH
SUCH PERFECTION.
YEAH.
LEN...
HE'S GOTTEN EVEN BETTER...
CLAP CLAP CLAP CLAP
CLAP CLAP CLAP CLAP CLAP CLAP CLAP CLAP
RAAH

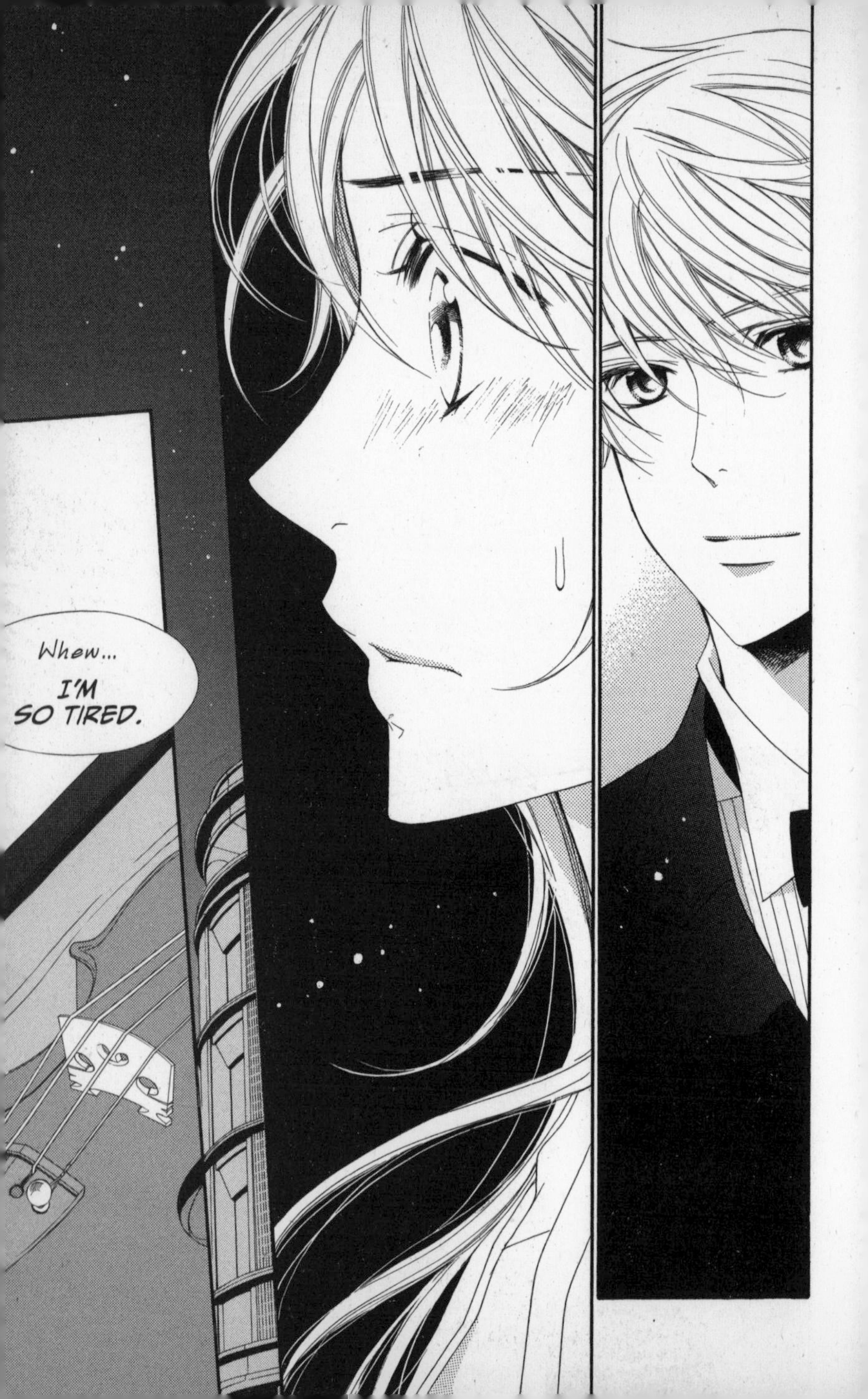
Whew... I'M SO TIRED.

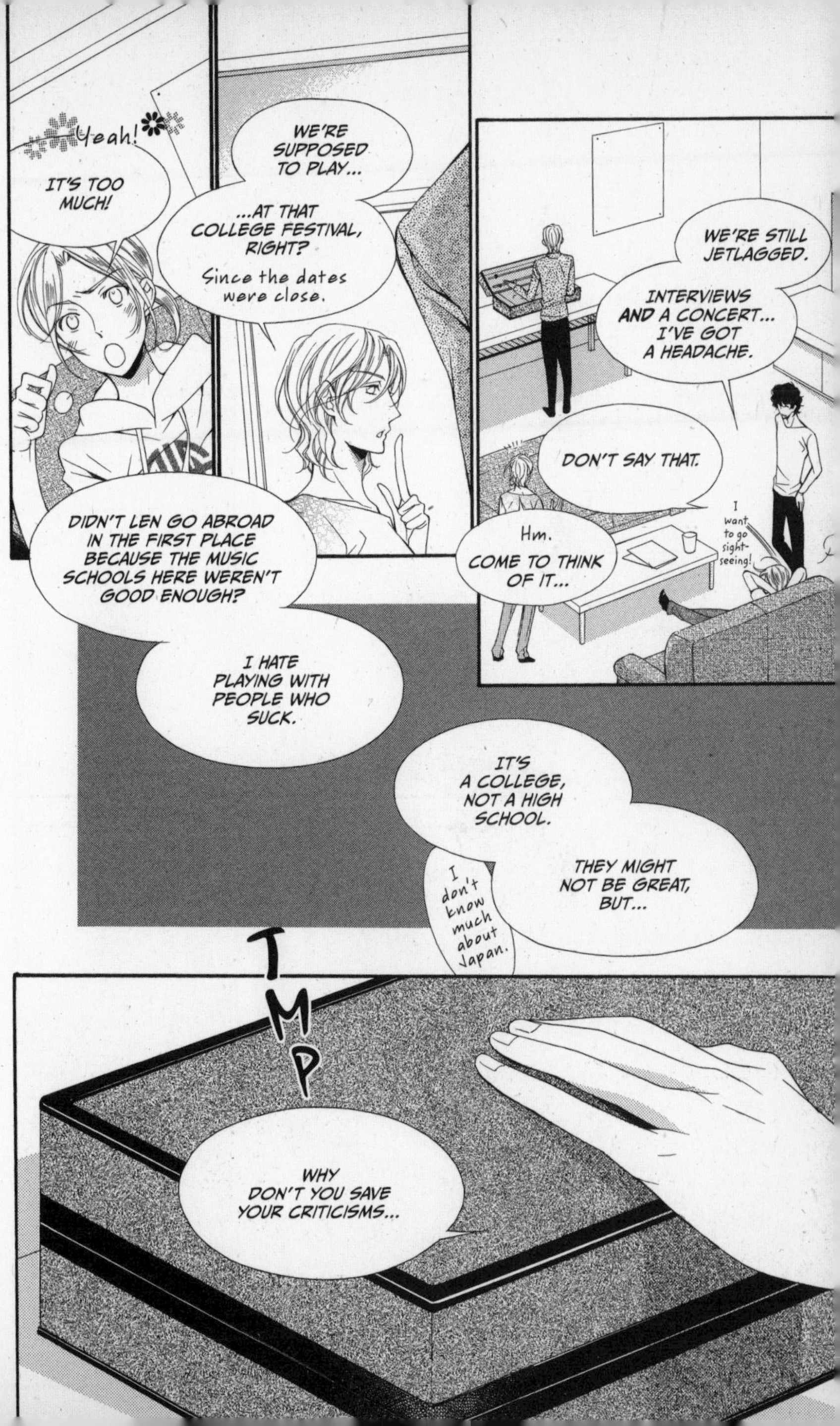
WE'RE STILL JETLAGGED.
INTERVIEWS AND A CONCERT... I'VE GOT A HEADACHE.
DON'T SAY THAT.
I want to go sight-seeing!
Hm.
COME TO THINK OF IT...
WE'RE SUPPOSED TO PLAY...
...AT THAT COLLEGE FESTIVAL, RIGHT?
Since the dates were close.
Yeah!
IT'S TOO MUCH!
DIDN'T LEN GO ABROAD IN THE FIRST PLACE BECAUSE THE MUSIC SCHOOLS HERE WEREN'T GOOD ENOUGH?
I HATE PLAYING WITH PEOPLE WHO SUCK.
IT'S A COLLEGE, NOT A HIGH SCHOOL.
THEY MIGHT NOT BE GREAT, BUT...
I don't know much about Japan.
TMP
WHY DON'T YOU SAVE YOUR CRITICISMS...

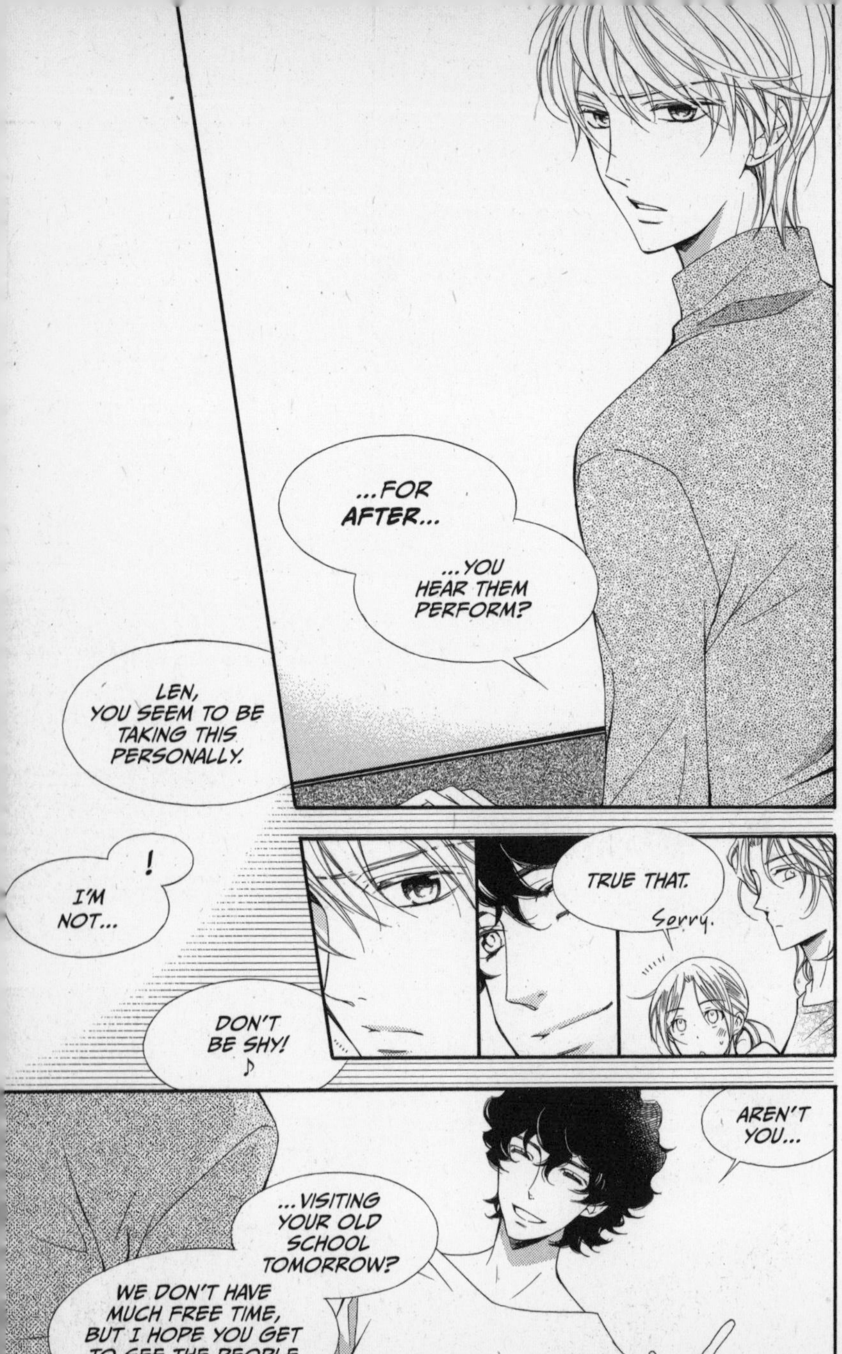
...FOR AFTER...
...YOU HEAR THEM PERFORM?
LEN, YOU SEEM TO BE TAKING THIS PERSONALLY.
!
I'M NOT...
DON'T BE SHY! ♪
TRUE THAT.
Sorry.
AREN'T YOU...
...VISITING YOUR OLD SCHOOL TOMORROW?
WE DON'T HAVE MUCH FREE TIME, BUT I HOPE YOU GET TO SEE THE PEOPLE YOU'VE MISSED.

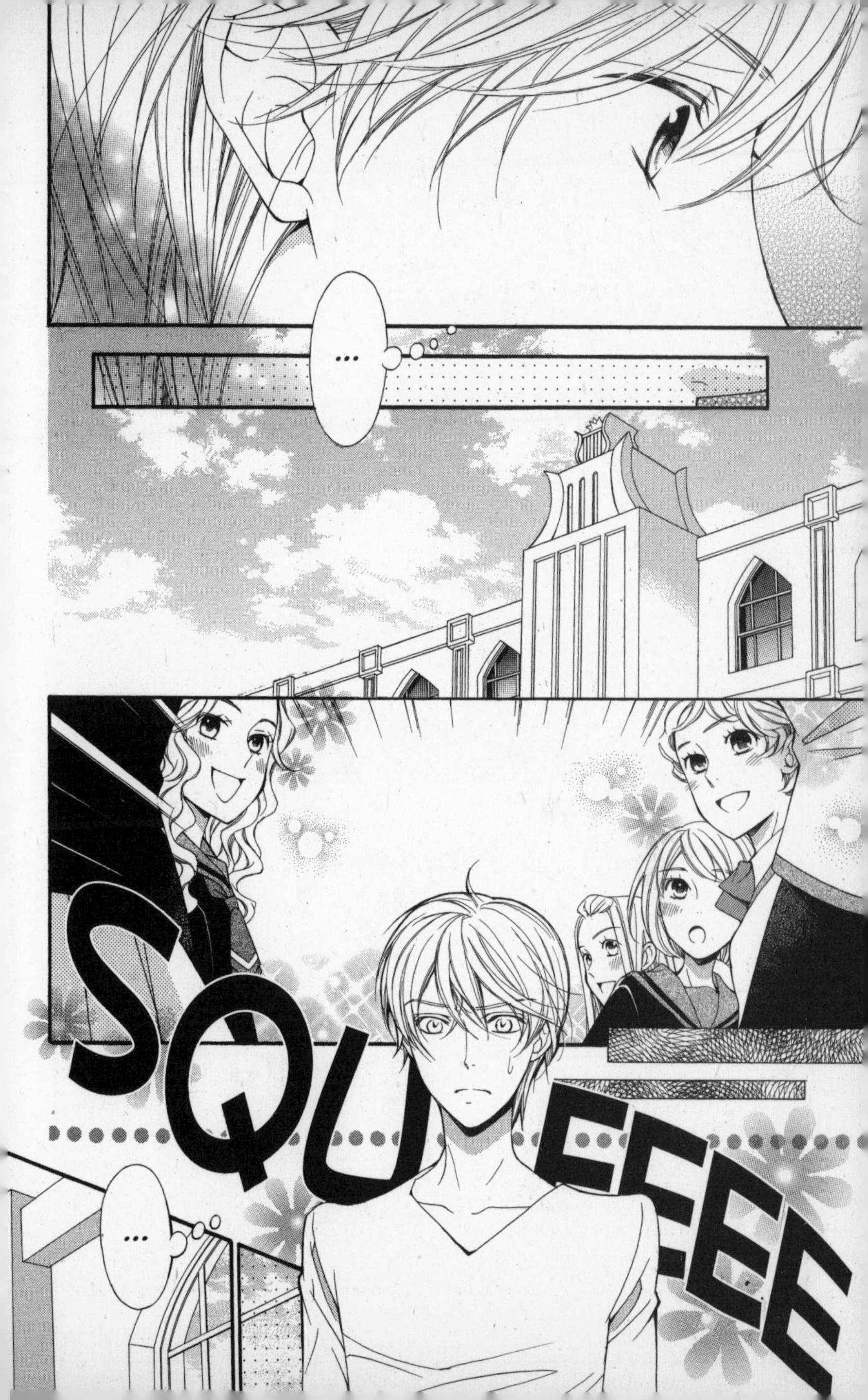
...
SQUEEEE
...

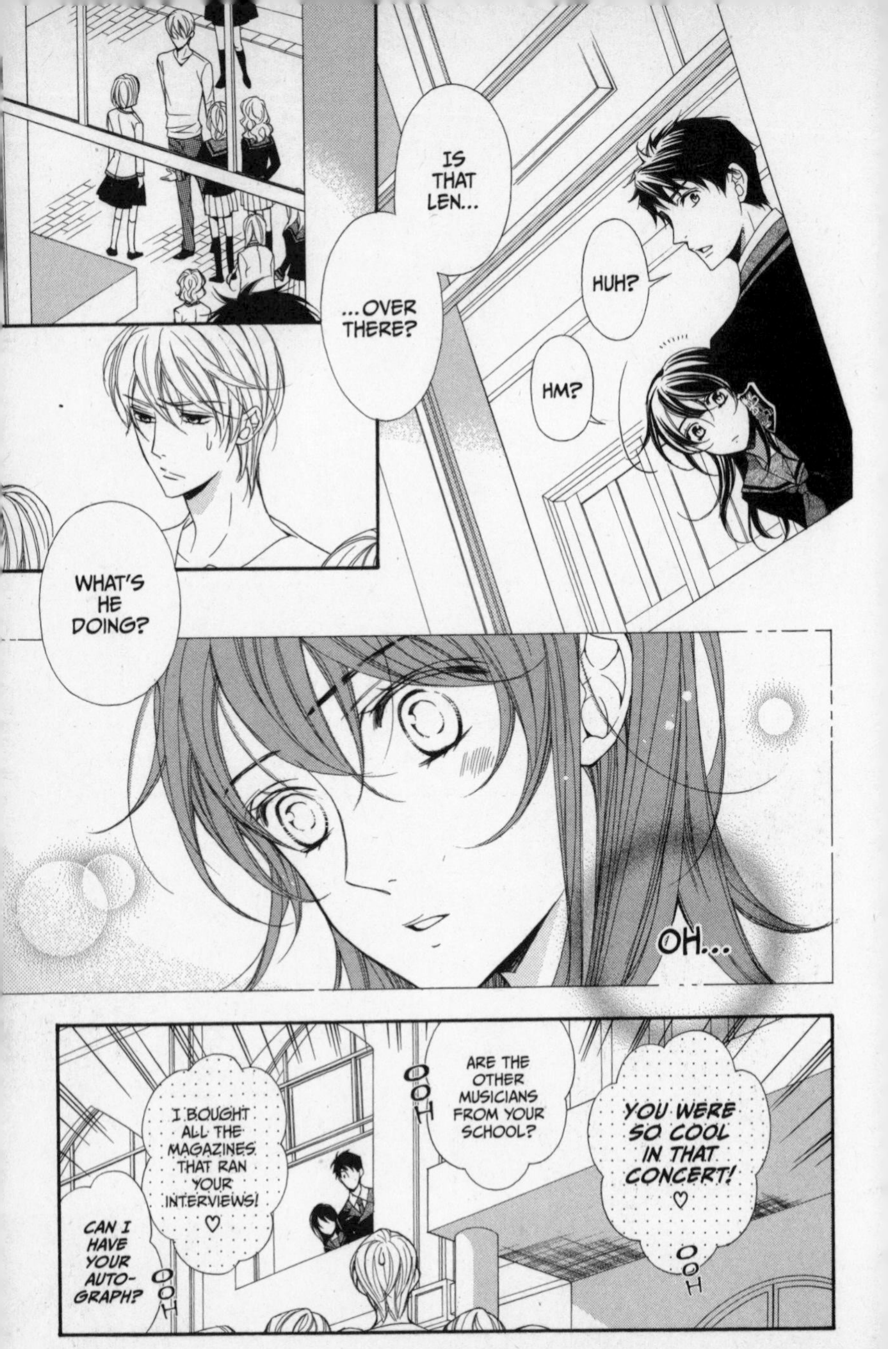
HUH?
HM?
IS THAT LEN...
...OVER THERE?
WHAT'S HE DOING?
OH...
YOU WERE SO COOL IN THAT CONCERT! ♡
OOH
ARE THE OTHER MUSICIANS FROM YOUR SCHOOL?
OOH
I BOUGHT ALL THE MAGAZINES THAT RAN YOUR INTERVIEWS! ♡
CAN I HAVE YOUR AUTO-GRAPH?
OOH

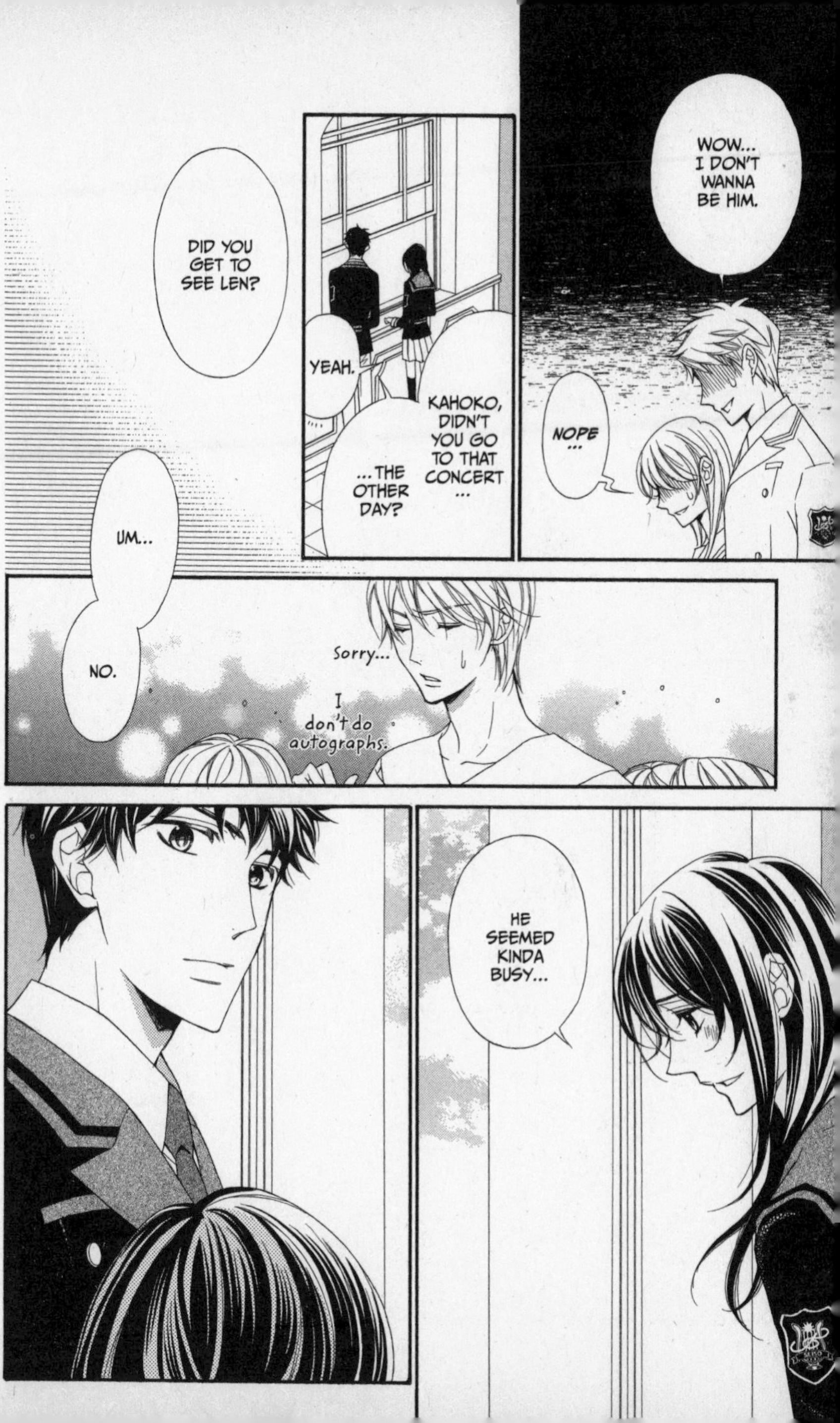
WOW... I DON'T WANNA BE HIM.
NOPE...
KAHOKO, DIDN'T YOU GO TO THAT CONCERT...
...THE OTHER DAY?
YEAH.
DID YOU GET TO SEE LEN?
UM...
NO.
Sorry...
I don't do autographs.
HE SEEMED KINDA BUSY...

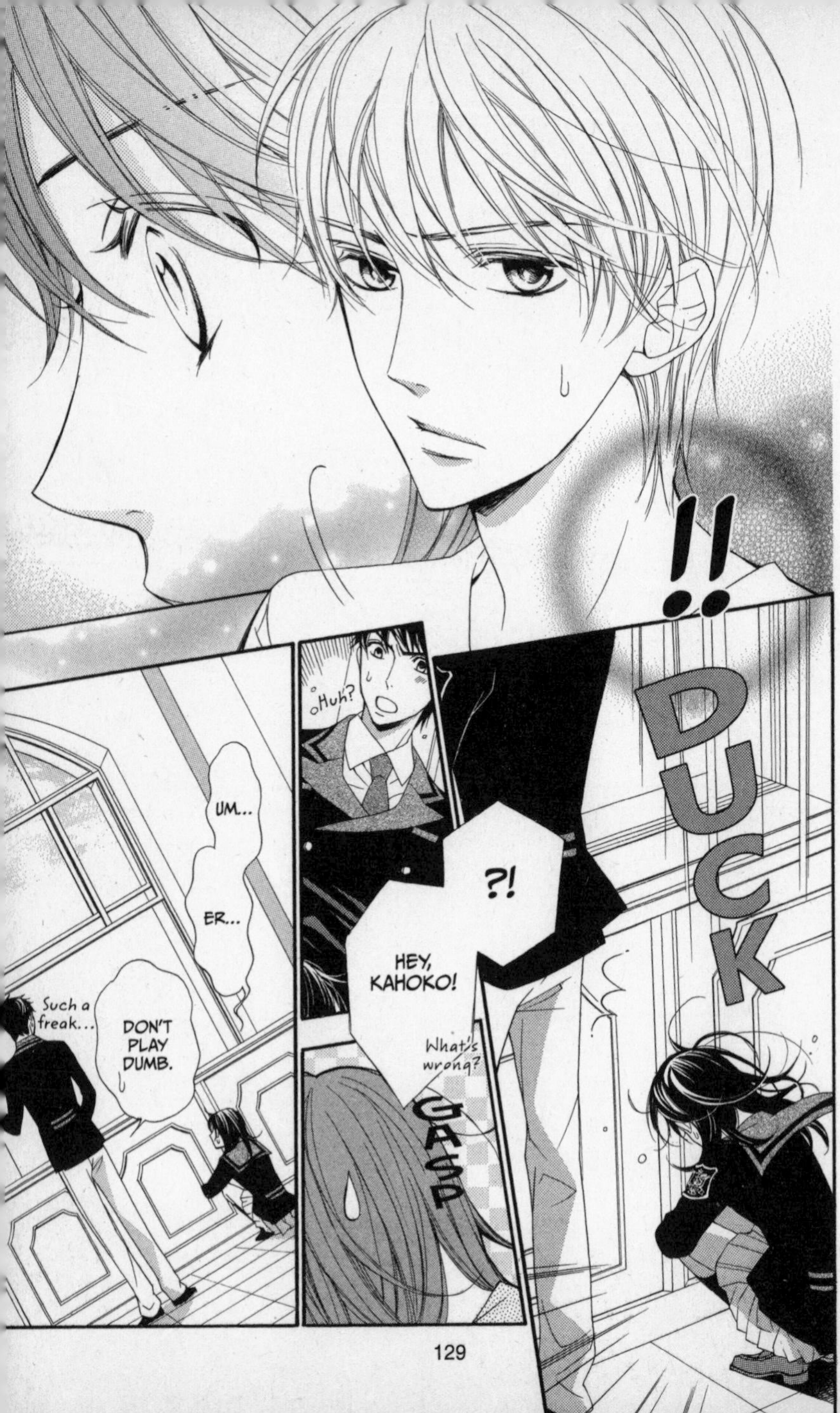
!!
DUCK
?!
HEY, KAHOKO!
What's wrong?
Huh?
GASP
UM...
ER...
DON'T PLAY DUMB.
Such a freak...

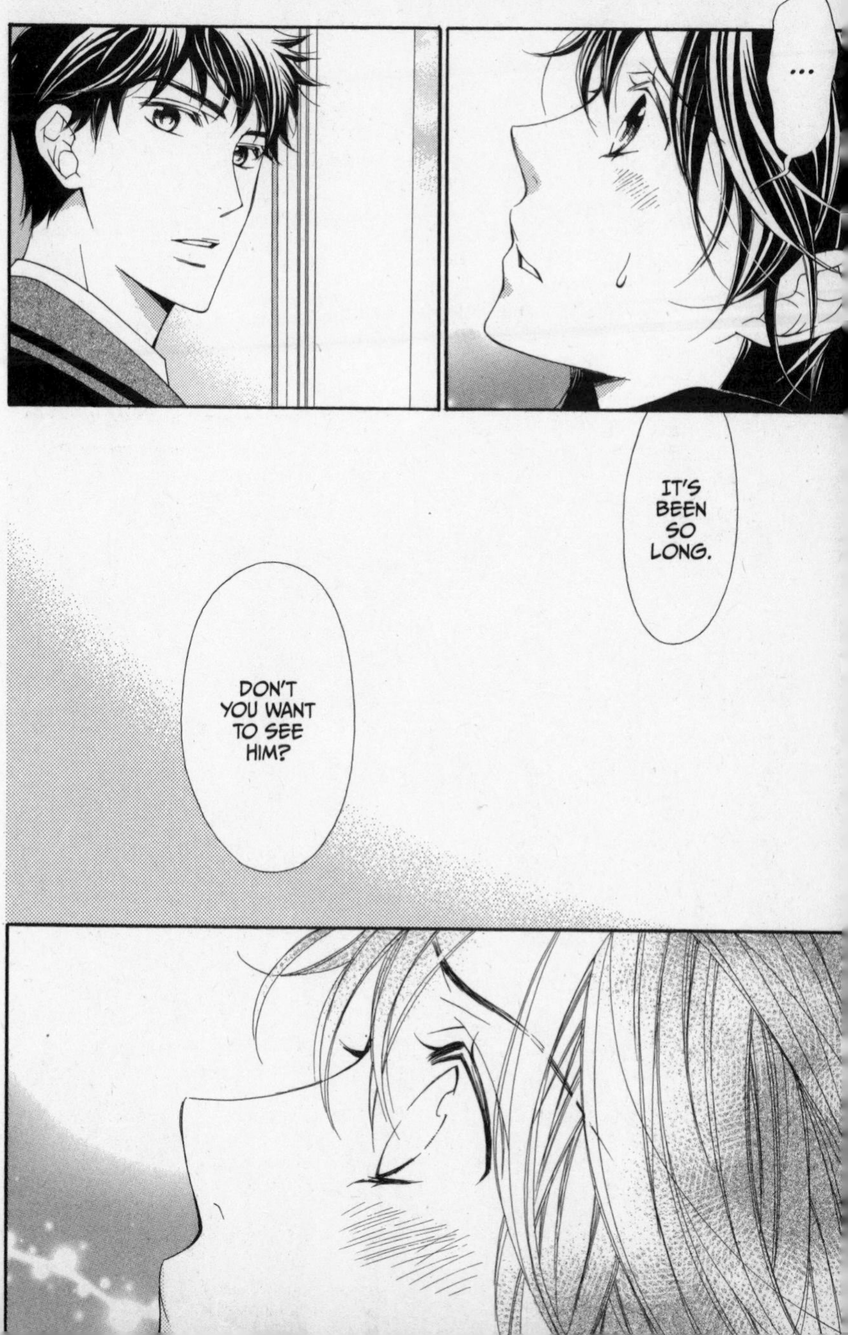
...
IT'S BEEN SO LONG.
DON'T YOU WANT TO SEE HIM?

Ryotaro probably wouldn't experiment with fashion much. But there was so much adorable artwork submitted by people who wanted to see him in cute outfits! He doesn't look as cute when I draw him, though...

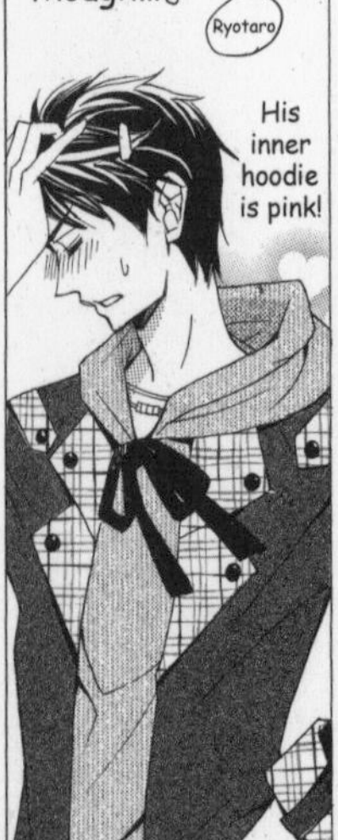
Ryotaro
His inner hoodie is pink!

BY MOMO FROM YAMAGATA

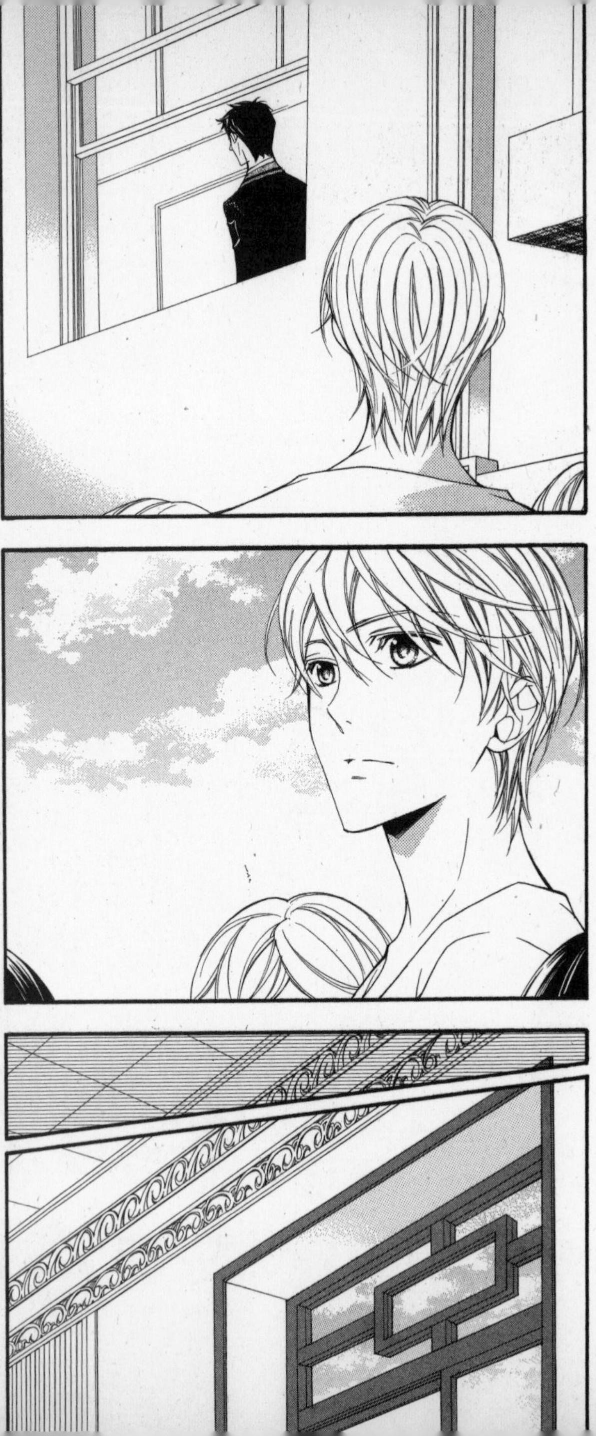

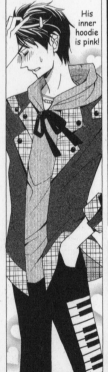

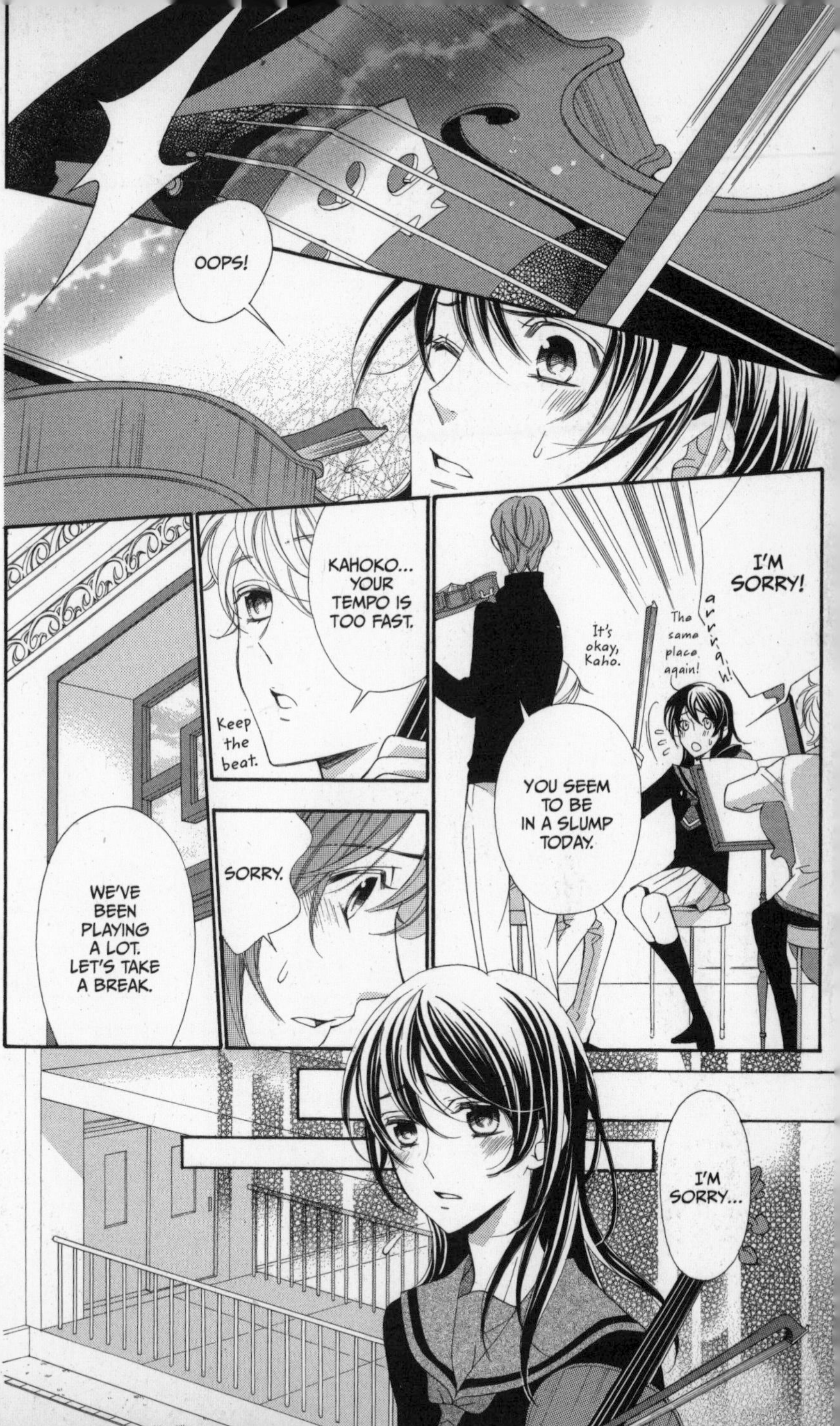
OOPS!
I'M SORRY!
arrrgh!
The same place again!
It's okay, Kaho.
YOU SEEM TO BE IN A SLUMP TODAY.
KAHOKO... YOUR TEMPO IS TOO FAST.
Keep the beat.
SORRY.
WE'VE BEEN PLAYING A LOT. LET'S TAKE A BREAK.
I'M SORRY...

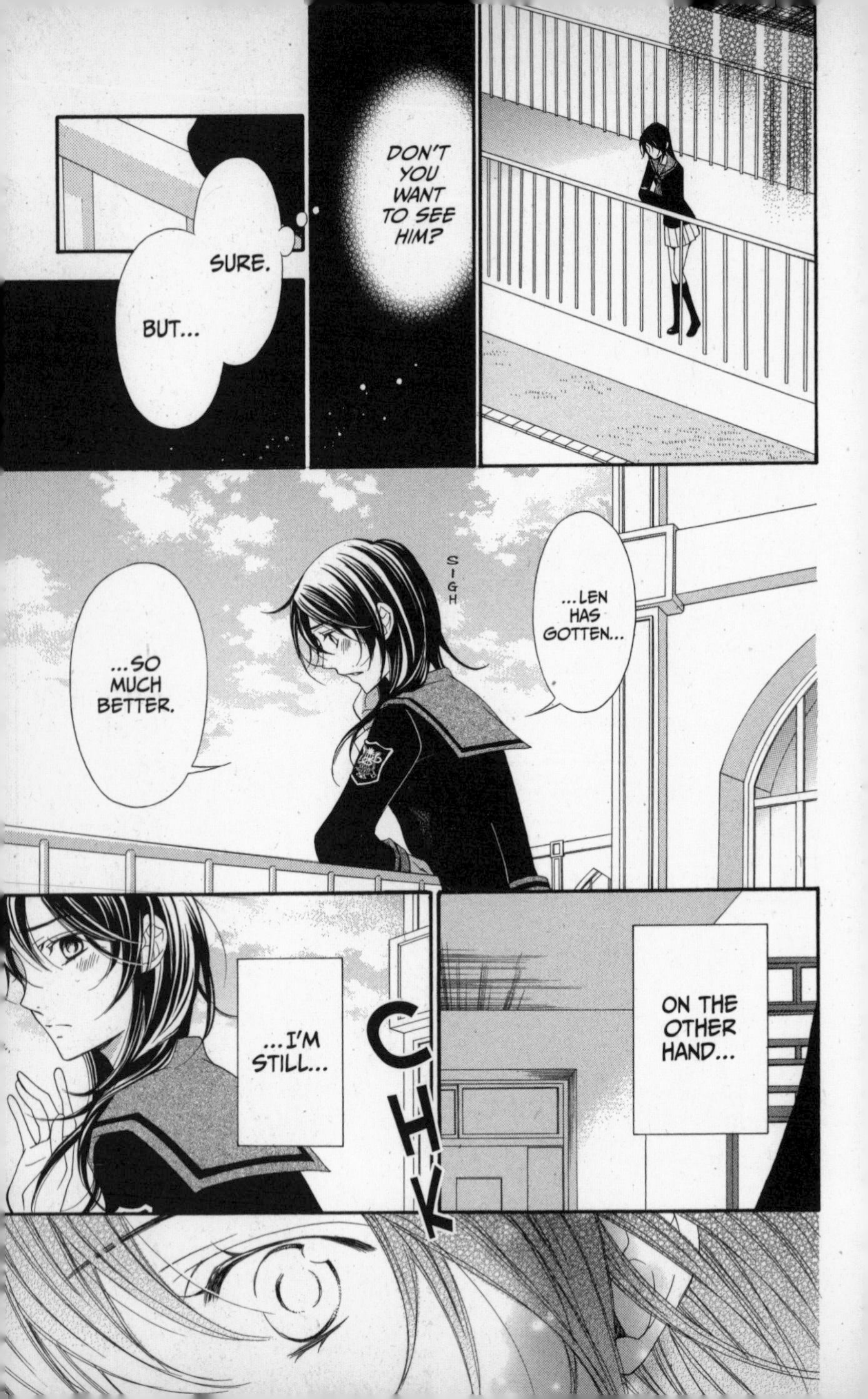
DON'T YOU WANT TO SEE HIM?
SURE.
BUT...
...LEN HAS GOTTEN...
SIGH
...SO MUCH BETTER.
ON THE OTHER HAND...
...I'M STILL...
CHK

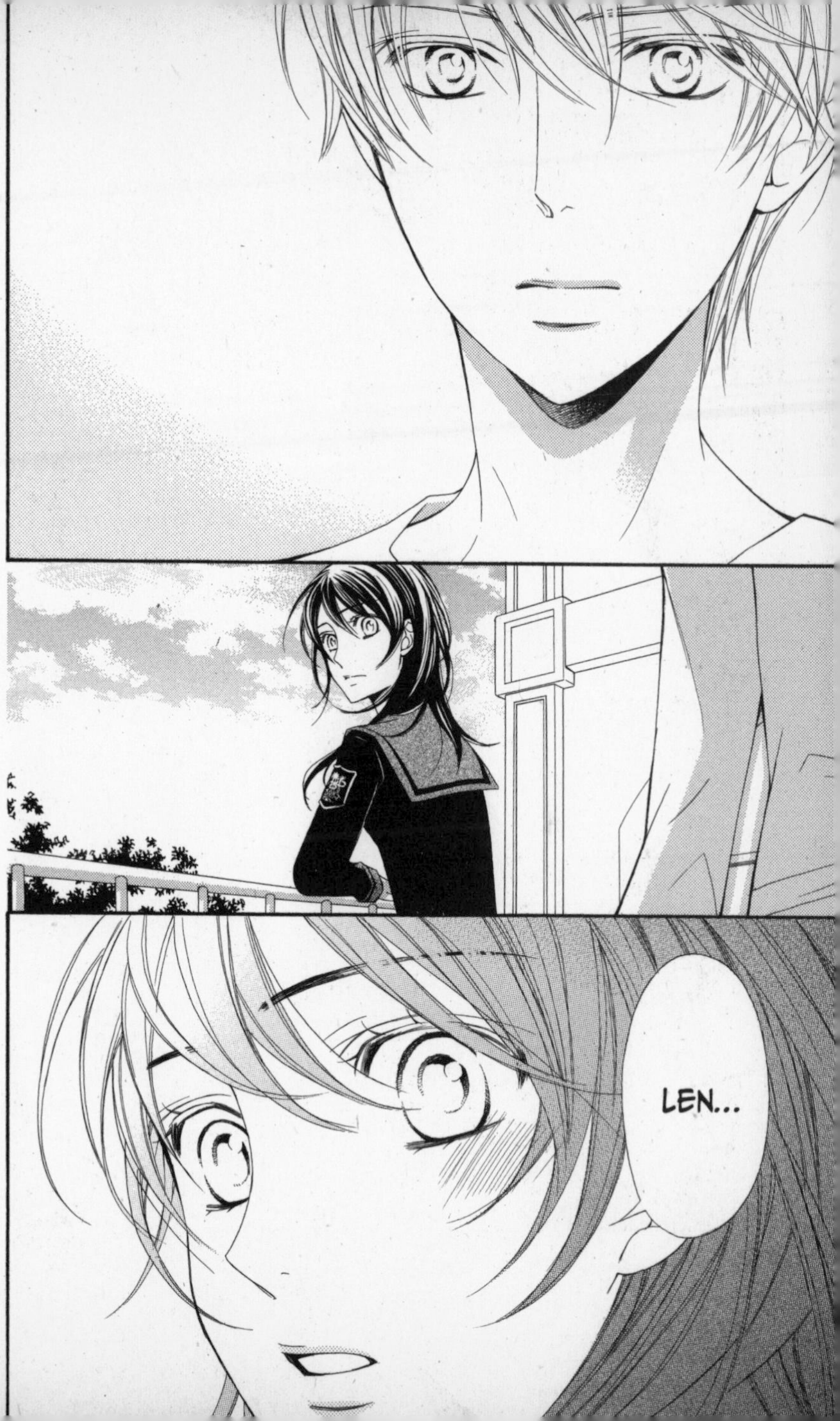
LEN...

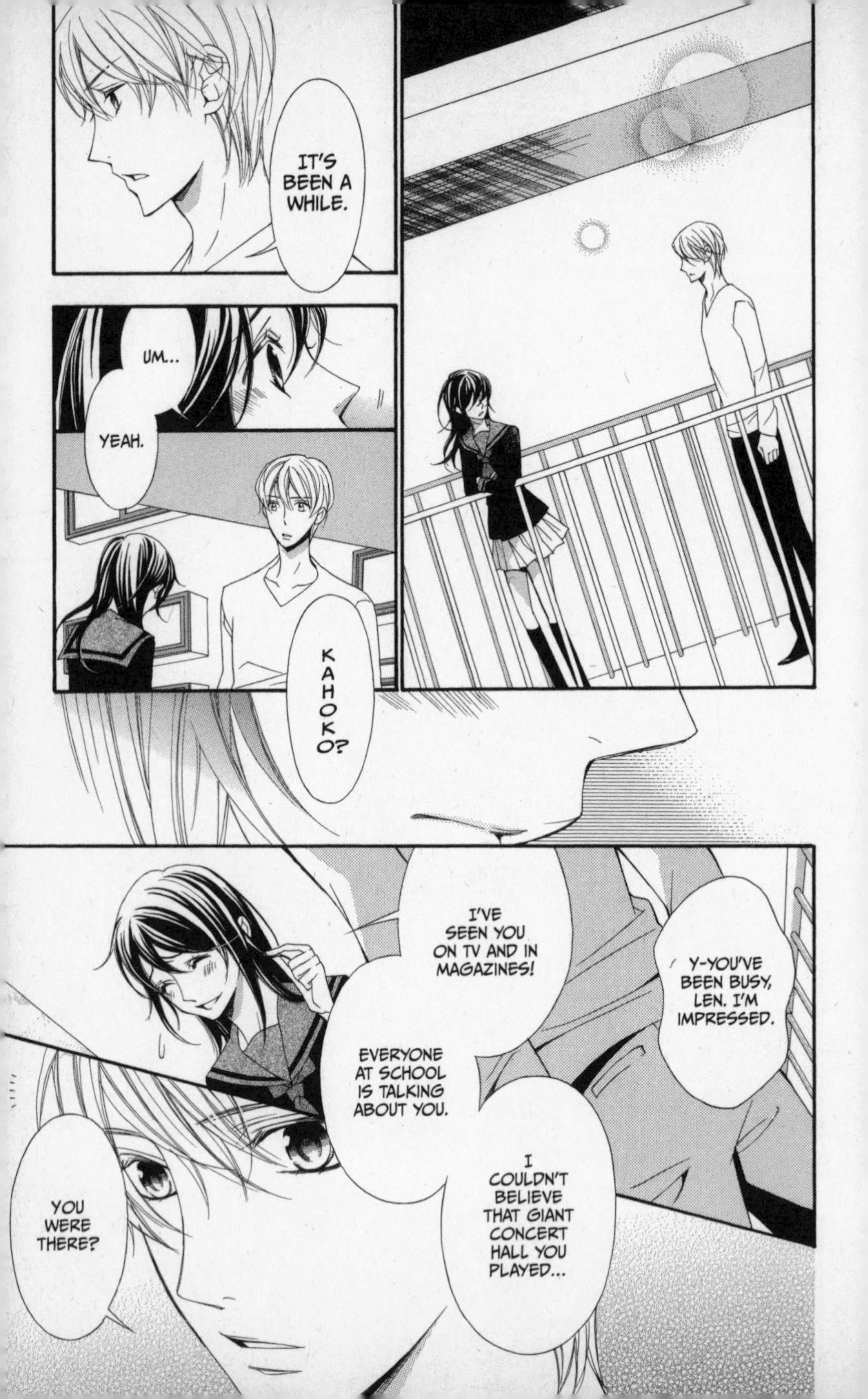
IT'S BEEN A WHILE.
UM...
YEAH.
KAHOKO?
Y-YOU'VE BEEN BUSY, LEN. I'M IMPRESSED.
I'VE SEEN YOU ON TV AND IN MAGAZINES!
EVERYONE AT SCHOOL IS TALKING ABOUT YOU.
I COULDN'T BELIEVE THAT GIANT CONCERT HALL YOU PLAYED...
YOU WERE THERE?

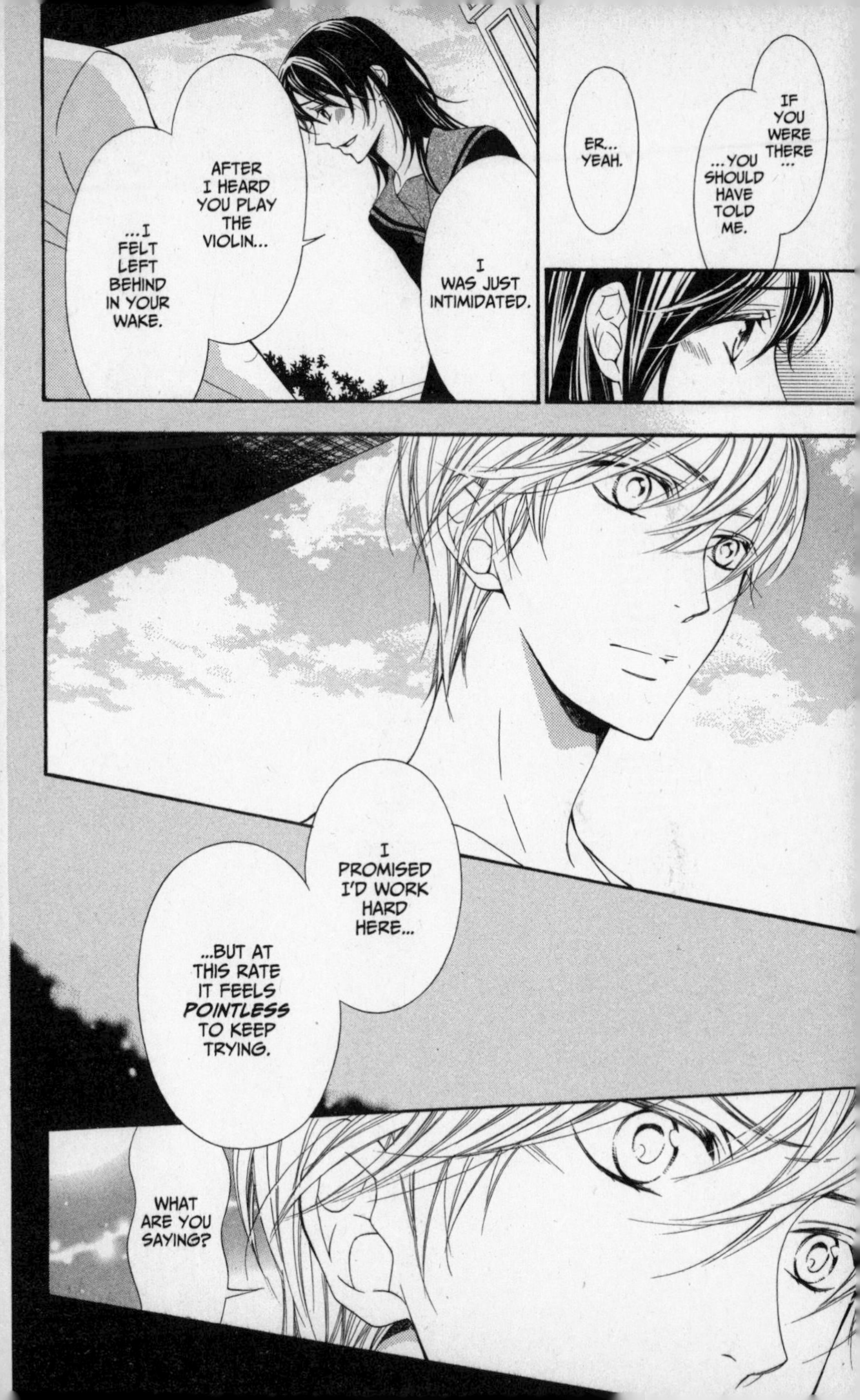
IF YOU WERE THERE...
...YOU SHOULD HAVE TOLD ME.
ER... YEAH.
I WAS JUST INTIMIDATED.
AFTER I HEARD YOU PLAY THE VIOLIN...
...I FELT LEFT BEHIND IN YOUR WAKE.
I PROMISED I'D WORK HARD HERE...
...BUT AT THIS RATE IT FEELS *POINTLESS* TO KEEP TRYING.
WHAT ARE YOU SAYING?

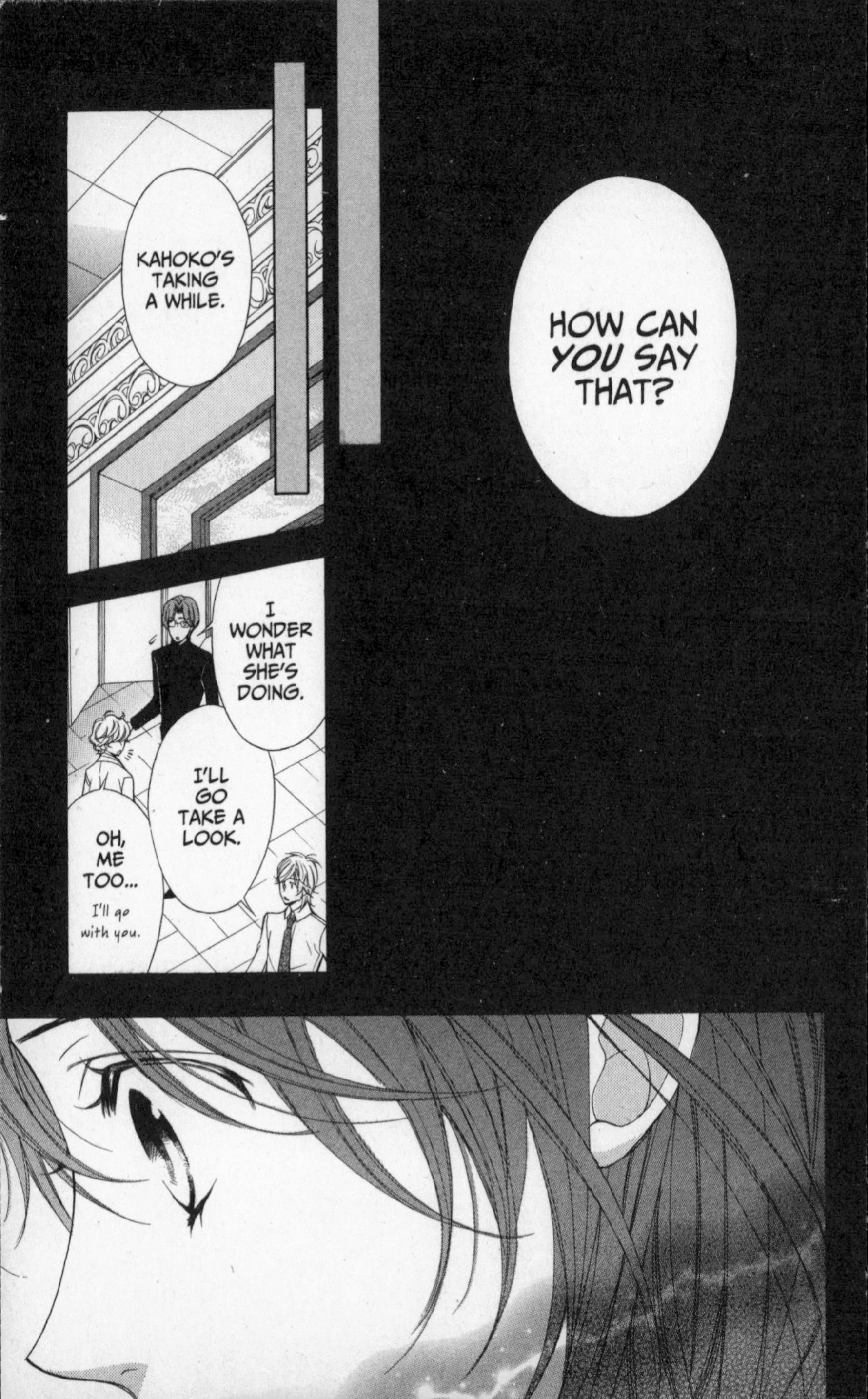
HOW CAN YOU SAY THAT?
KAHOKO'S TAKING A WHILE.
I WONDER WHAT SHE'S DOING.
I'LL GO TAKE A LOOK.
OH, ME TOO...
I'll go with you.

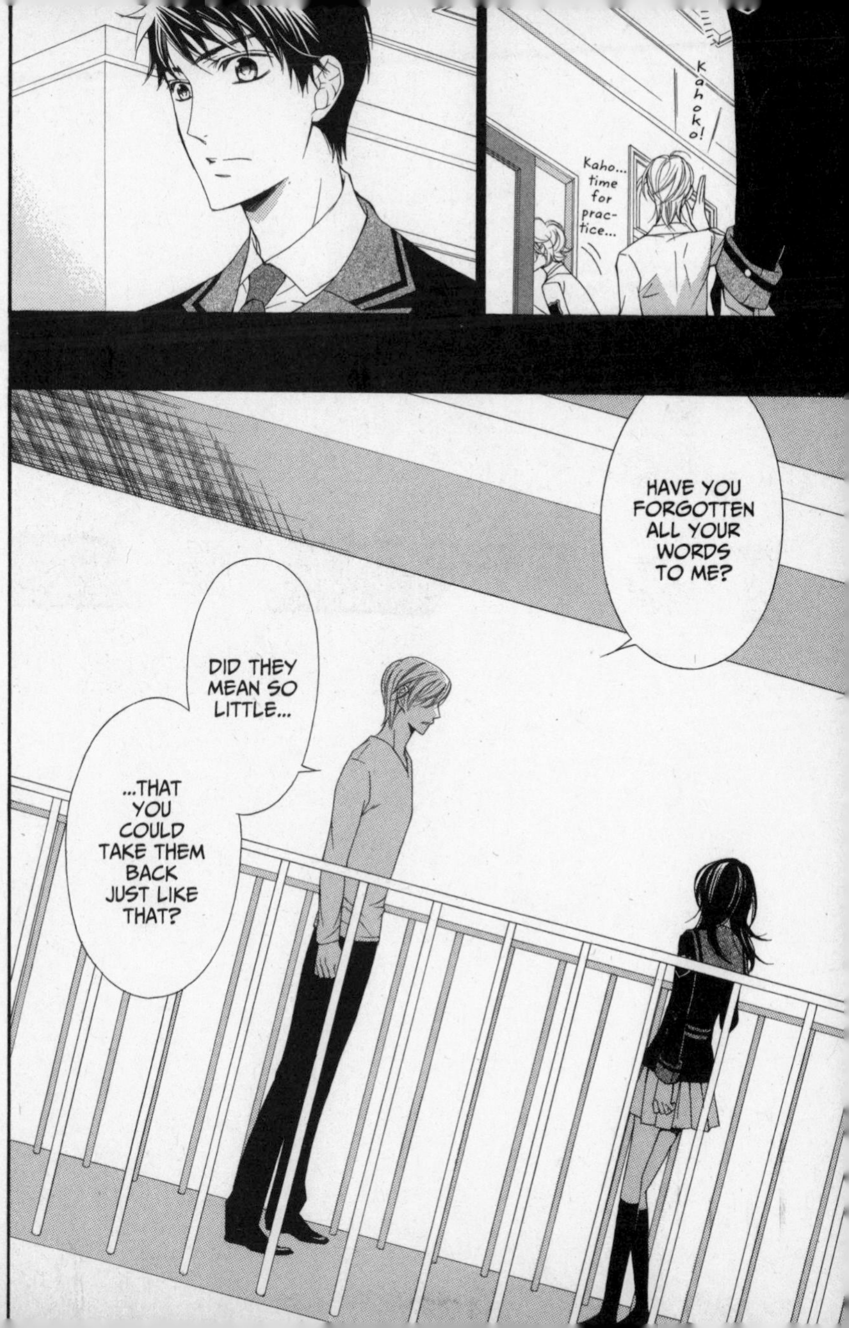
Kahoko!
Kaho... time for prac-tice...
HAVE YOU FORGOTTEN ALL YOUR WORDS TO ME?
DID THEY MEAN SO LITTLE...
...THAT YOU COULD TAKE THEM BACK JUST LIKE THAT?

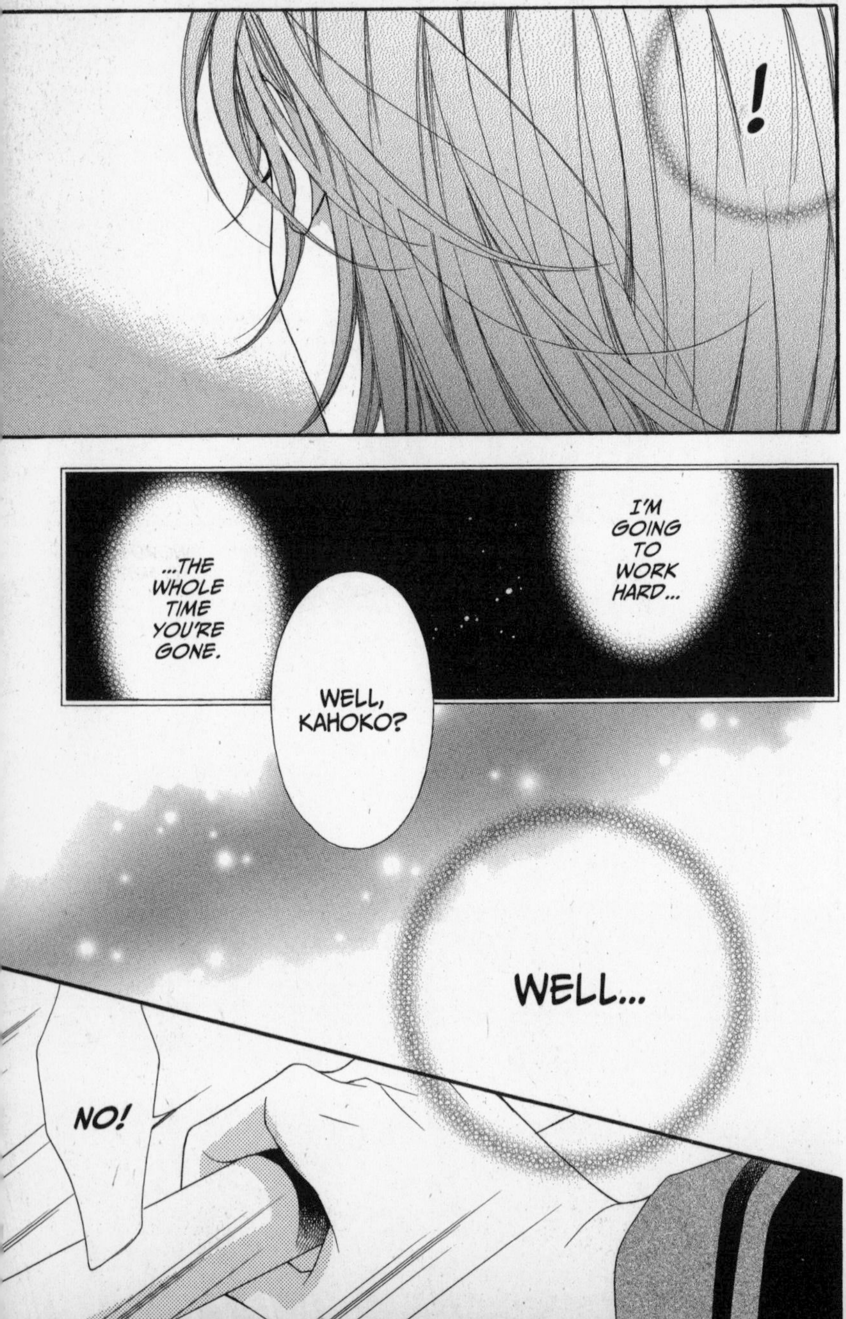
!
I'M GOING TO WORK HARD...
...THE WHOLE TIME YOU'RE GONE.
WELL, KAHOKO?
WELL...
NO!

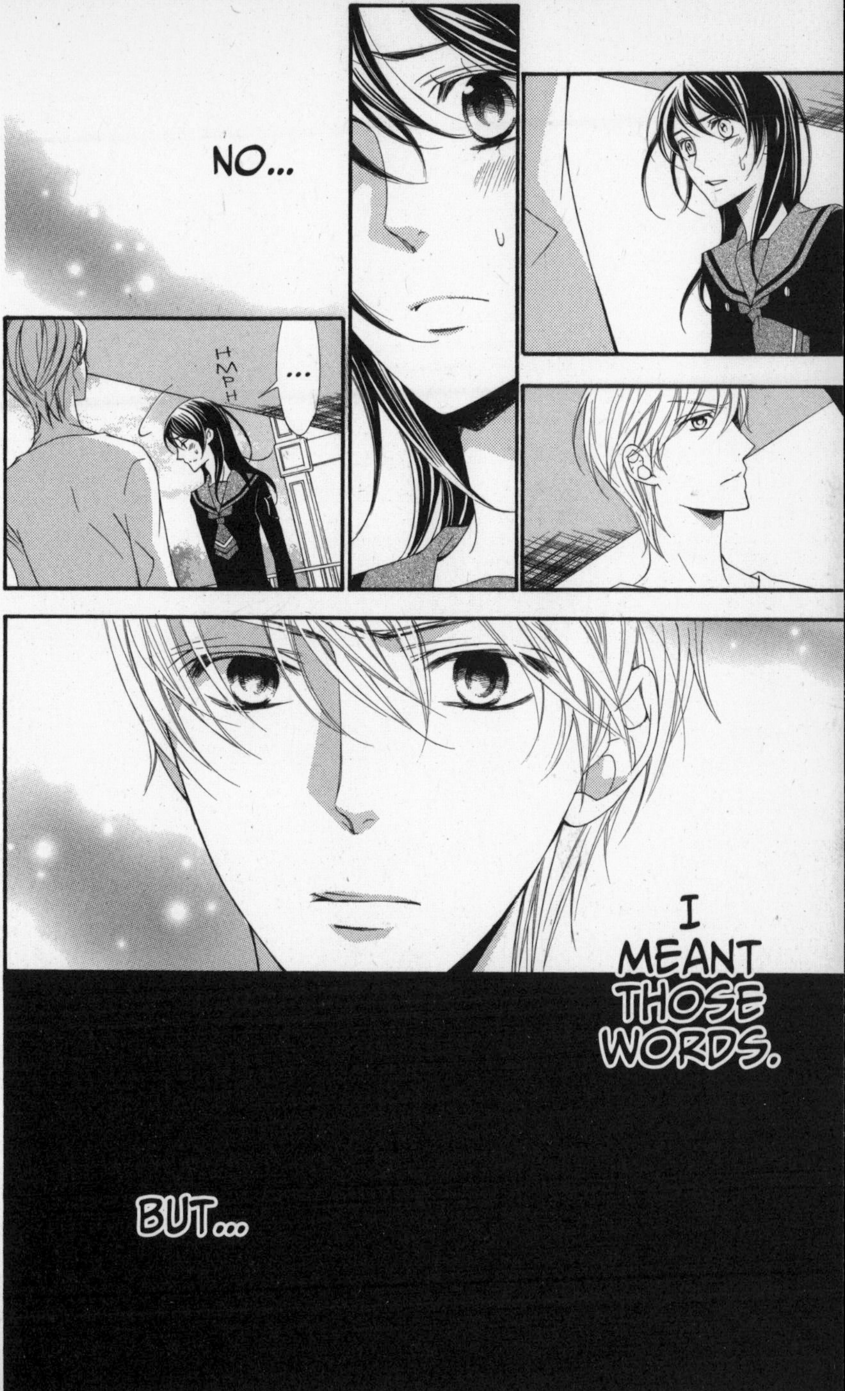
NO...
HMPH
...
I MEANT THOSE WORDS.
BUT...

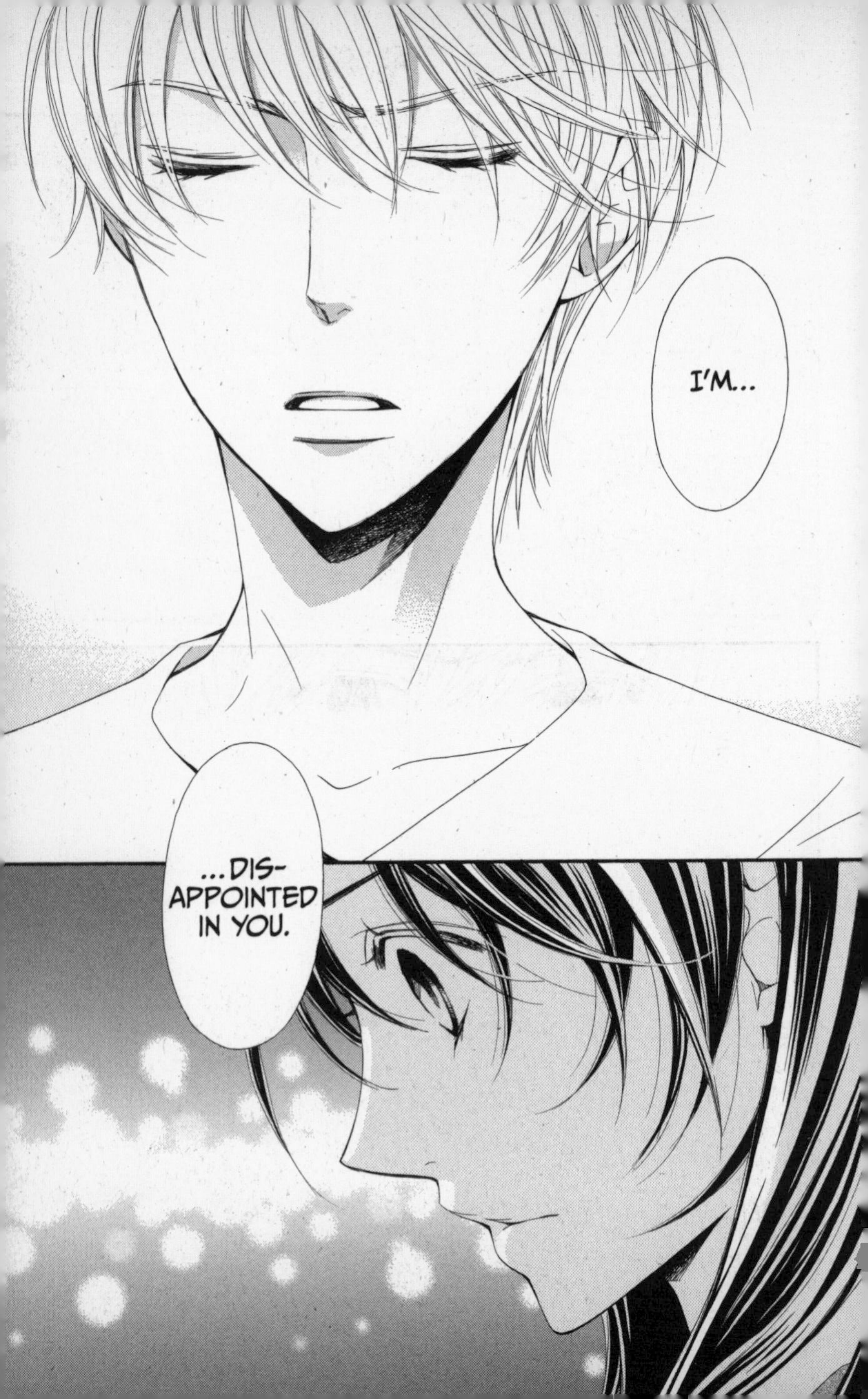
I'M...
...DIS-
APPOINTED
IN YOU.

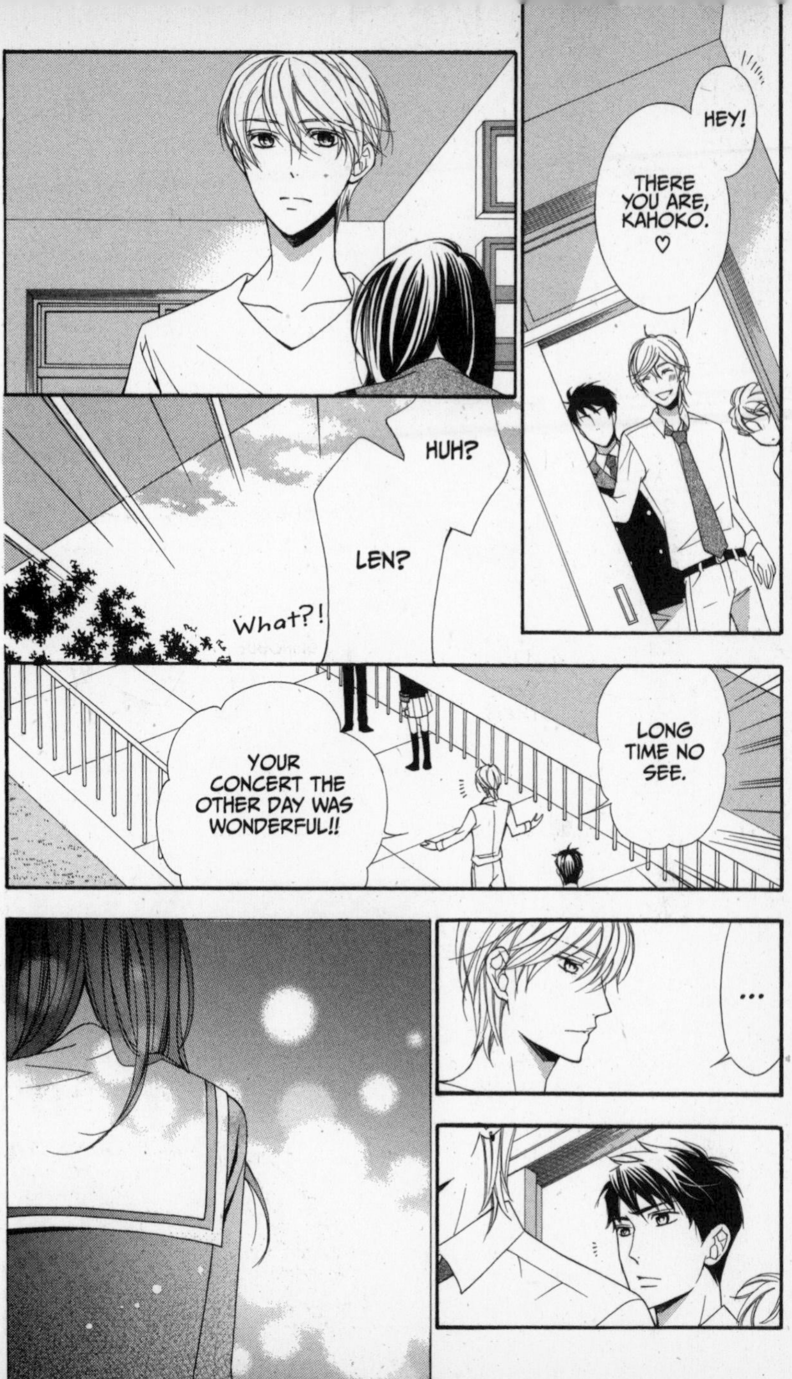
HEY!
THERE YOU ARE, KAHOKO. ♡
HUH?
LEN?
What?!
LONG TIME NO SEE.
YOUR CONCERT THE OTHER DAY WAS WONDERFUL!!
...

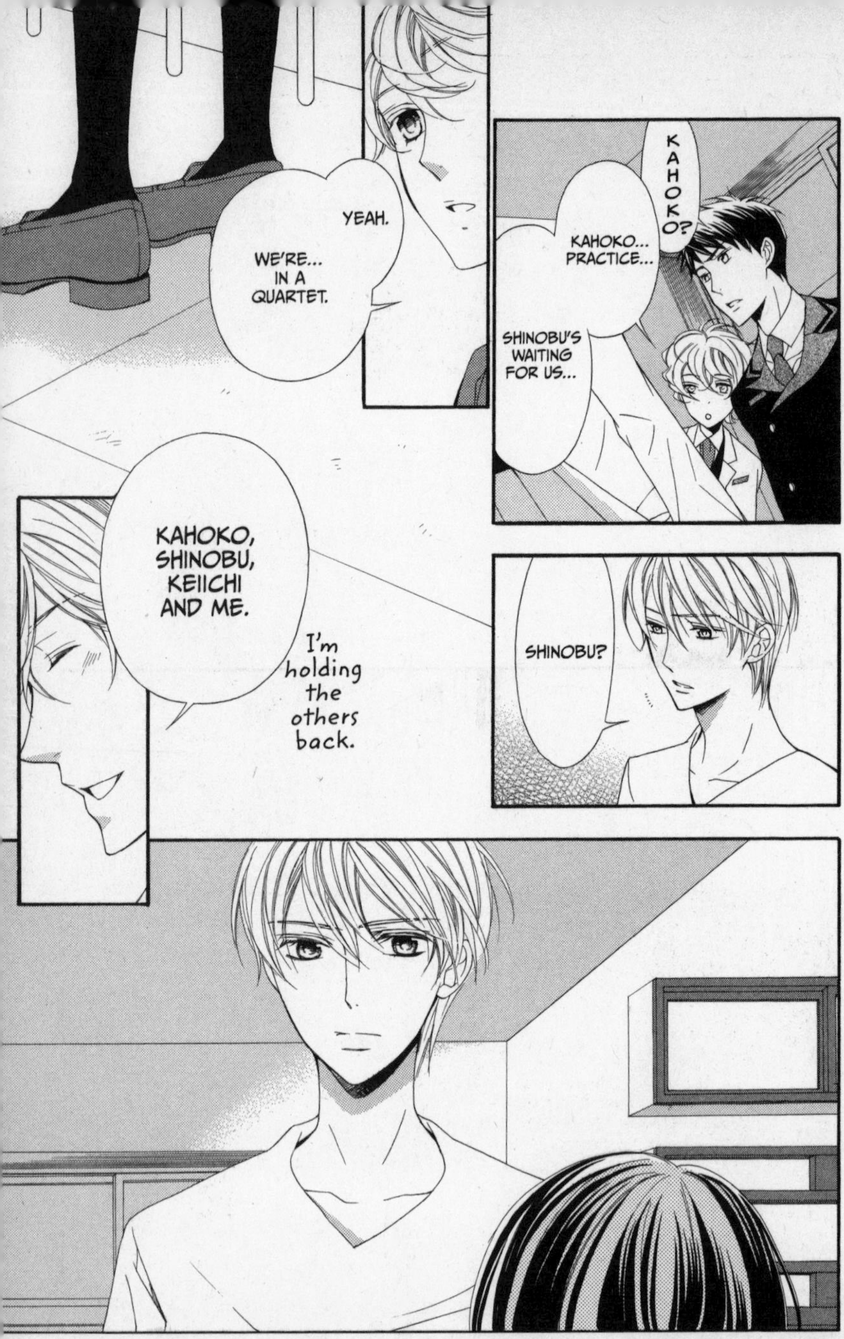
KAHOKO?
KAHOKO... PRACTICE...
SHINOBU'S WAITING FOR US...
YEAH.
WE'RE... IN A QUARTET.
SHINOBU?
KAHOKO, SHINOBU, KEIICHI AND ME.
I'm holding the others back.

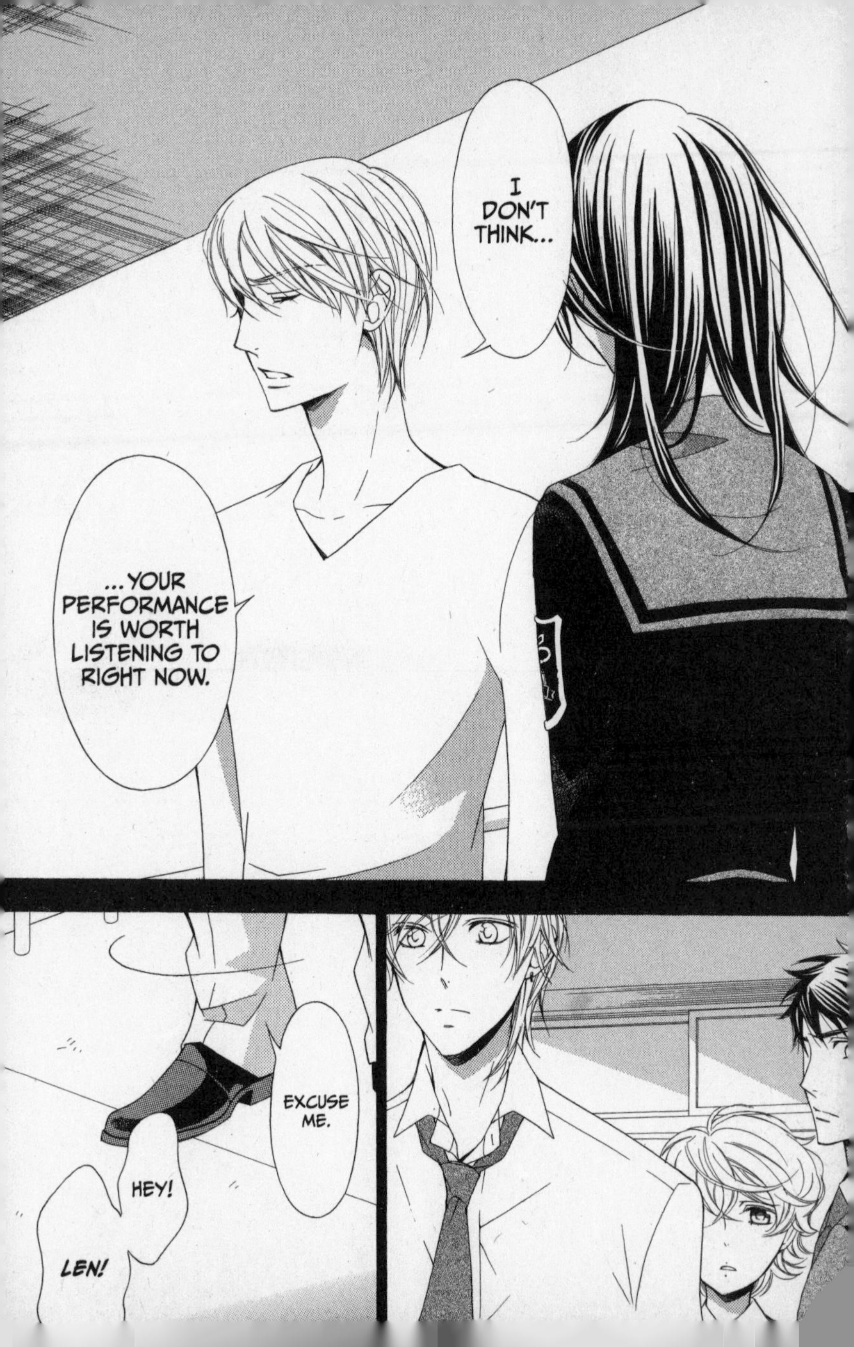
I DON'T THINK...
...YOUR PERFORMANCE IS WORTH LISTENING TO RIGHT NOW.
EXCUSE ME.
HEY!
LEN!

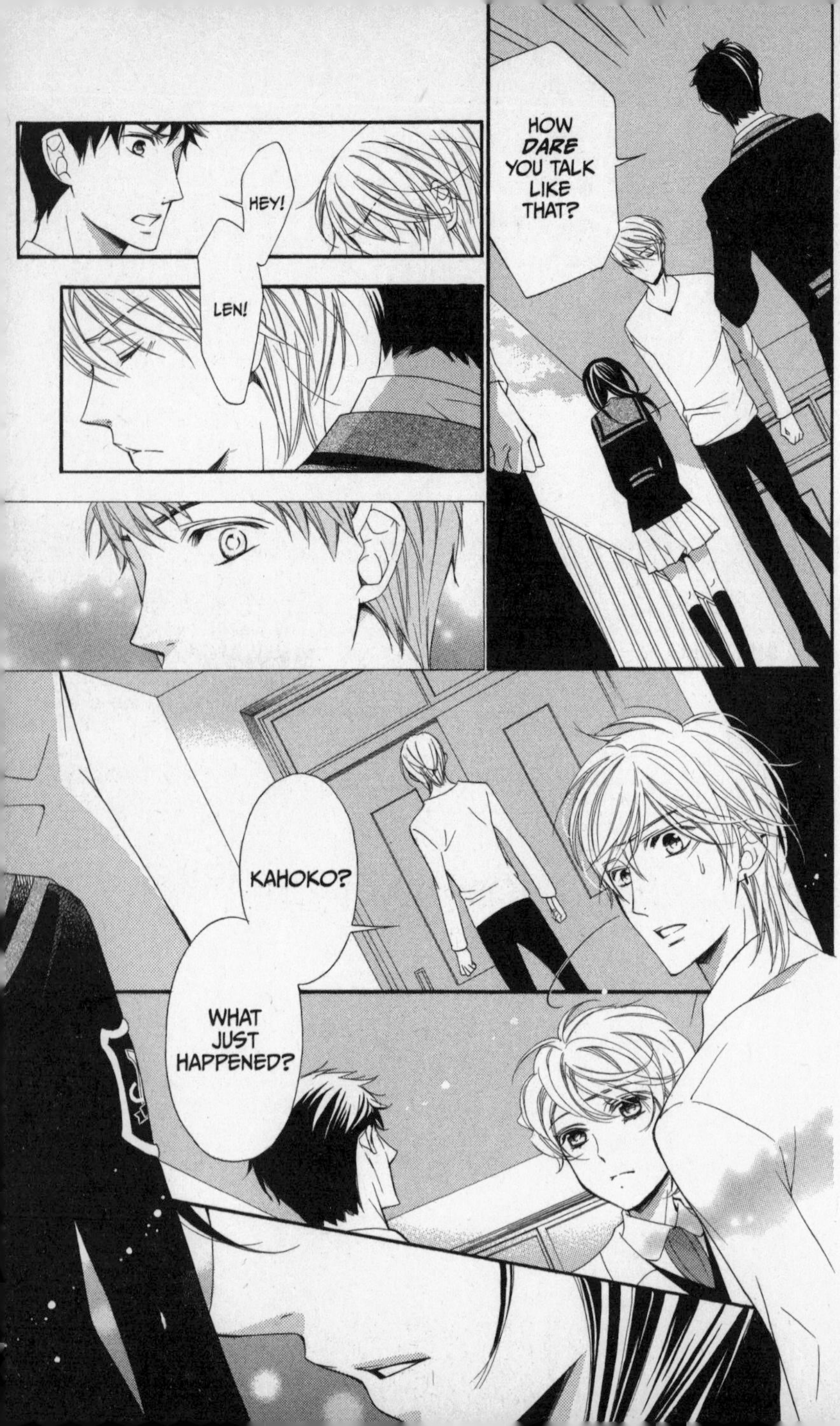
HOW DARE YOU TALK LIKE THAT?
HEY!
LEN!
KAHOKO?
WHAT JUST HAPPENED?

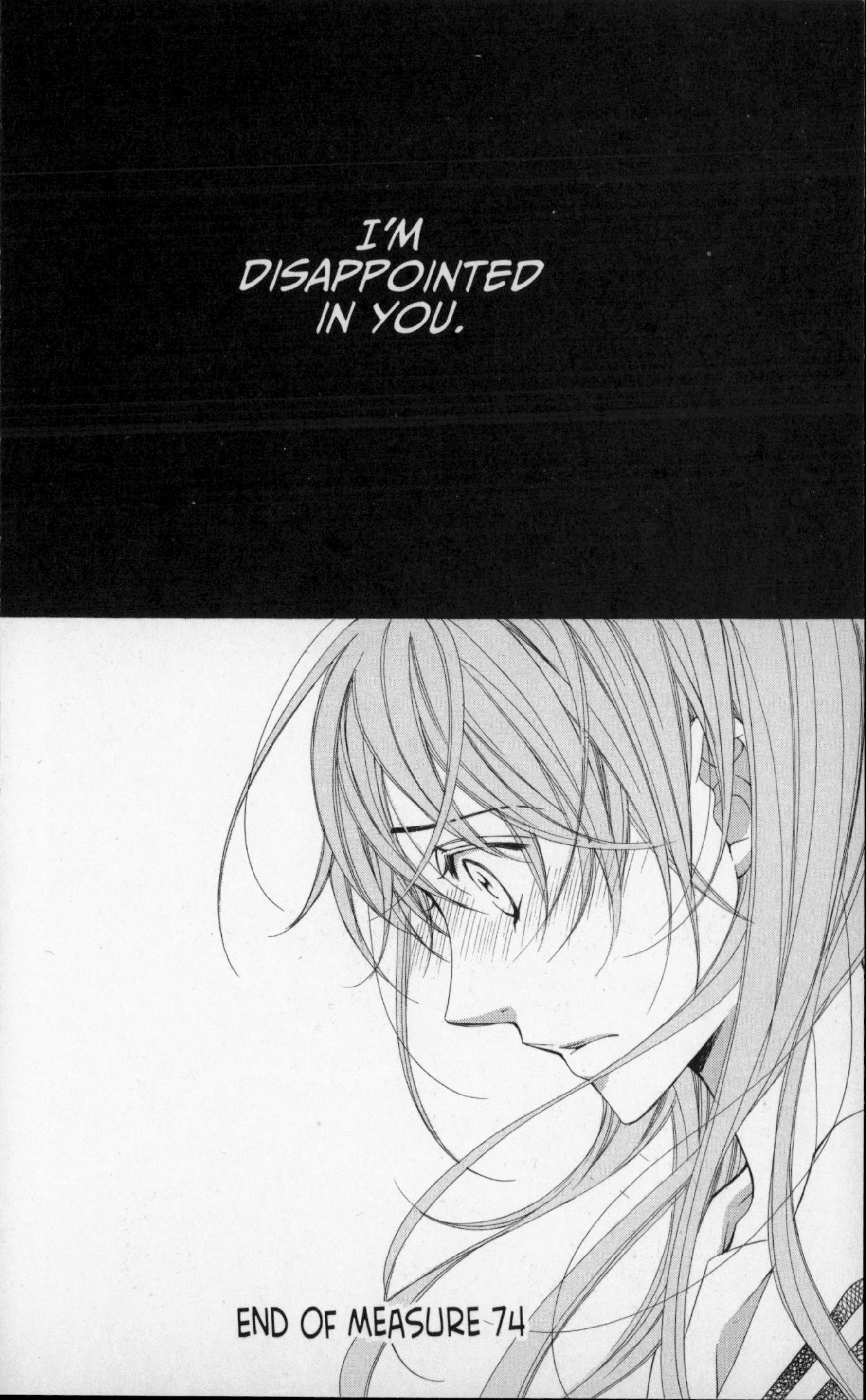
I'M DISAPPOINTED IN YOU.
END OF MEASURE 74

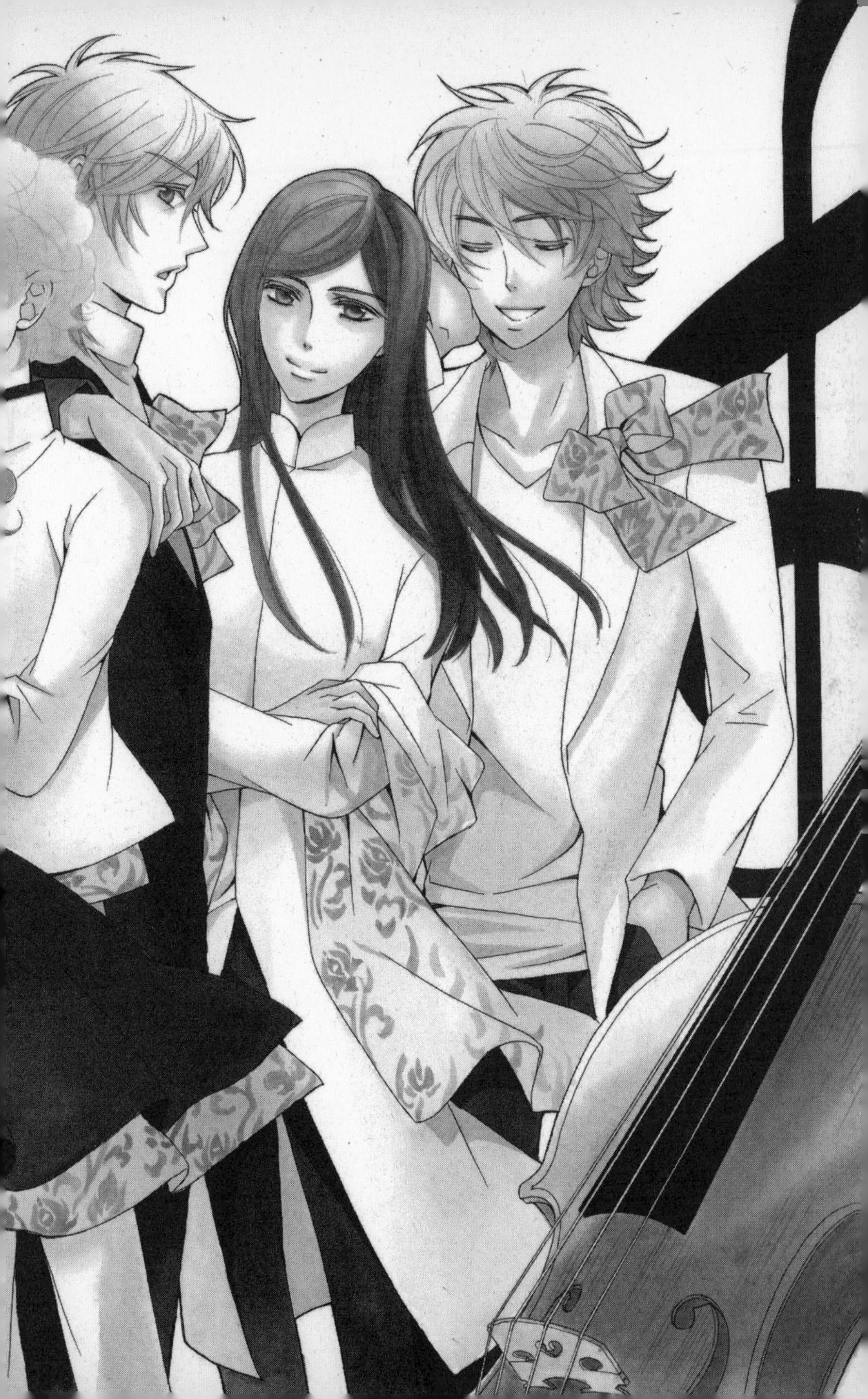

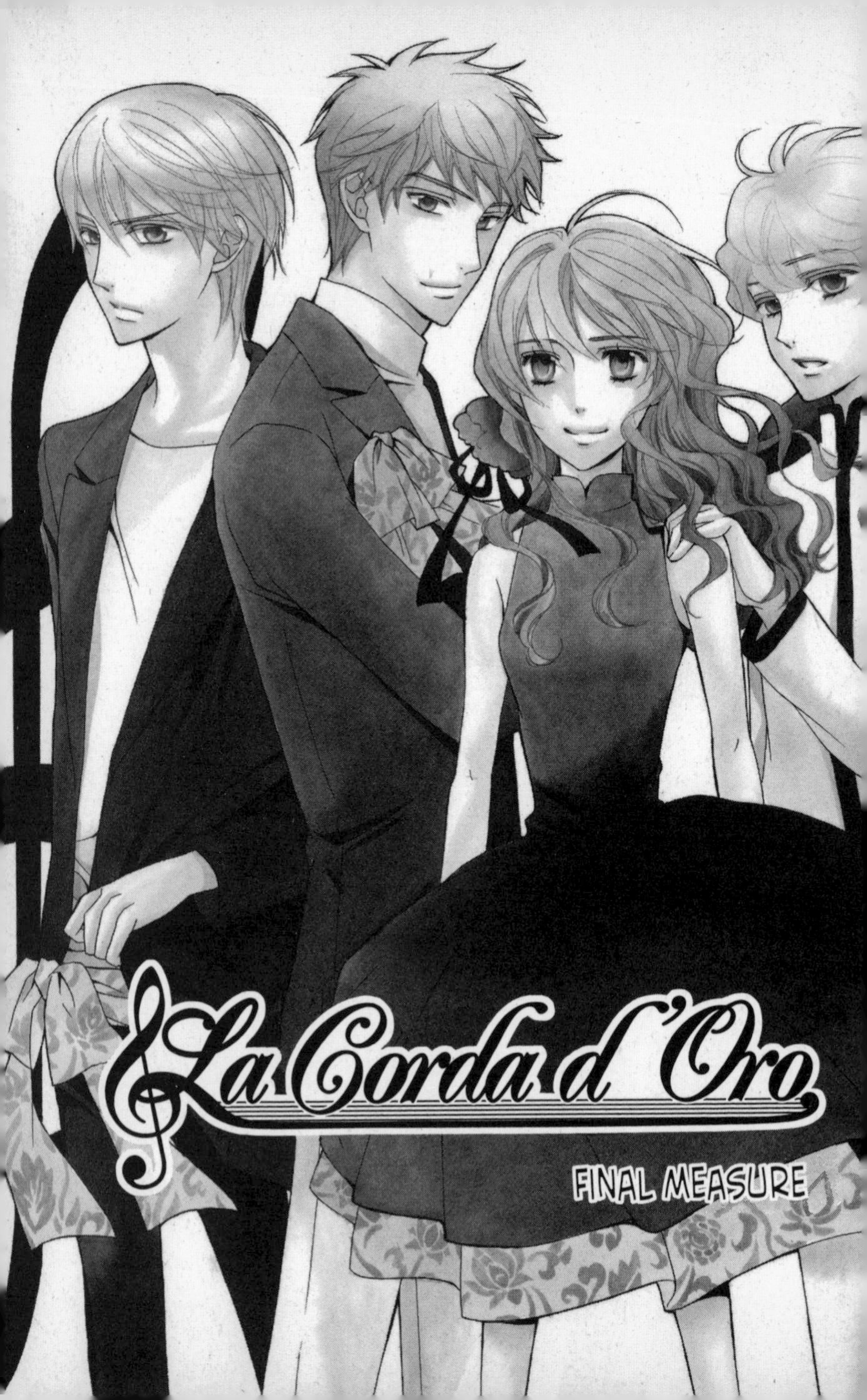
La Corda d'Oro
FINAL MEASURE

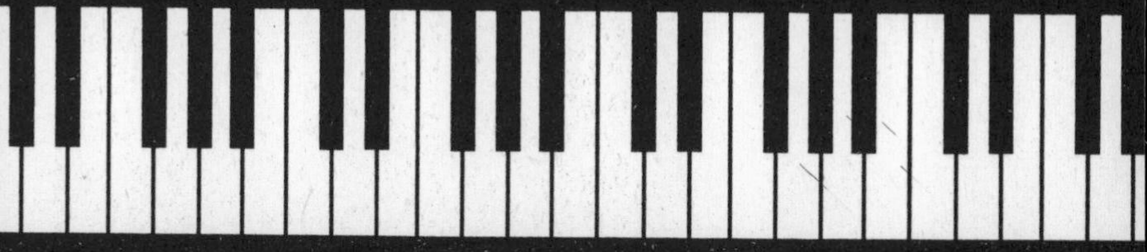

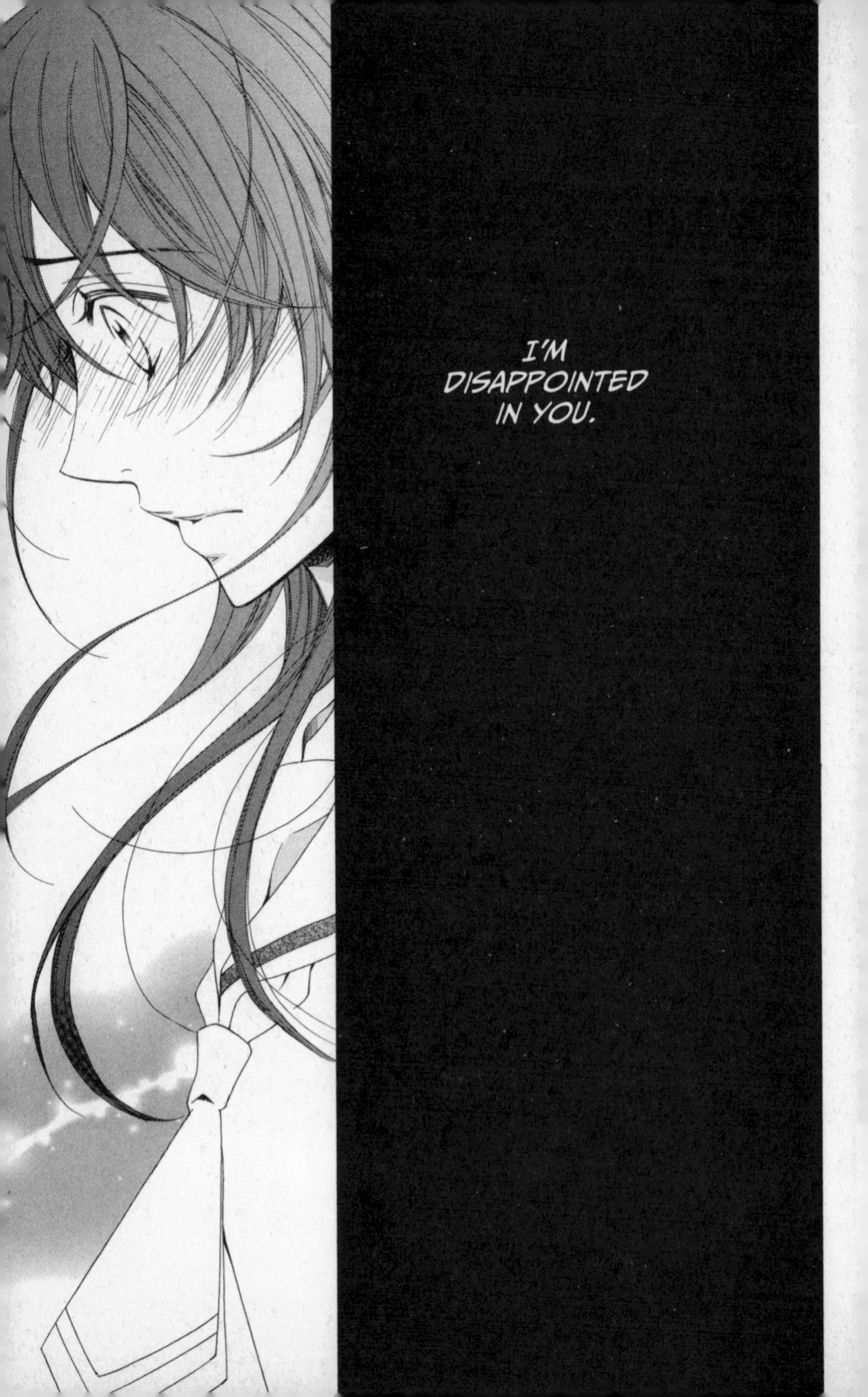
I'M DISAPPOINTED IN YOU.

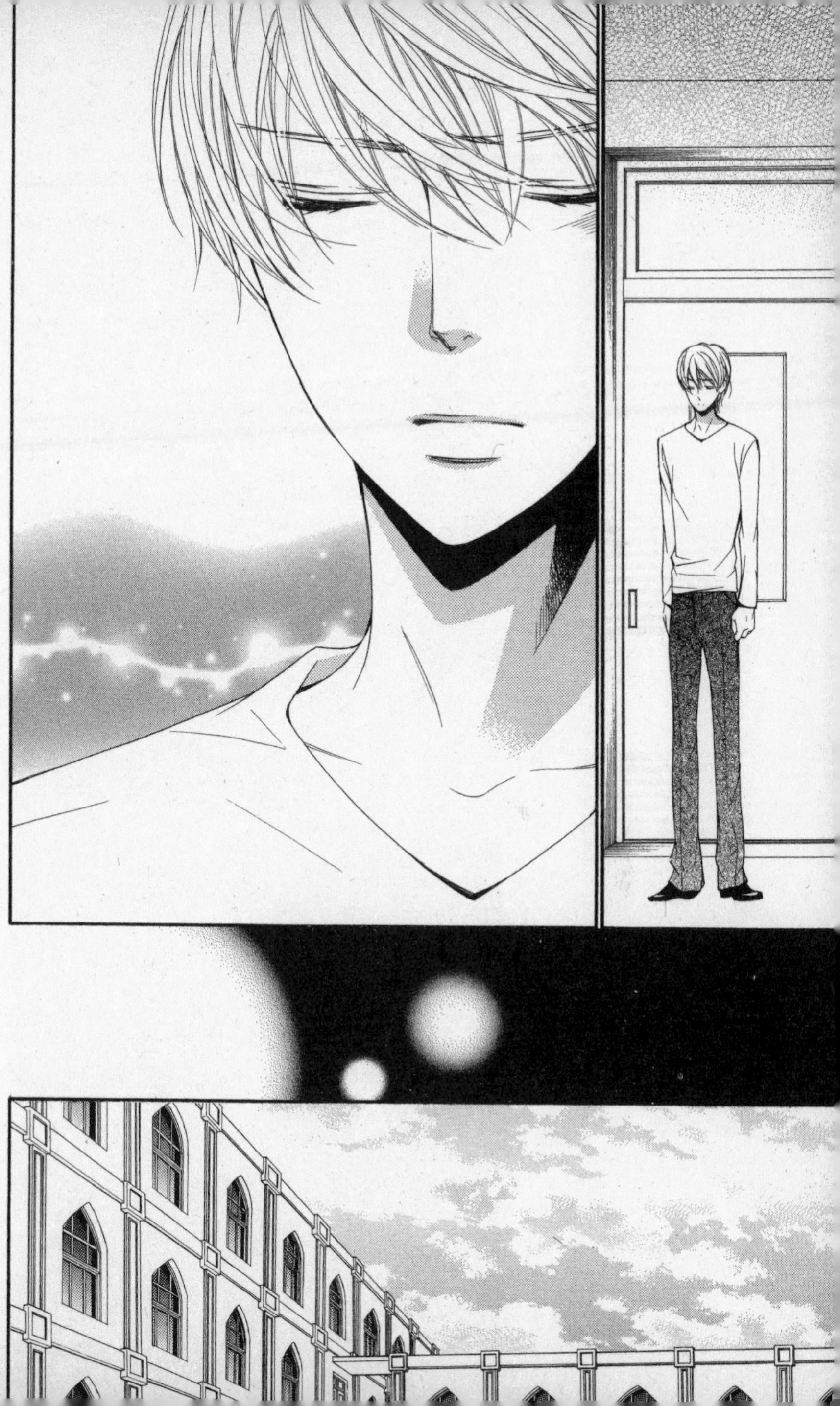

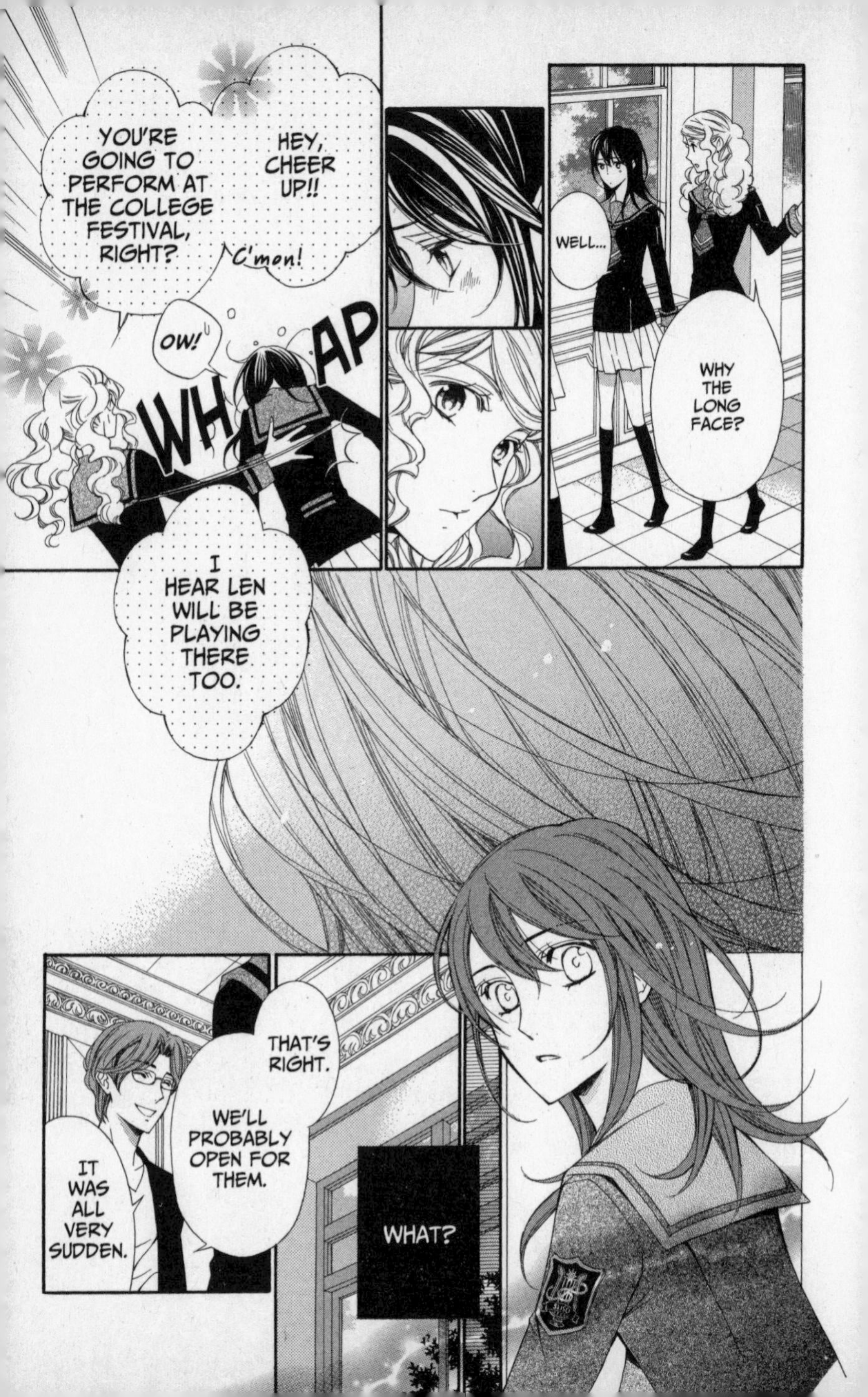

WHY THE LONG FACE?
WELL...
HEY, CHEER UP!!
C'mon!
YOU'RE GOING TO PERFORM AT THE COLLEGE FESTIVAL, RIGHT?
WHAP
OW!
I HEAR LEN WILL BE PLAYING THERE TOO.
WHAT?
THAT'S RIGHT.
WE'LL PROBABLY OPEN FOR THEM.
IT WAS ALL VERY SUDDEN.

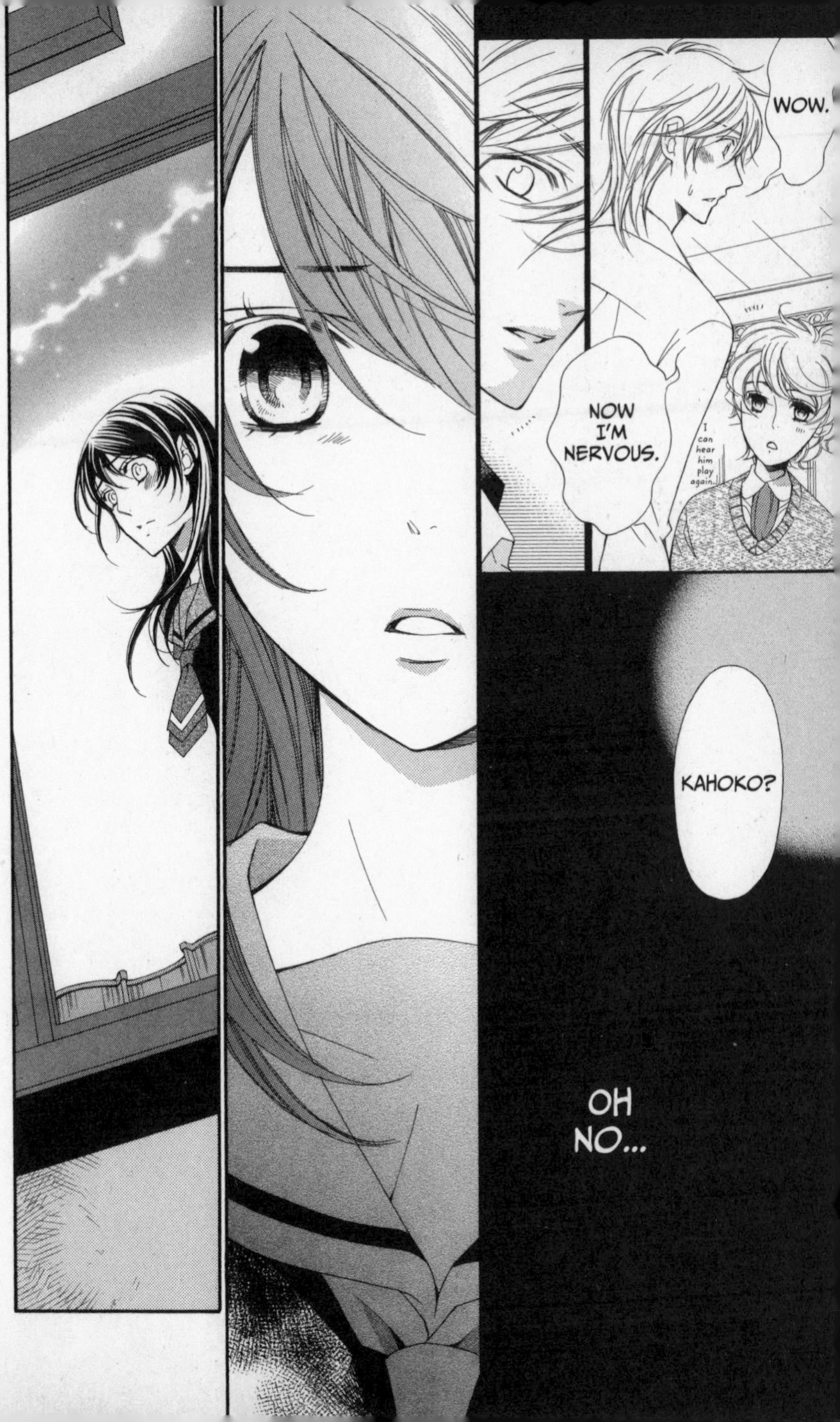
WOW.
I can hear him play again...
NOW I'M NERVOUS.
KAHOKO?
OH NO...

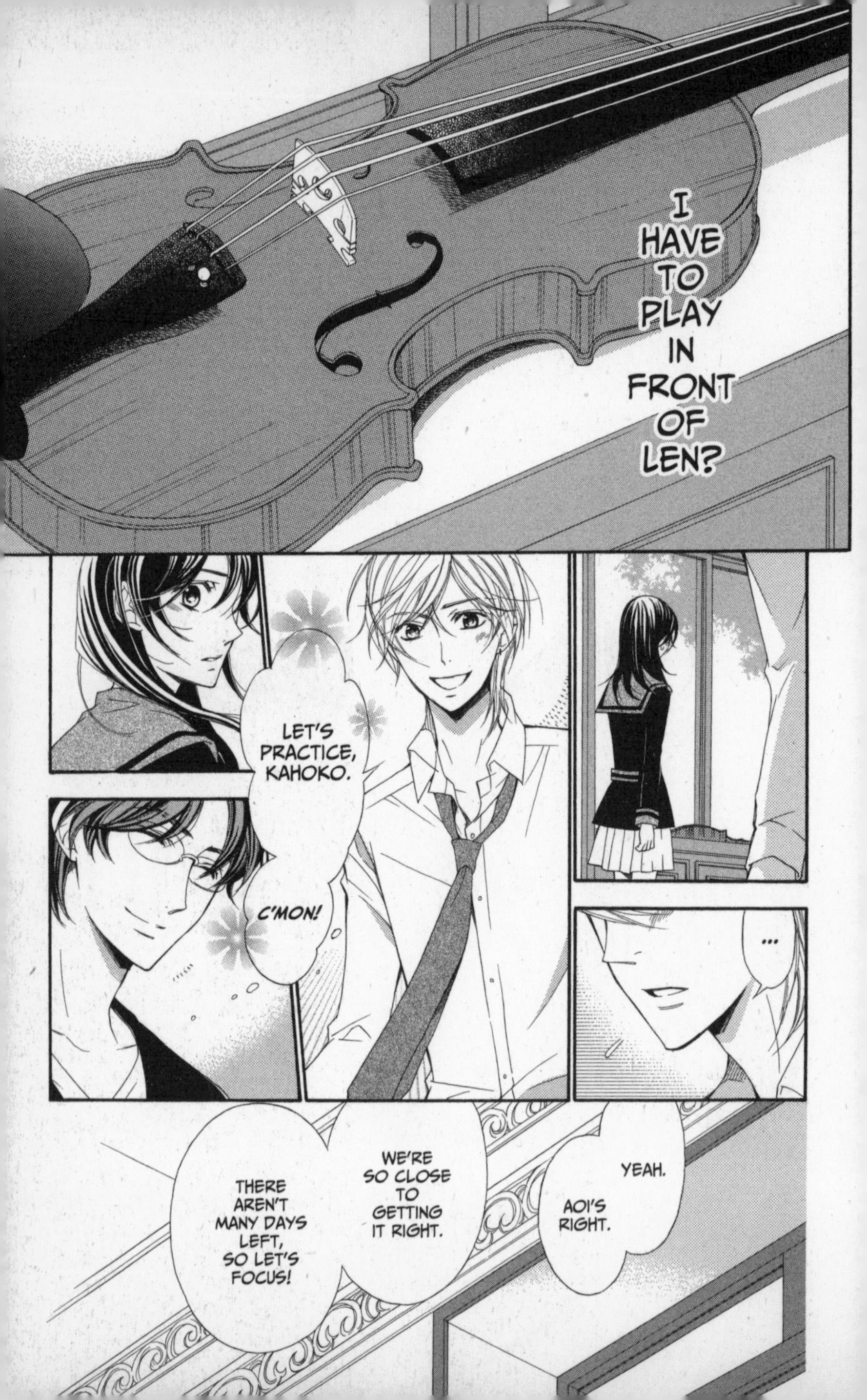
I HAVE TO PLAY IN FRONT OF LEN?
...
LET'S PRACTICE, KAHOKO.
C'MON!
YEAH.
AOI'S RIGHT.
WE'RE SO CLOSE TO GETTING IT RIGHT.
THERE AREN'T MANY DAYS LEFT, SO LET'S FOCUS!

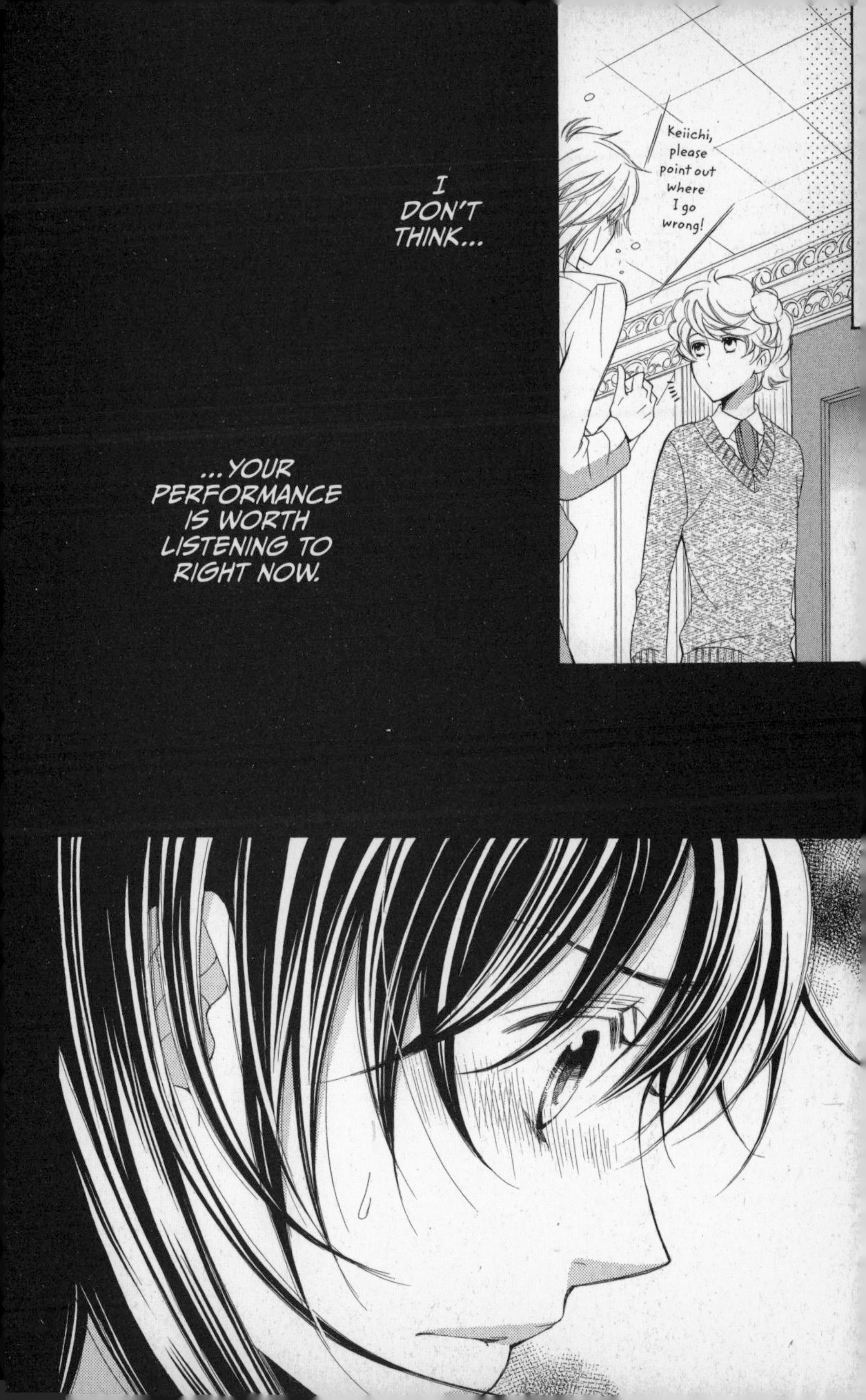
Keiichi, please point out where I go wrong!
I DON'T THINK...
...YOUR PERFORMANCE IS WORTH LISTENING TO RIGHT NOW.

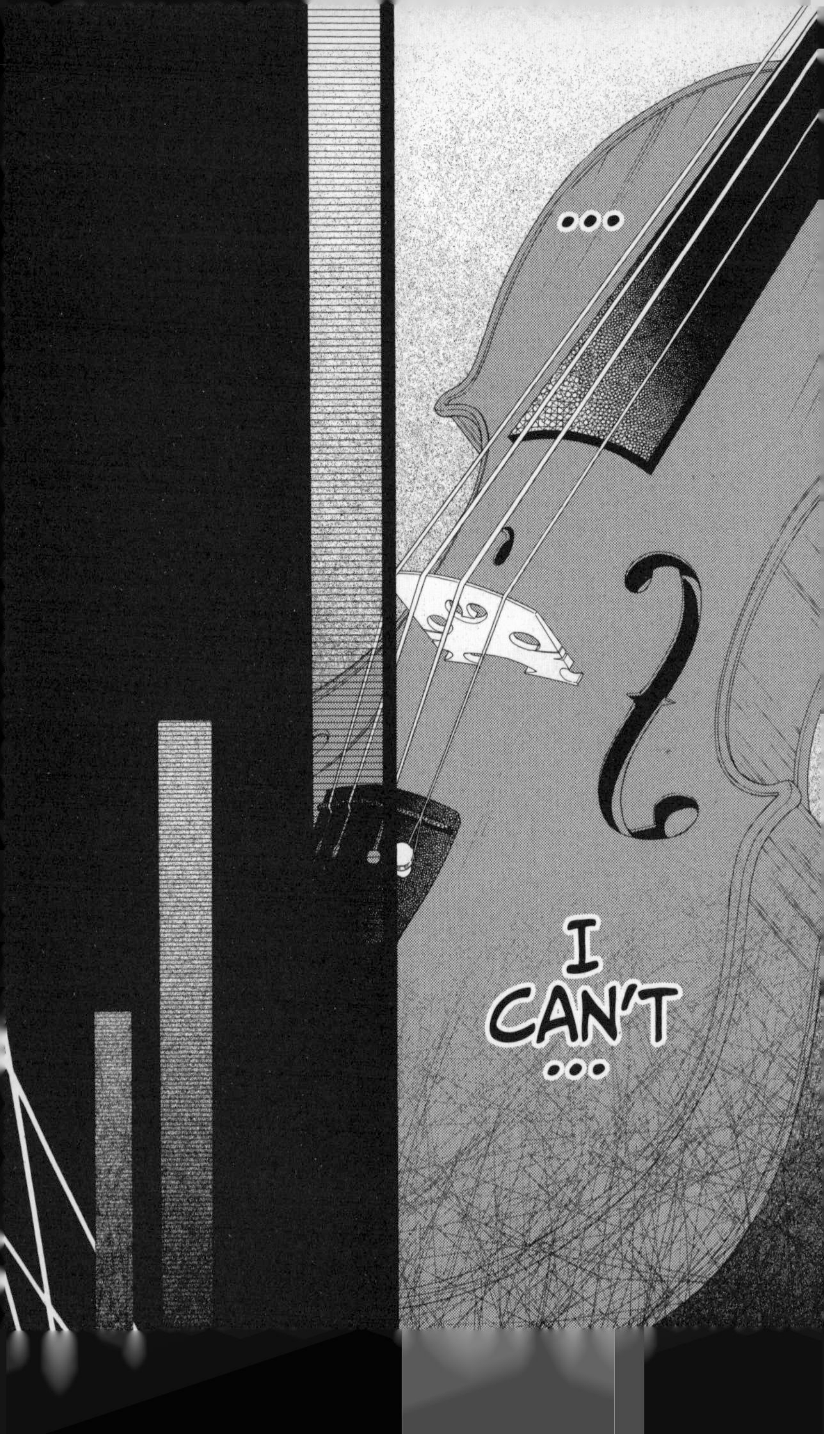
...
I CAN'T ...

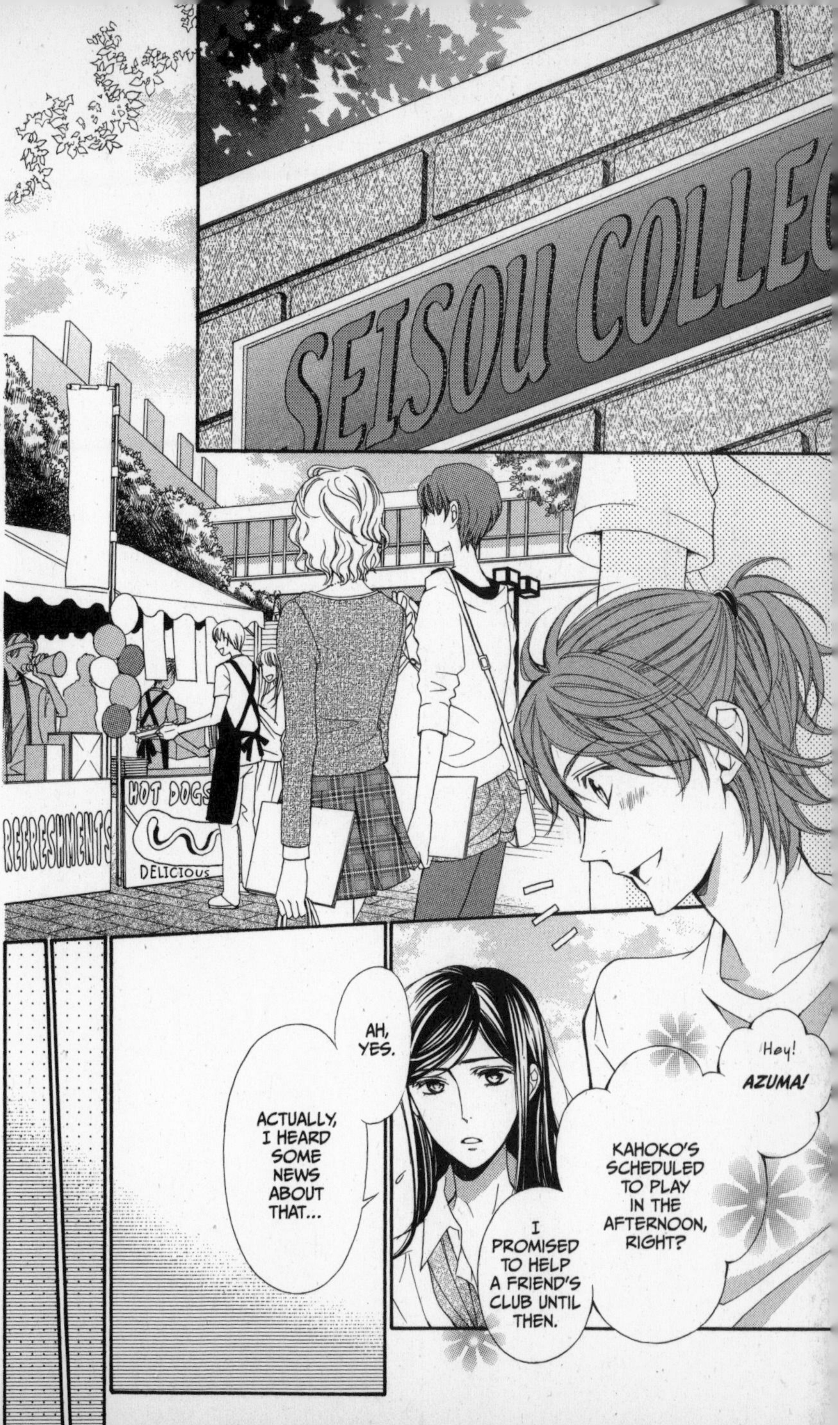
SEISOU COLLE
HOT DOGS
REFRESHMENTS
DELICIOUS
Hey! AZUMA!
KAHOKO'S SCHEDULED TO PLAY IN THE AFTERNOON, RIGHT?
I PROMISED TO HELP A FRIEND'S CLUB UNTIL THEN.
AH, YES.
ACTUALLY, I HEARD SOME NEWS ABOUT THAT...

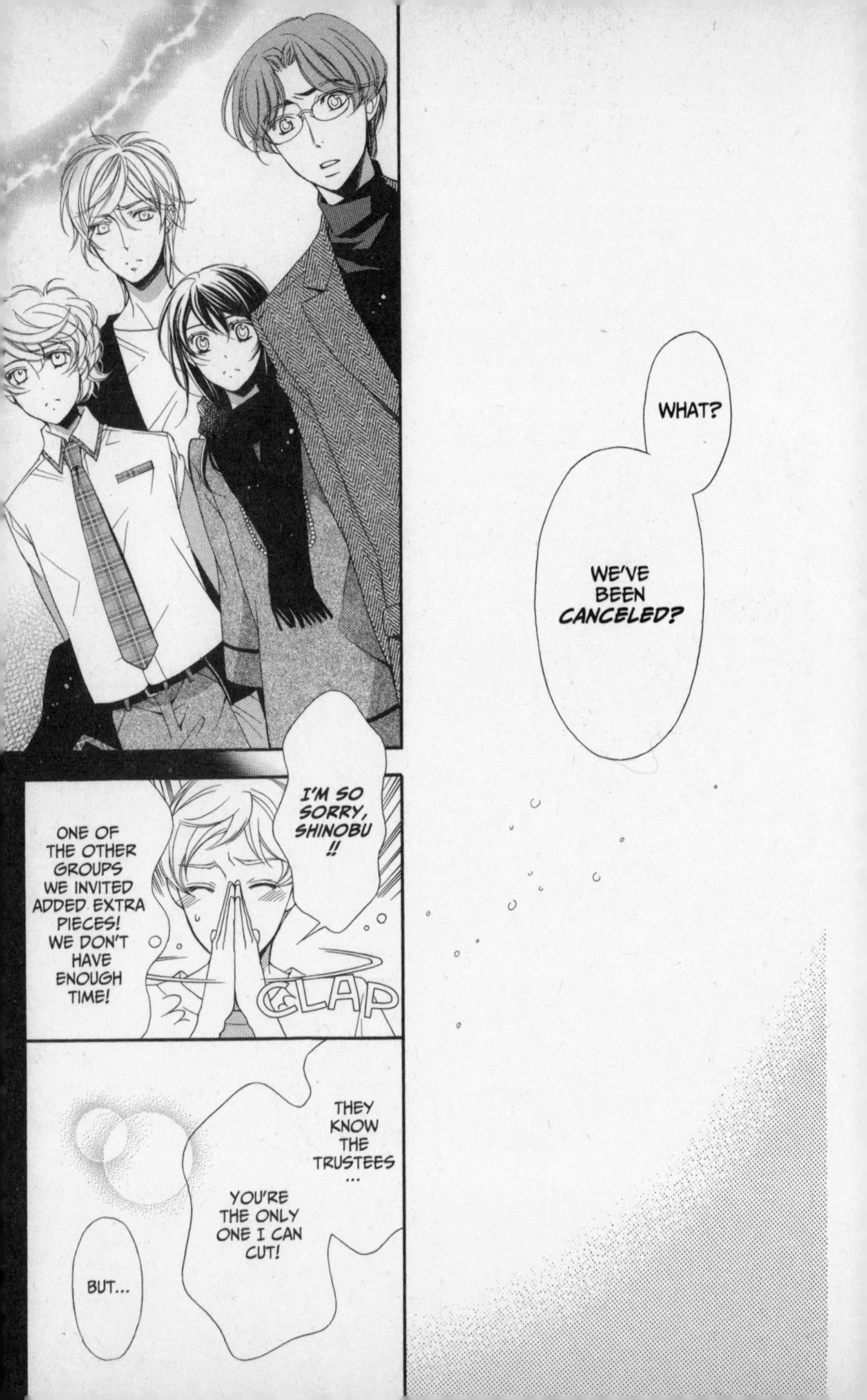
WHAT?
WE'VE BEEN CANCELED?
I'M SO SORRY, SHINOBU!!
ONE OF THE OTHER GROUPS WE INVITED ADDED EXTRA PIECES! WE DON'T HAVE ENOUGH TIME!
CLAP
THEY KNOW THE TRUSTEES...
YOU'RE THE ONLY ONE I CAN CUT!
BUT...

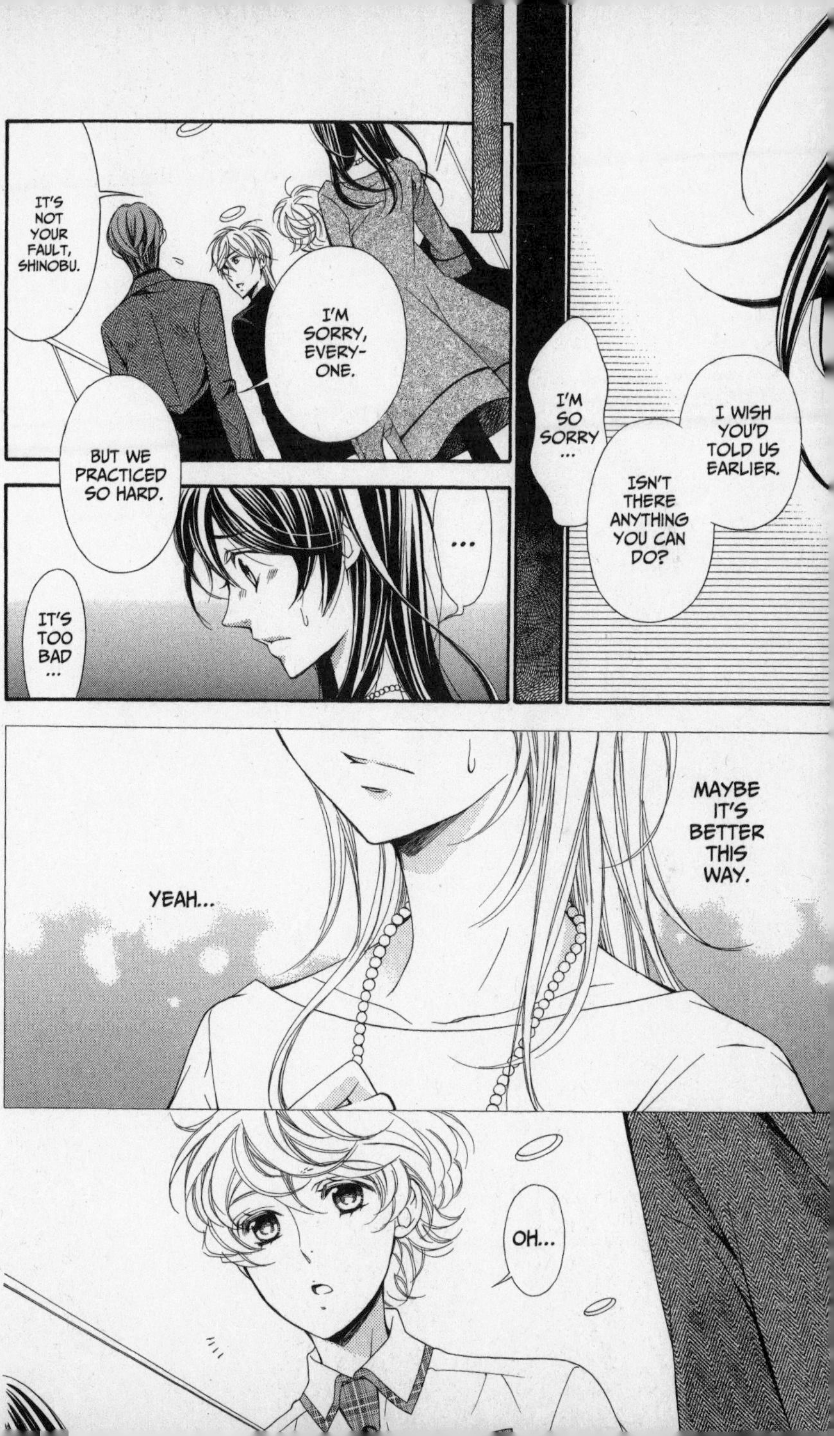
I WISH YOU'D TOLD US EARLIER.
I'M SO SORRY...
ISN'T THERE ANYTHING YOU CAN DO?
I'M SORRY, EVERYONE.
IT'S NOT YOUR FAULT, SHINOBU.
BUT WE PRACTICED SO HARD.
...
IT'S TOO BAD...
MAYBE IT'S BETTER THIS WAY.
YEAH...
OH...

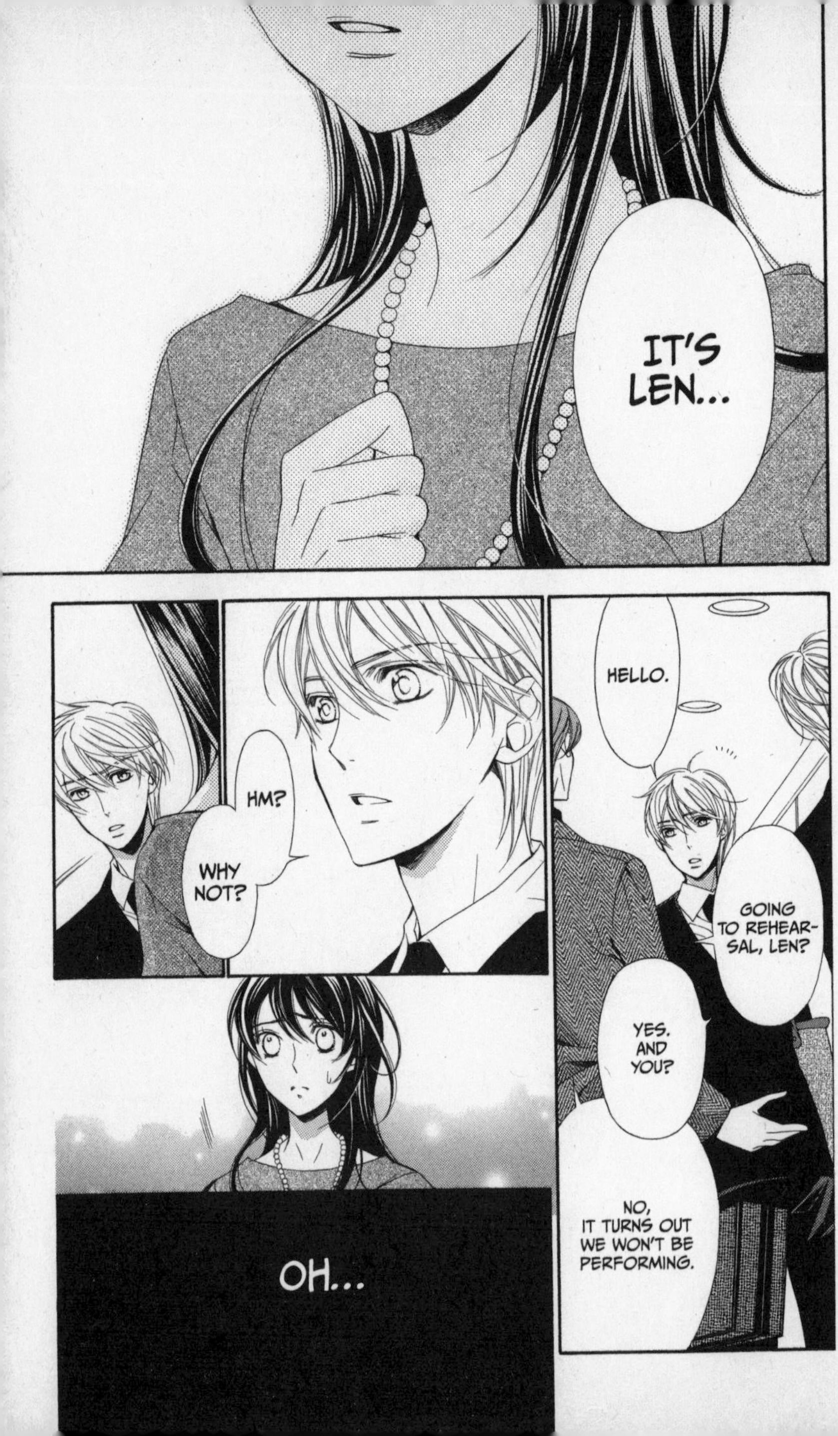
IT'S LEN...
HELLO.
GOING TO REHEAR-SAL, LEN?
YES. AND YOU?
NO, IT TURNS OUT WE WON'T BE PERFORMING.
HM? WHY NOT?
OH...

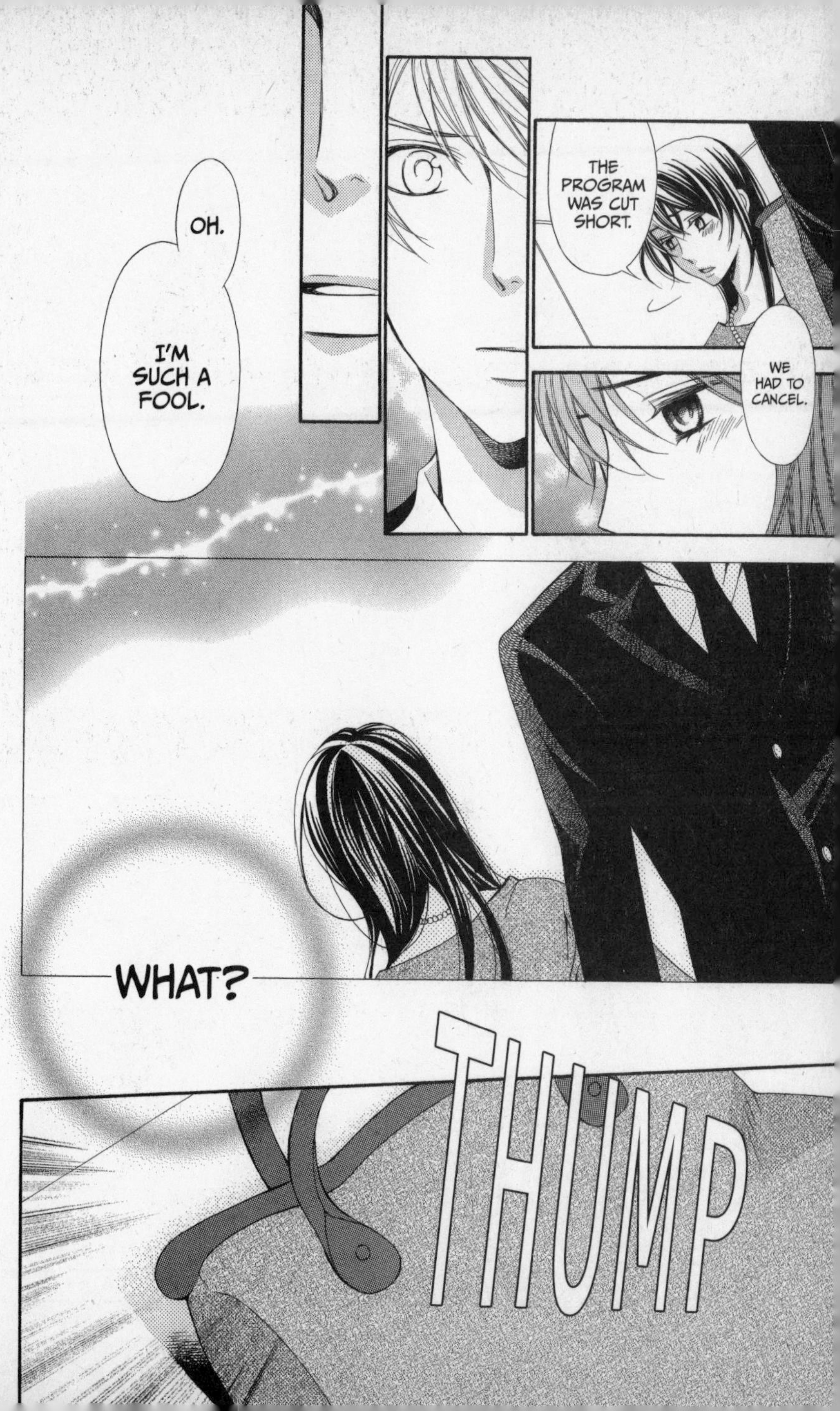
THE PROGRAM WAS CUT SHORT.
WE HAD TO CANCEL.
OH.
I'M SUCH A FOOL.
WHAT?
THUMP

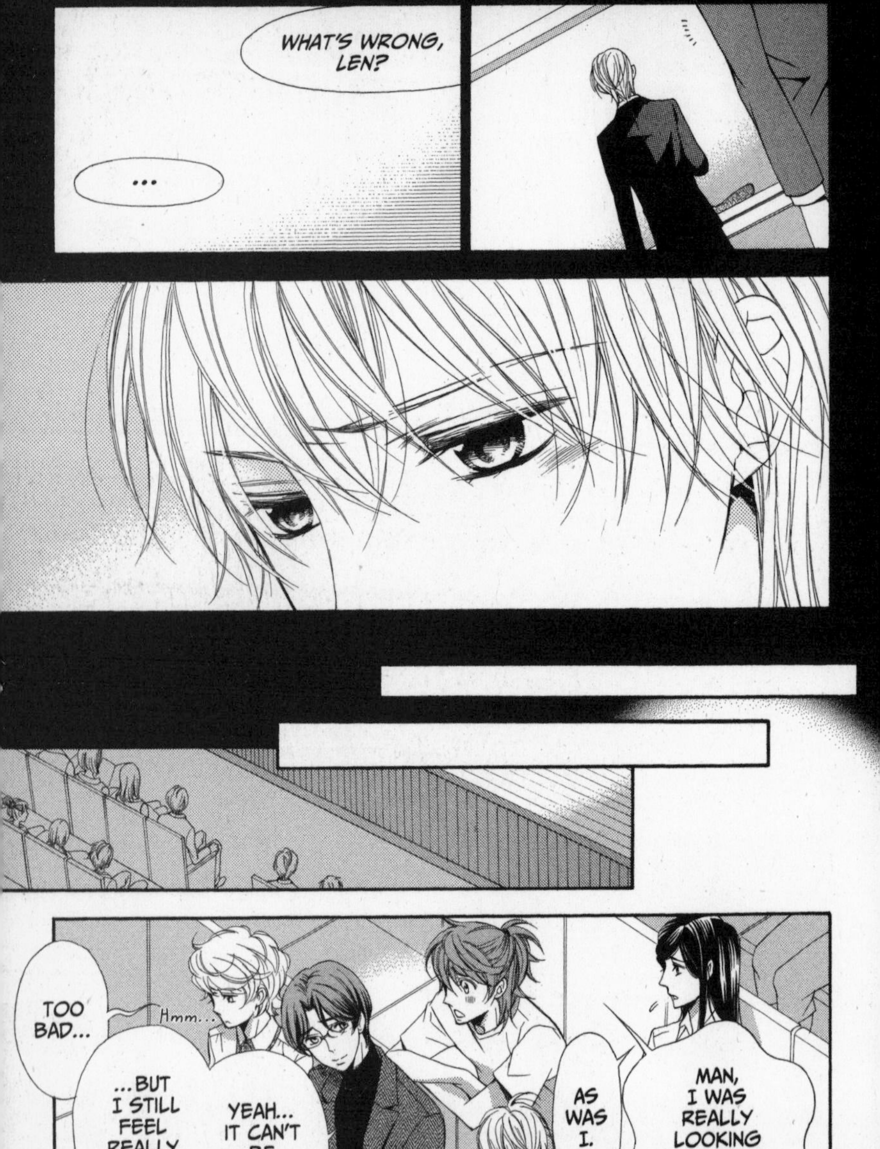
WHAT'S WRONG, LEN?
...
MAN, I WAS REALLY LOOKING FORWARD TO THIS.
AS WAS I.
YEAH... IT CAN'T BE HELPED...
...BUT I STILL FEEL REALLY BAD.
Hmm...
TOO BAD...

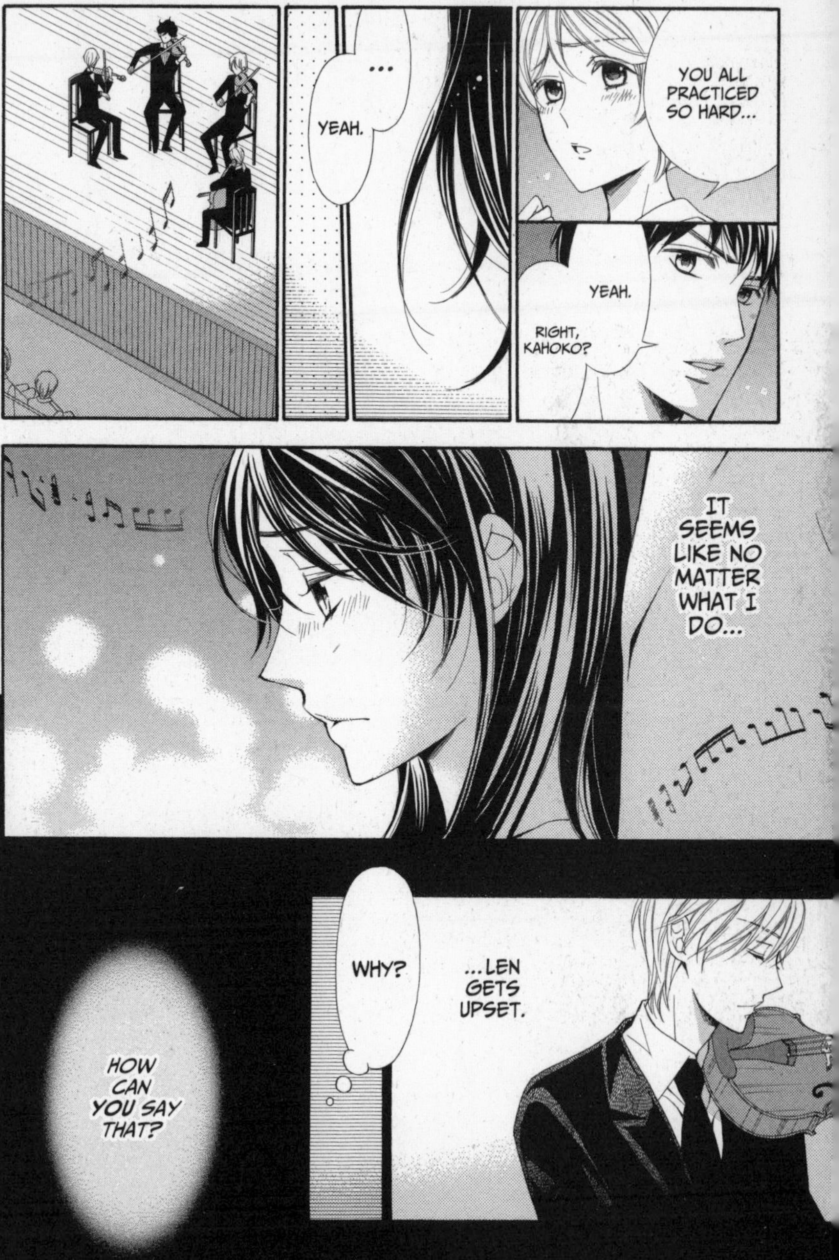
YOU ALL PRACTICED SO HARD...
YEAH.
RIGHT, KAHOKO?
... YEAH.
IT SEEMS LIKE NO MATTER WHAT I DO...
...LEN GETS UPSET.
WHY?
HOW CAN YOU SAY THAT?

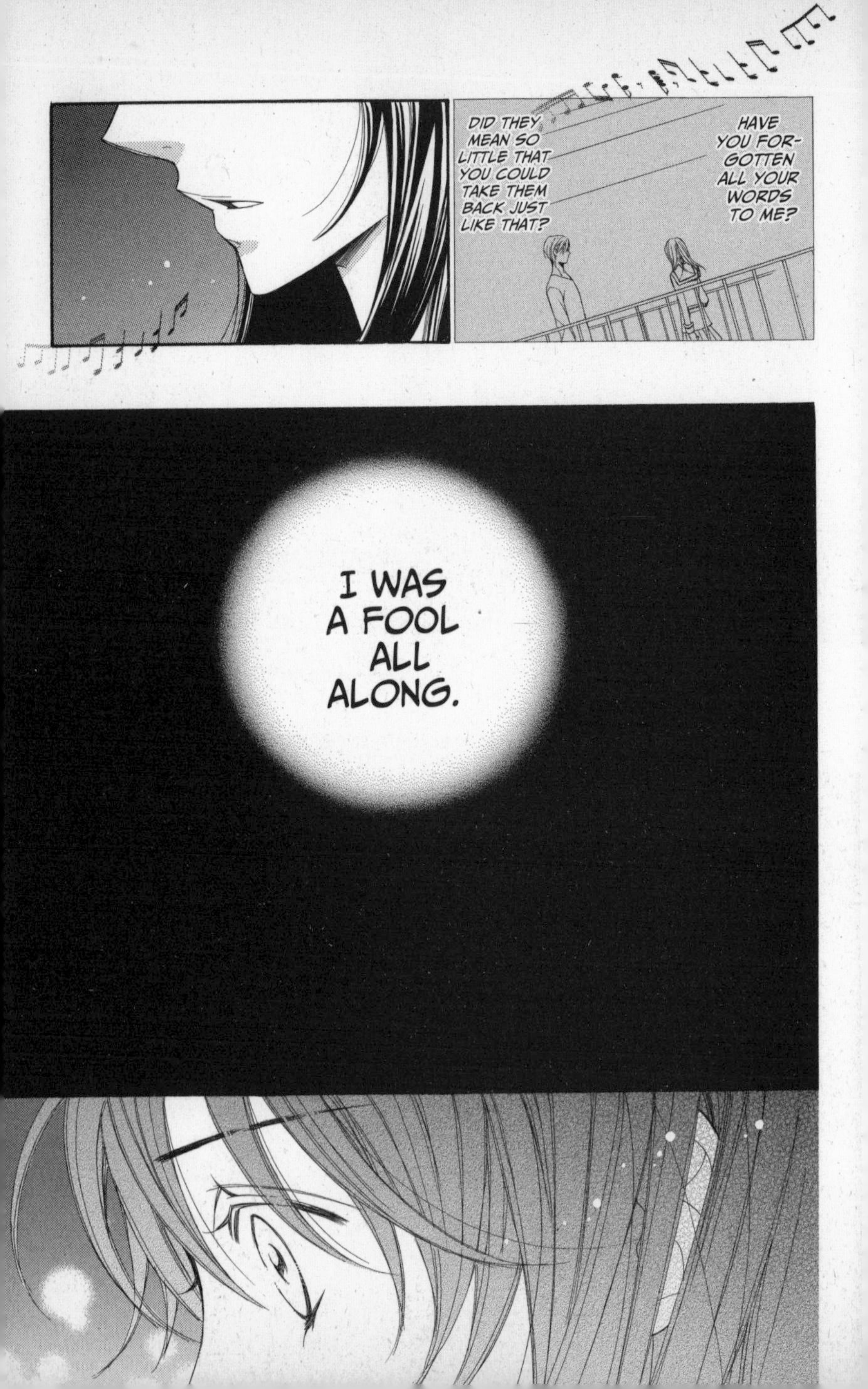
HAVE YOU FOR-GOTTEN ALL YOUR WORDS TO ME?
DID THEY MEAN SO LITTLE THAT YOU COULD TAKE THEM BACK JUST LIKE THAT?
I WAS A FOOL ALL ALONG.

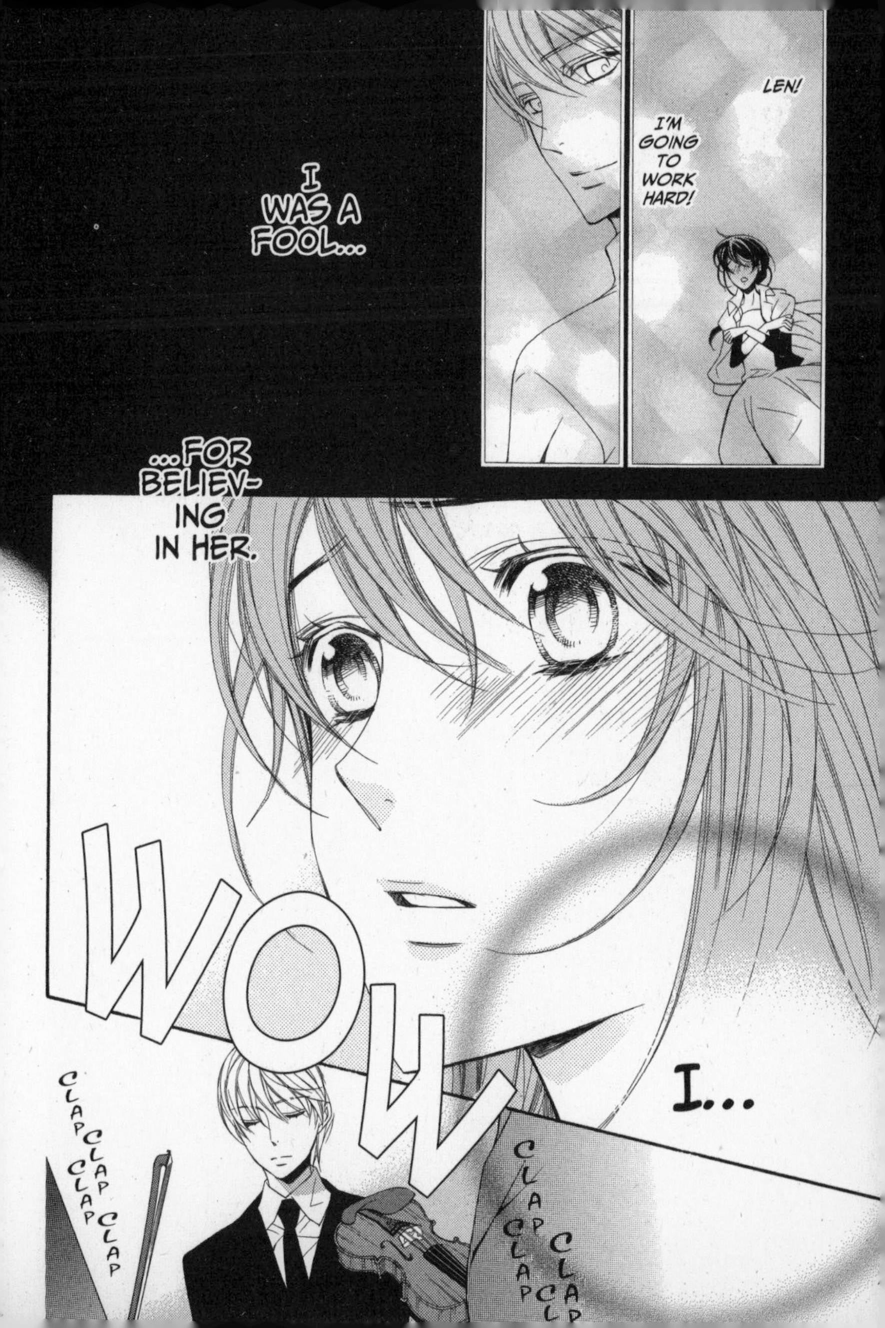
LEN!
I'M GOING TO WORK HARD!
I WAS A FOOL...
...FOR BELIEV-ING IN HER.
I...
WOW
CLAP CLAP CLAP
CLAP CLAP CLAP
CLAP CLAP CLAP

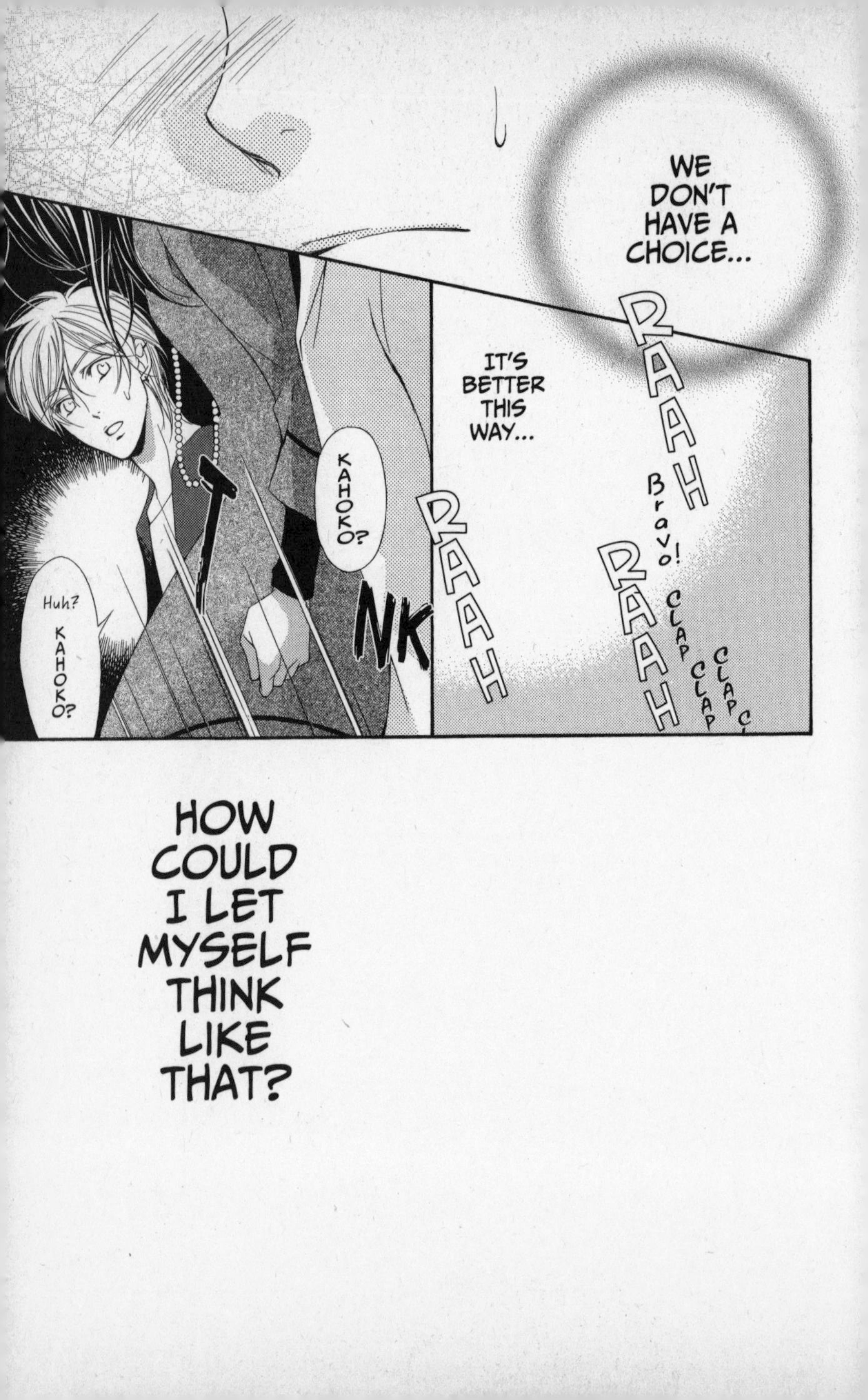
WE DON'T HAVE A CHOICE...
RAAAH
Bravo!
RAAAH
CLAP CLAP CLAP C
IT'S BETTER THIS WAY...
RAAAH
NK
KAHOKO?
Huh? KAHOKO?
HOW COULD I LET MYSELF THINK LIKE THAT?

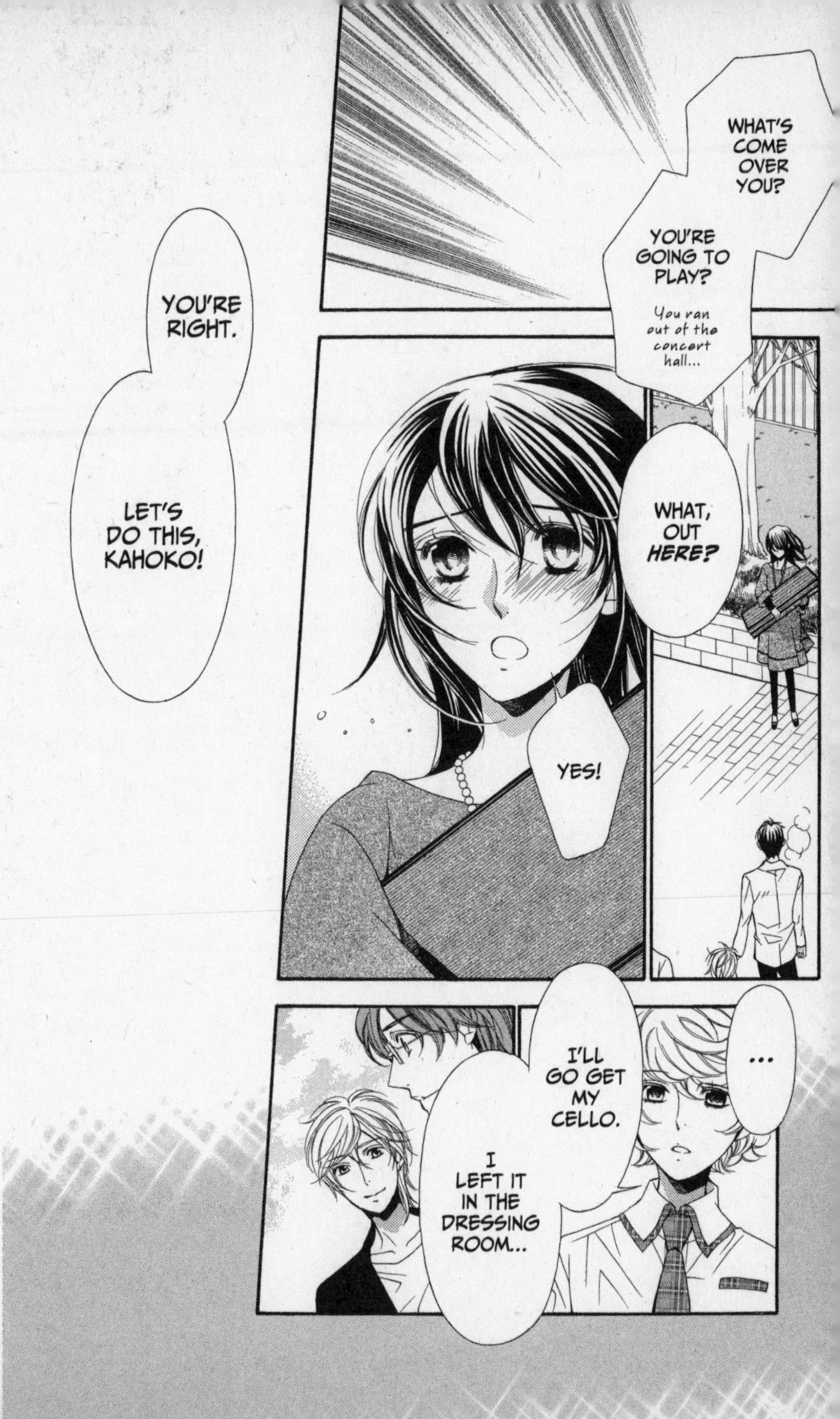
WHAT'S COME OVER YOU?
YOU'RE GOING TO PLAY?
You ran out of the concert hall...
WHAT, OUT HERE?
YES!
YOU'RE RIGHT.
LET'S DO THIS, KAHOKO!
...
I'LL GO GET MY CELLO.
I LEFT IT IN THE DRESSING ROOM...

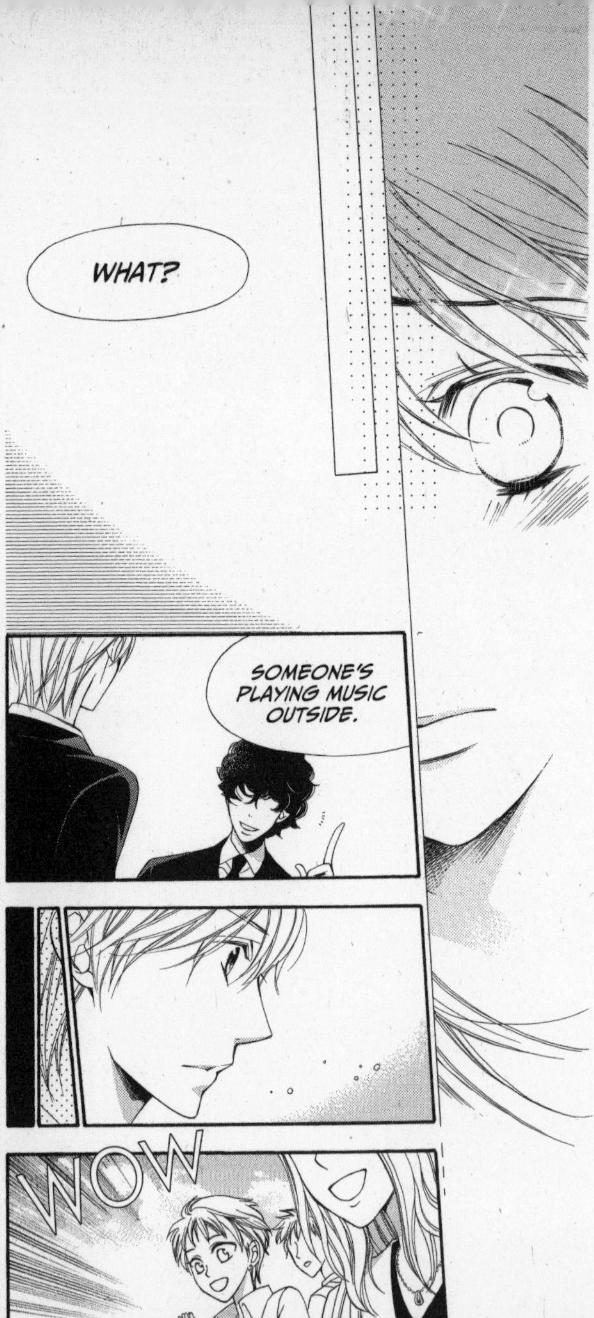
WHAT?
SOMEONE'S PLAYING MUSIC OUTSIDE.
WOW

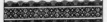

There were other wonderful illustrations and a great variety of outfits. Thanks so much for sending them!

Other sweep-you-off-your-feet lines: ↓

"Come sit a little closer."
"It's not like I was waiting for you...or anything."
"I'd like to stay with you longer..."
"Stay close to me."
"I see you're captivated by me."

There were too many!

One person submitted a fairy date with Len cosplaying as Lili!! ↓

Like this.

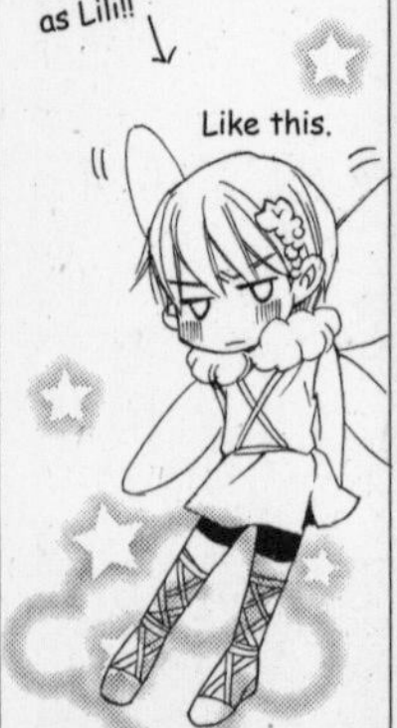

BY KYOKA FROM AICHI

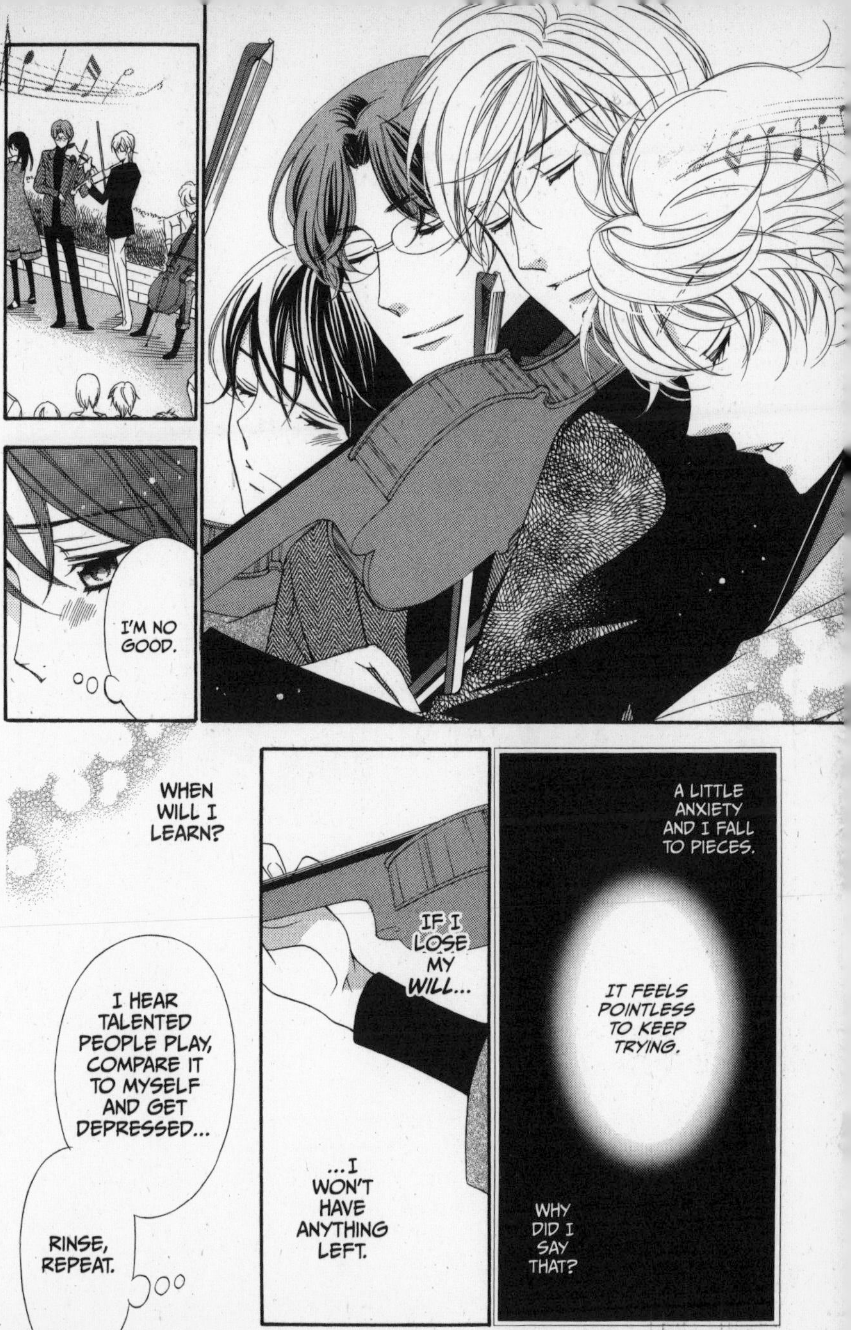
I'M NO GOOD.
A LITTLE ANXIETY AND I FALL TO PIECES.
IT FEELS POINTLESS TO KEEP TRYING.
WHY DID I SAY THAT?
IF I LOSE MY WILL...
...I WON'T HAVE ANYTHING LEFT.
WHEN WILL I LEARN?
I HEAR TALENTED PEOPLE PLAY, COMPARE IT TO MYSELF AND GET DEPRESSED...
RINSE, REPEAT.

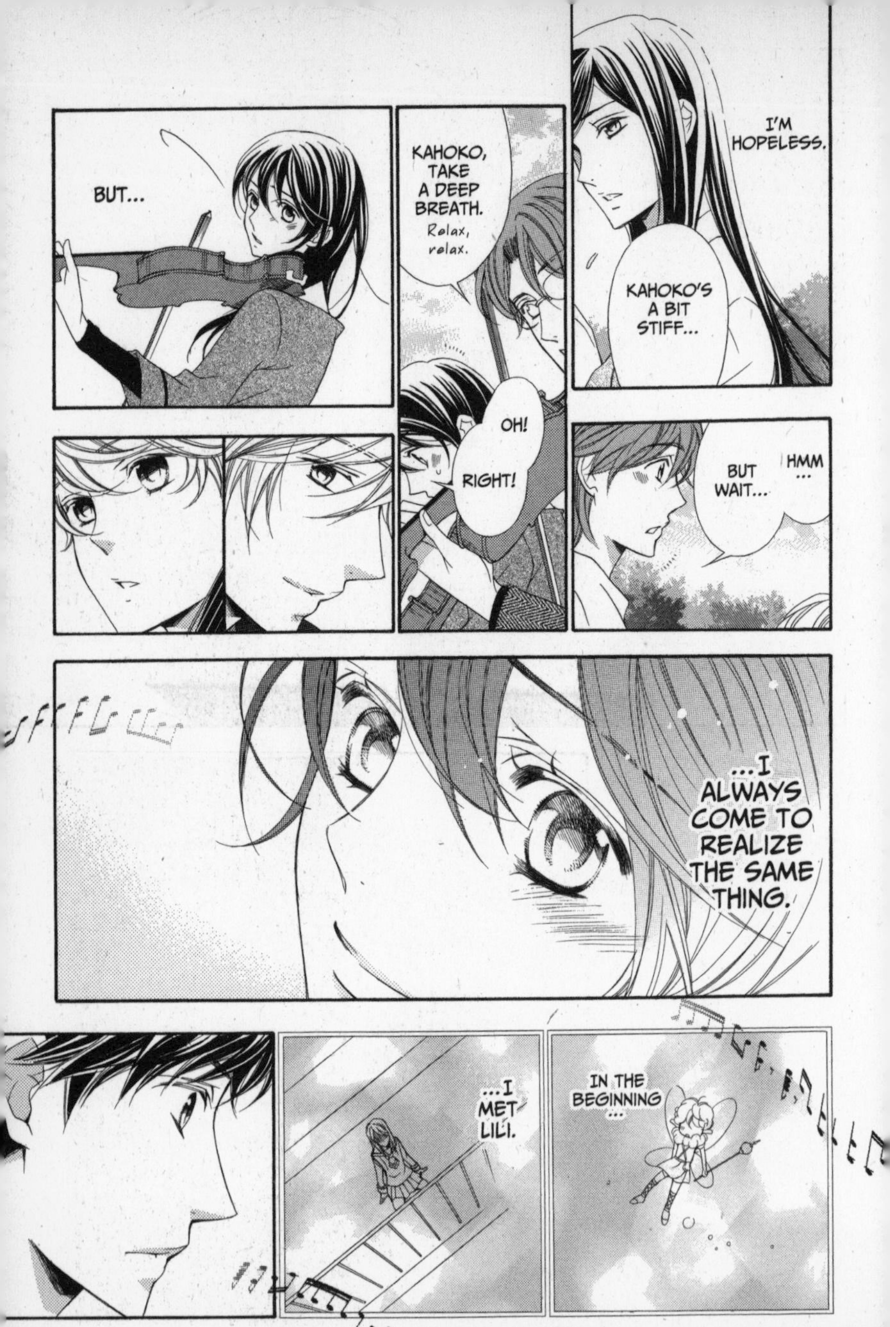
I'M HOPELESS.
KAHOKO'S A BIT STIFF...
KAHOKO, TAKE A DEEP BREATH. Relax, relax.
BUT...
HMM ...
BUT WAIT...
OH!
RIGHT!
...I ALWAYS COME TO REALIZE THE SAME THING.
IN THE BEGINNING ...
...I MET LILI.

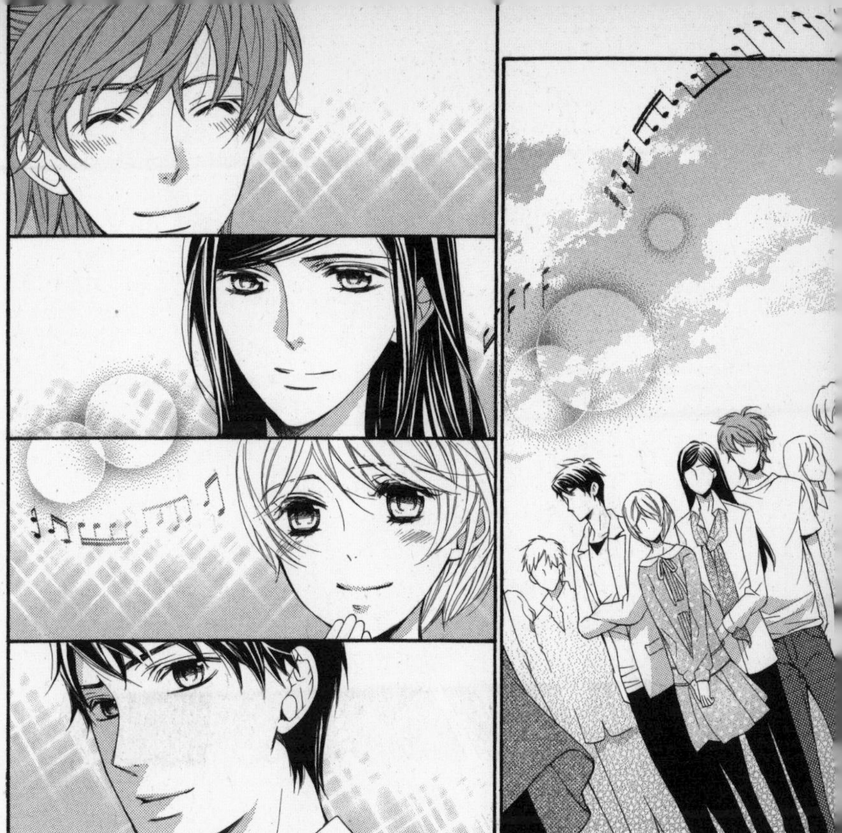

THEN
I GOT
TO KNOW
EVERYONE.

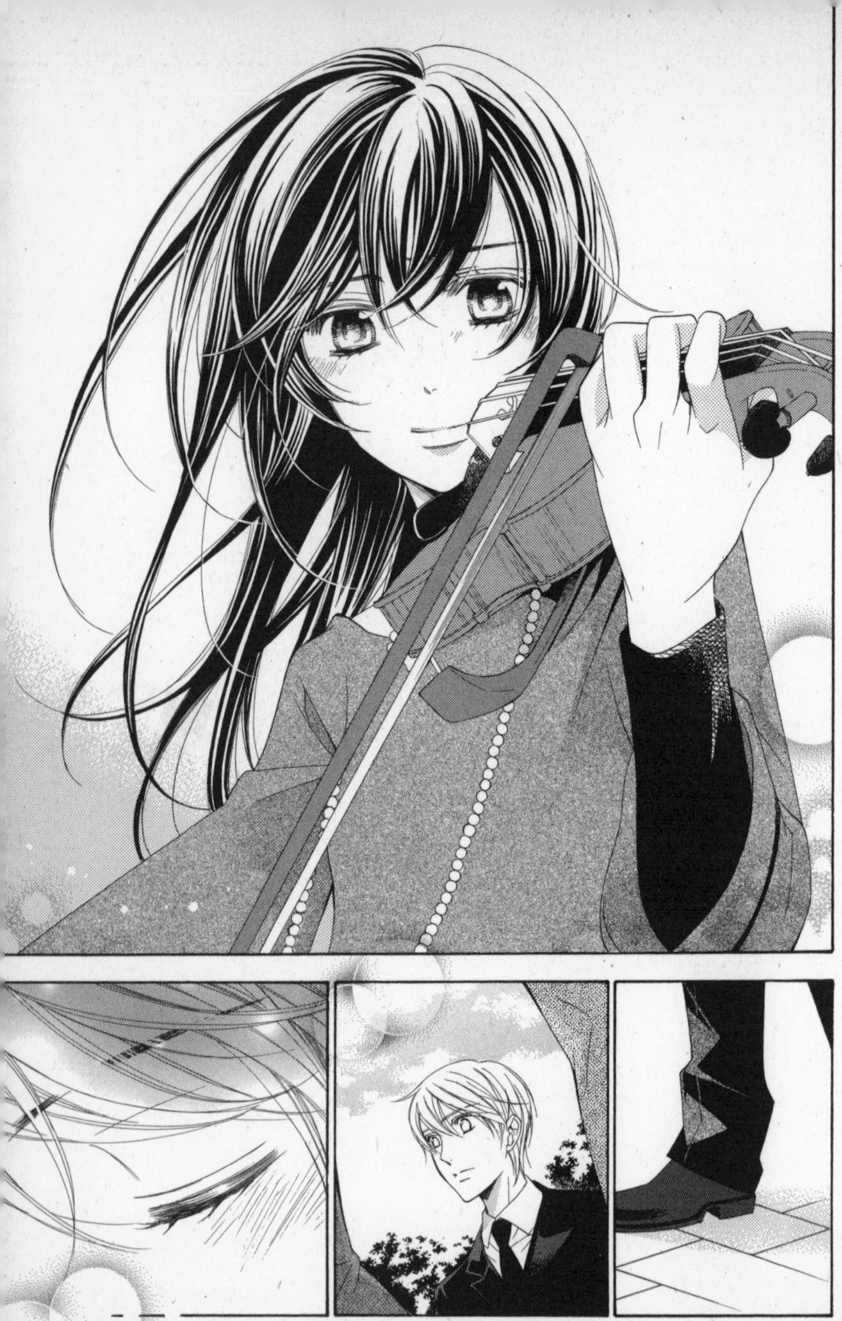

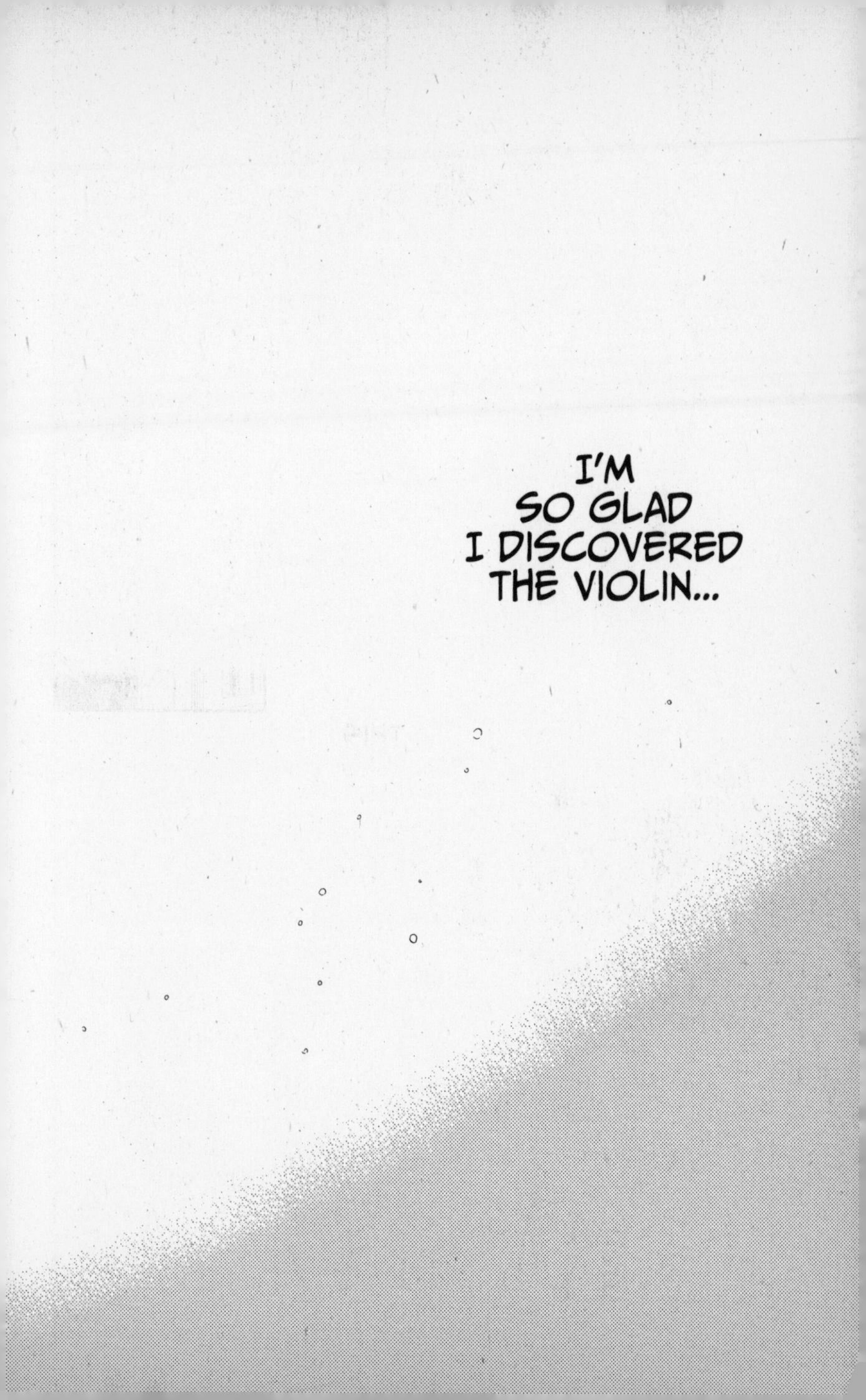
I'M SO GLAD I DISCOVERED THE VIOLIN...

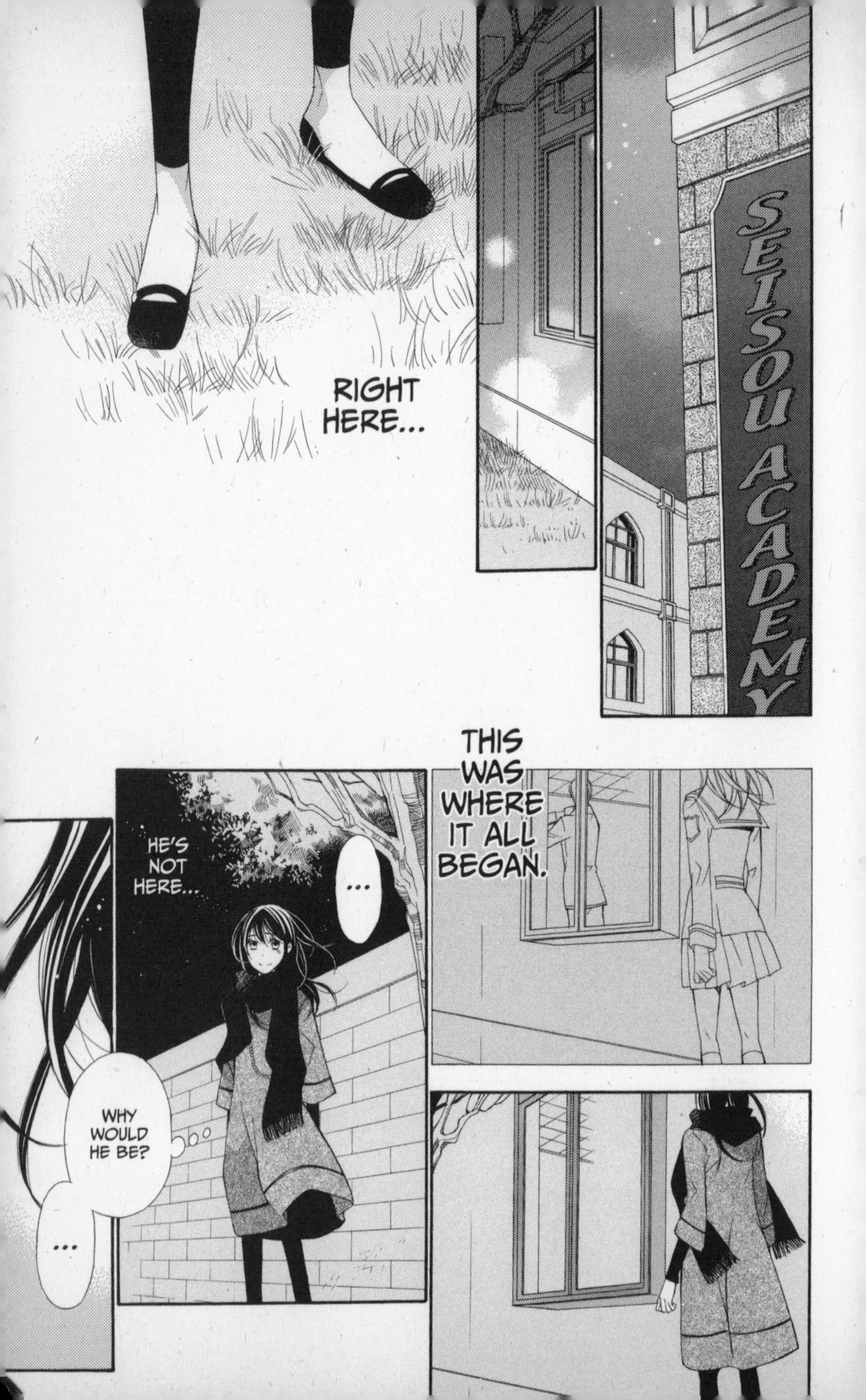
SEISOU ACADEMY
RIGHT HERE...
THIS WAS WHERE IT ALL BEGAN.
HE'S NOT HERE...
...
WHY WOULD HE BE?
...

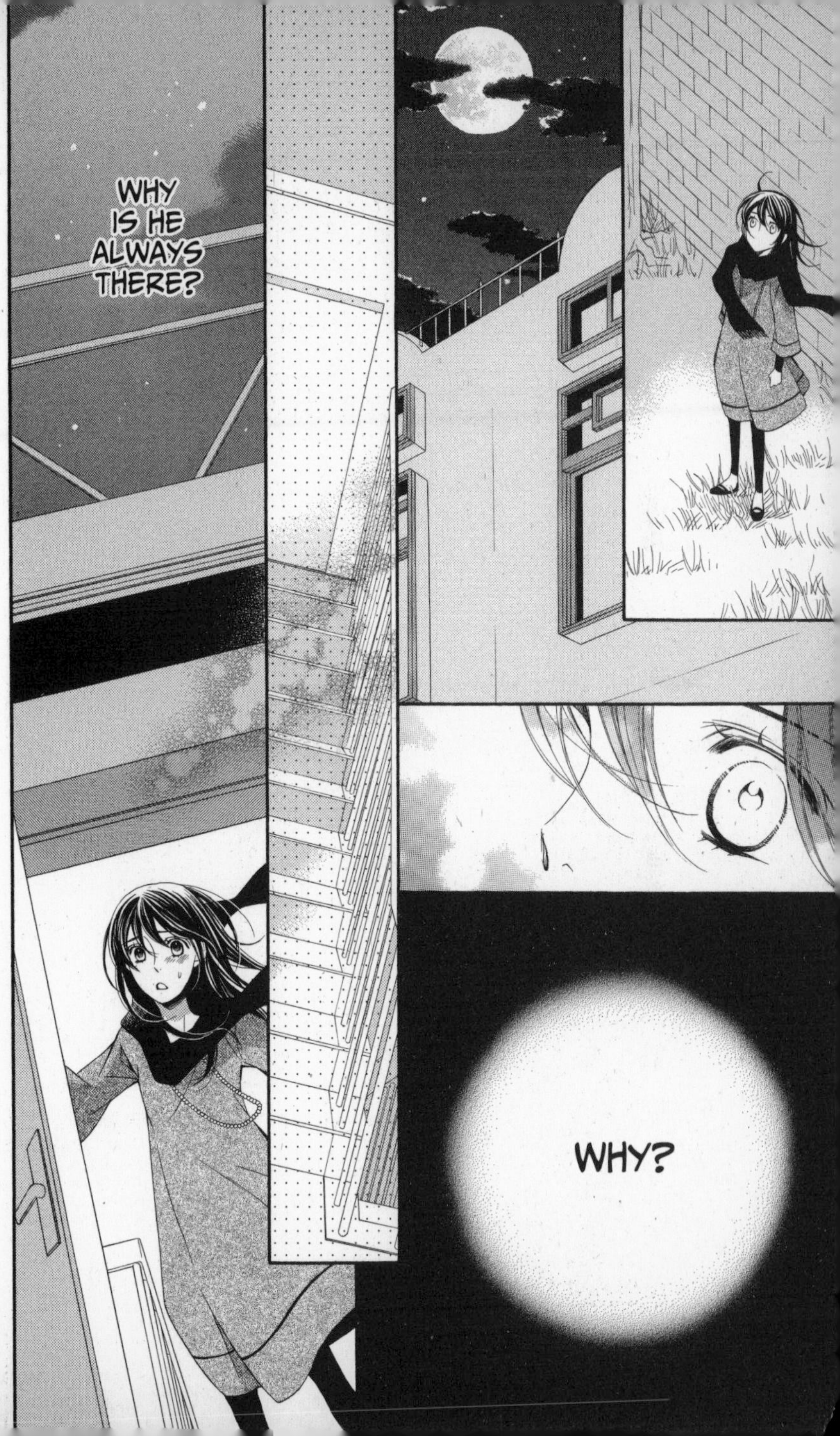
WHY IS HE ALWAYS THERE?
WHY?

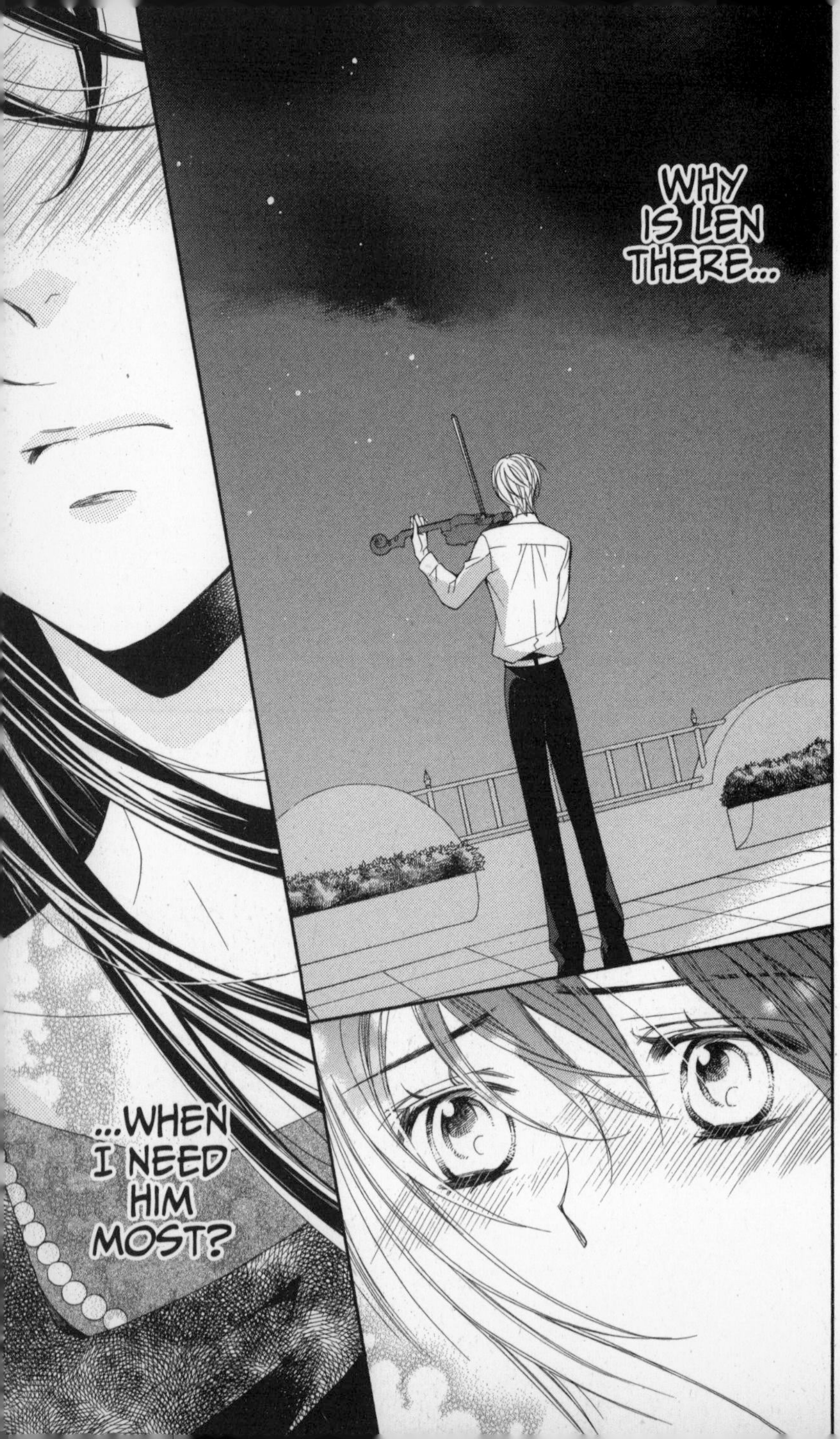
WHY IS LEN THERE...
...WHEN I NEED HIM MOST?

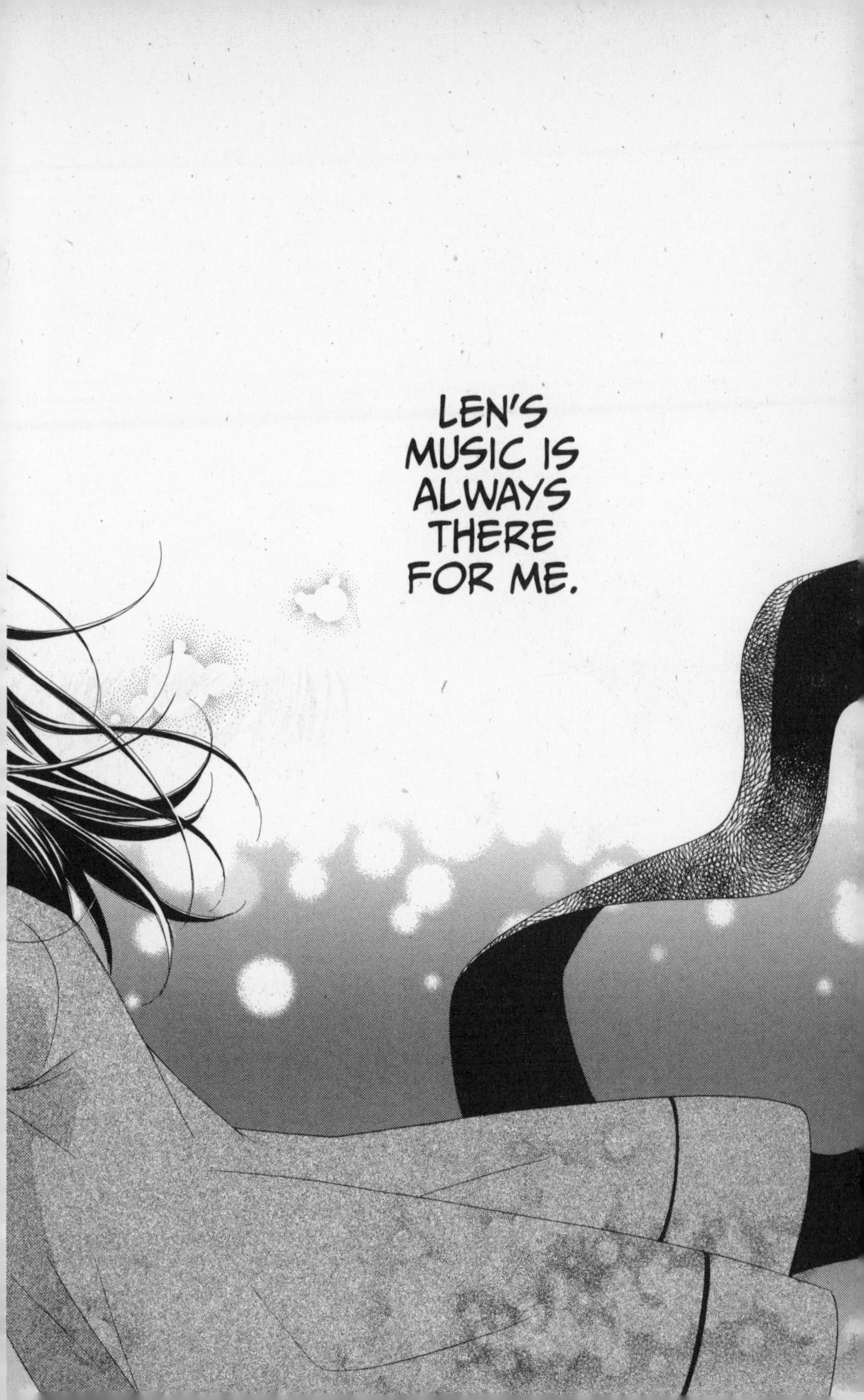
LEN'S MUSIC IS ALWAYS THERE FOR ME.

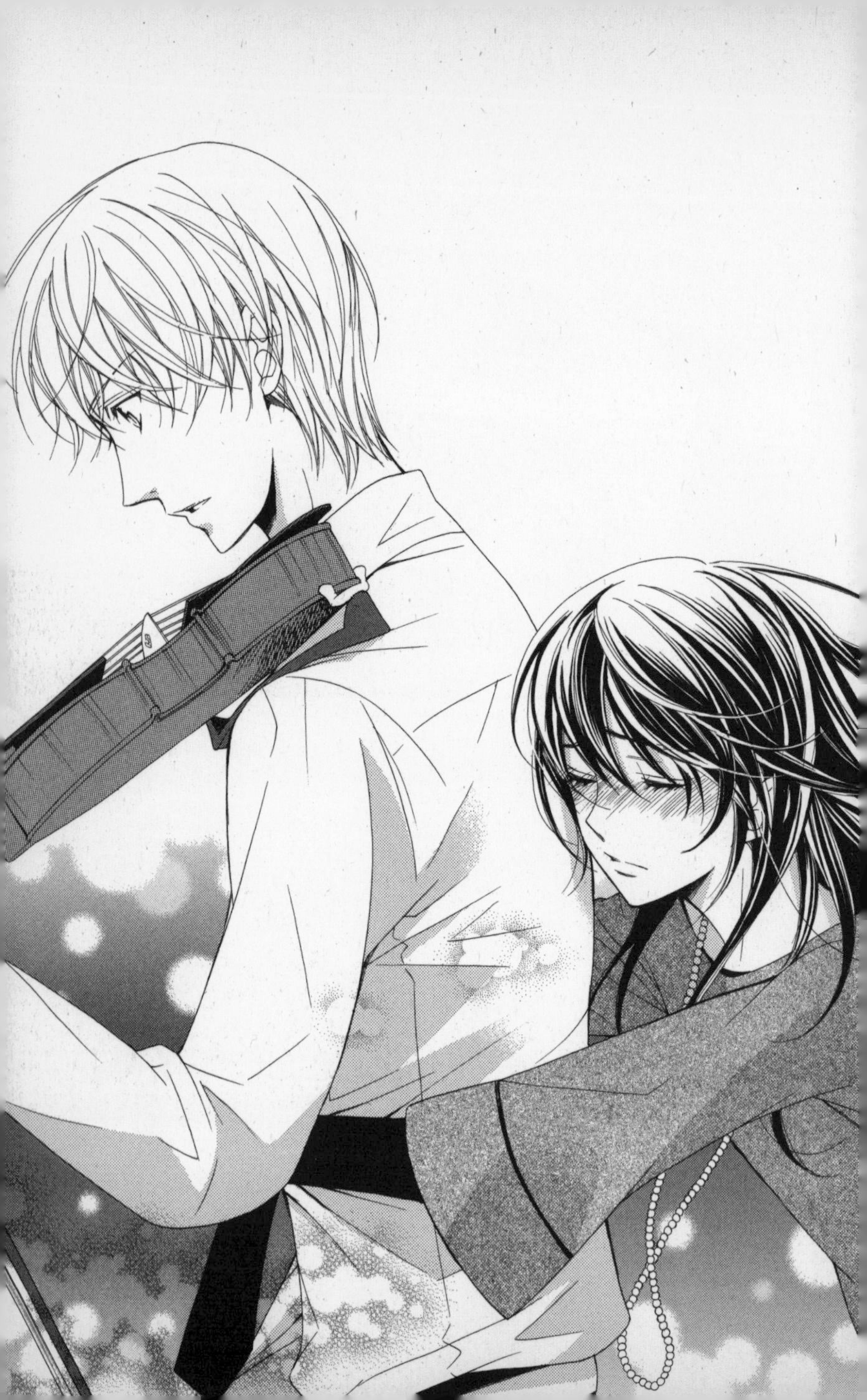

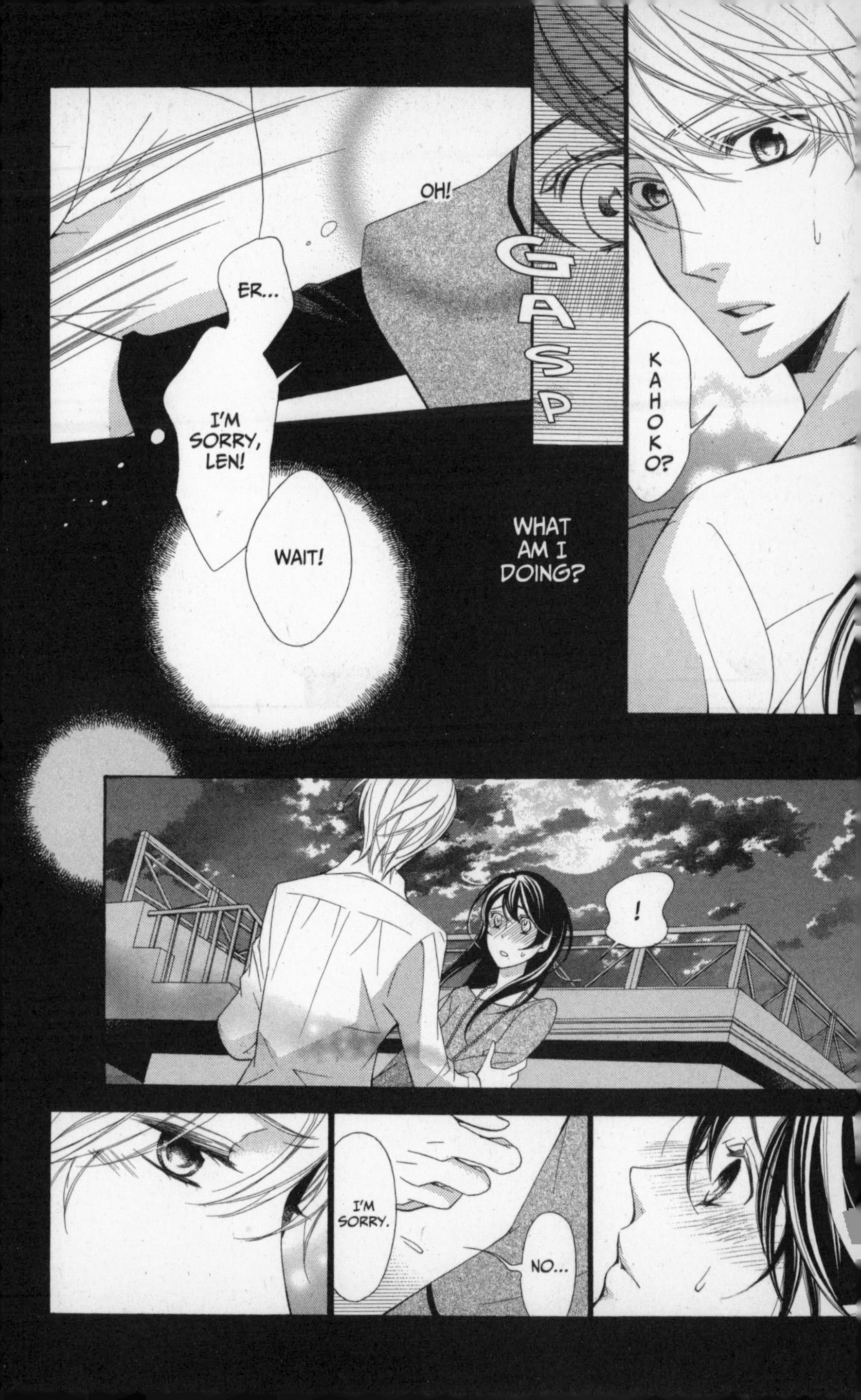
KAHOKO?
GASP
OH!
ER...
I'M SORRY, LEN!
WAIT!
WHAT AM I DOING?
!
NO...
I'M SORRY.

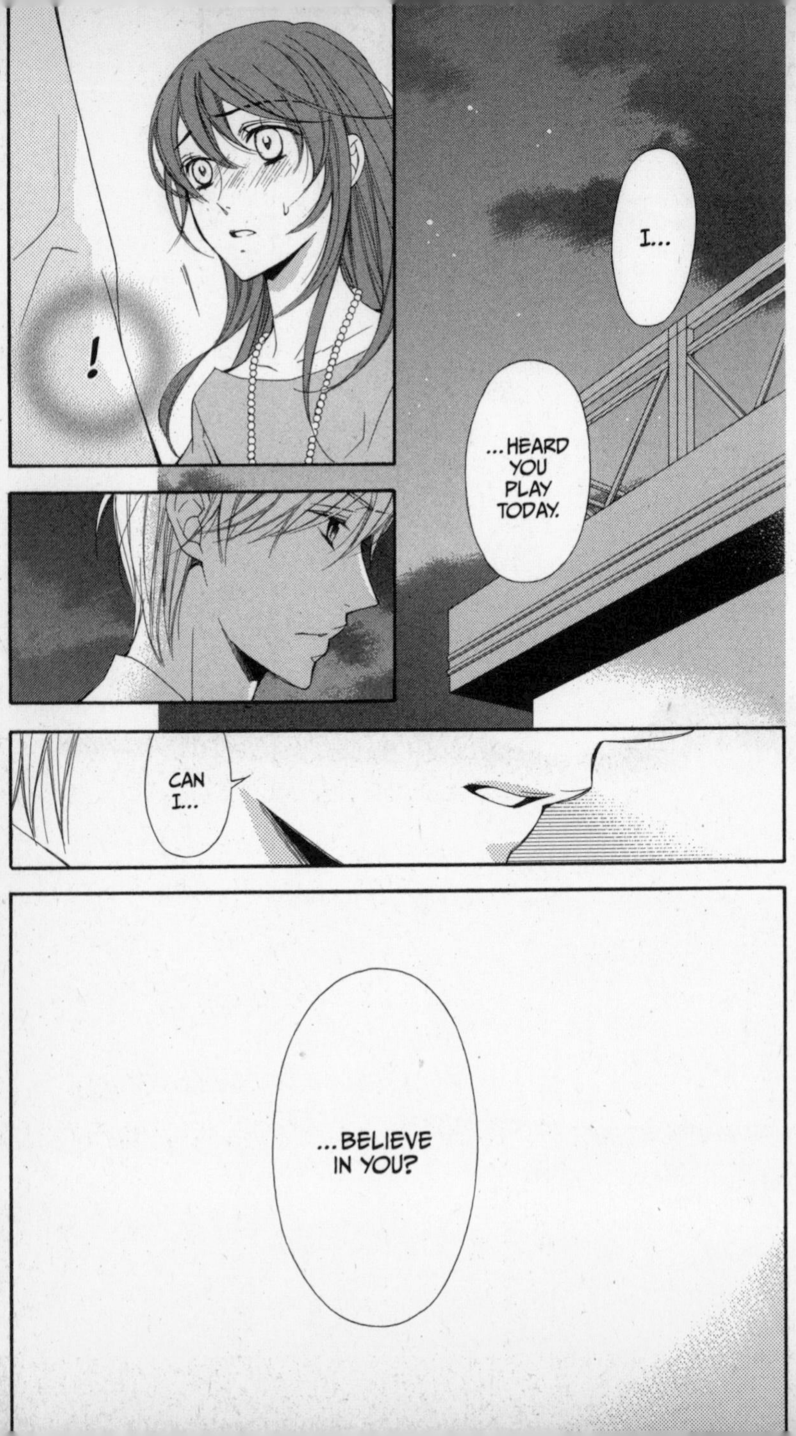
I...
...HEARD YOU PLAY TODAY.
!
CAN I...
...BELIEVE IN YOU?

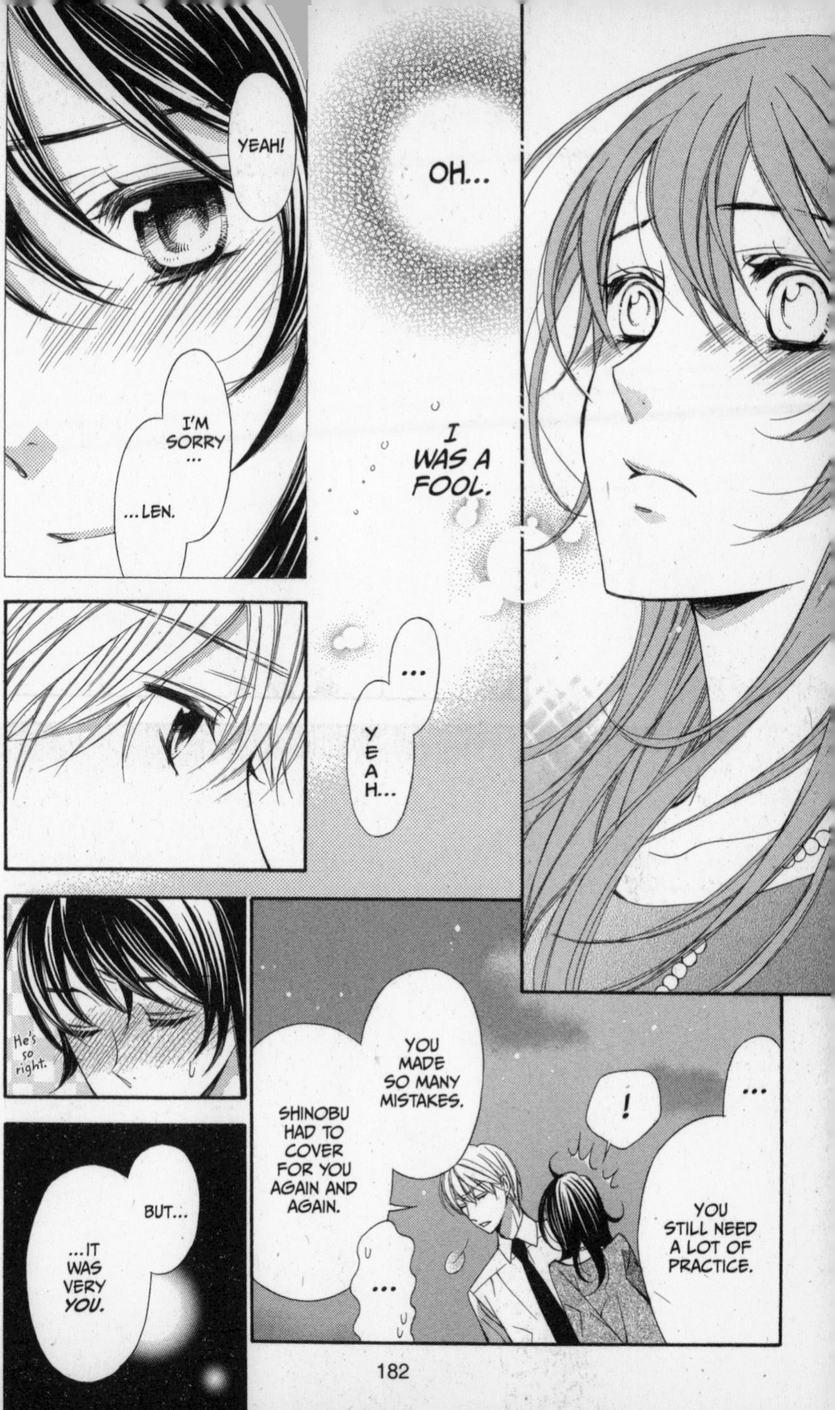
OH...
I WAS A FOOL.
YEAH!
I'M SORRY ... ...LEN.
... YEAH...
...
YOU STILL NEED A LOT OF PRACTICE.
!
YOU MADE SO MANY MISTAKES.
SHINOBU HAD TO COVER FOR YOU AGAIN AND AGAIN.
...
He's so right.
BUT...
...IT WAS VERY YOU.

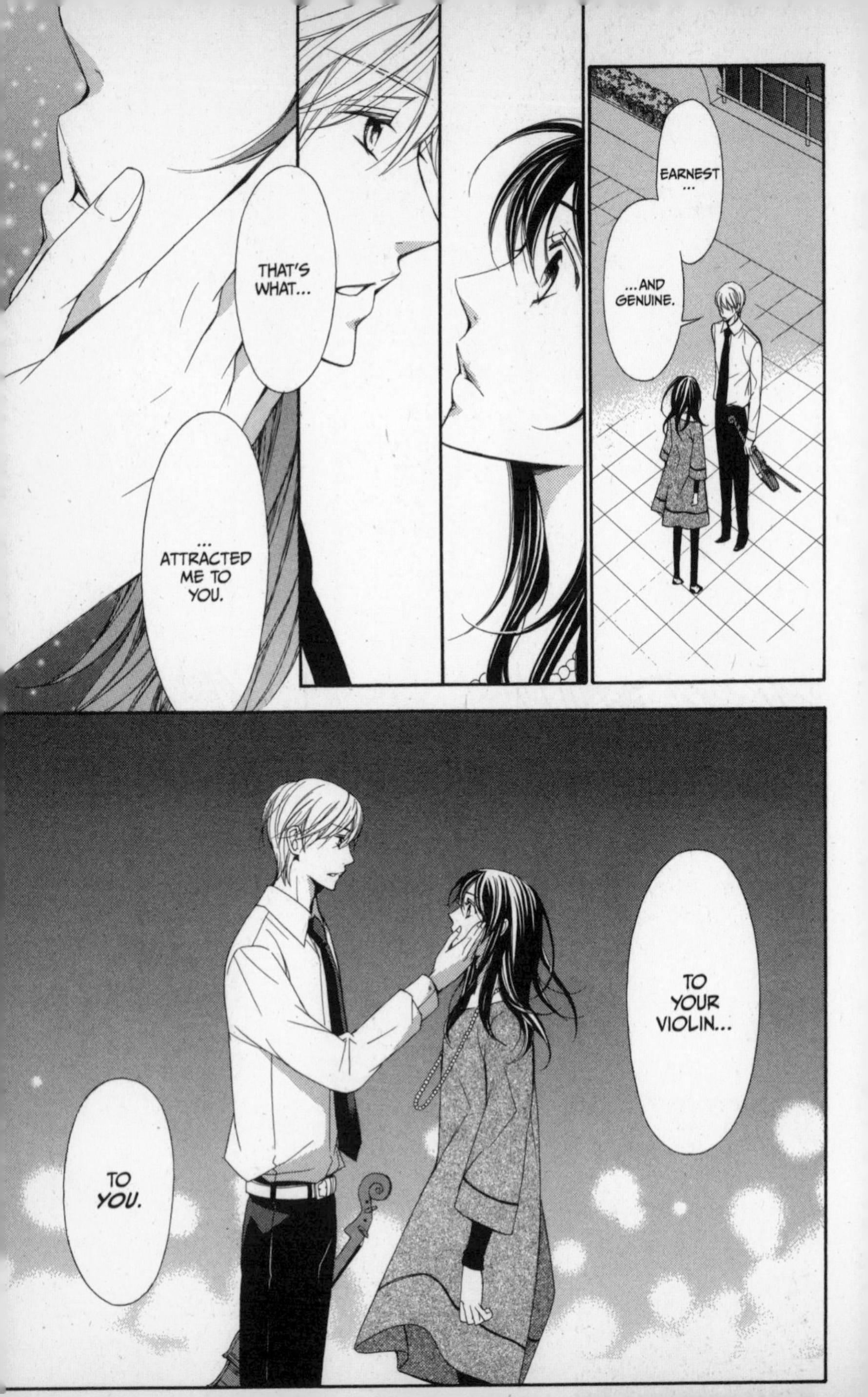
EARNEST ...
...AND GENUINE.
THAT'S WHAT...
... ATTRACTED ME TO YOU.
TO YOUR VIOLIN...
TO YOU.

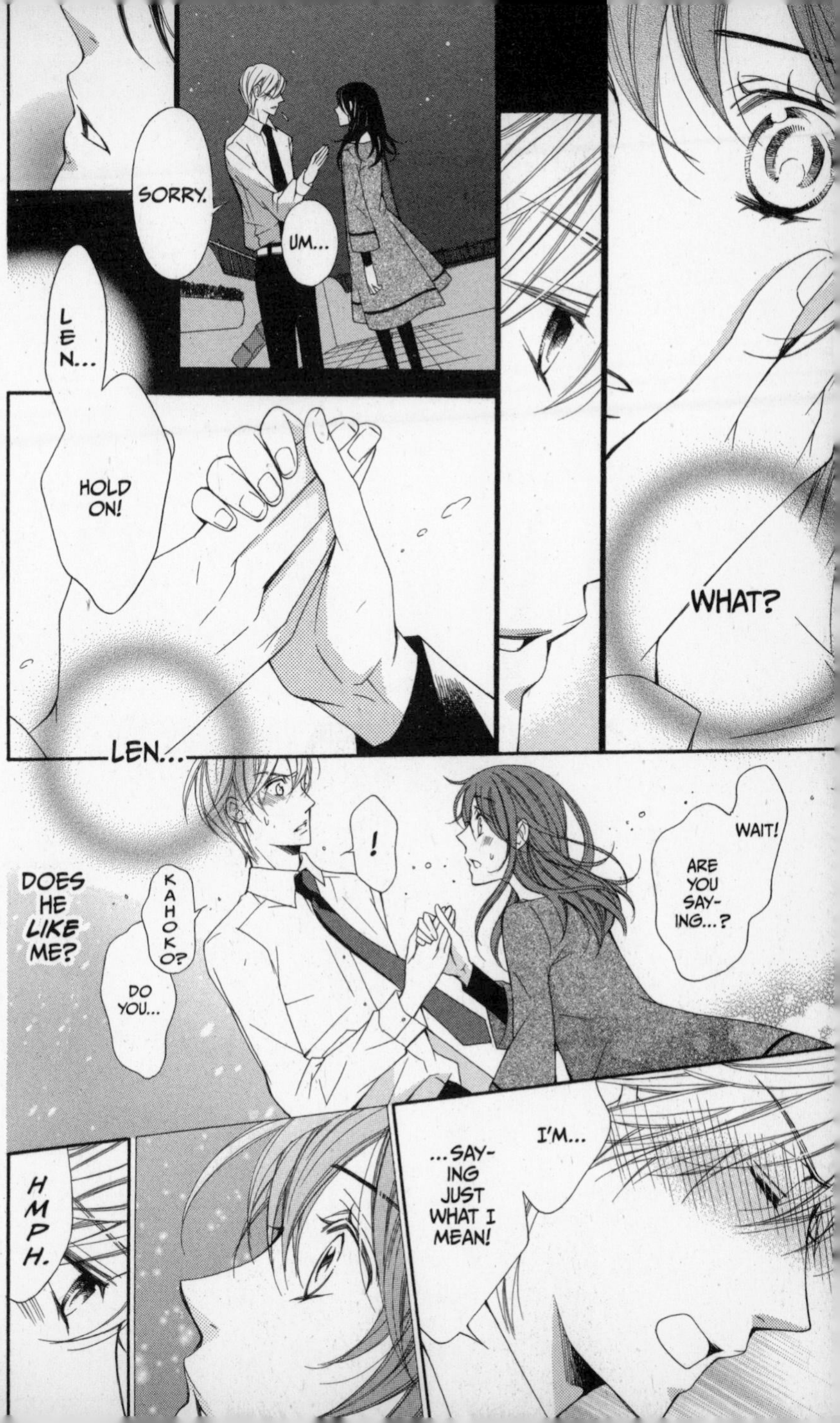
WHAT?
SORRY.
UM...
LEN...
HOLD ON!
LEN...
WAIT!
ARE YOU SAYING...?
!
KAHOKO?
DOES HE LIKE ME?
DO YOU...
I'M...
...SAYING JUST WHAT I MEAN!
HMPH.

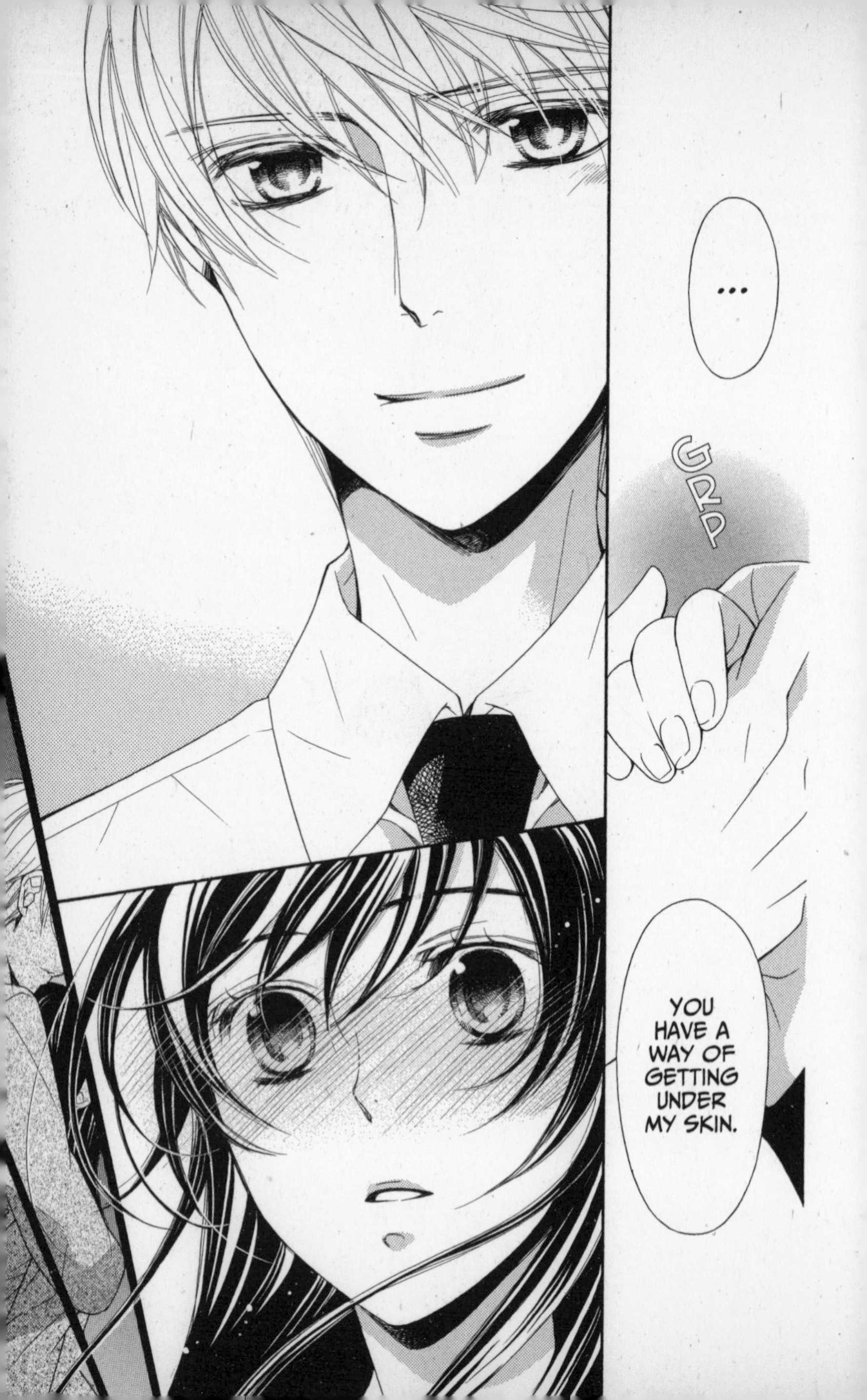
...
GRP
YOU HAVE A WAY OF GETTING UNDER MY SKIN.

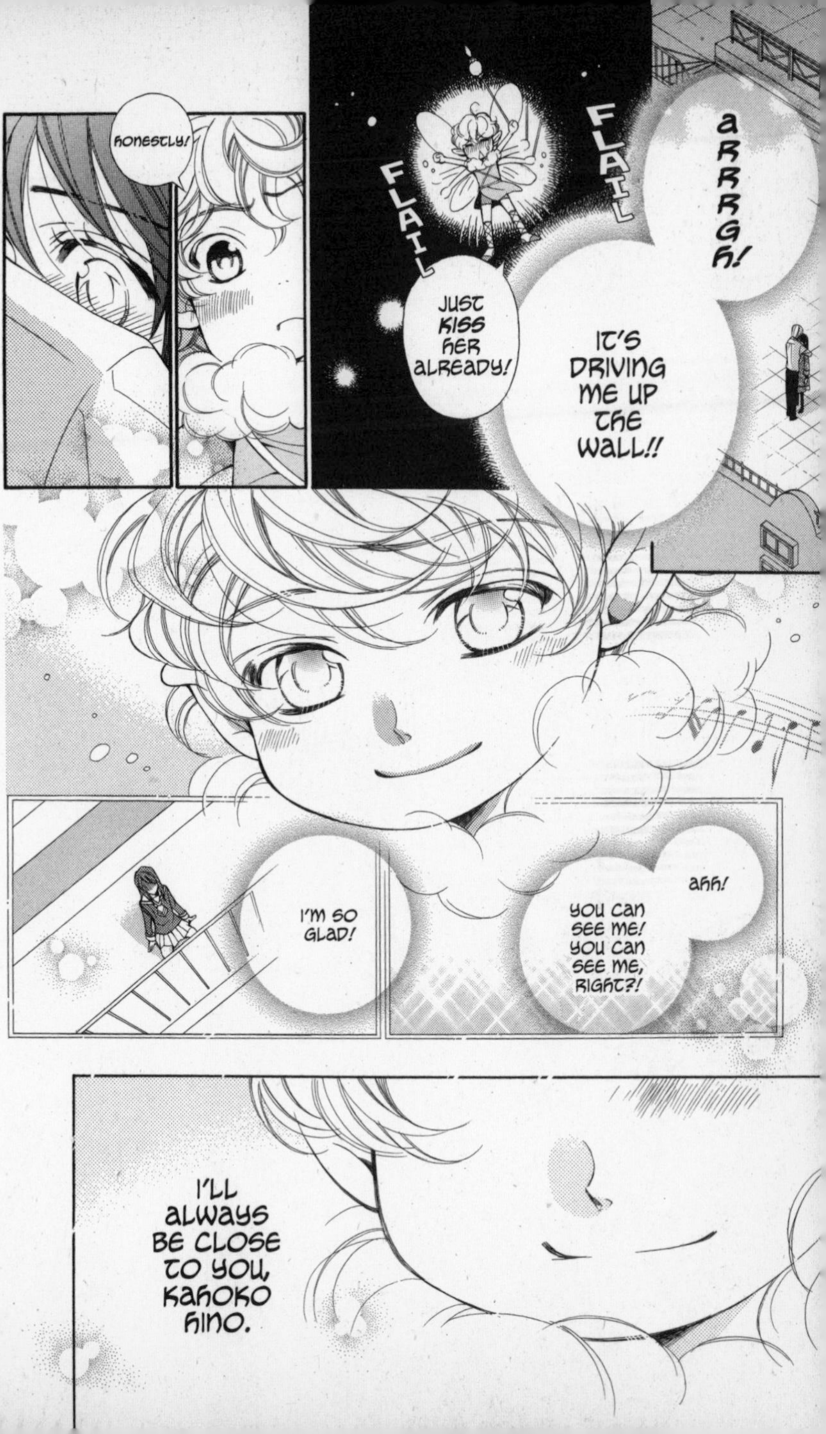
ARRRGH!
IT'S DRIVING ME UP THE WALL!!
FLAIL
FLAIL
JUST KISS HER ALREADY!
HONESTLY!
AHH!
YOU CAN SEE ME! YOU CAN SEE ME, RIGHT?!
I'M SO GLAD!
I'LL ALWAYS BE CLOSE TO YOU, KAHOKO HINO.

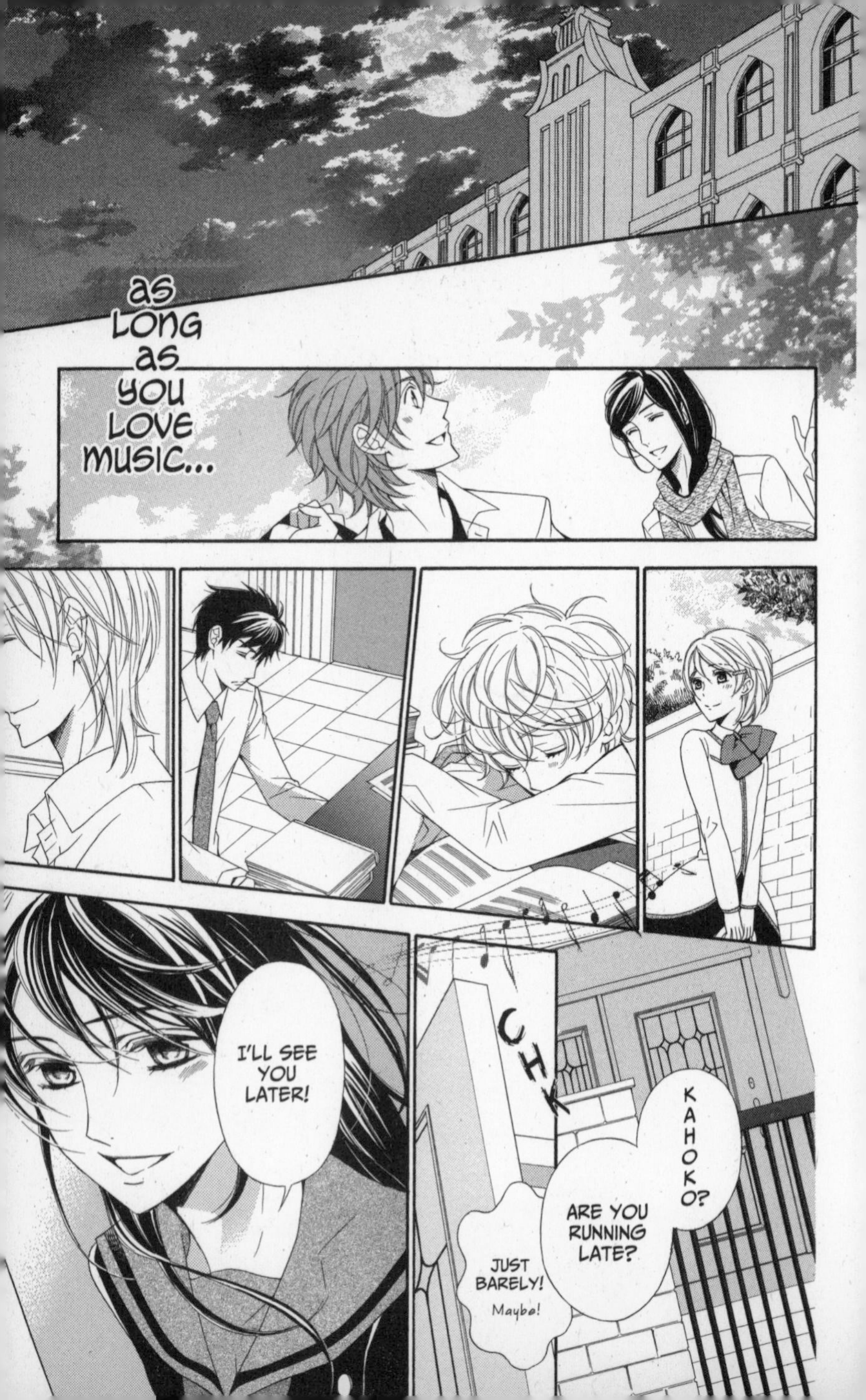
as long as you love music...
CHK
KAHOKO?
ARE YOU RUNNING LATE?
JUST BARELY!
Maybe!
I'LL SEE YOU LATER!

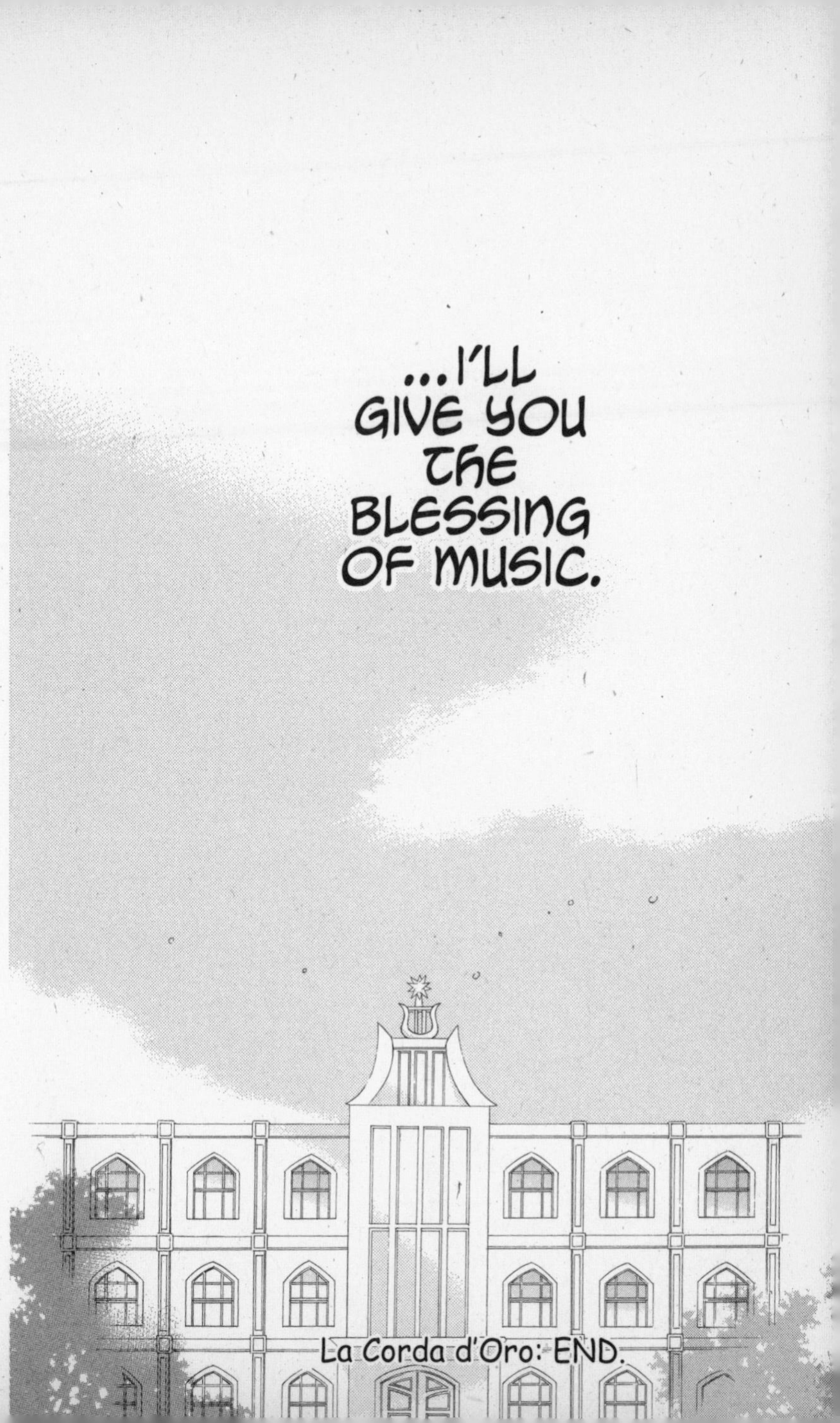
...I'LL GIVE YOU THE BLESSING OF MUSIC.
La Corda d'Oro: END.

Special Thanks

M.Shiino
N.Sato
C.Nanai
M.Morinaga

Afterword

The story has successfully reached its conclusion. I was introduced to the world of *La Corda d'Oro* when they chose me as the game's character designer, and then they offered me the opportunity to draw the manga. It was my first serial, and I worked feverishly every month. Now I look back and realize that I've been with these characters for a long time. It's a relief, yet also sad, to have it come to an end... Yes.

Thank you so much for following *La Corda* all this way. I always read the letters you send me! There were so many points of entry...people who first discovered it through the game or the anime, or started playing the game after reading the manga... I'm very grateful. There are so many great incarnations of *La Corda* now!
(My family thinks the anime version of Ryotaro is the coolest.)

Kahoko's adventure in the manga may be over, but the world of *La Corda* will continue in games and fan events and such, so please keep following us! (There, I snuck in a little advertisement.) I'd also like to thank all the assistants who helped me. They're excellent, fast workers, and I don't deserve them. They're masters at drawing the Seisou Academy campus. They've been such a huge help...thanks. And my editors, three different ones if I count back to when I started the character design process. I'm sorry for all the problems I've caused... They're such strong women, and I'm always amazed by how much energy they have. Thank you, Ms. T, Ms. I and Ms. T (two Ts...)!!

And the people at Koei, who go over my illegible rough drafts, and T who puts the finishing touches on the graphic novel collections (another T...). I'm so grateful to so many people.

And to all the characters of *La Corda d'Oro*...thank you.

Yuki Kure

Yuki Kure made her debut in 2000 with the story *Chijo yori Eien ni* (Forever from the Earth), published in monthly *LaLa* magazine. *La Corda d' Oro* is her first manga series published. Her hobbies are watching soccer games and collecting small goodies.

LA CORDA D'ORO
Vol. 17
Shojo Beat Edition

**STORY AND ART BY
YUKI KURE**

ORIGINAL CONCEPT BY
RUBY PARTY

English Translation & Adaptation/Mai Ihara
Touch-up Art & Lettering/HudsonYards
Design/Amy Martin
Editor/Shaenon K. Garrity

Printed in Canada

Published by VIZ Media, LLC
P.O. Box 77010
San Francisco, CA 94107

10 9 8 7 6 5 4 3 2 1
First printing, May 2013

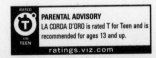

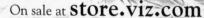